Systemic Perspectives on Discourse, Volume 1

Selected Theoretical Papers from the 9th International Systemic Workshop

edited by

James D. Benson
and
William S. Greaves

Glendon College, York University
Toronto, Canada

Volume XV in the Series
ADVANCES IN DISCOURSE PROCESSES
Roy O. Freedle, editor

 ABLEX PUBLISHING CORPORATION
NORWOOD, NEW JERSEY 07648

Library of Congress Cataloging in Publication Data

International Systemic Workshop (9th: 1982: Toronto, Ont.)
   Systemic perspectives on discourse.

   (Vol. 15–16 in the series Advances in discourse processes)
   Contents: v. 1. Selected theoretical papers from the 9th International Systemic Workshop—v. 2. Selected applied papers from the 9th International Workshop.
   Includes bibliographies and indexes.
   1. Systemic grammar—Congresses.   2. Discourse analysis—Congresses.   I. Benson, James D.   II. Greaves, William S.   III. Title.   IV. Series: Advances in discourse processes; 15–16.
P149.I57   1982   401'.41   84–28466
ISBN 0–89391–193–3 (v. 1)
ISBN 0–89391–202–6 (v. 2)

Ablex Publishing Corporation
355 Chestnut Street
Norwood, New Jersey 07648

Contents

Preface to the Series

Roy O. Freedle
Series Editor

This series of volumes provides a forum for the cross-fertilization of ideas from a diverse number of disciplines, all of which share a common interest in discourse—be it prose comprehension and recall, dialogue analysis, text grammar construction, computer simulation of natural language, cross-cultural comparisons of communicative competence, or other related topics. The problems posed by multisentence contexts and the methods required to investigate them, while not always unique to discourse, are still sufficiently distinct as to benefit from the organized mode of scientific interaction made possible by this series.

Scholars working in the discourse area from the perspective of sociolinguistics, psycholinguistics, ethnomethodology and the sociology of language, educational psychology (e.g., teacher–student interaction), the philosophy of language, computational linguistics, and related subareas are invited to submit manuscripts of monograph or book length to the series editor. Edited collections of original papers resulting from conferences will also be considered.

Volumes in the Series

Introduction

The articles in this volume have been selected from papers delivered at the 9th International Systemic Workshop, held at York University in Toronto, in August 1982. These workshops are held annually to bring together linguists working in the neo-Firthian tradition. The 9th ISW was the first held outside Great Britain, and the articles in the volume reflect the growing North American interest in Systemic Linguistics.

The tone of the workshop is established in the remarks of the two keynote speakers: M. A. K. Halliday gives a personal account of the background of Systemic Linguistics, and Ruqaiya Hasan discusses the centrality of context, deriving from Malinowski, in systemic work. Indeed, the keynote speakers make clear the way in which an orientation towards discourse is integral to systemic theory.

Although this volume contains theoretical articles (the companion volume being *Systemic Perspectives on Discourse: Selected Applied Papers from the 9th International Systemic Workshop*), as Halliday observes, "applied" and "theoretical" are not wholly adequate disciplinary divisions. A case in point is the computerized systemic grammar being developed by Mann and Matthiessen, reported on in this volume, which puts the fundamental principle of networks to an operational test.

The articles in this volume range from grammatical questions such as transitivity to more explicit considerations of discourse, including discussions of register, genre, and intertextuality. The volume concludes with a series of articles on phonology, which reflects the importance of the spoken mode for practictioners of systemic linguistics. All the articles have in common an underlying concern with the way in which language can be described in terms of systemic semantic choice, and show in a comprehensive way the contribution that systemic linguistics continues to make to the study of text and discourse.

This volume is the end product of a long process, and the editors wish to acknowledge the generous support of many individuals and institutions. The Workshop could not have been held outside Great Britain without the help from The British Council, The British Academy, The Social Sciences and Humanities Research Council of Canada, the York University Dean of Research, Dean of Graduate Studies, Ad Hoc Fund, Master of Winters College, Principal of Glendon College, and Applied Linguistics Research Working Group. Manuscript preparation was supported by Glendon College and we were fortunate in the assistance we received from Elissa Asp, and especially Karen Malcolm who prepared the index and skillfully contributed to the process of editing the volume. We are also indebted to our colleague Michael Gregory for valuable advice at several stages.

James D. Benson
William S. Greaves

Systemic Background 1

M. A. K. Halliday
University of Sydney
Australia

The Ninth Systemic Workshop is the first one to bear the title 'International'. It is, of course, the first to be held outside Britain; but I take it that it is not the crossing of the Atlantic Ocean that makes this occasion distinctively international—Canadian participants, after all, have been crossing in the other direction from the very beginning—nor is it, by the same token, the fact that more than one nation is represented. What the label 'international' conveys is perhaps more a difference of orientation. The Systemic Workshop has never been an exclusive affair; but it grew up as a forum to which people came in order to exchange ideas with those who were closest to them. This is a very rational form of behaviour, common among all human groups; and it is particularly valuable in intellectual activities, where the community of outlook, and the shared goals and assumptions, preclude any need for posturing or protesting one's right to exist, and encourage a real dialogue in which ideas flow freely and mental jams can be unblocked. But there is a time, also, for talking and listening to others; and this year's more heterogeneous gathering brings together 'systemicists', both theoretical and applied (and most systemicists are in fact both, this being one of the main reasons for adopting this approach), with others who would not think of themselves as systemicists but who have influenced systemic theory and perhaps been influenced by it.

The theme of the workshop is "Applications of Systemic Theory", and this suggests to me that it is in the context of what can be done with the theory that we shall be seeking to exchange ideas. The theory has evolved in use; it has no existence apart from the practice of those who use it. Systemic theory is a way of doing things. If the English language permitted such extravagances I would name it not with a noun but with an adverb; I would call it 'Systemically'. I have never found it possible, in my own work, to distinguish between the activities of working on the theory and using the theory to work on something else. The interesting diversification of ideas that shows up when systemicists get together is not so much a taking of different positions on abstract theoretical issues as a diversity in the kinds of activities in which they are engaged. The debate that arises from these differences of perspective is very much more positive and fruitful than the rather sterile confrontation that takes place when people take a stand on some theoretical point largely as a means of establishing their individual identity.

There are a lot of different doings represented at this Workshop, and enumerating some of these will perhaps give a flavour of what systemic theory is about:

- interpreting the nature, the functions and the development of language
- understanding the role of language in expressing, maintaining and transmitting the social system, in home, neighbourhood, school and other domains of the context of culture
- helping people to learn language, whether mother tongue or other languages, whether children or adults; and to use language effectively as a means of learning and in a variety of contexts of situation
- helping people to overcome language disorders, educational or clinical: 'slow learners', 'backward readers', aphasics, the mentally handicapped &c.
- understanding the nature of discourse, and of functional variation in language ('register'); studying particular types of discourse (classroom, medical &c.) for practical purposes such as the training of teachers and of specialists in the field
- understanding the nature of 'value' in a text, and the concepts of verbal art, rhetoric, and literary genres; gaining access to literature through the careful study of such texts
- using computers to analyse and generate discourse; developing a grammar for decoding and encoding, and a semantic representation to direct and interpret the grammar
- exploring a range of practical activities where language is involved: forensic issues, readability and complexity measures, communication in institutional settings and so on
- relating language to other semiotic systems and to the ideological patterns of the culture

This is a rather broad spectrum of doings, and it reflects the broad foundation on which systemic theory is built. The workshop brochure refers to the theory as being 'neo-Firthian'; and although I have never used that label myself, I have always made it clear that the most important influence on my own thinking came from my teacher J. R. Firth. Those who know Yorkshire—once described by Mary Abercrombie as 'the Texas of England'—will recognize the significance of the fact that we are both Yorkshiremen, and indeed grew up in the same home town (but in fact you do not need to have heard of Wharfedale in order to take this point—you only need to have heard of Whorf). It is from Firth, of course, that the concept of 'system' is derived, from which systemic theory gets its name; and unlike most of the other fundamental concepts, which were common to many groups of post-Saussurean linguists, particularly in Europe, the system in this sense is found only in Firth's theoretical framework.

Firth himself always emphasized his debt to the work of others. Among his predecessors and contemporaries, he held Hjelmslev in particularly high regard (though he thought Saussure overrated); he spoke admiringly of Trubetzkoy, Benveniste, Whitehead, Wittgenstein; but above all he acknowledged what he owed to Malinowski. Dr. Hasan's paper traces the genesis of the Malinowskian element in Firth's thinking, especially the origins of contextual theory, which was the foundation of Firth's functional analysis of meaning as 'serial contextualization'. I would like to take the story a little further by referring to the work of my own seniors and immediate precursors, who obviously were not part of Firth's inheritance but from whom I have learnt the greater part of whatever I have been able to apply. I feel I should apologize for expressing this in personal terms as a kind of catalogue of 'these have influenced me'; this is done partly to keep it short, but also because to represent it in third person language as 'the origins of systemic theory' would be to impute a questionable objectivity to something that is inevitably more in the nature of autobiography.

First, then, I would like to mention Firth's own younger colleagues, especially W. S. Allen, R. H. Robins, Eugenie Henderson and Eileen Whitley. Eugenie Henderson's work showed what it meant to be 'polysystemic', and demonstrated how to describe the phonology of a language in prosodic terms. Allen showed how to describe grammar, as well as phonology, in a Firthian way, and how to compare systems across languages. Robins built up a coherent picture of system-structure theory and—uniquely at that time—placed it in another contextual dimension, that of the history of linguistics. Eileen Whitley developed a deep insight into prosodic analysis; and also, very importantly, into Firth's conception of a text.

Of those on the western side of the Atlantic, the names that were most familiar to us were those of Sapir, Bloomfield and Fries: Sapir as the leading exponent of anthropological linguistics, Bloomfield mainly for his descriptive work, especially his Menomini studies, and Fries for his clearly stated methodology and for his interest in, and influence on, language education. The more immediate impact, however, came from their successors: from Hockett, who examined the foundations of structuralist linguistics, questioned them and was thus prepared for the developments to come; from Harris, who showed just how far one could go with these assumptions and where they could lead no further; from Gleason, who presented a systematic overall model for students and teachers, and then developed his own stratal viewpoint and his theory of narrative; and from Pike, who provided a solid foundation in phonetics, a functional theory of grammar and an explicit commitment to the cultural context of language.

One other scholar who had a profound effect on my own thinking was a linguist whom of course I never met, Benjamin Lee Whorf. Whorf, developing concepts derived from Sapir and before him Franz Boas, showed how it is that human beings do not all mean alike, and how their unconscious ways of meaning are among the most significant manifestations of their culture. Whorf's notion of the cryptotype, and his conception of how grammar models reality, have hardly yet begun to be taken seriously; in my opinion they will eventually turn out to be among the major contributions of twentieth century linguistics.

Next I would like to mention five other scholars from whom I gained rich and, to me, new and exciting insights into language. Walter Simon, Professor of Chinese at

London University, taught me what linguistic scholarship meant: to focus on language as an object of study, to take the text seriously, and to combine honesty with imagination in the construction of a theory. In China, Luo Changpei gave me a diachronic perspective and an insight into a language family other than Indo-European; and Wang Li taught me many things, including research methods in dialectology, the semantic basis of grammar, and the history of linguistics in China. When I first tried to teach linguistics, in a very disorganized way, David Abercrombie provided a model of how it should be done; he also provided a lucid and totally unbiased account of the principles of speech and of writing, and placed these studies in their historical perspective. Angus McIntosh demonstrated the scope and direction of a humanist linguistics, one that neutralized the opposition between arts and sciences; this he backed up in his own work by a farsighted commitment to a longterm programme of structured research (something I have never been able to achieve), which is now coming to a notable culmination.

At the risk of turning this into too much of a personal statement, I would like to round this part off by referring to some of my own contemporaries. I shall not try to make reference to those with whom I have been most closely associated in the work on systemic theory; it would take far too long to give even a remotely adequate account, and most are, happily for me, present on this occasion. But there have been a few other special acquaintances with whom I have interacted over the years, exchanging ideas when possible and always learning from them in the process.

Jeffrey Ellis was my first trackmate in exploring the (to me) unknown terrain of linguistics. Many years ago we wrote an article together, on temporal categories in the Chinese verb, which would have been my first academic publication; but the journal editor who had accepted it died suddenly, and it was rejected by his successor and so never appeared. Through Ellis I knew the late Denis Berg, who worked on 'conceptual-functional grammar' when no one else would hear of it; and Jean Ure, who introduced the notion of register and has subsequently developed it in a systemic framework in the teaching of English to speakers of other languages. Trevor Hill initiated me into what would now be called socio-linguistics, and Kenneth Albrow worked with me on intonation and rhythm; both Hill and Albrow mastered Firth's prosodic phonology and wrote simple introductions to it, a thing which none of Firth's own colleagues ever felt the necessity to do. Peter Strevens organized the field of applied linguistics into a coherent and powerful domain of language study, in which we have continued to collaborate at a distance. And Ian Catford provided a unique understanding of human speech production, as well as a broad comparative knowledge of languages of different parts of the world.

Further afield, I came to know Sydney Lamb; at out first talk, in a Georgetown bar masquerading as a pub, where we drank the beer from his home state, it became obvious that our ideas were compatible, and we have maintained the intertranslatability of systemic and stratificational theory ever since. He reawakened my interest in the computer as a research tool in linguistics, which had been aroused when I had worked with Margaret Masterman and Frederick Parker-Rhodes in the Cambridge Language Research Unit in the late fifties. Sydney Lamb was the first to show that it is possible to make grammar explicit and computable without discarding the achievements of descriptive linguistics and the understanding of language that grew out of them.

At about the same time I came to know Basil Bernstein, philosopher and thinker, and the first social theorist to build language into his explanatory scheme. From him we have learnt just what it is that is achieved through language—the transmission, maintenance and modification of the patterns of a culture—and hence what we, as linguists, have to be able to explain by means of our own theories. From Bernstein I learnt also, for the second time in my life, that linguistics cannot be other than an ideologically committed form of social action.

Thirdly during the nineteen sixties, I began working closely with language educators; and at University College London, in the Programme in Linguistics and English Teaching, a team of primary and secondary teachers combined with linguists to work on problems of language development in school, from initial literacy through to multifunctional English in the upper forms of high school. There were two of the team who participated from start to finish: David Mackay, and Peter Doughty. Peter Doughty brought a conception of English in secondary education which was so far ahead of his time that now, twenty years later, we are at last seeing some of his ideas introduced as innovations. David Mackay transformed an impoverished notion of 'reading' into a rich conception of language development in the infant and junior school; his work was followed up by the creation of the 'Centre for Language in Primary Education' of the Inner London Education Authority, an institution which might justly have been named after him.

My concern here is with the systemic background; it would be impossible in this space to review work in systemic theory itself, which in any case is the substance of most of the present volume. But in order to bring the background up-to-date, let me refer briefly to three of the salient motifs of the past fifteen years which have provided part of the context for recent systemic work. These are: language and social reality, language and human development, and language in the machine.

George Herbert Mead (1934) regarded talk as one of the two forms of social action—the other one was play—by which an individual built up his identity; and in a series of penetrating and sympathetic studies Erving Goffman described the regulation and maintenance of this identity, under both normal and pathological conditions. Harvey Sacks came nearer to showing how language actually served these functions in a number of brilliant (but unpublished) *explications de texte*, which still however made no reference to the language system. Meanwhile Berger and Luckman (1966) had described what they called the 'reality-generating power of conversation'. The work of Gunther Kress and his collaborators, in language and ideology (Kress and Hodge 1979; Fowler, Hodge, Kress and Trew 1979), and of Benjamin N. and Lore M. Colby (1981), in the study of culturally pregnant texts such as religious narrative, have shown the potential of systemic theory as a theory of text and system for interpreting texts as ideological documents, bringing out their significance for the construction of the social semiotic.

Advances in developmental linguistics have introduced a new dimension into language education, especially in the early and middle childhood years. Educators such as Kenneth and Yetta Goodman, Jerome Harste and Martha King have been focussing explicitly on language development in their approach to reading and writing and to all aspects of the learning process, and Sinclair and Coulthard (1975) have shown how the linguistic analysis of the classroom throws light on educational practice. In Britain, Canada, the United States and Australia there is ongoing collaboration between linguists and educators using systemic theory, for the study of classroom discourse and of children's conversation, oral narrative and writing. Jay Lemke's (1982) work on science education uses a close linguistic analysis to reveal the underlying ideological structures of the education process.

The main contribution from linguistics to these activities is the study of discourse, and what makes systemic linguistics particularly relevant is its orientation towards the text. From the start it has been used in text analysis projects, such as the coding of the Nuffield Foreign Languages Teaching Materials Project Child Language Survey (Hasan 1965, Handscombe 1966), the O.S.T.I. Programme in the Linguistic Properties of Scientific English (Huddleston, Hudson, Winter & Henrici 1968), as well as in stylistic and literary studies (see especially Hasan 1964, Spencer & Gregory 1964), and studies of register variation (eg. Benson & Greaves, 1973). A recent extension is its use in text generation by computer. Systemic theory had been employed before in artificial intelligence research (Winograd 1972, Davey 1979); but to use a systemic grammar as the basis of a text generation program would be uneconomical (since it is difficult to write systemic minigrammars) unless such a program was intended to become an exportable system that could be adapted to the needs of any user. This however is what William Mann set out to achieve, in the 'Penman' project at the Information Sciences Institute of the University of Southern California; and there for the first time a comprehensive systemic grammar of English is being implemented on a computer. This is reported on in another paper in this volume, by Mann and Matthiessen (see also Mann 1983, Mann & Matthiessen 1983). Eventually it should be possible to test the thesis that such a grammar is invertible, by constructing a systemic parsing program on the lines first sketched out by B. N. Colby and Mark James.

These very sketchy references will perhaps serve to bring out what I think is a salient feature in the evolution of systemic theory: its permeability from outside. By 'outside' I mean not only outside itself, from other theories of language such as tagmemics and stratification theory, but also from outside linguistics, from disciplines for which language is not the object of study but rather an instrument for some other purpose—where this other purpose may be, in turn, either the study of some other object, such as human development or culture, or a body of praxis such as the teaching of foreign languages. Systemic theory has never been walled in by disciplinary boundaries; this is not to imply that the concept of a discipline is vacuous, but that a discipline is defined not by what it studies but by the questions it seeks to answer, so that in order to understand language, which is what the questions of linguistics are about (the noun 'language' is of course a grammatical metaphor—Peter Doughty preferred to talk about 'languaging' to show that our object of study is more process than entity), we have to study many other things besides, and hence a linguistic theory has to be a means of intersemiotic translation, interfacing with other theories of social meaning and so facilitating the input of findings from elsewhere.

The value of a theory lies in the use that can be made of it, and I have always considered a theory of language to be essentially consumer-oriented. In many instances the theorist is himself also and at the same time a consumer, designing a theory for application to his own task; in others he may be working together with a group of consumers, designing a theory for their particular needs. (Sometimes he may set up as 'pure' theorist on his own, without any particular consumers in mind; or thinking of a particular target group but without actually consulting them—the fate of 'constrastive linguistics' is a good example of how this tends to limit the usefulness of the work.) Since there are so many tasks for which one needs a theory of language, any particular theory is likely to be, or very quickly to become, a family of theories—still on speaking terms, one hopes, and with a personal rather than positional family role system. This is why there is no orthodox or 'received' version of systemic theory, such as may arise with self-contained systems that are impervious to influences from outside, when some sort of 'standard' version comes to be defined by the stance adopted vis-à-vis certain issues that are identified from within.

Systemic theory is more like language itself—a system whose stability lies in its variation. A language is a 'metastable' system; it persists because it is constantly in flux. This does not mean that we cannot characterize a particular language, but that our characterization of it has to incorporate this feature. Similarly we can state certain essential characteristics of systemic theory (cf. Fawcett 1983). Let me try to enumerate some of those that are most central to our present theme.

1) A language is not a well-defined system, and cannot be equated with 'the set of all grammatical sentences', whether that set is conceived of as finite or infinite. Hence a language cannot be interpreted by rules defining such a set. A language is a semiotic system; not in the sense of a system of signs, but a systematic resource for meaning—what I have often called a 'meaning potential' (Halliday 1971). Linguistics is about how people exchange meanings by 'languaging'.

Part of the synoptic representation of a semiotic system is an account of its structure, the organic part-whole relationships that are known in linguistics as constituency. Because of the historical association of linguistics with writing— linguistics begins when a language is written down, and so made accessible to conscious attention; so grammar evolved as a grammar of written language— constituency has tended to occupy the centre of attention; so much so that my early (1961) paper 'Categories of the theory of grammar' was entirely misread (by Paul Postal 1967) as a theory of constituent structure, and the same mistake was made by Terence Langendoen in his book *The London School of Linguistics* (1968), which makes no reference at all to Firth's concept of 'system'. In systemic theory, constituency is treated as a small, though essential, part of the total picture; and it is treated in a specific way, using ranks (which are the folk-linguistic notion of constituency,

incidentally, and also that which is embodied in writing systems) instead of immediate constituents for the bracketing, and functions instead of classes for the labelling.
These are not arbitrary choices; there are good reasons why philosophical theories
of language, which tend to be formal and sentence-oriented, use maximal bracketing and class labels, whereas ethnographic theories, which tend to be functional and
discourse-oriented, use minimal bracketing and functional labels.

What distinguishes systemic theory is that its basic form of synoptic representation is not syntagmatic but paradigmatic; the organizing concept is not structure, but
system (hence the name). Since language is a semiotic potential, the description of a
language is a description of choice. The various levels, or strata, of the semiotic
'code' are interrelated networks of options. The constituent structure is the realization of these options, and hence plays a derivative role in the overall interpretation.

2) Closely allied to this is the fact that constituent structure at the 'content' level
is part of an integrated lexicogrammar (as distinct from a syntax with lexicon
attached) seen as natural, i.e. non-arbitrary. There are two distinct, though related,
aspects to this non-arbitrariness, one functional the other metafunctional. (i) Every
structural feature has its origin in the semantics; that is, it has some function in the
expression of meaning. (This is unaffected by whether semantics and lexicogrammar are treated as one stratum or as two.) (ii) The different types of structure tend to
express different kinds of meaning, as embodied in the metafunctional hypothesis;
and constituency is simply one type of structure, that which typically represents the
experiential metafunction—the reflective component in our meaning potential. But
whereas our experience is largely organized into particulate forms of representation,
our interpersonal meanings—the active component—are expressed more prosodi-
cally, as field-like structures; and the texture is provided by the periodic, wave-like
pattern of discourse, in which prominence is achieved by beginnings and endings
(of clauses, paragraphs and so on). Like the water I was contemplating at Niagara
Falls, language is at once particle, wave and field (cf. Pike 1959); and depending on
which kind of meaning we want to be foregrounded, so our representation of its
structure needs to adapt to the appropriate mode.

3) The heart of language is the abstract level of coding that is the lexicogrammar. (I see no reason why we should not retain the term 'grammar' in this, its
traditional sense in linguistics; the purpose of introducing the more cumbersome
term 'lexicogrammar' is simply to make explicit the point that vocabulary is also a
part of it, along with syntax and morphology.) A lexicogrammar is not a closed,
determinate system; and this fact has three consequences for systemic theory and
practice. First, grammar cannot be modelled as new sentences made out of old
words—a fixed stock of vocabulary in never-to-be-repeated combinations. On the
one hand, we process and store entire groups, phrases, clauses, clause complexes
and even texts; this is a crucial element in a child's language development. On the
other hand, we constantly create new words, and even now and again new morphemes. The higher the rank, the more likely a given instance is to be in some sense
a first occurrence; but there is nothing remarkable about that. Secondly, and closely
related to the last point, the lexicogrammatical system of a language is inherently

probabilistic. It has been readily accepted that the relative frequency of words is a systematic feature of language, but this principle has not generally been extended to grammatical systems; yet it is a fundamental property of grammar that, at least in some systems, the options are not equiprobable, and this can be built in to the representation of a grammatical network. The principle is an important one because it is likely that one of the significant differences between one register and another is a difference of probabilities in the grammar (this again is to be expected, since it is clearly true of the vocabulary—different registers display different lexical probabilities). Thirdly, grammar is indeterminate in the sense that there are often two or more possible grammatical interpretations of an item, each of which relates it to a different set of other items, thus making a particular generalization of a paradigmatic kind. This may affect anything from an entire system—transitive and ergative interpretations of English transitivity would be a case in point—to a single instance, where alternative analyses can be suggested for some item in a particular text.

4) A fourth assumption of systemic theory is that language is functionally variable; any text belongs to some register or other. (Dialect variation is also functional, of course, as the symbolic vehicle of social structure; but the term 'functional variety' refers to register). The different kinds of situation that collectively constitute a culture engender different kinds of text; but if we understand the semiotic properties of a situation we can make predictions about the meanings that are likely to be exchanged, in the same way that the interactants make predictions, and in so doing facilitate their own participation. The notions of field, mode and tenor, together with the subsequent distinction into personal and functional tenor, provided an initial conceptual framework for characterizing the situation and moving from the situation to the text; and much current work in systemic theory is directed towards the construction of an adequate model of register and genre, taking into account the context of situation, the rhetorical structure of the text and the higher-level semiotics that make up the context of culture. This is an essential step in any adequate interpretation of language as a social semiotic, within the tradition that I referred to above as 'ethnographic' as opposed to 'philosophical' linguistics; but it also has important educational applications, for example in the development of children's writing (Martin & Rothery 1980/1). In general, as remarked above, differences among different registers are likely to be found in the relative weightings assigned to different systems: the orientation towards different metafunctions and different options in semantics. In some instances, however, more clearcut distinctions emerge; for example the different kinds of complexity associated respectively with speech and writing.

5) Systemic theory accepts the Saussurean concept of how the system is represented by the observed *actes de parole*. But, as I see it at least, this has to be interpreted as Hjelmslev interpreted it; first in the framework of system and process, where the process (text) 'instantiates' the system, and secondly, with a distinction between instantiation and realization. The latter refers to the stratal organization of the system (and therefore also of the process) whereby the expression is said to 'realize' the content.

To take the latter point first: we assume that language is stratified. The number of strata ('levels', in Firth's terminology) that we recognize, and the kind of relationship between strata, will tend to depend on the questions we are asking and the problems we are trying to solve. For example, for certain purposes we may want to work with a Hjelmslevian model of content and expression, the only stratal boundary being the Saussurean line of arbitrariness; this is a way of pushing the grammar so far towards the interface as to incorporate the semantics within it. For other purposes, such as the study of language development, especially the move from protolanguage to language, we may want to interpret the lexicogrammar as a third, purely abstract, level of coding that gets 'slotted in' between the two interface levels of semantics and phonology. We may want to add other, higher-level strata to accommodate a theory of register, or to represent the knowledge base in a text generation program. It is the basic concept of stratification that is important.

Secondly, whereas Saussure, in separating *langue* from *parole,* drew the conclusion that linguistics was a theory of *langue,* systemic theory follows Hjelmslev in encompassing both. For a linguist, to describe language without accounting for text is sterile; to describe text without relating it to language is vacuous. The major problem perhaps is that of interpreting the text as process, and the system as evolution (its ontogenesis in the language development of children): in other words, of representing both the system and its instantiation in dynamic as well as in synoptic terms. Dynamic models of semiotic systems are not yet very well developed, and this is one of the problems that theorists of language now have to solve.

6) It is a general feature of semiotic systems that they develop and function in a context, and that meaning is a product of the relationship between the system and its environment—where that environment may be another semiotic system. For language, the context of the system is the higher level semiotics which it serves to realize; hence it is the stratal representation that allows us to interpret the context of the system (Malinowski's 'context of culture'). It is in this sense that semantics is an interface ('interlevel', in earlier terminology), namely when we are considering it as the relationship between the lexicogrammar and some higher-level semiotic. The context of a text, on the other hand, is Malinowski's 'context of situation': the configuration of semiotic processes that are constitutive of its rhetorical structure and shape its ideational, interpersonal and textual characteristics. Systemic theory has always been explicitly contextual, in both these senses, offering contextual explanations for such problems as how children learn language from what goes on around them and how language provides a grid for the construction of models of experience.

7) Finally, given the tradition to which it belongs, it is to be expected that those using systemic theory have tended to take a particularist rather than a generalist position with regard to linguistic categories. In part, this has been to avoid claiming universality for categories such as 'cases', or phonological features, that seemed far too specific to bear such a theoretical load, but equally, perhaps, from the knowledge that, while no one is likely to question the identity of all languages at a sufficiently abstract level, for most purposes for which linguistic theory is used it is

the DIFFERENCES among languages that need to be understood—while in those applications where only one language is concerned, the universality or otherwise of its categories is irrelevant.

I am not suggesting for a moment that these observations are acts of faith to which all 'systemicists' subscribe; but that it is an inclination to adopt viewpoints such as these that leads people to explore the potential of systemic theory. What is perhaps a unifying factor among these who work within this framework is a strong sense of the social accountability of linguistics and linguists. Systemic theory is designed not so much to prove things as to do things. It is a form of praxis. I have often emphasized that language, both in its nature and in its ontogenetic development, clearly reveals a dual function; it is at once, and inseparably, a means of action and a means of reflection. Linguistics, as metalanguage, has to serve the same twofold purpose. Systemic theory is explicitly constructed both for thinking with and for acting with. Hence—like language, again—it is rather elastic and rather extravagant. To be an effective tool for these purposes, a theory of language may have to share these properties with language itself: to be non-rigid, so that it can be stretched and squeezed into various shapes as required, and to be non-parsimonious, so that it has more power at its disposal than is actually needed in any one context.

Systemic theory, then, is a way of thinking about language and of working on language—and through language, on other things. But it is also a symbolic system; and, as every infant knows, symbols do not affect things, only people. Thus 'applying' linguistics is using a linguistic theory to act on people. But thinking about language is also, of course, thinking about people, since there is no language other than in people's acts of meaning; so that action and reflection in linguistics are not very clearly separated activities. Just as, in the evolved adult language, mood and transitivity are mapped into a single clause, so that one cannot mean in one way without also meaning in the other, so in reflecting on how people communicate we are likely to be also acting on their communicative processes. It seems to me that this is a perspective which most systemicists share, and which emerges strongly in the papers assembled in the present volume.

REFERENCES

Abercrombie, David. (1965). *Studies in Phonetics and Linguistics*. London: Oxford University Press (Language & Language Learning **10**).

———. (1967). *Elements of General Phonetics*. Edinburgh: Edinburgh University Press.

Albrow, Kenneth H. (1962). The phonology of the personal forms of the verb in Russian, *Archivum Linguisticum* **14**.

———. (1968). *The Rhythm and Intonation of Spoken English*. London: Longmans (Schools Council Programme in Linguistics and English Teaching, Paper **9**).

Allen, W. Sidney. (1953). Relationship in comparative linguistics. *Transactions of the Philological Society 1953*.

———. (1956). Structure and system in the Abaza verbal complex. *Transactions of the Philological Society 1956*.

Bazell, C. E., Catford, J. C., Halliday, M. A. K. & Robins, R. H. (eds.) (1966). *In Memory of J. R. Firth*. London: Longmans (Longmans' Linguistics Library).

Benson, James D. & Greaves, William S. (1973). *The Language People Really Use*. Agincourt, Ontario: The Book Society of Canada.

Berger, Peter L. & Luckmann, Thomas. (1966). *The Social Construction of Reality: a treatise in the sociology of knowledge*. London: Allen Lane (Penguin Press).

Bernstein, Basil. (1971). *Class, Codes and Control I: theoretical studies towards a sociology of language*. London: Routledge & Kegan Paul (Primary Socialization, Language and Education).

————. (1975). *Class, Codes and Control III: towards a theory of educational transmissions*. London: Routledge & Kegan Paul (Primary Socialization, Language and Education). 2nd ed., 1977.

Bloomfield, Leonard. (1962). *The Menomini Language*. New Haven, CT & London: Yale University Press.

Butler, C. S. (1979). Recent developments in systemic linguistics. *Linguistics and Language Teaching: Abstracts* **12.**

Catford, J. C. (1965). *A Linguistic Theory of Translation*. London: Oxford University Press (Language and Language Learning **8**).

————. (1977). *Fundamental Problems in Phonetics*. Bloomington, IN: Indiana University Press.

Colby, Benjamin N. & Colby, Lore M. (1981). *The Daykeeper: the life and discourse of an Ixil diviner*. Cambridge, MA & London: Harvard University Press.

Davey, Anthony. (1979). *Discourse Production*. Edinburgh: Edinburgh University Press.

Doughty, Peter. (1976). *Language, "English" and the Curriculum*. London: Edward Arnold (Schools Council Programme in Linguistics and English Teaching).

Doughty, Peter, Pearce, John & Thornton, Geoffrey. (1972). *Exploring Language*. London: Edward Arnold (Schools Council Programme in Linguistics and English Teaching).

Ellis, Jeffrey. (1958). General linguistics and comparative philology. *Lingua* **7.** Reprinted in Ellis (1966).

————. (1966). *Towards a General Comparative Linguistics*. The Hague: Mouton (Janua Linguarum Series Minor **52**).

Ellis, Jeffrey & Halliday M. A. K. (1951). Temporal categories in the Modern Chinese verb (unpublished).

Fawcett, Robin P. (1983). Language as a semiological system: a reinterpretation of Saussure. In John Morreall (ed.), *The Ninth LACUS Forum*. Columbia, SC: Hornbeam Press.

Firth, J. R. (1935). The technique of semantics. *Transactions of the Philological Society 1935*. Reprinted in J. R. Firth, *Papers in Linguistics 1934–1951*. London: Oxford University Press, 1957.

————. (1945). Wartime experiences in linguistic training. *Modern Languages* **26.**

————. (1957). Synopsis of linguistic theory. In J. R. Firth (ed.), *Studies in Linguistic Analysis* (Special Volume of the Philological Society). Oxford: Blackwell. Reprinted in Palmer, F. R. (ed.), *Selected Papers of J. R. Firth 1952–59*. London: Longman (Longman Linguistics Library), 1968.

Fowler, Roger, Hodge, Bob, Kress, Gunther, & Trew, Tony. (1979). *Language and Control*. London: Routledge & Kegan Paul.

Fries, Charles Carpenter. (1940). *American English Grammar*. New York: Appleton-Century-Crofts (National Council of Teachers of English, English Monograph **10**).

Gleason, H. A., Jr. (1966). The organization of language: a stratificational view. *Monograph Series on Languages and Linguistics* **17** (Georgetown University Institute of Languages and Linguistics).

————. (1965). *Linguistics and English Grammar*. New York: Holt, Rinehart & Winston.

————. (1968). Contrastive analysis in discourse structure. *Monograph Series on Languages and Linguistics* **21** (Georgetown University Institute of Languages and Linguistics). Reprinted in Makkai & Lockwood, 1973.

Goffman, Erving. (1963). *Stigma: notes on the management of spoiled identity*. Englewood Cliffs, NJ: Prentice-Hall.

————. (1967). *Interaction Ritual: essays on face-to-face behaviour*. Garden City, NY: Doubleday (Anchor Books).

Goodman, Kenneth & Goodman, Yetta M. (1979). Learning to read is natural. In Resnik, Lauren B. & Weaver, Phyllis B. (eds), *Theory and Practice of Early Reading* I. Hillsdale, NJ: Erlbaum.

Halliday, M. A. K. (1961). Categories of the theory of grammar. *Word* **17.3.**

———. (1971). Language in a social perspective. *The Context of Language (Educational Review,* University of Birmingham **23.**3). Reprinted in M. A. K. Halliday, *Explorations in the Functions of Language.* London: Edward Arnold (Explorations in Language Study), 1973.

———. (1979). Modes of meaning and modes of expression: types of grammatical structure, and their determination by different semantic functions. In Allerton, D. J., Carney, Edward & Holdcroft, David, (eds.), *Function and Context in Linguistic Analysis: essays offered to William Haas.* Cambridge: Cambridge University Press.

Handscombe, R. J. (1966). *The First Thousand Clauses: a preliminary analysis.* Leeds, England: Nuffield Foreign Languages Teaching Materials Project.

Harris, Zellig S. (1951). *Methods in Structural Linguistics.* Chicago, IL: University of Chicago Press.

———. (1955). From phoneme to morpheme. *Language* **31.**

Harste, Jerome C. & Burke, Carolyn L. (1977). A new hypothesis for reading research. In Pearson, P. D. (ed.), *Reading: Theory, Research and Practice.* Clemson, SC: National Reading Conference.

Hart, N. W. M., Walker, R. F. & Gray, B. (1977). *The Language of Children: a key to literacy.* Reading, MA: Addison-Wesley.

Hasan, Ruqaiya. (1964). *A Linguistic Study of Contrasting Features in the Style of two Contemporary English Prose Writers.* University of Edinburgh Ph.D. thesis.

———. (1965). *Grammatical Analysis Code.* Leeds, England: Nuffield Foreign Languages Teaching Materials Project.

Henderson, Eugénie, J. A. (1951). The phonology of loanwords in some Southeast Asian languages. *Transactions of the Philological Society 1951.* Reprinted in F. R. Palmer (ed.), 1970.

———. (1966). Towards a prosodic statement of Vietnamese syllable structure. In Bazell, C. E. et al. (eds.), 1966.

Hill, Trevor. (1958). Institutional linguistics. *Orbis* **7.**

———. (1966). The technique of prosodic analysis. In Bazell, C. E. et al. (eds.), 1966.

Hjelmslev, Louis (1961). *Prolegomena to a Theory of Language.* trans. J. Whitfield. Madison, WI: University of Wisconsin Press. (Danish original: Copenhagen, 1943.)

Hockett, Charles, F. (1954). Two models of grammatical description. *Word* **10.**

———. (1961). Linguistic elements and their relations. *Language* **37.**

———. (1968). *The State of the Art.* The Hague: Mouton.

———. (1967). *Language, Mathematics and Linguistics.* The Hague: Mouton.

Huddleston, R. D., Hudson, R. A., Winter, E. O. & Henrici, A. (1968). *Sentence and Clause in Scientific English.* Communication Research Centre, University College London. (O.S.T.I. Programme in the Linguistic Properties of Scientific English, Final Report.)

King, Martha & Rentel, Victor. (1979). Toward a theory of early writing development. *Research in the Teaching of English* **13.**

Kress, Gunther & Hodge, Robert. (1979). *Language as Ideology.* London: Routledge & Kegan Paul.

Lamb, Sydney M. (1966). On the mechanization of syntactic analysis. In Hays, David G. (ed.), *Readings in Automatic Language Processing.* New York: American Elsevier.

———. (1964). Stratificational linguistics as a basis for machine translation. Tokyo: Seminar on Mechanical Translation (mimeo). Reprinted in Makkai & Lockwood (eds.), 1973.

———. (1966). *Outline of Stratificational Grammar.* Washington, D.C.: Georgetown University Press.

———. (1974). Dialogue. In Herman Parret (ed.), *Discussing Language.* The Hague: Mouton (Janua Linguarum Series Maior **93**).

Langendoen, Terence D. (1968). *The London School of Linguistics: a study of the linguistic theories of B. Malinowski and J. R. Firth.* Cambridge, MA: M.I.T. Press (Research Monograph **46**).

Lemke, J. L. (1982). *Classroom Communication of Science.* (N.S.F. Project, Final Report.) ERIC no. **222 346.**

———. (forthcoming). The language of science teaching. In Shirley Brice Heath (ed.), *Language in the Professions.* Cambridge: Cambridge University Press.

Mackay, David, Thompson, Brian & Schaub, Pamela. (1970). *Breakthrough to Literacy: Teacher's Manual*. London: Longman. (Schools Council Programme in Linguistics and English Teaching.) (2nd (illustrated) ed., 1978.)

Makkai, Adam & Lockwood, David G. (eds.). (1973). *Readings in Stratificational Linguistics*. University, AL: University of Alabama Press.

Malinowski, Bronislaw, (1923). The problem of meaning in primitive languages. Supplement I to C. K. Ogden & I. A. Richards, *The Meaning of Meaning*. London: Kegan Paul. (International Library of Psychology, Philosophy and Scientific Method.)

Mann, William C. (1983). *An Overview of the Nigel Text Generation Grammar* and *An Overview of the Penman Text Generation System*. Information Sciences Institute, University of Southern California. (ISI/RR-830-113,114.)

Mann, William C. & Matthiessen, Christian M. I. M. (1983). *Nigel: a systemic grammar for text generation*. Information Sciences Institute, University of Southern California. (ISI/RR-83-105.)

Martin, J. R. & Rothery, Joan. (1980–1). *Writing Project: Report 1980, 1981*. Linguistics Department, University of Sydney.

McIntosh, Angus. (1961). Patterns and ranges. *Language* **37**. Reprinted in McIntosh & Halliday, 1966.

McIntosh, Angus & Halliday, M. A. K. (1966). *Patterns of Language: papers in general, descriptive and applied linguistics*. London: Longmans (Longmans' Linguistics Library).

Mead, George, H. (1934). *Mind, Self and Society: from the standpoint of a social behaviourist*. Morris, Charles W. (ed.). Chicago, IL & London: University of Chicago Press.

Monaghan, James (1979). *The Neo-Firthian Tradition and its Contribution to General Linguistics*. Tübingen, Germany: Niemeyer (Linguistische Arbeiten **73**).

Palmer, F. R. (ed.). (1970). *Prosodic Analysis*. London: Oxford University Press (Language and Language Learning **25**).

———. (1968). *Selected Papers of J. R. Firth 1952–1959*. London: Longmans (Longmans' Linguistics Library).

Pike, Kenneth, L. (1943), *Phonetics: a critical analysis of phonetic theory, and a technic for the practical description of sounds*. Ann Arbor: University of Michigan Press.

———. (1943). Taxemes and immediate constituents. *Language* **19**.

———. (1954–1960). *Language in Relation to a Unified Theory of the Structure of Human Behaviour*. Glendale, CA: Summer Institute of Linguistics. (2nd ed., The Hague: Mouton, 1967.)

———. (1959). Language as particle, wave and field. *The Texas Quarterly* **2**.

Postal, Paul, M. (1967). *Constituent Structure*. 2nd ed. IJAL (Indiana University Research Center in Anthropology, Folklore and Linguistics, Publication **30**).

Robins, R. H. (1957). Aspects of prosodic analysis. *Proceedings of the University of Durham Philosophical Society* **I**, Series B (Arts), I. Reprinted in Palmer (ed.), 1970.

———. (1961). John Rupert Firth. (obituary). *Language* **37**.

———. (1963). General Linguistics in Great Britain 1930–1960. In Mohrmann, Christine, Norman, F. W. & Sommerfelt, Alf (eds.). *Trends in Modern Linguistics*. Utrecht, The Netherlands: Spectrum.

Sinclair, John McH., Jones, S. & Daley, R. (1970). *English Lexical Studies*. Department of English, University of Birmingham. (O.S.T.I. Project C/LP/08 Final Report.)

Sinclair, John McH., & Coulthard, Malcolm. (1975). *Towards an Analysis of Discourse: the English used by teachers and pupils*. London: Oxford University Press.

Spencer, John & Gregory, Michael. (1964). An approach to the study of style. In Nils Erik Enkvist, John Spencer & Michael Gregory, *Linguistics and Style*. London: Oxford University Press (Language and Language Learning **6**).

Strevens, Peter. (1965). *Papers in Language and Language Teaching*. London: Oxford University Press (Language & Language Learning **9**).

———. (1977). *New Orientations in the Teaching of English*. London: Oxford University Press.

Turner, Geoffrey J. (1970). A linguistic approach to children's speech. In Turner, Geoffrey J. & Mohan, Bernard A. (eds.), *A Linguistic Description and Computer Programme for Children's Speech*. London: Routledge & Kegan Paul (Primary Socialization, Language & Education).

Ure, Jean. (1982). "Introduction: approaches to the study of register range." In Ellis, Jeffrey & Ure, Jean (eds.), *Register Range and Change*. Berlin: Mouton (International Journal of the Sociology of Language **35**).

————. (in press). *Patterns and Meanings: an introduction to systemic grammar and its application to the description of registers in contemporary English*. London: Allen & Unwin.

Ward, Dennis (ed.) (1972). *Report of the Contemporary Russian Language Analysis Project*. Language Centre, University of Essex.

Whitley, Eileen, M. (1966). Contextual analysis and Swift's Little Language of the *Journal to Stella*. In Bazell, C. E., Catford, J. C., Halliday, M. A. K. & Robins, R. H. (eds.), *In Memory of J. R. Firth*. London: Longmans (Longmans Linguistics Library).

Whorf, Benjamin Lee. (1941). The relation of thought and habitual behaviour to language. In Spier, Leslie (ed.), *Language, Culture and Personality: essays in memory of Edward Sapir*. Menasha, WI: Sapir Memorial Publication Fund. Reprinted in Whorf, 1956.

————. (1945). Grammatical categories. *Language 21*. Reprinted in Whorf, 1956.

————. (1956). *Language, Thought and Reality: selected writings*, Carroll, John B. (ed.). Cambridge, MA: M.I.T. Press.

Winograd, Terry. (1972). *Understanding Natural Language*. Edinburgh: Edinburgh University Press.

Meaning, Context and Text—   **2**
Fifty Years after Malinowski

Ruqaiya Hasan
Macquarie University
Australia

Perhaps a more accurate title for this paper would have been *Malinowski Forty Years after Himself*, for in fact, I am not concerned here with reviewing developments in the study of meaning, context and text since his time; rather, my primary concern is a review of the traditional reviews of Malinowski. Any comparison of his position with that of some of the famous modern authorities in these areas is largely incidental upon this primary concern. The time seems ripe—both historically and academically—for such an enterprise. Historically, we are close to the first centenary of Malinowski's birth, and we are just four decades away from his last writings. But more important is the change in the academic scene: the recent revolution against the so-called Chomskian revolution in linguistics cannot but draw attention to Malinowski. There has grown a practice, in the past decade, among linguists, anthropologists, AI specialists—in fact just about anyone interested in language—to begin their own discussion of some linguistic problem by first drawing attention to the inadequacies of the present day linguistic models. As an example let me quote Schank and Abelson, AI specialists, who claim that "linguistics has managed to miss the central problems", because linguists have concerned themselves with

> . . . considerations of semantics at the level of 'can one say this? Will it mean something?'. People already know what they want to say and that it is meaningful. (Schank & Abelson 1977:7)

They also criticize linguists for having failed to understand understanding. For this failure they offer the following reasons:

> . . . semantic features are considerably more important than linguists had generally been willing to acknowledge . . . there has been increasing recognition that context is of overwhelming importance in the interpretation of text. Implicit real world knowledge is very often applied by the understander, and this knowledge can be very highly structured. The appropriate ingredients for extracting the meaning of a sentence, therefore, are often nowhere to be found within the sentence. (Schank & Abelson 1977:9)

To Malinowski, writing in 1923, approximately half a century before Schank & Abelson, none of this would have sounded particularly revolutionary or even original. In this early essay he claimed that:

. . . utterance and situation are bound up inextricably with each other and the context of situation is indispensable for the understanding of the words. Exactly as in the reality of spoken or written language, a word without *linguistic context* is a mere figment and stands for nothing by itself, so in the reality of a spoken living tongue, the utterance has no meaning except in the *context of situation*. (Malinowski 1923:307)

I must admit I find Malinowski's formulation preferable to that of Schank & Abelson's, for, in him, there is not the hidden assumption that the knowledge of the world is sharply distinct from the knowledge of language. For Malinowski there was a continuity between words and action, between social knowledge and social semiotic, the recognition of which is only just beginning to become fashionable amongst those dealing with language. But in making these comments I am anticipating myself, so let me begin again—and this time with a personal anecdote.

I was asked a few months ago if I could name a small book on Malinowski, such as perhaps Culler's *Saussure*. True to the Malinowski-Firth prediction, my text was affected by the properties of its linguistic context; so I asked: "How about Fontana Modern Masters?". I was told that they do not have one. I have checked personally since, and surely enough, Malinowski is no modern master. This state of affairs seems to me quite typical; and it is typical both of Malinowski and of intellectual fashions in the academic world. Let me develop this comment.

First, it is typical of Malinowski to miss the Modern Masters series. After all, Raymond Firth's *Man and Culture: An Evaluation of the Work of Bronislaw Malinowski* opens as follows:

This book has been written because some of us have thought for a long while that too little attention has been paid to the work of Bronislaw Malinowski. (R. Firth 1957:1)

With very minor adjustments, I too could have begun my paper with these same words without violating any truth conditions! Of course, Raymond Firth was concerned mainly with Malinowski the anthropologist, about whom Edmund Leach comments:

. . . Malinowski transformed ethnography from the museum study of items of custom into the sociological study of systems of action. (Leach 1957:119)

Coming from Edmund Leach, this is high praise indeed, for he is not entirely uncritical of Malinowski's contributions to his chosen field. However, insofar as boundaries in the realm of knowledge have any reality, I shall not be concerned in this paper with Malinowski as an anthropologist. By taking this position, I wish to claim a neutral stance about his hypotheses regarding the origins of cultural institutions. Though quite obviously the same teleological stance is carried over into his thinking about language, the situation appears somewhat different, as I hope will emerge later. An early appraisal of Malinowski's contribution to linguistics comes from a close contemporary, J. R. Firth:

The most outstanding anthropological contribution to linguistics in recent years is Malinowski's Supplement to Ogden & Richards' *Meaning of Meaning*. (J. R. Firth 1930:150)

And, again writing in *Man and Culture,* he declared:

> We can be proud to include him as one of the makers of linguistics as we now
> understand it in this country. (J. R. Firth 1957:94)

Though not as caustic in his criticism as Edmund Leach, J. R. Firth could hardly be
described as an unquestioning admirer of Malinowski's views on language. I mention this to emphasize the fact that the appraisals presented above are taken from
discerning readers. They are, thus, doubly interesting as they highlight the fact that
despite being a scholar of appreciable stature, Malinowski typically did not attract
as much attention as might have been expected. The question naturally arises: why
has his work been so undervalued? Malinowski's main contribution to linguistics—
as Firth was quick to recognize—was his enunciation of the relationship between
language and the context of situation. Today most literature in linguistics, whether
concerned with models for the description of language as system, or for text production, text comprehension or for translation, recognizes the centrality of similar ideas
under such impressive labels as *knowledge of the world, belief system, logic of
conversation,* and so on. I doubt if these high-sounding concepts are better reasoned
out today, made more objective, theoretically more viable or even more explicit
than Malinowski's own description of context of situation or of culture. Why has
the modern terminology caught on, bringing such prestige to the creators? and why
is reference to Malinowski still an occasion for his denigration? I suggest that these
questions can bear serious investigation, providing useful insight into the conven-
tion-bound behaviour of the academic community.

I shall myself make a modest beginning in this direction by saying a few words
about intellectual fashions, which far from being seen as mere fashions, are regarded by the pundits as totally self-evident, logically sound truths. Note the good
company Malinowski keeps in being ignored by Fontana Modern Masters. The
series includes neither Boas, nor Sapir nor Firth—and of course, to think of Whorf
in this connection would be total anathema. To turn Bolinger's phrase around
(Bolinger 1968), our minds are so in the grip of scholarly misrepresentations (Alford 1980, Hasan 1975, Hasan 1978) that I despair of Whorf ever getting a fair
hearing. But one may ask: what have Boas, Sapir, Firth and Whorf in common with
Malinowski? I would suggest that what they have in common is their commitment
to the essentially social foundation for one's ability to function as an individual.
Despite crucial differences, each one thought of language as inextricably bound up
with culture, of culture as a force essential to the shaping of the individual, while for
each the essence of linguistics is, to use Whorf's expression, "the quest of meaning" (Whorf 1956:73). In other words, these linguists can be grouped together by
virtue of the fact that they attach importance to precisely the two factors for the
neglect of which Schank & Abelson criticize today's linguists—namely, commitment to statements of meaning (Firth 1957a) and an acceptance of the centrality of
social context both in the creation and the interpretation of the text.

I suggest that in the consistent neglect of a group of the above type lies the
second aspect of what is typical in Malinowski missing the Modern Masters series.

By tacit common consent it is typical of our time to either ignore such scholars of language, or if they are noticed, it is equally typical for them to be misrepresented. Note for example that when Schank and Abelson criticize modern linguistics for underplaying semantics and for ignoring context, they do not seem to be at all aware of the existence of any of these scholars: for them—as for many—linguistics is largely synonymous with the Chomskian revolution, one of whose main contributions to the field is precisely to accentuate this questionable dissociation of language from the life of the speech community. It is hard to choose between this neglect and such misrepresentation of, for example, Malinowski's position as can be found in the writings of F. R. Palmer or Geoffrey Leech, to mention but two. In this respect, Whorf is probably the most misrepresented of all. A galaxy of impressive names springs to mind immediately—Black (1959), Bolinger (1968), Brown (1976), Cole and Scribner (1974), Greenberg (1954), Hockett (1954), Berlin & Kay (1969) and Lenneberg (1971)—each claims to have proved that the Whorfian hypothesis is untenable; ironically, it remains to be demonstrated that what they have refuted is actually the Whorfian hypothesis!

There is a danger that these comments might be read as an effort to politicize academic evaluation—worst still, they may be attributed to paranoia. So let me add at once that in drawing attention to the neglect and the misrepresentation of sociologically oriented linguistics, I do not imply any conscious academic conspiracy. However, there remains the fact that all ideology, including academic ideology, thrives by keeping the other point of view out of view. One may not set out consciously to achieve this aim, but vast differences in ideology inevitably lead to a failure in sharing the assumptions and following the motivation behind an enterprise. Notwithstanding the Gricean maxims (Grice 1975), at least in academic pronouncements it is not automatically and unquestionably evident what constitutes sufficient evidence for saying what one does say—much less, what it means to be truthful, or relevant. Inevitably, if the structure of beliefs, aims and attitudes is at variance, failures in textual interpretations are bound to occur. Instead of finding metaphors, such a reader arrives at a metamorphosis of the message. The five scholars I have named have all—except perhaps Boas—suffered in this respect. They are assigned views which they can be shown not really to hold; their position is exaggerated beyond recognition, rendering their views so untenable as to be suitable only for a merciful oblivion.

I think it is useful to enquire further into the reasons for failure in communication in this specific case. It seems to me that, in the first place, culture as the main driving force in the life of the individual is not a theme that is readily favoured—least of all in linguistics. We insist on seeing the individual as a free agent in a free society, the sole architect of his own destiny, himself the shaper of his own personality. And more relevant to the discussion here, we see him as the most significant element in the production of his parole, if not in the creation of his langue. To be sure, the immediate source of behaviour lies in the individual—and I mean not simply Saussure's executive side of language (Saussure 1916:13) but also, in an important sense, the motivational and intentional elements of behaviour must be traced, at least in the first instance, to the individual. But this does not seem to me to be the end of the enquiry into behaviour. If 'individual-ness' is at the core of behaviour, it also seems important to point out that the belief in the autonomy of the human organism turning itself into an individual is neither intuitively obvious nor empirically substantiated. Individuality and inter-subjectivity are mutually dependent notions and that argues for a social base for the construction of individuality. If we dissociate the individual from his cultural context, so that most of what is significant to the construction of his individuality is by definition a-social, then, logically the final mainsprings of intention, motivation and execution have to be sought not so much in the social environment as within the organism. And this, in the last resort, leads to a biologism whose popular name in linguistics is the 'innateness hypothesis'. This popular stance on the individual appears all the more reasonable to us, since in the literature there is no outright rejection of the possibility of cultural differences. However, while we recognize cultural differences, we also render them harmless by relegating them to surface phenomena which have only secondary importance in human affairs. The deepest stratum, it is argued, consists of the innate species-specific attributes which are ipso facto universal; culture-specific facts—if there are any—are simply surface phenomena. These attitudes are implicit in the ways in which we talk about meanings, understanding, perception and cognition. So we say that the semantic space for mankind is the same; or we insist on the centrality of 'the knowledge of the world' rather than of 'acculturation' to understanding; and so far as perception and cognition are concerned, they are basically the same across the human race. According to this philosophy, the physical is far more fundamental, far more 'real' than the social. Metaphorically speaking we overplay Freud and underplay Durkheim.

This preoccupation of modern linguistics with innateness—this insistence on the primacy of intra-organic approach to language (Halliday 1974)—is not a breakaway, revolutionary movement. Chomsky has rightly implied, by referring to distant authorities (1965), that this is a dominant stance on the Western intellectual scene, which takes different shapes to suit the current dominant ideology. Today's concern with a clear distinction between deep and surface phenomena is simply a new version of an old academic fashion. Given the intellectual convention of glorifying the innate properties of the human brain, it appears superfluous to ask: what are the factors—if any—which affect the actual development of the potential of this marvellously designed instrument? Those who suggest, like Mead (1934), that unlike the human brain, the human mind is a social phenomenon, remain on the periphery of our deliberations about language. This is not because there is a necessary conflict between accepting the universal innate properties of the human brain and acknowledging that the actualization of this potential is subject to social environment (Halliday 1974, 1977a). Rather it is because academic conventions dictate that the individual be seen as the fulcrum of the social universe. We see then that there is a considerable ideological gulf between those committed to this latter convention and those for whom the essential foundation for individuality is social in nature. Failure in communication between these two groups is not surprising once we see clearly the differences between their basic assumptions. Malinowski, without doubt, belonged to the sociologically oriented group of scholars—as did Boas, Sapir and Whorf and Firth. The misrepresentation and obscurity from which they have suffered might be described as 'an ideologically induced low academic visibility'.

I intend to argue that, whatever his shortcomings as an anthropologist might have been, Malinowski's contribution to linguistics deserves less perfunctory, less pejorative and a more serious treatment than it has so far received. I will argue this by focussing mainly on issues relating to meaning, context and text, since in my opinion it is in these domains that Malinowski made his main contributions to the study of language. I will begin by enquiring into Malinowski's views on the relationship between meaning and context; here it would be important to describe the nature of the central problem that Malinowski attempted to solve. This will take us into a consideration of the Saussurean notion of sign. I will argue that to see the relationship between meaning and context in the way that Malinowski saw it implies a recognition of the centrality of text to the study of language. Since the three concepts are closely linked, a consideration of one naturally merges into that of the other(s) and the boundaries may not be as clear as my programmatic assertion suggests.

Let me begin then with meaning and Malinowski. Most semanticists would agree with Palmer that:

> The problem of semantics is not the search for an elusive entity called 'meaning'. It is rather an attempt to understand how it is that words and sentences can mean at all. . . . (Palmer 1981:29)

Despite the risk of some oversimplification, it would be essentially correct to claim that the pre-occupations in modern semantics fall under two distinct areas. First there is the concern with questions relating to how a linguistic unit, of whatever size, comes to have the meaning that it does have. To quote Searle:

> How does it happen that when people say, "Jones went home" they almost always mean Jones went home and not, say, Brown went to the party or Green got drunk. (Searle 1969:3)

Secondly there is the concern with devising techniques following which an explicit representation can be made of the meanings that the linguistic units are perceived to have. It seems to me that important as the second concern is, the first constitutes the substance of our theory of linguistic meaning. And, notwithstanding linguists' disdainful attitude to Malinowski, I would claim that he made his major contribution in this central area of semantics.

It is a commonplace of linguistics that the basic problem—namely, "how it is that words and sentences can mean at all"—arises from the principle which Saussure described as 'the arbitrariness of the sign' (Saussure 1916:67). This principle according to Saussure lies at the centre of language; it

> . . . dominates all linguistics . . . its consequences are numberless . . . (and) not all of them are equally obvious at first glance. . . (Saussure 1916:68)

A detailed discussion of arbitrariness would be out of place here; nonetheless it seems appropriate to provide a brief account of what Saussure meant by arbitrariness of the linguistic sign and to draw attention to some of its immediate implications. This would help to define sharply the problem to which Malinowski addressed himself. I believe that *The Course* contains sufficient evidence to support the view that Saussure thought of the sign's arbitrariness from two points of view, only one of which is invariably recognized by modern linguists of all persuasions. This widely recognized aspect of the sign's arbitrariness is described by Culler in the following words:

> There is no natural or inevitable link between the signifier and the signified. . . .
> There is no intrinsic reason why one signifier rather than another should be linked
> with the concept 'dog'. (Culler 1976:19)

The signifier is un-motivated in the sense that it "actually has no natural connection with the signified" (Saussure 1916:69). Seen from this point of view, the line of arbitrariness between the signifier and the signified coincides with the line which divides the level of phonology from the rest of the language system (Halliday 1977*b*). This, as I pointed out before, is the aspect of the sign's arbitrariness which is recognized everywhere in linguistics; however, the second aspect is not so well publicized, but I believe it is equally important.

Whereas the first aspect of the sign's arbitrariness is concerned with the relation between the signifier and the signified, the second is concerned with the relation between the signified and extra-linguistic reality. In *The Course* (or at least in its English translation) the term 'signified' is often inter-changeable with 'idea', 'concept' and even 'thought'. Saussure was concerned with arguing that the signified does not pre-date the signifier—that language is not a simple naming system.

> Psychologically our thought—apart from its expression in words—is only a shape-
> less and indistinct mass. Philosophers and linguists have always agreed in recogniz-
> ing that without the help of signs we would be unable to make a clear-cut, con-
> sistent distinction between two ideas. Without language, thought is a vague,
> uncharted nebula. There are no pre-existing ideas, and nothing is distinct before the
> appearance of language. . . . The characteristic role of language with respect to
> thought is not to create a material phonic means for expressing ideas but to serve as
> a link between thought and sound, under conditions that of necessity bring about
> the reciprocal delimitation of units. (Saussure 1916:111–112)

The context of the discussion, the repeated assertions and the nature of the examples (pp 111–122) strongly support the interpretation that in Saussure's view the relationship of the signified to the extralinguistic universe was not a strictly rational one. Concepts—or signifieds—are not in a one to one relation with extra-linguistic things. Had this been the case then one could have argued, quite reasonably, for the pre-existence of the signifieds. And had it been possible to hold this latter claim, then it would have been reasonable to think of the signifier simply as a means of expression for the signified.

If words stood for the pre-existing concepts, they would all have exact equivalents in meaning from one language to the next; but this is not true. (Saussure 1916:116)

The physical properties of the phenomena around us do not contain within them any principle whereby they themselves might be segmented into 'referent' units. The fact that a certain domain of physical experience is referred to, in one language, by *mutton* and *sheep*, while in another, the same sense data is referred to only by *mouton*, could not possibly be governed by a rational, non-arbitrary principle. Thus the relationship between the signified and the bits of the extra-linguistic reality to which it relates (by signification) is itself arbitrary—and this is the second, less widely recognized, aspect of the arbitrariness of the linguistic sign. To accept these views about the arbitrariness of the linguistic sign is tantamount to the rejection of the existence of any rational principle(s) for predicting what aspect of extra-linguistic reality any sign might be applicable to. And yet, this is just a conservative interpretation. A more radical view is to hold with Hjelmslev (1953) that reality itself is relative, that it is given a shape—aspects of it are imbued with salience for the speakers of a language—largely because of the operation of the linguistic signs themselves.

These two aspects of the sign's arbitrariness give rise to most of the productive problems in the study of language. Of these the most relevant to my topic is the question of the identity, the value and the signification of the linguistic sign. I suggest that Saussure was able to provide a clearer indication of how he saw a sign's identity and value to be established, but that about signification he had relatively less to say. It is at least a theoretical commonplace of linguistics today that the identity and the value of a sign are determined by treating both the signifier and the signified as "purely relational entities". Thus the value of the plural in a three-term system—eg in Sanskrit—is different from its value in a two-term system—eg in French (Saussure 1916:116). If the nature of language is systemic, as Firth maintained (Firth 1957a), this systemic quality is entailed by the arbitrary nature of the linguistic sign. In the last resort, the value and identity of the linguistic sign is the function of its systemic nature.

Saussure maintained a clear distinction between value and signification. 'Value' is the function of relations between entities of the same order—between, say, the dime and the dollar; the value of a dime resides in its relation to a quarter, a nickel, a penny etc. Its signification, by contrast, resides in "what it can be exchanged for" (Saussure 1916:115); ie. in its relation to entities of a different order. In the case of the dime, for example, one might ask what fixed quantity of bread or milk one might be able to buy with it. The contrast between value and signification is quite clear from this Saussurian example. Value is system-internal, being defined by the relation of one sign to another in the system. This as is well recognized, brings it closest to the 'sense' of a sign (Lyons 1968, 1977). Signification, on the other hand, is not a system-internal relation; it is concerned with the relation between the sign and what the sign is a sign for. This brings the term 'signification' quite close to at least one interpretation of the term 'reference'.

Clear as the distinction is, I believe, it would go against Saussure's intentions to give the impression that the two concepts are independent of each other. Saussure made signification sub-servient to value. He claimed that without the systemic relations (which determine the value of the sign), "signification would not exist" (Saussure 1916:117); if the signification of French *mouton* and English *mutton* is not entirely identical, this is because their value is not identical; indeed it could not be, given that they participate in two distinct systems. When the relationship is expressed this way, it would appear logical to suppose that so long as the value of the sign can be established without dependence upon its signification, one should be home and dry; the theory would be free of problems and both aspects of the meaning of a sign would have a clear status. Unfortunately, this does not happen, and before long we find ourselves kneedeep in muddy waters.

If we ask: what kind of relations are essential to the determination of the value of a sign, the standard answer will invoke the concepts of 'syntagm' and 'paradigm'. But I an not convinced that Saussure's "associative bonds" are entirely inter-changeable with "paradigm", especially if by paradigm is meant a set of items capable of acting as fillers in a slot. This conception of paradigm is more in tune with, for example, Zellig Harris' 'distributional sets' and carries the implication that paradigms can be constructed without awareness of the signification of signs (Harris 1951). It seems obvious that Saussure did not intend his associative bonds to be based entirely on structural relations at the level of grammar. Consider, for example, his treatment of the French word *enseignement* (teaching). I would draw attention, here, particularly to the bond that, according to Saussure, holds between *enseignement* and *apprentissage, education*. It is quite obvious that the quality of the bond between the items here is such that neither, say, *finissage* nor *imploration* could be included in the set. If *enseignement, apprentissage* and *education* con-stitute members of a paradigm, then this paradigm can be characterized only as a set 'belonging to the same general area of signification'—what we would describe today, perhaps, as the same semantic field.

If this reading is accepted, there is an unavoidable, and I believe an intentional, circularity in Saussure's treatment of value and signification. To the question: How is signification of a sign determined?, we have the answer: By its value. To the question: How is the value of a sign determined?, we have the answer: By its associative bonds, one of which is the bond of similar signification. We arrive, then, at an impasse; no signification without value, but equally, value is unknowa-ble without signification. This provokes the observation that despite a long and resolute tradition, the ultimate basis for sense relation does not—indeed, could not—lie entirely in the value of the signs; the various conventionally recognized sense relations must rely equally strongly on the referential potential—the significa-tion—of the signs. Seen from this point of view, what began apparently as the subservience of signification to value, resolves itself into a mutually defining rela-tion. At the same time, it could be maintained that in another sense Saussure saw signification as primary—after all, the raison d'etre of the language sign is not so that it can enter into system(s) of relations; if there is any reason for its existence it is so that it can signify something. Despite this, *The Course* fails to solve the problem of how the relation of signification is to be thought of. The question hangs in the air: given that linguistic sign is arbitrary, how do we know that a sign, say, *dog* applies to this or that class of phenomena, how do we know that people mean Jones went home when they produce the sentence *Jones went home?*

Of course, I am not suggesting that there are no answers in *The Course* at all; only that the answers themselves are problematics. Thus one of the answers, as I have pointed out at some length, is: by knowing the value of the signs. Another answer to be found in the discussion is: by knowing the conventions of the speech community. I have drawn attention to a serious problem in the first answer: it gives with one hand what it takes away with the other. Let me now point to another problem which is inherent in both these answers—this is the problem of the novice trying to learn the language. How, for example, would an infant break into a system of this kind? Obviously not by first constructing the total network of relations into which the signs enter. This would be impossible, both theoretically, because of the interdependence of value and signification, and biologically, in view of the baby's cognitive capacities at this stage. And, if we say that the child learns both value and signification concurrently by being exposed to the conventions of his speech community, the question still remains: how are the conventions of a language made accessible to an immature novice? It is my belief that Malinowski's main contributions to semantics lay in his attempts to provide an answer to this basic question. Interpreted thus, his work does not run counter to Saussure's; rather, it complements it—it developes suggestions that were no more than hints in Saussure's own writing.

It was for a good reason that Malinowski raised the question of the infant learning how to mean. Palmer has recently rejected the relevance of this question to the study of meaning. He believes that:

> We shall not solve problems of semantics by looking at a child learning language, for an understanding of what he does raises precisely the same problems as those of understanding what adults do in their normal speech. (Palmer 1981:23)

Obviously not all problems in semantics are solved by looking at the child's learning of language. However, Palmer seems to have overstated his case, for there are undeniable differences between the adult and the child. It is only in the case of the adult that the question of an appeal to the notion of semantic competence can be at all entertained, as, for example, by Geoffrey Leech when he concludes his discussion of the ambiguous phrasal verb *put on* as follows:

> It is part of our COMPETENCE (the rules, categories etc that we know by virtue of being speakers of the English language) to know that *put . . . on* has at least the three dictionary meanings. (Leech 1974:80)

And, a few lines later, he goes on to add:

> We have a justification for ignoring as far as possible the study of context where it interferes with the study of competence. At least we see that the study of meaning-

in-context is logically subsequent to the study of semantic competence. . . . (Leech 1974:80)

Whatever the position for the adult, these claims cannot be made with regard to the infant; even an extreme nativist approach would baulk at the idea of innate semantic competence whereby the value and signification of each linguistic sign is already present within the folds of the baby's brain.

This debate is central to a clarification of Malinowski's position. His main interest was not the search for a methodology for the description of the contents of an adult's already existing semantic competence; rather, the question he sought to answer was: how is such semantic competence created? Two important things follow from this starting point. First, unlike Leech, for Malinowski, the meaning of linguistic units—the value and the signification of the sign—is not a given fact. The question of how this meaning should be described is logically subsequent to the question of how the semantic content of a sign is determined in the first place—in Palmer's words "how it is that words and sentences mean at all". Secondly, this preoccupation of Malinowski's provides a rational explanation for the putting together of certain varieties of language, which grouping at first sight appears ill-assorted. What is in common to "the infantile uses of words, of primitive forms of significance and of prescientific language among ourselves", (Malinowski 1923:318) is the fact that in each of these, language has:

> . . . an essentially pragmatic character; . . . . it is a mode of behaviour, an indispensable element of concerted human action. (Malinowski 1923:316)

I am tempted to suggest that Malinowski saw the pragmatic function of language as the primary one, precisely because of its centrality to the problem of signification. If a sign system is as pervasively arbitrary as the system of language is, then the only way the signification of signs can begin to be learnt—semantic competence begin to be created—is through the regularity of the correspondence between the sign and what the sign stands as the sign of. From this point of view, those contexts are more important in which such correspondence is immediately observable. And in the nature of things, these contexts happen to be the ones where language has a pragmatic function:

> The pragmatic relevance of words is greatest when these words are uttered within the situation to which they belong and uttered so that they achieve an immediate practical effect. For it is in such situations that words acquire their meaning. (Malinowski 1935:52)

It is in the environment of such a discussion that Malinowski makes a claim for the

> . . . dependence of the meaning of each word upon practical experience, and of the structure of each utterance upon the momentary situation in which it is spoken. (Malinowski 1923:312)

Interestingly, it is also in this type of textual environment that the widely misrepresented, and by now infamous, sentences of Malinowski occur.

> *In its primitive uses*, language functions as a link in concerted human activity, as a piece of human behaviour. *It is a mode of action, not an instrument of reflection.* (italics mine) (Malinowski 1923:312)

Much has been written about these views of Malinowski's. Often a reader might come across comments which leave the impression that Malinowski only discussed primitive situations, or that Malinowski's view on the relationship of context to language were made only with reference to primitive languages; often, through a juxtaposition of their names, a reader might be lead to believe that there is no appreciable difference between Bloomfield and Malinowski so far as their views on meaning are concerned; often the impression will be given that language as "a mode of action, not an instrument of reflection" is a characterization which Malinowski applied indiscriminately to all uses of language. Not one scholar appears to have noticed that there is something peculiar about Malinowski's use of the words 'pragmatic' and 'action'—that the domain of their signification in his writings is much wider than it is in our normal usage. This latter point will be discussed below, but here are a couple of quotations to substantiate my claim that Malinowski's position has been misrepresented in the above ways.

> It is noticeable that the situations to which Malinowski, Bloomfield and Morris naturally turn when they want to illustrate the contextualist thesis are all 'primitive' in one sense or another. In fact, contextualism in its crudest form . . . is incapable of dealing with any but the most unsophisticated circumstances in which linguistic communication occurs (say, telling a story, giving a lecture, gossiping about the neighbours, reading a news bulletin) observing the situation in which speaker and listener find themselves will tell little, if anything, about the meaning of the message. (Leech 1974:74)

The 'contextualist thesis' of Malinowski is about as different from that of Bloomfield's as Saussure's structuralism is different from that of Harris'; and perhaps both differ appreciably from Morris. Granting the limitations of a short introductory book, the fact should still not be overlooked that these are the ways in which academic profiles are constructed: the view that Malinowski's 'situation' is the same as Bloomfield's is widespread. No matter how practical the reasons for juxtaposing the two names, the result in my opinion is mis-information. Further, not all situations which Malinowski discusses could possibly be said to be 'primitive', even if we grant that the only sophisticated uses are those involving displaced language and/or abstract notions; the situations he discussed in some detail included displaced language as in the telling of story, gossip, boast, magical and religious rituals and decision making. Although Malinowski's account of how context of situation operated in the interpretation of, say, a story is far from satisfactory, it is incorrect to suggest that he avoided all but the most simplistic situations such as perhaps those for the use of direct directives. Finally, the reason Malinowski insisted on the primacy of 'pragmatic' contexts, in the sense in which he used the word, is well stated in Leech's words. It brings home the point that the relationship between words and context of situation is variable. As Malinowski put it "the pragmatic relevance of words is greatest when these words are uttered within the situation in which they belong. . ." (Malinowski 1935:52); this did not preclude the recognition on his part—rather it implied it—that there exist contexts of situation with a qualitatively different relationship to language (see for example his discussion of stories and rituals in *Coral Gardens and Their Magic* 1935). To give the impression, even if inadvertently, that there is any disagreement on this point between Leech's position and that of Malinowski's would be erroneous. Let me add also, that to Malinowski we owe the insight—which, incidentally, will always elude atomistic theories of meaning—that the actual environment in which one encounters a text is never irrelevant to its full interpretation; this is quite evident if we compare the interpretations of Shakespeare across the centuries.

Consider now another opinion:

> Malinowski's remarks about language as a mode of action are useful in reminding us that language is not simply a matter of stating information. But there are two reasons why we cannot wholly accept his arguments. First, he believed that the 'mode of action' aspect of language was most clearly seen in the 'basic' needs of man as illustrated in the languages of the child or of primitive man. He assumed that the language he was considering was more primitive than our own and thus more closely associated with the practical needs of the primitive society. (Palmer 1981:52)

It is true that in his earlier work Malinowski (1923) expressed the belief that word and action were so closely related only in primitive languages—ie languages of the primitive communities. But in his later publications, he revised this view.

> I want to make it quite clear that I am not speaking here only of the Trobriand language, still less of native speech in agriculture. I am trying to indicate the character of human speech in general and the necessary methodological approach to it. Every one of us could convince himself from his own experience that language in our own culture often returns to its profoundly pragmatic character. Whether engaged in a technical manipulation, purusing some sporting activity, or conducting a scientific experiment in a laboratory or assisting each other by word and deed in a simple manual task—words which cross from one actor to another do not serve primarily to communicate thought: they connect work and correlate manual and bodily movements. Words are part of action and they are equivalents to action. (Malinowski 1935:8–9)

Now, one may react violently against Malinowski's views on language and thought, on the basis of this extract; however, so far as Palmer's criticism is concerned it loses a good deal of its force. As we see, the mode of action aspect applies universally to human languages, not simply to infantile and primitive ones, though in the latter, it is more marked as also in 'unscientific language among ourselves' (Malinowski 1923:318). Leaving the infant aside for the moment, I would read this as a claim about register. That the register repertoir of non-literate communities does differ from that of the literate ones is now a recognized fact (Goody 1968, 1977); that the role of language as instrument, as a mode of action, is variable across context types is also undeniable. Although Malinowski remarked on the structural peculiarities of primitive languages, in his writings on the context of situation it is the diatypic aspect of their 'primitiveness' which he drew attention to most frequently:

> . . . written statements are set down with the purpose of being self-contained and self-explanatory. A mortuary inscription . . . a chapter or statement in a sacred book . . . a passage from a Greek or Latin philosopher . . . one and all of these were composed with the purpose of bringing their message to posterity unaided, and they had to contain this message within their own bounds.
>
> To take . . . a modern scientific book, the writer of it sets out to address every individual reader who will peruse the book and has the necessary scientific training . . . we might be tempted to say metaphorically that the meaning is wholly contained in or carried by the book.
>
> But when we pass from a modern civilized language, . . . to a primitive tongue, never used in writing . . . there it should be clear at once that the conception of meaning as *contained* in an utterance is false and futile. (Malinowski 1923:306–7)

It appears, then, that although Palmer is right in criticising Malinowski for thinking in terms of primitive and civilized languages, he is wrong in attributing to him the view that the action mode of language is applicable only to infantile and primitive languages; obviously, Malinowski thought of these simply as two of the environments which function as the domain, par excellence, for the operation of language in its action mode. That words as ''equivalents to action'' are more likely to be found in extempore spoken use of language in the course of ''concerted human activities'' seems to me quite undeniable; and that 'primitive' communities characteristically lack a written mode of expression also appears obvious. But what about the infant? Is Malinowski justified in thinking that language as a mode of action is a primary stage in the ontogeny of language? Does a consideration of the child learning language help us to solve any problems in semantics, or is it a fruitless pursuit as Palmer suggests?

Recent studies—not only the functionally oriented ones (Halliday 1975, 1979, Bullowa 1979, Wells 1981), but any others which consider meaning as central to human language (Brown 1973, Bruner 1972, Clark 1973, Dore 1974, Greenfield & Smith 1976, Karmiloff-Smith 1979 and others) provide more than just a sufficient hint that Malinowski's views on the development of language in the young child were surprisingly near the mark. Definitely the action mode of language is one of the very few which comes to the fore in the earliest proto-linguistic and linguistic systems of communication employed by the child.

> The child acts by sound at this stage and acts in a manner which is both adapted to the outer situations, to the child's mental state and which is also intelligible to the surrounding adults. (Malinowski 1923:319)

For the young child, his vocal symbols are 'equivalents of action', and they are of value because they are capable of producing action on the part of others. If it is true that in learning language, the child is learning how to mean, then certainly the child's earliest experiences in (proto-)linguistic communication are of interest. At birth the baby has no access to the verbal signs of the mother tongue—he recognizes neither the signifier nor the signified—but in a few years' time he has constructed a system of relations whereby most of the signs he uses will be imbued with the meanings conventional to his speech community. To study this process cannot but increase our understanding of how a linguistic unit comes to have a meaning in the life of an individual; and this is certainly an important question in semantics. In his discussion of language development, Malinowski argued that:

> In all the child's experience, words *mean* in so far as they act and not in so far as they make the child understand and apperceive. (Malinowski 1923:321)

According to Malinowski, the function of language as an instrument of reflection arises at a later stage; he seems to argue that both in the history of the human race and of the individual, the use of language as a mode of action is primary; its use as a mode of reflection is historically later. Hence it is often described as 'secondary' or 'derived'. The suggestion that ontogeny is a replication of phylogeny is beyond proof, but so far as the individual infant is concerned, recent research supports the hypothesis of the primacy of the pragmatic function for the young child. But what does this say about the learning of meaning?

It would be misleading to imply that Malinowski provided a detailed answer to this question, but certainly his argument is coherent and clear. In the first place one has to remember the characteristic quality of the pragmatic environment; it is here that there is 'the dependence of the meaning of each word upon practical experience'; language acts upon the environment.

> . . . a small child acts upon its surroundings by the emission of sound which is the expression of its bodily needs and is, at the same time, significant to the surrounding adult. The meaning of this utterance consists in the fact that it defines the child's wants and sets going a series of actions in his social environment. . . . As inarticulate sounds pass into simple articulations, these at first refer to significant people, or else are vague indications of surrounding objects, above all of food, water, and favoured toys or animals. . . . As soon as words form . . . they are also used for the expression of pleasure or excitement . . . (but) it is when they are used in earnest that they mobilize the child's surroundings. Then the uttered word becomes a significant reaction adjusted to the situation, expressive of the inner state and intelligible to the human *milieu*. (Malinowski 1935:6)

The child learns the meanings of the signs of his mother tongue because for the most part the words he is concerned with occur in conjunction with the surrounding social reality. His case then runs parallel to the so-called savage:

> The meaning of a word arises out of familiarity, out of ability to use, out of the faculty of direct clamouring as with the infant, or practically directing as with primitive man. A word is used always in direct active conjunction with the reality it means. (Malinowski 1923:322–3)

The determination of the domain of signification is not a sudden thing—it occurs largely because of the regularity of correlation between the sign and what the sign is a sign of. Equally, the value of a sign is not determined in one fell swoop for a baby; the regular patterns of use in the child's social milieu must play a role in this process and this could be effective only where there is a good deal of 'referential transparency'. This referential transparency is ensured for the greater portion of the signs in those environments where language acts as instrument. Recent studies—especially those in the child's learning of the lexicon—have drawn attention to the phenomena of 'over-extension' and 'narrowing'. The evidence appears strong that the approximate mastery of the acoustic shape of the sign—ie, the signifier—cannot be confused with the mastery of the signified. The child appears to go through a stage where both the value and the signification of the mother tongue signs are in the process of being internalized. Both the sense and reference—the value and the signification—relations have to grow side by side, before the child can reach the stage of approximation to the adult system. In the interim, the child's use—and understanding—of a mother-tongue-like-sign is not the same as in the adult's usage—in other words, the sign does not have the meaning for the child which the adult's dictionary credits the sign with. To study the processes whereby the child's meaning of a sign approximates the adult's meaning of that sign is to study—at least partially—how a linguistic unit comes to have meaning at all. Malinowski was well aware of these implications of the study of 'infantile' utterances:

> . . . I believe this problem will have to be studied in infantile speech if we are to arrive at the most important foundations for the science of semantics: I mean the problem of how far and through what mechanisms speech becomes to the child an active and effective force which leads him inevitably to the belief that words have a mystical hold on reality. (Malinowski 1935:65)

I am suggesting that Malinowski's answer to Saussure's problem of signification was to introduce the concept of context of situation and of culture. This latter, he some times described as the 'context of reference' (1935:51). The question how a linguistic sign such as 'dog' comes to signify extralinguistic phenomena belonging to the class DOG is answered by saying that the process involves an active experience of the word in conjunction with reality within a culturally recognizable context of situation. This is the primary means of entry into the language system. Note that ultimately, the appeal is to convention; but, unlike Saussure, Malinowski provides a clearer indication of what is essential—or at least one aspect of what is essential—to the learning of conventions. The view that the pragmatic context provides the most hospitable environment for the learning of conventions is interestingly in agreement with Lewis' view that conventions arise and are ratified in co-operative problem solving (Lewis 1968). Essentially, then, for Malinowski, meanings are social. He rejected the strong Western tradition of treating meaning as mental entities—concepts and the like.

There is indeed a danger in thinking of meaning as a concept. As Austin complains, there is a tendency to treat concept—perhaps because the word is a noun—as ''an article of property, a pretty straightforward piece of goods'' (Austin 1979:41), which can be part of the 'furniture' of man's mind. Once this step is taken, we may find ourselves recognizing a simple ''commonsense reality'' with

Leech—namely that, "meaning is a mental phenomenon and it is useless to pretend otherwise" (Leech 1974). But claims about the 'mental-ness' of phenomena can mean such different things; one needs to be clear how the expression is used. There is a very obvious sense in which every piece of knowledge is mental. Whatever the child's or adult's understanding of the linguistic sign *dog*, this understanding is surely stored in the brain; further, it is only because of the structure of the brain that it is possible for humans to arrive at understandings of this sort. But in a rather important sense it does not make the meaning of the sign *dog* a mental phenomenon; the dictionary may be located in the brain but the specific details relating to each entry in the dictionary originate not in the brain but in the social human milieu. Meaning and mind are created in a social environment, through social agencies as Luria (1976) has argued on a basis stronger than that of sheer speculation. By placing an emphasis on the role of cultural contexts in the learning of meaning, Malinowski provides support for Saussure's claim that the discipline of linguistics is an important part of the science of semiology.

This is part of what I was drawing attention to by an earlier comment that Malinowski is not in opposition to Saussure. Not only does he agree with Saussure in believing that, as a sign system, language is embedded in the social life of a community, but also he seems to take into account the existence of the language internal relations—its systematicity—which were emphasized by Saussure. Whatever his reservations might have been against the Durkheimian principle of 'conscience collective', he does not deny the most crucial characteristic of language—namely its coherent inner structure, and the centrality of this to the 'meaningfulness' of a sign. This is obvious from his treatment of a part of the semantic field of 'garden site' in Kiriwinian. In dealing with the relations between such signs of the language as *buyagu, odila, yosewo, baleko, bagula* etc, he shows that he has a fairly sophisticated notion of the linguistic sign. The discussion is concluded as follows:

> The definition of the word consists partly in placing it within its cultural context, partly in illustrating its usage in the context of opposites and of cognate expressions. (Malinowski 1935:16)

Nor is it possible to maintain the view that Malinowski was so simpleminded as to advocate the naming theory of meaning. Consider:

> It is obvious that words do not live as labels attached to pieces of cultural reality. Our Trobriand garden is not a sort of botanical show with tags tied on to every bush, implement or activity. (Malinowski 1935:21)

His terminology surely differs from ours, but I doubt if his understanding of the relations into which signs enter is any less advanced. Consider, for example, the following passage:

> . . . words do not exist in isolation . . . words are always used in utterances. . . .
> A one-word sentence, such as a command . . . may . . . be significant through its
> context of situation only. Usually a one-word sentence will have to be explained by

connecting it with utterances which preceded it or which follow. To start with single words . . . is the wrong procedure. But this I do not need to elaborate; for it is now a commonplace of linguistics that the lowest unit in language is the sentence not the word . . . even the sentence is not self-contained, self-sufficient unit of speech. Exactly as a single word is . . . meaningless and receives its significance through the context of other words, so a sentence usually appears in the context of other sentences and has meaning only as a part of a larger significant whole. (Malinowski 1935:22)

In these words of Malinowski, we have a precursor to J. R. Firth's view of meaning as a "complex of contextual relations" (Firth 1957*a*:19).

Malinowski was ahead of his time in drawing attention to the relevance of context of situation to the study of language as he was also in predicting the importance of functional approaches to dvelopmental linguistics. At the same time he was, without doubt, one of the few scholars first to point out the need for treating the text as central to the interpretation of the linguistic units of all sizes. For him, unlike Lyons, the language system was not a set of sentences (Lyons 1977:585); it was a resource for the living of communal life in culturally created contexts, which implies, from the very beginning, the recognition of text as a significant unit of linguistic analysis. That these intuitive insights were not developed by him into a well articulated coherent theory is certainly true (Palmer 1981:53); but this does not throw into doubt the acuteness of his insight, especially when we realize that today, even half a century after him, such a theory cannot be found in the currently valued reflections of the often-cited authorities in the areas of pragmatics, developmental linguistics, semantics and discourse analysis. To focus here simply on the connection between meaning and text, far from treating sentence as "the lowest unit in language" as Malinowski suggested, the main preoccupation of semantic experts till very recently has been with isolated words. Progress—thanks to logic and philosophy—has meant a shift of interest from words to sentences. But these too now receive attention each in isolation from its textual environment. In fact, since most examples are conjured up by linguists trying to prove a point, these can have no textual environment—they arise out of nothing, lead into nothing and themselves are nothing compared to the naturally functioning sentences of a 'live tongue' used in the service of everyday activity.

What is most remarkable about Malinowski's hypotheses regarding meaning, context and text is the fact that his approach spans rather than exaggerates the distance between langue and parole. With his view of the social context as playing a crucial role in the transmission of language to the next generation, and with text—by implication—functioning as a bridge between the context and the system, it is easier to see the dialectic between parole and langue whereby the system is shaped by the process while the process itself is an instantiation of the system. That the hypothesis of some such dialectic between langue and parole is essential to the theory of linguistics has been argued convincingly by sociolinguists (Labov 1972, Weinreich, Labov & Herzog 1968); that it is also essential to the solution of at least some of the problems in the study of meaning is rarely recognized (Halliday 1973, 1978). To set up a dissociation between system and process—between langue and parole—of the type that Lyons appears to recommend (1977:622 ff.) leaves us in the midst of many problems. His sharp distinction between system-sentence and text-sentence appears to be motivated by a desire to maintain a clear boundary between competence and performance; and there is more than a hint in Lyons that 'linguistics proper' is concerned with competence, while performance is the domain of stylistics and sociolinguistics (Lyons 1977:585). It is clear that such a view runs counter to Malinowski's position; for him context is not something to which one appeals simply in order to find the appropriate interpretation of some multivalent lexeme such as *plant* (Lyons 1977:582) or *put on* (Leech 1974:80); nor is it a device for simply sorting out the local situational referents of deixis or ellipsis. Malinowski's view of how context functions in the creation and use of the verbal symbolic system would do all this, but more. For him it constitutes the ever-present series of semiotic frames in conjunction with which the signification of the linguistic signs is defined. It is the wider matrix within which the sign operates so that it acquires a value in the system and a signification in the world of active experience.

It is difficult to accept Lyons' contention that a set of system-sentences constitutes the 'language system' (Lyons 1977:586). There is no advantage in thinking of language as a set of sentences, even if we add the qualification of infinity to the set. Rather, language is a network of systemic relations, the systematicity of which permits the generation of any number of sentences—language is not a product; it is a principle. There is sufficient evidence in our ignorance of how to account for comprehension and production of ordinary day-to-day discourse to permit the claim that this undue emphasis on sentence as the central concern of linguistics has been unfortunate for the development of the field. It is now widely recognized that no matter how rich our description of the sentence might be, it can never hope to throw light on the real unit of human interaction—namely the text (van Dijk 1977, Petofi 1978, Hasan 1979). Even more importantly, no framework for the description of the sentence can be complete, without the means of relating it to its environment—both linguistic and extra-linguistic. This naturally implies that there has to be some kind of systematic relationship between a system sentence and its analogous text-sentence. If this relationship is one of abstraction whereby system sentences are "derived from utterances by the elimination of all the context-dependent features of utterances" (Lyons 1977:588), it is difficult to see why system-sentences must be regarded as central to 'linguistics proper', while text-sentences are not. After all, it seems reasonable to suggest that the latter would subsume the properties of the former—not the other way round. In the Malinowskian conception of the relation between sign and context, there is no aspect of the meaning of a sign—its value or signification—that is, as it were, constructed by the speech community in isolation from the context. For example, according to this view, the interpretation of the so-called 'de-contextualized' declarative sentence type as STATEMENT is based simply on the fact that in a wide range of actual contexts, this sentence type most frequently has the function of STATEMENT. In other words, it is how this type functions as a text-sentence that gives its analogous system-sentence a particular value. In my opinion a more powerful—because more comprehensive—model of semantics is one which could provide a systematic account of how classes of text-sentences are interpreted by normal speakers; this must of necessity subsume their interpretation as system-sentences.

The concept 'decontextualization' is intriguing. Lyons (1977:589) defines it, at least implicitly, as "the elmination of all the context-dependent features of utterances" (p. 588), and later in the discussion of the interpretation of an elliptical sentence it is said to "consist in supplying some element or elements from the preceding co-text" (p. 589). In other words, the de-contextualization of a text-sentence consists in the explicitization of all implicit encoding devices whether endophoric or exophoric (Halliday & Hasan 1976, 1980, Hasan 1984a, 1979). But surely this explicitization is subject to as regular rules as any other set of rules. More accurately, while the most specific interpretation of, say, the pronoun *he* would vary from one context of situation to the other, there is no doubt that *he* has a general meaning, which transcends instantial details (Hasan 1975). This general meaning may be stated as ONE (CO-)TEXTUALLY IDENTIFIED (QUA SI) HUMAN MALE, where (co-)textual identification would equal co-reference to the nearest explicitly mentioned one human male, unless there is good reason to reject this equation. The good reasons for the rejection of the equation, if any, will be found within the sentence under focus or in the accompanying text. Thus de-contextualization is not merely local and random; a large part of de-contextualiza-tion—which in everyday contact with language is simply 'interpretation' after all—is entirely systematic even if the details of the system may not be wholly obvious to us at this point in the development of linguistics. From whatever point of view one looks at the distinction between system-sentence and text-sentence, the theoretical value of this distinction appears questionable, unless one were to trivialize the notion text-sentence to mean sentences which contain errors of performance a la Chomsky. Sentence, after all, is just sign—though one of an order different from other orders of signs; it seems more viable to think of language as a set of con-current systems of options, where the selection of some path(s) is actualized as a particular sentence, this actualization itself being motivated by the context of situa-tion in which the speaker happens to find himself. Whatever Malinowski's short-comings as a theoretician, for him context of situation was not simply a cure for ambiguity, nor a search-light for picking out the specifics; for him, it was integral to the study of language since in his view the creation of semantic competence depends entirely on the systematic operation of language in social context—and, more basic than that, it provides a viable hypothesis of how the signification of signs is estab-lished for the members of a speech community. At least at the moment we have no better theory of signification, even though I might concur with Palmer (1981) that Malinowski's pronouncements lacked theoretical coherence.

I hope I have demonstrated both Malinowski's contribution to the Saussurian theory of meaning and his far from naive view of the nature of the linguistic sign system. It seems amazing, then, that instead of getting acclaim and recognition, he has more often earned criticism. Consider, for example, E. Leach who upbraids him for the shallowness of his pragmatism. Tracing the origin of the movement of pragmatism to C. S. Peirce, Leach comments highly favourably on the quality of Peirce's work, which, according to him, is:

> . . . now recognized as one of the major influences leading to the development of mid-twentieth-century logical positivism. William James was a friend and colleague of Peirce. . . . Where Pierce was austere, retiring, philosophic, James was a public figure, a missionary propagandist with a wide popular appeal. James' pragmatism is a creed rather than a philosophy. . . . Malinowksi's pragmatism is that of James' rather than Peirce'. (Leach 1957:121–122)

Regretfully, I was not able to consult Gallie (1952) whom Leach quotes as an authority on this issue, but my reading of Ayer (1968), Moore (1961) and of Smith (1978) does not agree with Leach's reading of Gallie to the extent that James should appear shallow by comparison with Peirce. These scholars draw attention to the difference between the two; Peirce is more arcane and possibly more abstract but there seems to be no suggestion that James is to be regarded as no philosopher. So if Malinowski's pragmatism is shallow it seems to me the blame cannot be laid at James's door. But is Malinowski's pragmatism shallow?

Ignoring his application of pragmatism to his theory of needs and to culture and cultural institutions in general, if I ask the above question simply with regard to language, my answer would be: 'no'. And the best I can do to prove the validity of this answer is to compare Peirce's ideas with those of Malinowski's on the child's 'acquisition of semantic competence'. Further, a comparison of Malinowski's pragmatism with that of modern pragmatists—ie. the speech act theorists, should be of interest. So first, here is Moore's view of Peirce's position on the child just learning to speak his mother tongue:

> Suppose some fine autumn day that his (ie. the child's) father takes him out for a walk. They climb a hill and at the top of the hill, the child encounters an object which he touches and finds to occasion an experience of roughness. He says to his father, "what's that?". His father replies, "That is a tree." Thus the word "tree" now means to the child something such that if he touches it he will have an experience of roughness. The child leans against the tree to rest and finds that the tree supports him. He now adds to the meaning of the tree the idea that a tree is an object such that if he leans against it he will have the experience of being supported. Suppose his father now cuts the tree down and takes part of it home and puts it in the fireplace from which there presently comes warmth. The child's meaning of tree now grows to include the idea that a tree is an object such that if he cuts it down and puts it in the fireplace he will experience warmth. The next summer he learns that objects called trees are green in summer, that if one sits under them in summer he will feel cooler etc. etc. Thus what the child means by a tree continues to grow as his experiences grow. When he gets to the point where he has had all of the commoner experiences of a tree, his meaning of "tree" will coincide with that held by most people, and he will have no difficulty knowing what they mean by "tree". (Moore 1961:50)

Comparing this with the earlier citations from Malinowski, at least on this issue, there seems to be no serious difference between the austere philosopher Peirce and the shallow pragmatist Malinowski, except that Malinowski's pragmatic contexts, having their origin in the wider context of culture, appear far more natural than Peirce's imaginary situations which have a certain degree of artificiality, common to events conceived of a-socially. This is not to claim that Malinowski is a better semiotician or a deeper philosopher, but simply to demonstrate that on the question of how the linguistic conventions are learnt by a child there is not much to choose between the two—definitely Malinowski is no shallower than Peirce. When we turn to a comparison of Malinowski with the speech act theorists, not surprisingly, we find passages in the former which could easily have occurred in the writing of, say, Austin. This is perhaps to be expected, for after all *How to Do Things with Words* is a collection of Austin's William James Lectures. Austin would have no hesitation in accepting that

> Words are parts of action and they are equivalents to action (Malinowski 1935:9)

or that

> . . . in all communities, certain words are accepted as potentially creative of acts. You utter a vow, or you forge a signature and you may find yourself bound for life to a monastery, a woman or a prison. (Malinowski 1935:53)

It would be quite wrong to give the impression that there is no difference between Malinowski and speech act theorists, who are normally philosophers. The speech act theorists have been much concerned with enquiry into the linguistic realizations of classes of speech acts (Austin 1962, Cole & Morgan 1975, Sadock 1974, Searle 1969, 1979, etc.); Malinowski never worked at that level of detail, but on the other hand, it should be added that his main aim in writing about language was not to present a detailed description of any part of the form. The second main difference that springs to mind in comparing Malinowski with philosophers of language is that he does not share their distrust of ordinary language. He would agree with Austin when the latter claims that ''words are our tools'' (Austin 1961:181). But there they would part company for Austin goes on to add:

> . . . and as a minimum, we should use clean tools . . . and we must forearm ourselves against the traps that language sets us. (Austin (1961:181)

Such logophobia is entirely absent from Malinowski. Perhaps, at the risk of stereotyping, there is a generalization to be made here. Just as philosophers characteristically display a distrust of ordinary language (Halliday 1977*a*), find it inadequate, full of traps and prone to falsity, so sociologists and anthropologists treat the ordinary language as an institution largely above question. One consequence of this difference is manifested in their respective views of reality. The philosopher's reality is given by nature; and is made up largely of physical phenomena. It makes contact with man through individual minds, while each individual mind is in many ways simply an echo of the other individual minds. Not so with the anthropologist. For him the world is largely made up of and through the symbolic systems for communication. So reality is largely inter-subjectively defined. In this respect, Malinowski and the speech act theorists are true to type. Austin, who is perhaps one of the few socially aware philosophers, maintains that

> Words are not . . . facts or things: we need therefore to prise them off the world, to
> hold them apart from and against it, so that we can realize their inadequacies and
> arbitrariness and can re-look at the world without blinkers. (Austin 1961:182)

This is the type of orientation that is responsible for the creation of the gap between
'the knowledge of the world' and 'the knowledge of language'. Malinowski's
position is radically different. Astonishing as this claim may sound to those whose
acquaintance with Malinowski is second-hand, for him the world was made of
language—at least those parts of the world which are crucial to the living of life. I
am aware this reading goes against the popular view voiced by Leech who claims
that for Malinowski "meaning is reducible to observable context" (Leech 1974:74)
but a reading of section V of the *Ethnographic Theory of Language* leaves me no
option but to reject Leech's view. Let me present a few segments from this section:

> Let us first consider the power of words in their creative supernatural effects.
> Obviously we have to accept here the intent and the mental attitude of those who
> use such words. If we want to understand the verbal usage of the Melanesian we
> must . . . stop doubting or criticizing his belief in magic, exactly as, when we want
> to understand the nature of Christian prayer and its moral force, or of Christian
> sacramental miracles, we must abandon the attitude of a confirmed rationalist or
> sceptic. *Meaning is the effect of words on human minds and bodies and, through
> these, on the environmental reality as created or conceived in a given culture.* (my
> italics) (Malinowski 1935:53)

Having attempted to show how tenuous the distinction between the imaginary and
the real is, Malinowski goes on to conclude:

> . . . in every community—among the Trobrianders quite as definitely as among
> ourselves—there exists a belief that a word uttered in certain circumstances has a
> creative, binding force.

> This creative function of words in magical or in sacramental speech, their binding
> force in legal utterances . . . in my opinion constitutes their real meaning.

> Take again the verbal act of repentance in the Roman Catholic confession of sins,
> or again the sacramental act of Absolution administered verbally by the Father
> Confessor: here words produce an actual change in the universe which, though
> mystical and imaginary to us agnostics, is none the less real for the believer.
> (Malinowski 1935:54–55)

With these statements so clearly speaking for Malinowski, I find it difficult to
imagine how he could be accused of "crude contextualism".

One explanation for misreadings of Malinowski might lie in the way he used
certain favourite words. For example the discussion of the creative power of words
from which the above quotations were taken is prefaced as follows:

> . . . to arrive at an understanding of meaning we have to study the dynamic rather
> than the purely intellectual function of words. (Malinowski 1935:52)

This might appear an astonishing claim to us since today knowledge structure and a
world created out of beliefs would be regarded as 'mental phenomena'. Most

pragmatists would agree with Malinowski when he declares that "language is primarily an instrument of action." But I doubt if they would accept the examples he provides of the "two peaks of this pragmatic power of words." The first of these is "to be found in certain sacred uses", for example in

> . . . magical formulae, sacramental utterances, exorcisms, curses and blessings and most prayers. All sacred words have a creative effect, usually indirect, by setting in motion some supernatural power, or, when the sacramental becomes quasi legal, in summoning social sanctions.

The other peak is to be found in environments where characteristically one may find a high frequency of directives. Examples would be:

> An order given in battle, an instruction issued by the master of a sailing ship, a cry for help, are as powerful in modifying the course of events as any other bodily act. (Malinowski 1935:52–53)

Passages such as these lead one to suggest that it is probably not Malinowski's view of verbal meaning which is problematic; the real problem might lie in his use of such words as 'intellectual', 'reflection' and 'abstract contemplation', as it might do in his insistence that the function of language as the creator of reality is simply an instance of language operating as a mode of action. Malinowski's usage of the words 'pragmatic' and 'action' is at least as idiosyncratic as Peirce's use of the expression 'practical consequences' in the definition of meaning. Such a wide domain of signification for the word 'pragmatic' is definitely at variance from the practices of most modern pragmatists, as a brief glance at their handling of meaning in literature will easily demonstrate (Levin 1976, van Dijk 1976, Searle 1979).

One of the most outstanding differences between Malinowski and the present day speech act theorists lies in Malinowski's idea that an isolated sentence is a fiction, since the natural unit of interaction is a text. This implies that sentences are neither comprehended nor produced apart from their context where the word 'context' subsumes both verbal and extra-verbal environment. Such an orientation to sentences would have been useful to the speech act theorists, since the speech act status of utterances cannot be determined entirely by examining the sentence-internal properties (Hasan 1982). This much is quite obvious from the current discussions of the indirect directives (Searle 1979; Sadock 1974). Although most descriptions of indirect speech acts must make a reference to the co-text, such reference remains a-theoretical and ad hoc.

These same remarks can be made with regard to the speech act theorist's view of social context. From its very inception (Austin 1962), it has been obvious that the notion 'context of situation' is absolutely crucial to any reasoned description of speech acts; nonetheless there is an ad hoc quality to their invocations of this concept. If one accepts with Palmer that Malinowski's context is 'pre-theoretical', then one would have to grant that the speech act theorist's concept of context is definitely no better. For them too context is a 'bit' of real situation; there is, of course, the difference that for Malinowski situation was fundamentally a social entity, for the speech act theorist it is more physical than social, but this is to be expected from their orientation. These comparative remarks are not intended to suggest that the work in speech act theory is less worthy of our attention or that as a semiotician Peirce is not an important figure. The aim has been simply to argue that when it comes to a comparison of Malinowski with these scholars in respect of their treatment of context of situation they have no edge on Malinowski. In fact Malinowski's conception of the role of context in the determination of the signification of a linguistic sign is much closer to that of Peirce's. To ask the question: how is it that a hearer knows that a promise is a promise? and to answer that he does so because he knows the set of conditions that must be satisfied by an utterance before it can be taken as a promise, is only half the story. Malinowski tried to demonstrate how it is that a listener gets to know the set of condition whose satisfaction counts as a promise. Naturally the question is important only if you believe that the rules for promising are not universal, but culturally variable and that their knowledge is not innate.

I have argued so far that Malinowski has been misrepresented; that his contribution to linguistics has been undervalued; that his concept of context of situation is much richer, and his views on its place in the theory of language description is far more viable than he has been given credit for. I have suggested that the reason behind this misrepresentation is his unfashionable adherence to 'anti-mentalism', and that this anti-mentalistic stance appears to be exaggerated by his rather idiosyncratic usage of a certain class of words. With a certain degree of good-will, such as we exercise in the reading of many modern favourites, his writings would not appear as unreasonable, as mindless as they do through the standard short quotes and the traditional comments included in most writings dealing with his work. Certainly, once his orientation, and the aim of his endeavour are taken into account, Malinowski's achievement does not appear mean. He was, after all, no linguist; his aim was not to produce viable descriptions of specific classes of linguistic units. More sobering, the entire debate on the centrality of context of situation to the theory of meaning was activated simply by his desire to show that the translation of ethnographic data consists in the difficult task of encapsulating a series of cultural contexts which may be quite foreign to the language in which they are being translated. To my knowledge no one has yet presented a better definition of an adequate translation and much work in the processing of information by AI specialists would imply that comprehension could be defined simply as the degree of success in the reconstitution of the verbally encapsulated context. That Malinowski arrived at important theoretical conclusions from the consideration of a purely practical problem is of interest to those of us who prefer to think of the relation between theory and practice as a constant dialogue, each improving the other by the continued interaction. In this view, linguistics is not an intellectual game concerned with superbly organized form without content; it is a field of knowledge eminently useful to mankind. In the words of Whorf:

> . . . the forces studied by linguistics are powerful and important . . . its principles
> control every sort of agreement among human beings, and, . . . sooner or later it
> will have to sit as judge while the other sciences bring their results to enquire into
> what they mean. (Whorf 1956:232)

I grant that these pronouncements sound incurably romantic; but that might be because, at heart, we remain such confirmed rationalists. Certainly, there is no hope of developing linguistics in the ways that Whorf had in mind, unless we are willing to assign as great an importance to meaning as we have done to form, until we are willing to see language not simply as a species-specific phenomenon, but also as one which is equally importantly culture-specific—until we can think of language not simply as a mental organ, ours despite our unique selves, but also as a social institution shaped according to our cultural identity—in short until we are willing to recognize the implications of linguistics being a branch of semiology. I suppose that anthropologists, whose main stock in trade is culture, are more willing to grant that the variable across cultures is as significant as the universal; Malinowski was no exception.

The flaws in Malinowski's programmatic design for the description of language to which I now turn, arise precisely because he is first an anthropologist, and only secondarily a linguist. That his notion of the context of situation was not abstract enough to be used as a general framework was first pointed out by J. R. Firth (1957a), who commented that Malinowski's context was only a bit of the social process, an actual set of events in rebus. It is certainly true that Malinowski never focussed on extra-linguistic situation with a view to systematically abstract from it just those factors which were relevant to the functioning of language. Thus a systematization of the type we find in Firth (1957), Halliday (1957, 1959), Halliday et al. (1964) and Hymes (1964)—and following them, others—is not to be encountered in Malinowski's writings; while he was fully alive to the elements of the context of situation which interact with language, he simply failed to create a 'schematic construct'. Critical remarks, such as these, are sometimes understood— as, for example, by Leech and Palmer—to imply that for Malinowski context equalled actual observable situation. This is certainly a misrepresentation since observations such as the following cannot be reconciled with a 'crude contextualist' position; (the comments below are with reference to the interpretation of the term *buyagu*):

> First we had to remind the reader of the general context of situation . . . ; that is, to indicate the social, legal and technical arrangements by which a portion of cultivable soil is ear-marked for next year's gardens. . . . Then I give the . . . approximate. . . . English label 'garden site'. . . . But this . . . term has to be redefined by fuller English circumlocutions. . . . These circumlocutions obviously derive their meaning from the reader's knowledge of how land is cultivated in the Trobriands. . . . Throughout its analysis . . . the word is progressively defined by reference to the ethnographic description, supplemented by additional information concerning linguistic usage. . . . Thus the definition of a word consists partly in placing it within its cultural context, partly in illustrating its usage in the context of opposites and of cognate expressions. (Malinowski 1935:15–16)

Again the power of the words to create reality as in magical incantations and religious rituals to which Malinowski draws attention (1935, Div. V), can hardly be reconciled with a 'crude contextualist' position, in which the linguistic sign and the physical thing named by the sign are held to be in a one-to-one (observable) correlation. I would suggest that such a misinterpretation of Malinowski's position arises from his failure to draw a clear distinction between context as a schematic construct and the material situational setting within which an interactive event takes place. It is obvious that such a distinction is essential not only in the description of displaced language but also in throwing light on the ancillary function of language which is characteristically associated with predominantly pragmatic environments (Halliday 1977, Ure 1971, Hasan 1973, 1980, 1981).

Perhaps the problems inherent in Malinowski's account of how a narrative— whether historical chronicle, fiction or myth—comes to be understood by the listener, arises partly from the above failure. While he is to be commended for pointing out the necessity for the recognition of more than one contextual frame in the description of the narrative, his treatment leaves much to be desired. Malinowski separated the context of narration—the outer context—from the context which is encapsulated within and is reconstitutable from the language of the narrative—the inner context, referring to the former as primary and to the latter as secondary.

> When incidents are told or discussed among a group of listeners there is, first, the situation of that moment made up of the respective social, intellectual and emotional attitudes of those present. Within this situation, the narrative creates new bonds and sentiments by the emotional appeal of the words. (Malinowski 1923:312–3)

This outer context, to which Malinowski refers as primary or direct, encloses another—a secondary or indirect context:

> A narrative is associated also indirectly with one situation to which it refers . . . the words of a tale are significant because of previous experiences of listeners; . . . narrative speech is derived in its function, and it refers to action only indirectly, but the way in which it acquires its meaning can only be understood from the direct function of speech in action . . . the referential function of a narrative is subordinate to its social and emotive function. (Malinowski 1923:313)

The above extracts present all the essentials of the Malinowskian view of how a narrative is comprehended. There appears to be no advance on this position though it is, perhaps, more lucidly expressed a decade later in *Coral Gardens*. Much can be said in criticism of this stance; in fact, much has already been said though sometimes the basis for the criticism is itself not justified. Let me quote Palmer as an example:

> . . . he discusses narrative, the telling of stories; but here surely, the context is the same at all times—the story-teller and his audience, whatever the story. If context is to be taken as an indication of meaning, all stories will have the same meaning. Malinowski's solution was to invoke 'secondary context', the context within the narrative; but that has no immediately observable status and can no more be objectively defined than the concepts or thoughts that he was so eager to banish from discussion. (Palmer 1981:53)

In this extract, Palmer is making three claims. In the first place he assumes that the outer, primary context for story telling is invariable; secondly he claims that Malinowski's secondary context is created to repair the 'deficiency' arising from the invariable quality of the primary one. And, finally, he discounts the secondary context on the ground that for Malinowski, context always had to be 'immediately observable', which quite obviously would not be the case with the secondary context. So the entire framework is faulty. I think Palmer can be refuted on all counts, without necessarily having to accept that Malinowski's account of story-telling is above criticism.

Palmer's assumption that Malinowski's primary context would be invariable is open to question. True that the role-relation of story-teller and audience is invariable. But this does not argue that everything else in the primary context would be always invariable, quite apart from the fact that differences in the nature of the carriers of these roles would itself create variation. Malinowski does allow for this by recognizing the importance of the 'social, intellectual and emotional attitudes of those present'; but apart from this, he also draws attention to the variety of purposes for which stories may be told and the difference that this variation would make to how the words of the story are understood by the listeners (1935:46 ff.). These are perceptive remarks on Malinowski's part as can be shown if we take an example from the familiar Western culture: Hamlet in the bush (Bohannan 1971) is different from Hamlet on the Elizabethan stage; and Hamlet in the modern classroom is different from both—it is a moot point how far the 'story' remains the same for these audiences. Malinowski's informal framework for the primary context takes into account many of the sources of such differences. But not having a schematic construct, he is unable to clarify how despite the identity of the contextual variables relevant to story-telling, there are likely to exist significant differences of the actual contextual configuration (Hasan 1964, 1978, 1980, 1984b) from one occasion to another. For this he can certainly be criticized, but it is wrong to suggest that his account of primary context presupposes uniformity of meaning.

Malinowski does not appear to be aware of the implications of his own comments. Although in *The Problem of Meaning* he was concerned mainly with pre-literate communities, the later work often makes comparative statements involving literate communities as well. He never seems to have recognized that at least in literate communities—and possibly also in the pre-literate ones—two outer contexts rather than one would have to be postulated: one, the context of story-creation, including two separable strands—the biographic and the artistic, and secondly the context of story-narration (Hasan 1964, 1979, 1984b). All else being equal, the greater the distance between these two outer frames the greater the difficulty in comprehension; and if this is the case, it does support Malinowski's hypothesis of the relevance of the outer context(s) to understanding the meanings of the story. Thus Palmer's contention that the postulate of an outer context implies invariance is quite without any basis; the criticism that Malinowski failed to follow his own lead is far more justified. And since the problem of invariance does not exist, the notion of secondary context could not be seen as a solution to it! Rather, the postulate of secondary context is needed in

order to account for a relationship between language and situation which is different
from the primary pragmatic type of relationship. As Malinowski commented:

> In a narrative words are used with what might be called a borrowed or indirect
> meaning. The real context of reference has to be reconstructed by the hearers even
> as it is being evoked by the speaker. (Malinowski 1935:46)

It is true that, as Palmer claims, 'the context within the narrative . . . has no
immediately observable status' and cannot be 'objectively defined'. So what is
Malinowski's own account of this relationship?

> . . . the real meaning of words, the real capacity for visualising the contents of a
> narrative, are *always* derived from a personal experience, physiological, intellec-
> tual and emotional . . . *such experience is invariably connected with verbal acts.*
> A narrative type of utterance is, therefore, comprehensible *by the reference of the
> statements to past personal experiences in which words were directly embedded
> within the context of situation.* (italics mine) (Malinowski 1935:46)

I have claimed above that Malinowski is not a crude contextualist for whom context
has to be always observable. The above extract argues that the 'invoked context'
can be reconstructed *only if* the hearers have had a direct experience of the words of
the story within a pragmatic context prior to encountering them in the story. The
acceptance of this position does not commit one to meaning as 'concept or thought';
it simply commits one to a memory for the meaning of signs previously encountered
and understood through the mediation of a pragmatic context of situation. Thus
once again Palmer's criticism is not to the point. This does not mean that Malinowski's position is unassailable. There are at least two very serious objections.

It is not at all obvious to what extent the reconstructed context has to be a replica
of some directly experienced context. If a close degree of resemblance is a necessary condition for the ability to comprehend the meanings of the 'narrative utterances', then the more fantastic the tale, the more problematic the Malinowskian
solution. How could one account for the hearer's comprehension of Dylan Thomas'
Adventures in Skin Trade or for Kafka's *Metamorphosis?* And we would definitely
have to write off James Joyce as sheer nonsense, unless we turned our backs to
Malinowski at this point. If resemblance between the reconstructed context and
directly experienced context is not necessary, Malinowski's account has offered no
hypothesis how the words of the narrative can be used to reconstruct a context in
which they were never experienced.

Secondly, if it is true that the meanings of the narrative utterances are derived
from a primary pragmatic context, it follows that stories could not be used for the
learning of new meanings. In fact, Malinowski acknowledges this to be the case;
having described a variety of pragmatic contexts, he goes on to add:

> . . . in such situations we have speech used in a primary, direct manner. It is from
> such situations that we are most likely to learn the meaning of words, *rather than
> from a study of derived uses of speech.* (my italics) (Malinowski 1935:46–47)

Anyone who has ever taught a foreign language knows very well that this claim is untenable. Stories can be used and are used for the teaching of new words, which, in the last resort, means for the teaching of the meanings of these words. It is at this point that I would like to make my major criticism of Malinowski. His main fault lies in the fact that he was never able to visualize the implications of language being a system. This is, of course, not to say that he did not see language as a system—he certainly did as I have tried to argue earlier with reference to his treatment of the semantic field of garden site. He, however, did not seem to realize that the very inter-relatedness of the terms within the linguistic system acts as an advantage, once an effective entry into the system has been made. To give a very simple example, if the sign system of Urdu is a closed book to you, it does not help if I say that /tʃhori/ is synonymous with /leRki/ while /tʃora/ is an antonym to both. But if I were to add that the value and signification of /tʃhora/ covers approximately the same area as the sign *lad* does in English, the rest would be clear. Although my example assumes a foreign language learning situation, this does not affect the main point I am making here. It is this systematicity of language which also permits its use as a meta-language, permitting paraphrase, explication etc. And these too are ways of learning meaning, even though these means of learning how to mean cannot be used with the infant. It may be that having defined for himself a position which was indeed novel in linguistics—for let us not forget that *The Problem of Meaning* was first published in 1923, when Saussure was not a familiar name to even linguists—Malinowski felt impelled to single it out as the 'important unrecognized'. Further, as I pointed out earlier, Malinowski was, after all, not a linguist by training; it was only through his practice that he entered the field. Be it as it may, this failure to recognize the full implications of the systematicity of language constantly mars his statements about the relation of language to context. It is this fact, rather than his insistence on the primacy of the pragmatic function that acts as a hurdle to our complete acceptance of the Malinowskian position.

It is in keeping with this underestimation of the importance of systematicity that Malinowski never raised the question: what aspects of the context can always be reconstituted by the language of a narrative utterance—ie. a displaced text? Little wonder then that his context is not a schematic construct. Further, there is no occasion for raising the subsequent question which modern systemicists following Halliday (1970) ask: why is it that the language of a displaced text invariably permits the reconstitution of these and no other contextual phenomena? In a sense, to ask these two questions is to complete the circle of interdependence—or better still, the dialectic—between text, meaning and context.

In his introduction to *Man and Culture: an evaluation of the work of Bronislaw Malinowski*, Raymond Firth makes the following comments:

> . . . the main task Malinowski had set himself (was)—a dynamic interpretation of human behaviour in the widest range of cultural circumstances, in terms which were at once more theoretically sophisticated, and more realistic, than any then current. At that time, the tradition was that an anthropologist was primarily either a

theoretician or an ethnographer, and that the theory should be kept separate from the facts. It was part of Malinowski's contribution, not only to combine them, but to show how fact was meaningless without theory and how each could gain in significance by being consciously brought into relation. The main theoretical apparatus which he constructed over a decade and a half has proved unable, in the end, to bear the systematic weight he wished to put upon it. But much of it is still usable, and it has given many ideas to others, often unacknowledged by them.

The Malinowski legend sometimes takes an extreme form—as expressed in this student's examination answer: 'Because of his views Malinowski did not make abstractions and was at best a misguided theorist.' Such a distortion of his theoretical position ignores his keen preoccupation with methodology—and indeed his general interest in philosophical issues. (R. Firth 1957:2)

These remarks are made about Malinowski the anthropologist; but with very few alterations, they would express the position regarding Malinowski the linguist. I have attempted to show in this essay how the 'legend has taken an extreme form' in linguistics, and how 'too little attention has been paid to the work of Bronislaw Malinowski'. Unlike the authors of *Man and Culture,* I have no personal allegiance to Malinowski, but in the light of revived interest in the so-called pragmatics, it seems appropriate to point out that we gain nothing by either ignoring him or by keeping alive legends which take extreme form. The handling of the concept of context in present day speech act theory, which appears to me in no way better articulated than Malinowski's, should give us a pause if nothing else does. Even if we are willing to ignore his achievements—and these were considerable as I have argued—let us at least not ignore the real shortcomings of his position, for retracing an erroneous path with great aplomb is far less excusable than making mistakes in the very first exploration.

REFERENCES

Alford, D. K. H. (1980). The demise of the Whorf hypothesis. Mimeo. Berkeley, CA: University of California.
Austin, J. L. (1961). *Philosophical Papers.* 3rd ed. Urmson, J. O. & Warnock, G. J. (eds.) 1979. Oxford: O.U.P.
———. (1962). *How to Do Things with Words.* Page refs. to (1980) 2nd ed. Sbisa, M. & Urmson, J. O. (eds.). Oxford: O.U.P. paperback.
Ayer, A. J. (1968). *The Origins of Pragmatism.* London: Macmillan.
Berlin, B. & Kay, P. (1969). *Basic Color Terms.* Berkeley, CA: University of California Press.
Bohannan, L. (1971). Shakespeare in the bush. In *Conformity and Conflict: Readings in cultural anthropology.* Spradley, J. P. & McCurdy, D. W. (eds.). Boston, MA: Little, Brown & Co.
Black, M. (1959). Linguistic relativity: The views of B. L. Whorf. *Philosophical Review,* **68.**
Bloomfield, L. (1935). *Language.* London: Allen & Unwin.
Bolinger, D. L. (1968). *Aspects of Language.* New York: Harcourt, Brace & Jovanovich.
Brown, R. (1976). Reference: In memorial tribute to Eric Lenneberg. *Cognition,* **4.**
———. (1973). *A First Language.* Cambridge, MA: Harvard University Press.
Bruner, J. S. (1972). Nature and uses of immaturity. *American Psychologist,* **27** no. **8.**

Bullowa, M. (1979). *Before Speech: The beginning of interpersonal communication.* Cambridge, England: C.U.P.

Chomsky, N. (1965). *Aspects of the Theory of Syntax,* Cambridge, MA: MIT Press.

Clark, E. (1973). What's in a word? On the child's acquisition of semantics in his first language. In Cognitive Development and the Acquistion of Language. Moore, T. E. (ed.). New York: Academic Press.

Cole, M. & Scribner, S. (1974). *Culture and Thought: A psychological introduction.* New York: John Wiley & Sons.

Cole, P. & Morgan, J. L. (eds.) (1975). *Syntax & Semantics, Vol. 3: Speech Acts.* New York: Academic Press.

Culler, J. (1976). *Saussure.* Fontana Modern Masters Series. Glasgow, Scotland: Fontana/Collins.

Dore, J. (1974). A pragmatic description of early language development. *Journal of Psycholinguistic Research, 3.*

Dressler, W. U. (1978). *Current Trends in Textlinguistics.* Berlin: deGruyter.

Firth, J. R. (1930). *Speech.* London: Ernest Benn. References are to the reprint in *The Tongues of Men, and Speech* (1964). London: Oxford University Press.

————. (1957). Ethnographic analysis and language with reference to Malinowski's views. In *Man and Culture: An evaluation of the work of Bronislaw Malinowski.* London: Routledge & Kegan Paul. Page refs. to (1964) Harper Torchbooks. New York: Harper and Row.

————. (1957a). *Papers in Linguistics 1934–1951).* London: O.U.P.

Firth, Raymond (ed.). (1957). *Man & Culture: An evaluation of the work of Bronislaw Malinowski.* London: Routledge & Kegan Paul. Page refs. to (1964) Harper Torchbooks. New York: Harper and Row.

Gallie, W. B. (1932). *Peirce and Pragmatism.* Cited in E. R. Leach. 1957.

Goody, J. (1968). *Literacy in Traditional Society.* Cambridge, England: C.U.P.

————. (1977). *The Domestication of the Savage Mind.* Cambridge: C.U.P.

Greenberg, J. H. (1954). Concerning inferences from linguistics to nonlinguistic data. In *Language in Culture: Conference on the interrelations of language and other aspects of culture.* Hoijer, Harry (ed.). Chicago, IL: University of Chicago Press.

Greenfield, P. M. & Smith, J. H. (1976). *Communication and the Beginning of Language: the development of semantic structure in one-word speech and beyond.* New York: Academic Press.

Grice, H. P. (1975). Logic and conversation. In *Syntax and Semantics, Vol. 3: Speech Acts.* Cole, P. & Morgan, J. L. (eds.). New York: Academic Press.

Halliday, M. A. K. (1957). Some aspects of systemic description and comparison in grammatical analysis. In *Studies in Linguistic Analysis,* special volume of the Philological Society. Oxford: Blackwell.

————. (1959). *The Language of the Chinese "Secret History of the Mongols".* Publication xvii of the Philological Society. Oxford: Blackwell.

————. (1970). Language structure and language function. In *New Horizons in Linguistics.* Lyons, J. (ed.). Harmondsworth, England: Penguin.

————. (1973). *Explorations in the Functions of Language.* London: Edward Arnold.

————. (1974). *Language and Social Man.* Schools Council Programme in Linguistics and English Teaching, Series II Vol. 3. London: Longmans.

————. (1975). *Learning How to Mean: Explorations in the development of language.* London: Edward Arnold.

————. (1977). Text as semantic choice in social contexts. In *Grammars and Descriptions.* van Dijk, T. & Petofi, J. S. (eds.). Berlin: de Gruyter.

————. (1977a). Ideas about language. In *Aims and Perspectives in Linguistics.* Occasional paper no. 1. Publication of ALAA.

————. (1977b). *Review of Jonathan Culler's Saussure.* A B C broadcast.

————. (1978). *Language as Social Semiotic.* London: Edward Arnold.

————. (1979). One child's proto-language. In *Before Speech: The beginning of interpersonal communication,* Bullowa, M. (ed.). Cambridge, England: C.U.P.

Halliday, M. A. K., McIntosh, Angus, & Strevens, Peter. (1964). *Linguistic Sciences and Language Teaching*. London: Longmans.

Halliday, M. A. K. & Hasan, Ruqaiya. (1976). *Cohesion in English*. London: Longmans.

——. (1980). *Text and Context: Aspects of language in a social-semiotic perspective*. Sophia Linguistica **VI**. Tokyo: Sophia University Press.

Harris, Zellig, S. (1951). *Methods in Structural Linguistics*. Chicago, IL: University of Chicago Press.

Hasan, Ruqaiya. (1964). *A Linguistic Study of Contrasting Features in the Style of Two Contemporary English Prose Writers*. Unpublished Ph.D. thesis. University of Edinburgh.

——. (1973). *Measuring the Length of a Text*. Mimeo.

——. (1978). The implications of semantic distance for language in education. To appear in *Proceedings of 10th ICAES*. (in press).

——. (1978a). Text in the systemic-functional model. In *Current Trends in Text-linguistics*. Dressler, W. U. (ed.). Berlin: de Gruyter.

——. (1979). On the notion of text. In *Text vs. Sentence: Basic Questions of Text-linguistics*. Petofi, J. S. (ed.). Hamburg: Helmut Buske.

——. (1980). What's going on: A dynamic view of context in language. In *The Seventh LACUS Forum*. Copeland, J. E. & Oavies, P. W. (eds.). Columbia, SC: Hornbeam Press.

——. (1979a). Language in the study of literature. Report on Workshop no. 6 from *Working Conference on Language in Education*. Sydney University Extension Programme & Department of Linguistics, August 19–24.

——. (1982). Situation and the definition of conversation. Paper presented at the *Multi-Disciplinary Workshop on the Analysis of Naturally Occuring Conversation: The MAP* At the Annenburg School of Communications, University of Pennsylvania, Nov. 17–20, under the leadership of Allen Grimshaw.

——. (1984a). Ways of saying: ways of meaning. In *The Semiotics of Culture and Language*. R. P. Fawcett, M. A. K. Halliday, S. M. Lamb, & A. Makkai (eds.). London: Frances Pinter.

——. (1984b). The structure of the nursery tale: an essay in text typology. In *Linguistica Testuale*. L. Coveri (ed.). Rome: Bulzoni.

Hjelmslev, L. (1953). *Prolegomena to a Theory of Language*. (Tr. F. J. Whitfield). Bloomington, IN: Indiana University Press.

Hockett, Charles T. (1954). Chinese versus English: an exploration of the Whorfian Theses. In *Language in Culture: Conference on the interrelations of language and other aspects of culture*, Hoijer, Harry (ed.). Chicago, IL: Chicago University Press.

Hoijer, Harry. (1954). *Language in Culture: Conference on the interrelations of language and other aspects of culture*. Chicago, IL: Chicago University Press.

Hymes, Dell H. (1964). The ethnography of speaking. In *Readings in the Sociology of Language*. Fishman, J. A. (ed.). The Hague: Mouton.

Karmiloff-Smith, A. (1979). *A Functional Approach to Child Language*. Cambridge, England: Cambridge University Press.

Labov, William. (1972). The social motivation of a sound change. In *Socio-linguistic Patterns*. Oxford: Basil Blackwell.

Leach, Edmund R. (1957). The epistemological background to Malinowski's pragmatism. In Firth, Raymond (ed.). (1957). *Man & Culture: An evaluation of the work of Bronislaw Malinowski*. London: Routledge & Kegan Paul. Page refs. to (1964) Harper Torchbooks. New York: Harper and Row.

Leech, Geoffrey. (1974). *Semantics*. Harmondsworth, England: Penguin.

Lenneberg, E. H. (1971). Language and cognition. In *Semantics: An interdisciplinary reader in philosophy, linguistics and psychology*. Cambridge, England: Cambridge University Press.

Luria, A. R. (1976). *Cognitive Development: Its cultural and social Foundation*. Cambridge, MA: Harvard University Press.

Levin, Samuel R. (1976). Concerning what kind of a speech act a poem is. In *Pragmatics of Language and Literature*. van Dijk, T. (ed.). Amsterdam: North-Holland.

Lewis, David K. (1968). *Conventions: A philosophical study*. Cambridge, MA: Harvard University Press.

Lyons, John. (1968). *Introduction to Theoretical Linguistics*. London: Cambridge University Press.

_____. (ed.) (1970). *New Horizons in Linguistics*. Harmondsworth, England: Penguin.

_____. (1977). *Semantics*. Cambridge, England: Cambridge University Press.

Malinowski, B. (1923). The problem of meaning in primitive languages. Supplement I to *The Meaning of Meaning*. Ogden, C. K. & Richards, I. A. Page refs. to (1959) Harvest Books. New York, N.Y.: Harcourt Brace & World.

_____. (1935). An ethnographic theory of language. Part IV of *Coral Gardens and Their Magic* 2. London: Allen & Unwin.

Mead, George H. (1934). *Mind, Self and Society*. Chicago, IL: Chicago University Press.

Moore, E. C. (1961). *American Pragmatism: Peirce, James and Dewey*. New York: Columbia University Press.

Morris, C. W. (1955). *Signs, Language and Behaviour*. Englewood Cliffs, NJ: Prentice-Hall.

Palmer, F. R. (1981). *Semantics*. 2nd ed. Cambridge, England: Cambridge University Press.

Petofi, Janos S. (1978). A formal semiotic text theory as an integrated theory of natural language. In *Current Trends in Text-linguistics*. Dressler, W. U. (ed.). Berlin: de Gruyter.

Sadock, Jerry M. (1974). *Toward a Linguistic Theory of Speech Acts*. New York: Academic Press.

de Saussure, F. (1916). *Course in General Linguistics*, Page refs. to (1966) New York: McGraw-Hill (Paperback Edition).

Schank, R. C. & Abelson, R. P. (1977). *Scripts, Plans, Goals and Understanding: An inquiry into human knowledge structures*. Hillsdale, NJ: Lawrence Erlbaum.

Searle, J. R. (1969). *Speech Acts: An essay in the philosophy of language*. Cambridge, England: Cambridge University Press.

_____. (1979). Indirect speech acts. In *Expression and Meaning: Studies in the Theory of Speech Acts*. Cambridge, England: Cambridge University Press.

_____. (1979a). The logical status of fictional discourse. In *Expression and Meaning: Studies in the Theory of Speech Acts*. Cambridge, England: Cambridge University Press.

Smith, John E. (1978). *Purpose and Thought: The meaning of pragmatism*. London: Hutchinson.

Ure, Jean. (1971). Lexical density and register differentiation. In *Applications of Linguistics: Selected papers of the second International Congress of Applied Linguistics*. Perren, G. & Trim, J. L. M. (eds.). Cambridge, England: Cambridge University Press.

van Dijk, T. A. (1977). Connectives in text grammar and text logic. In *Grammars and Descriptions*. van Dijk, T. A. & Petofi, J. S. (eds.). Berlin: de Gruyter.

_____. (1976). Pragmatics and poetics. In *Progamatics of Language and Literature*. Amsterdam: North-Holland.

Weinreich, U., Labov, W. & Herzog, M. 1. (1968). Empirical foundations for a theory of language change. In *Directions for Historical Linguistics: A symposium*. Austin, TX: University of Texas Press.

Wells, Gordon. (1981). *Learning through Interaction*. Cambridge, England: Cambridge University Press.

Whorf, Benjamin Lee. (1956). *Language, Thought and Reality: Selected Writings of Benjamin Lee Whorf*. Cambridge, MA: M.I.T. Press.

A Demonstration of the Nigel Text Generation Computer Program

3

William C. Mann
Christian M. I. M. Matthiessen
USC Information Sciences Institute
Los Angeles, California

How can a particular sentence be generated given the intention to communicate? This paper demonstrates a systemic grammar in use and its associated semantics, which is the core of a text generation program. The demonstration is a dramatization in which the actors play the roles of the major components of the program. The generation drama consists of the interactions of these components in the generation of the sentence *This gazebo was built by Sir Christopher Wren*. By the end of the generation, almost all major aspects of the grammar and its semantics will have been illustrated and explained in context.

The paper is a transcript of the actual demonstration; the mode is "written to be spoken to an audience."

1 INTRODUCTION TO THE DEMONSTRATION

Although the title of this paper announces a computer program demonstration, we have no computer here, and you won't have a chance to see a computer producing its outputs. That may be a relief, since computer program demonstrations can easily become obscure and mysterious.

We do have a computer program called Nigel that contains a large systemic grammar of English and is capable of generating a wide range of sentences. But instead of just running it for you, we'd like to give a more comprehensible view of Nigel, by another kind of representation of what it does—a generation drama.

Nigel was built as part of a larger text generation system called Penman. The research goal for Penman is to model the generation of fluent multiparagraph texts, in English, which correspond to given intentions to communicate. This is obviously an ambitious goal, since it involves in at least a token way many of the functions of authorship. The role of the computer is, in most ways, inessential. It gives us some methodological biases and serves as a tool for various kinds of experiments. But what you will see is not computational in any essential way. The only part of Penman which has been extensively developed so far is its grammar.

Two kinds of activities have taken most of our time in the last two years or so since we started building the grammar:

1. specifying all of the details well enough, and
2. making the grammar responsive to the intent, purpose or achievement goal of the speaker.

This morning we're going to concentrate on the second of these, i.e., making the grammar responsive to intent. Since the systemic framework is functionally organized, this is a problem of extending that functionalism so that it is very explicit. Consequently, we are really serving a much broader collection of goals than the origins of the project would suggest. This task has not turned out at all to be just an application of computation to the systemic framework. In some ways it has tested the functionalism of the systemic framework as a whole.

Our goal in the demonstration is to convey an informal understanding of a method for defining the semantics of the choices in a systemic grammar. We are not trying to convey any formal scheme. Rather, we would like to say: Here is an approach to defining the semantics of a systemic grammar, one which leads to examinable results.

We will proceed by first sketching the approach, and then showing how a particular sentence can be generated.

2 AN APPROACH TO THE SEMANTICS OF A SYSTEMIC GRAMMAR

How can a text be produced from an intention to communicate? Our general view is that there are text planning processes which are directly responsive to speakers' intentions to communicate, and that for monologue it is helpful to view them as logically prior to the activity of the grammar.

Presupposing this, how can a text be produced from a planful response to an intention to communicate? This is a question of method. The question can be answered by specifying a method of generation. Since methods are inherently processlike, and since, from our knowledge of language, we expect that the method will have a complex abstract structure, it must be specified, not by one process, but by a collection of processes which can work together to create the text. (Here we are using "process" in the sense of procedure, not in its grammatical sense, nor in the sense Hjelmslev used it.)

The definitional framework which is the basis of the Nigel grammar is just such a collection of processes. It is systemic and functional, and it has provisions for realization. It is based on the work of Halliday and other systemicists, with additional work by Halliday and major contributions by Christian Matthiessen and Bill Mann. The chooser and inquiry framework which we will describe was developed by Bill Mann and Christian Matthiessen.

Because the systemic framework is used, all grammatical control is in the choices; the focal concern is getting the choices right. This means more than just getting the range of possibilities right. The potential of the language must be applied, in each particular case, in a way which conforms to the speaker's intent.

To get the choices right we have added another stratum, a semantic one which adds two principal kinds of devices to the basic grammatical framework:

1. A set of choosers (also called ''choice experts'')
2. A set of inquiries

Choosers are explicit processes that are able to examine the case at hand and make a systemic choice. There is a separate, independent chooser for each system. So, the system expresses a particular set of alternatives of linguistic potential, and the chooser expresses the circumstances under which each particular choice is made. A chooser acts by performing a sequence of steps that is specified by its definition as a process.

The second kind of device, the inquiries, are questions that choosers can ask to help them understand the present case. Around Nigel there is a boundary. A chooser will typically present two or three inquries to the region beyond this boundary, what we call the Environment.[1] This environment has three parts:

1. **Knowledge Base:** knowledge which existed before the intention to communicate.
2. **Text Plan:** knowledge which was developed in response to the intention to communicate, but before entering the grammar.
3. **Text Services:** knowledge which is available to the grammar on demand.

The grammar has no direct access to any of these kinds of knowledge, because they are outside of the boundary. However, the boundary is really an interface, so the grammar can present inquiries at the interface, and receive answers. This is how it finds out everything it needs to know about the present case. We have tried to define all of these inquiries so that they do not demand any grammatical knowledge from the environment.

There are two forms of each inquiry: an English question and a corresponding formal inquiry form.

Because inquiries have an English form, the actions at the interface can be understood as a dialogue between the grammar, represented by the choosers of all the systems, and the environment.

---

[1] There is an obvious correspondence between ''environment'' and the Malinowskian/Firthian notion of context. However, the term ''environment'' will be used here, since it does not imply a detailed Firthian theory of context.

3 PRELIMINARIES TO THE GENERATION PROCESS

The Nigel computer program does all of the kinds of things that go on inside the boundary. It enters systems, runs chooser processes, presents inquiries to the interface, receives answers, makes choices and performs realizations.

As our demonstration we are going to present one of Nigel's dialogues, derived from a computer run in which a sentence was generated. We won't be using the computer directly; instead we will have people representing the various parts.

In Nigel, and so in our demonstration, initiative comes from the grammar. The general control of what happens comes from the entry conditions of the systems. It is not the case that the semantic stratum has its own control, does its work and presents the results to the grammar for realization. Instead, it is controlled by the entry conditions of the systems. This means that grammar and semantics work in synchrony.

To keep the various activities distinct, we have assigned different kinds of activities to be played as roles by different people:

- **Environment:** The environment is represented by Ruqaiya Hasan. She has three books which she consults in order to answer inquiries. They are called Knowledge Base, Text Plan and Text Services, representing the three kinds of knowledge in the environment.
- **Choosers:** There is one individual, Bill Mann, representing all of the different independent choosers: he asks questions, keeps track of some answers in the Function Association Table, and chooses.
- **Grammar:** All of the systems of the grammar are represented by Michael Halliday. He enters systems and keeps track of the selection expression.
- **Realizer:** All of the realization operations are also represented by Michael Halliday. He shows each realization as soon as it becomes definite.

Each of these represents very closely what the computer program does.

Grammar and Realizer represent the grammatical component or stratum. Grammar interacts with the Choosers, which represent the semantics collectively. The Choosers also interact with Environment. There is no direct interaction between Grammar and Environment: the Choosers mediate as an inter-level. The possible interactions are summarized diagrammatically in Figure 1.

There is an additional character in our drama, the narrator (played by Christian Matthiessen), whose function is to give comments at a meta-level.

```
ENVIRONMENT
   |
CHOOSERS
   |
GRAMMAR ———REALIZER
```

Figure 1. Role interactions

In Greenwich, in South East London, there is a small brick gazebo. This gazebo was built by
Sir Christopher Wren. It is a rather undistinguished structure, which might have been a task
set for homework when he was at school.

Figure 2. The gazebo text

Some activity will be suppressed to avoid tedious repetition. The grammar provides for many adjuncts, and for many modifiers in NominalGroups, but only a few
will be shown. We will not try to justify either content or methodology.

The work has involved a fair amount of innovation, and so, in presenting it to
you, there is a tradeoff between how much we can show of *how* we do things, on the
one hand, and how much we can explain *why* we do them that particular way, on the
other hand. The more we justify, the less we can show of our methods. This
particular session will have a minimum of justification and, we hope, a maximum of
useful demonstration of methods.

The situation as we enter the grammar is that the text plan already exists. This
plan is indexed into the knowledge of the subject matter, and both are available in
the environment. The sentence we are generating is the second sentence in the
paragraph represented in Figure 2 (derived from Halliday, 1970).

The order of entering the systems which we will meet is exactly the order that the
computer program actually employed. Often there were several systems which
could have been entered, and the particular selection was arbitrary. This leads to a
somewhat disconnected style, in which, for example, the program gets part way
through developing tense, hops off to do other things, and then returns to complete
the tense development much later. For purposes of presentation, the generation
process will be divided into thirteen sections, each represented by a section of the
system network of Nigel. Each section comprises one or more systems. The sections are as follows:

1. RANK: Rank; CLASS: ClauseClass; COMPLEXITY: ClauseComplexity
2. SECONDARY TENSE: NonDeicticPresent, ZNonDeictic Tense
3. TRANSITIVITY I: Location, Manner, Agency, ProcessType, AgentInsert
4. TRANSITIVITY II (MATERIAL TRANSITIVITY): DoingType,
   GoalInsertConflate
5. CLAUSE VOICE: EffectiveVoice, Agentivity
6. VERBAL VOICE: LexverbPasspart
7. MOOD I: Dependence, MoodType
8. MOOD II: IndicativeType, DeclarativeTag
9. THEMATIZATION: ThemeMarkingDeclarative
10. DEICTICITY: Deicticity, PrimaryTense
11. POLARITY: Polarity, PolarityMarkingPositive
12. SUBJECT PERSON: ThingSubject, IndicativeOtherSubjectNumber
13. LEXICALVERB TERMRESOLUTION: LexicalverbTermResolution

As features are chosen in these systems, the Grammar will accumulate a selection expression. For each section, we will show the current expression as it has been developed up to that point in the generation process. After the completion of the generation process, its results will be summarized and a complete selection expression is given below in section 5 (Figure 27).

As we go along generating *This gazebo was built by Sir Christopher Wren,* the Realizer will build the clause structure step by step. The final result, the complete clause structure, is also presented in section 5 (in Figure 28) and you can trace each step the Realizer takes in the figure.

Before we start generating, we need a couple of additional terms. There are elements of the text plan in the environment, and also elements of prior knowledge. The environment is always able to assign an arbitrary name to any such element, and to give that name as an answer to an inquiry. These names are called *Hubs.* Arbitrary mnemonic names are used as hubs, but the hubs should not be thought of as lexical items.

The grammar's set of symbols does not include any hubs, so it does not know any of the specific symbols which represent knowledge in the environment. It does not even know the symbol which represents the identity of the speaker. It keeps track of the environment's symbols by associating them with symbols of its own, starting over each time the grammar is entered. The place where it keeps these associations is called the Function Association Table. The Function Association Table will be developed throughout the generation process (tables 1, 2, 3, and so on). In these tables, the right column lists grammatical functions and the left column lists a hub for each grammatical function, lined up according to its association. For example, the first association is (hub:) WREN-GAZEBO (associated with function:) ONUS.

Whenever the grammar is entered, there is one symbol, ONUS, which already has an association in the Function Association Table (as in the present example in Table 1 below). This grammatical function always represents the largest unit to be generated on the present entry to the grammar. In the demonstration case, the hub associated with ONUS will be the environment's name for the plan to generate the second sentence of the paragraph.

Table 1. Function Association Table: Initial State

Hubs	Grammatical Functions
WREN-GAZEBO	ONUS

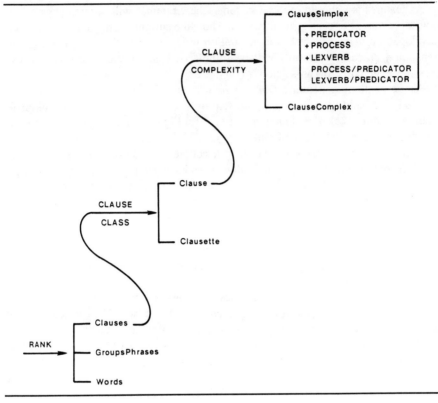

Figure 3. Rank, Class, and Complexity

4 THE GENERATION PROCESS

NARRATOR: *The drama begins with an association of WREN-GAZEBO with ONUS in the Function Association Table, which is presented in Table 1. The grammar can start—*

4.1 Rank, Class, and Complexity

4.1.1 Rank
GRAMMAR: We now enter the **Rank** system (see Figure 3). The choice options are Clauses, GroupsPhrases, and Words.

NARRATOR: *The grammar is a **single network** grammar, so **rank** is the least delicate system in this network. Consequently, the Rank*

Clauses, Clause, ClauseSimplex

Figure 4. Selection Expression, stage: (1)

Table 2. Function Association Table, Stage: (1)

Hubs	Grammatical Functions
WREN-GAZEBO-STATEMENT	SPEECH-ACT
NOW	SPEAKING-TIME
GAZEBO-BUILDING	PROCESS
HISTORIC-TIME	EVENT-TIME

system is always the first system entered whenever the grammar is entered, no matter what grammatical unit is being generated.

CHOOSER: Does WREN-GAZEBO (ONUS)[2] have an illocutionary force?

ENVIRONMENT: Yes, it has an illocutionary force.

CHOOSER: Then I choose feature Clauses, which is the first addition to the selection expression in Figure 4.

NARRATOR: *The rest of the questions by this chooser are for the purpose of adding information to the association table. Other choosers, for example the ClauseClass chooser right below, can use this information.*

CHOOSER: What is the concept which is the speech act aspect of WREN-GAZEBO (ONUS)?

ENVIRONMENT: The speech act aspect is called WREN-GAZEBO-STATEMENT.

CHOOSER: I'll put the association of WREN-GAZEBO-STATEMENT with SPEECH-ACT in Table 2.

CHOOSER: . . . and I'm finished in this chooser.

NARRATOR: *The preceding conversation illustrates much of the mechanism: The grammar controls the entry of systems. Given that a system is entered, the chooser of that system will ask one or more questions of the environment and choose according to the answers. There may be further questions to establish associations between a hub and a grammatical function. When the chooser of a system has been exhausted, it announces that it has finished.*

4.1.2 ClauseClass

GRAMMAR: We now enter the **ClauseClass** system. The choice options are Clause and Clausette.

NARRATOR: *The terms Clause and Clausette correspond to the terms major clause and minor clause.*

---

[2] The notation WREN-GAZEBO (ONUS) means "the hub WREN-GAZEBO associated with the function ONUS."

CHOOSER: Is the speech act WREN-GAZEBO-STATEMENT (SPEECH-
                 ACT) one which has a propositional parameter?
ENVIRONMENT: Yes, the act has a propositional parameter.
CHOOSER: Then I choose feature Clause (added to the selection ex-
                 pression in 4).
NARRATOR: *Again, the question which follows gathers information for
                 later use by systems developing tense; see 4.2 below.*
CHOOSER: What concept represents the current time, the time at which the
                 language is generated?
ENVIRONMENT: It's called NOW.
CHOOSER: I'll put the association of NOW with SPEAKING-TIME in
                 Table 2.
CHOOSER: . . . and I'm finished in this chooser.

4.1.3 ClauseComplexity
GRAMMAR: We now enter the **ClauseComplexity** system. The choice op-
                 tions are ClauseSimplex and ClauseComplex.
CHOOSER: Does expression of WREN-GAZEBO (ONUS) represent a
                 multiplicity of related processes rather than a single process?
ENVIRONMENT: It's a single process.
CHOOSER: Then I choose feature ClauseSimplex (added to selection ex-
                 pression in 4).
CHOOSER: What concept is the process aspect of WREN-GAZEBO
                 (ONUS), i.e., the one which governs the main verb?
ENVIRONMENT: It's called GAZEBO-BUILDING.
CHOOSER: I'll put the association of GAZEBO-BUILDING with PRO-
                 CESS in Table 2.
CHOOSER: What concept represents the time of occurrence or the re-
                 stricted portion of the time of occurrence of GAZEO-BUILD-
                 ING (PROCESS) which this mention of it has in view?
NARRATOR: *This is a somewhat obscure question. It is simply asking for a
                 symbol to represent the time at which the gazebo was built. In
                 general,* **inquiries** *are intended to encode the semantics of a
                 particular system and are phrased so that they will be suffi-
                 ciently explicit.*
ENVIRONMENT: All right, it occurred at HISTORIC-TIME.
CHOOSER: I'll put the association of HISTORIC-TIME with EVENT-
                 TIME in Table 2.
CHOOSER: Now, what is the set of applicable lexical items which are
                 denotationally appropriate for expressing GAZEBO-BUILD-
                 ING (PROCESS)?
ENVIRONMENT: The answer is a set of 15 terms (see Figure 5): the first 5 are
                 "build, built (as a past form), built (as an en-participle), build-
                 ing and builds. The other 10 are the corresponding forms of
                 "create" and "construct."

build	create	construct
builds	creates	constructs
built	created	constructed
built	**created**	**constructed**
building	creating	constructing

Figure 5. The initial termset for PROCESS

NARRATOR: *Nigel keeps track of sets of* candidate lexical items *for various grammatical functions. In this case, PROCESS will be associated with these 15 terms. Abstractly, there are two ways in which sets of candidate lexical items are constrained and denotational appropriateness is the first kind of constraint applied. Then grammatical constraints—such as the requirement that the lexical item be an en-participle—are used to filter the set of denotationally appropriate terms. Finally, the remaining indeterminacy is resolved on some other basis, such as register or frequency.*

    In this case, the grammar will apply grammatical constraints to reduce this set of 15 terms to 3 en-participles, and the final selection will be made from that set of 3.

CHOOSER: . . . and I'm finished in this chooser.

NARRATOR: *We are about to see the* realization process *in operation. There are 9 types of realization represented in this example. (1) One group builds and specifies the function structure of the unit being generated. These fall into two subgroups. The first includes* Insert, Conflate, *and* Expand. *Insert adds a new function to the structure (e.g., (Insert SUBJECT)). Conflate operates on two functions and specifies that they are the same constituent (e.g., (Conflate SUBJECT AGENT)). Expand specifies a constituent relationship between two functions (e.g., (Expand MOOD SUBJECT)). The second subgroup is made up of ordering operators,* Order, OrderAtEnd, *and* OrderAtFront.

    (II) The second group consists of operators that specify a grammatical feature, a lexical feature or a lexical item that realizes a functional constituent. Preselect specifies a choice to be made in realizing a constituent in a subsequent pass through the grammar. Classify specifies a required lexical feature and Lexify specifies a lexical item to be used.

    You can follow the steps in the realization process in the complete structure to be generated displayed in Figure 28.

    The Realizer will not perform realization for the features already selected.

Clauses, Clause, ClauseSimplex;
NoNonDeicticPresent, NoZNonDeicticTense

Figure 6. Selection Expression, stage: (2)

REALIZER: Insert PREDICATOR[3]
REALIZER: Insert PROCESS
REALIZER: Insert LEXVERB
REALIZER: Conflate LEXVERB PROCESS
REALIZER: Conflate PREDICATOR LEXVERB

4.2 Secondary Tense

4.2.1 NonDeicticPresent

GRAMMAR: We now enter the **NonDeicticPresent** system. The choice options are NoNonDeicticPresent and NonDeicticPresent.

NARRATOR: *These are the feature names from the grammar. Others might call them Progressive and NonProgressive.*

CHOOSER: Is the activity represented by GAZEBO-BUILDING (PROCESS) complete at the time represented by HISTORIC-TIME (EVENT-TIME)?

ENVIRONMENT: It is complete.

CHOOSER: Then I choose feature NoNonDeicticPresent and the feature is added to the selection expression (see Figure 6).

---

[3] In this script, realizations are shown in their formal forms. The realizer person reads these relations as follows:

Insert FF: We now insert the function FF in the structure.
Conflate FF GG: We now conflate function FF with function GG.
                      Symbol: +FF
Expand NN TT: We now expand function NN to have as a constituent function TT.
                      Symbol: NN(TT)
Classify FF LL: We now classify function FF with lexical feature LL.
                      Symbol: FF! LL
Preselect FF PP: We now preselect function FF to use grammatical feature PP.
                      Symbol: FF: PP
Lexify FF II: We now commit to using lexical item II to express function FF.
                      Symbol: FF= II
Order FF GG: We now order function FF before and adjacent to function GG in the structure.
                      Symbol: FF^GG
OrderAtEnd FF: We now order function FF to be the rightmost among those that descend from its mother.
                      Symbol: FF ^ #
OrderAtFront FF: We now order function FF to be leftmost among those that descend from its mother.
                      Symbol: #^ FF

NARRATOR: *The NonDeicticPresent chooser is an example of a chooser that is in the early stages of development; it is a placeholder for a more sophisticated chooser.*

CHOOSER: . . . and I'm finished in this chooser.

4.2.2 ZNonDeicticTense

GRAMMAR: We now enter the **ZNonDeicticTense** system (a secondary tense)—see Figure 7. The choice options are ZNonDeicticTense and NoZNonDeicticTense.

NARRATOR: *The tense we meet first in our development of the tense combination for the clause is ZNonDeicticTense; the Z indicates that its realization is rightmost in the tense expression.*

CHOOSER: What concept represents the time to which GAZEBO-BUILDING (PROCESS) is relevant?

NARRATOR: *This chooser question is part of a treatment of tense that fleshes out the semantics implicit in Halliday's grammatical analysis. It also draws on Reichenbach, particularly for the notion of relevant time (which he calls reference time), and adds some innovations of our own.*

ENVIRONMENT: It's HISTORIC-TIME.

CHOOSER: I'll put the association of HISTORIC-TIME with RELEVANT-TIME in Table 3.

CHOOSER: Is HISTORIC-TIME (RELEVANT-TIME) identical to HISTORIC-TIME (EVENT-TIME)?

ENVIRONMENT: Yes, they are the same.

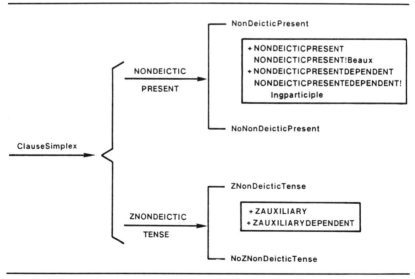

Figure 7. SECONDARY TENSE

Table 3. Function Association Table, Stage: (2)

Hubs	Grammatical Functions
WREN-GAZEBO	ONUS
WREN-GAZEBO-STATEMENT	SPEECH-ACT
NOW	SPEAKING-TIME
GAZEBO-BUILDING	PROCESS
HISTORIC-TIME	EVENT-TIME
HISTORIC-TIME	RELEVANT-TIME

CHOOSER: OK, I choose feature NoZNonDeicticTense (added to selection expression in 6).

NARRATOR: *The grammar of tense starts with the temporal location of the process (event/state) and specifies it with respect to the time of speaking, one step at a time—i.e., one tense at a time. Complex tenses are built up just as Halliday's names for them are—for example, past-in-future-in-present. Here there is no secondary tense: The realization of this particular feature, NonZNonDeicticTense, is zero, and the realizer will keep quiet.*

CHOOSER: . . . and I'm finished in this chooser.

4.3 Transitivity I

4.3.1 Agency

GRAMMAR: We now enter the **Agency** system—see Figure 8. The choice options are Middle and Effective.

CHOOSER: Is the process GAZEBO-BUILDING (PROCESS) one which conceptually has some sort of entity which causes the process to occur?

ENVIRONMENT: Yes, it is caused.

CHOOSER: What is the entity which caused or causes GAZEBO-BUILDING (PROCESS)?

ENVIRONMENT: The causer is SIR-CHRISTOPHER

CHOOSER: I'll put the association of SIR-CHRISTOPHER with CAUSER in Table 4.

CHOOSER: Now, is it preferable to mention the causative relation between SIR-CHRISTOPHER (CAUSER) and the GAZEBO-BUILDING (PROCESS) process?

ENVIRONMENT: Mention it.

CHOOSER: All right, I choose feature Effective, which is added to the selection expression in Figure 9.

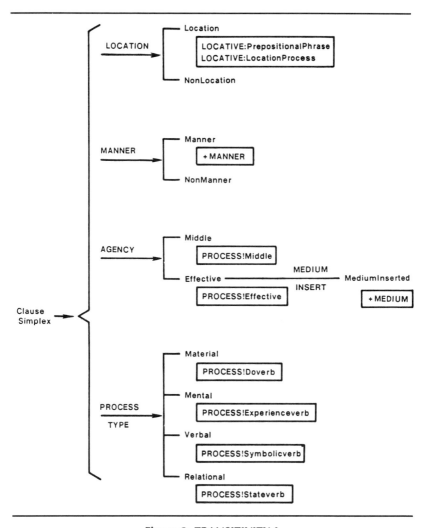

Figure 8. TRANSITIVITY I

CHOOSER: . . . and I'm finished in this chooser.
REALIZER: Classify PROCESS Effective
NARRATOR: *Classify is one of the realization operators, comparable to Preselect. It means: Require this lexical feature on the item realizing that function.*

4.3.2 MediumInsert
GRAMMAR: We now enter the Gate **MediumInsert**
REALIZER: Insert MEDIUM

Table 4. Function Association Table, Stage: (3)

Hubs	Grammatical Functions
WREN-GAZEBO	ONUS
WREN-GAZEBO-STATEMENT	SPEECH-ACT
NOW	SPEAKING-TIME
GAZEBO-BUILDING	PROCESS
HISTORIC-TIME	EVENT-TIME
HISTORIC-TIME	RELEVANT-TIME
SIR-CHRISTOPHER	CAUSER
GREENWICH	LOCATION
MEDIOCRITY	MANNER

NARRATOR: *In addition to the systems of the grammar, we have entities called* gates. *A gate is best thought of as the entry condition part of a system, with only one output feature. This feature can play the same role in the grammar in terms of realization, and be an input feature to other systems just as a feature in a system can. Even though only one output is possible, a gate can have a chooser that asks useful questions.*

MediumInsert is a gate, but it does not have a chooser. It is present entirely to carry the realization operation we just saw, "Insert MEDIUM".

4.3.3 Location

GRAMMAR: We now enter the **Location** system. The choice options are NonLocation and Location.

CHOOSER: Is there knowledge of the location where GAZEBO-BUILDING (PROCESS) occurred?

ENVIRONMENT: It's known.

CHOOSER: What is the most salient location aspect of the knowledge represented by GAZEBO-BUILDING (PROCESS)?

ENVIRONMENT: GREENWICH.

CHOOSER: I'll put the association of GREENWICH with LOCATION in Table 4.

Clauses, Clause, ClauseSimplex;
NoNonDeicticPresent, NoZNonDeicticTense;
Effective, MediumInserted, NonLocation, NonManner, Material

Figure 9. Selection Expression, stage: (3)

CHOOSER:	Is it preferable to express the knowledge represented by GREENWICH (LOCATION) or not?
ENVIRONMENT:	Withhold it.
CHOOSER:	Then I choose feature NonLocation (added to selection expression in 9).
CHOOSER:	. . . and I'm finished in this chooser.

4.3.4 Manner

GRAMMAR:	We now enter the **Manner** system. The choice options are NonManner and Manner.
CHOOSER:	Is there knowledge of the manner of performance or occurrence of GAZEBO-BUILDING (PROCESS)?
ENVIRONMENT:	It's known.
CHOOSER:	What is the most salient aspect of the manner of performance of GAZEBO-BUILDING (PROCESS)?
ENVIRONMENT:	MEDIOCRITY.
CHOOSER:	I'll put the association of MEDIOCRITY with MANNER in Table 4.
CHOOSER:	Is it preferable to express the knowledge represented by MEDIOCRITY (MANNER) or not?
NARRATOR:	*Notice that the wording is familiar, from its use in the Location chooser. Whenever a particular wording of a question reappears, as in this case, the same underlying formal inquiry is being addressed to the environment.*
ENVIRONMENT:	Withhold the expression of that knowledge.
CHOOSER:	Then I choose feature NonManner (added to selection expression in 9).
CHOOSER:	. . . and I'm finished in this chooser.

4.3.5 Process Type

GRAMMAR:	We now enter the **Process Type** system. The choice options are Material, Verbal, Mental, and Relational.
CHOOSER:	Does the process GAZEBO-BUILDING (PROCESS) represent a static condition or state of being?
ENVIRONMENT:	No, it doesn't represent a static condition or state of being.
CHOOSER:	Does the process GAZEBO-BUILDING (PROCESS) represent symbolic communication of a kind which could have an addressee?
ENVIRONMENT:	No, it isn't symbolic communication that could have an addressee.
CHOOSER:	Is GAZEBO-BUILDING (PROCESS) a process of comprehension, recognition, belief, perception, deduction, remembering, evaluation or mental reaction?
ENVIRONMENT:	No, it is not any of those.

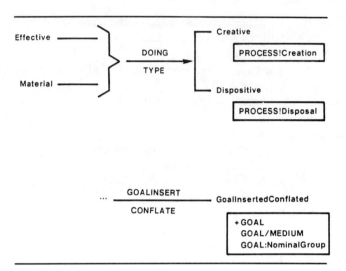

Figure 10. TRANSITIVITY II

CHOOSER: Then I choose feature Material (added to selection expression in 9).
CHOOSER: . . . and I'm finished in this chooser.
REALIZER: Classify PROCESS Doverb

4.4 Transitivity II

4.4.1 GoalInsertConflate

GRAMMAR: We now enter the **GoalInsertConflate** gate—see Figure 10, and activate the feature GoalInsertedConflated.
REALIZER: Insert GOAL
REALIZER: Conflate GOAL MEDIUM
REALIZER: Preselect GOAL NominalGroup
NARRATOR: **Preselect *associates a grammatical feature with a function. For each of the function bundles that carries preselections, the grammar will be reentered to develop the structure, and the preselected features will be chosen then. This gate, Goal-InsertConflate, is here in order to invoke the realization that we have seen on a particular combination of features. Beyond this point we will not be showing entry of any gates, unless there is associated inquiry. This means that some realizations will appear mysteriously, and some of the entry conditions will be satisfied mysteriously.***
CHOOSER: What is the entity which GAZEBO-BUILDING (PROCESS) affects or is directed toward?
ENVIRONMENT: It's called THE-GAZEBO.

Table 5. Function Association Table, Stage: (4)

Hubs	Grammatical Functions
WREN-GAZEBO	ONUS
WREN-GAZEBO-STATEMENT	SPEECH-ACT
NOW	SPEAKING-TIME
GAZEBO-BUILDING	PROCESS
HISTORIC-TIME	EVENT-TIME
HISTORIC-TIME	RELEVANT-TIME
SIR-CHRISTOPHER	CAUSER
GREENWICH	LOCATION
MEDIOCRITY	MANNER
THE-GAZEBO	GOAL
THE-GAZEBO	MEDIUM
SIR-CHRISTOPHER	ACTOR
SIR-CHRISTOPHER	AGENT

CHOOSER: I'll put the association of THE-GAZEBO with GOAL in Table 5.

NARRATOR: *As we'll see, choosers know how to transfer a hub from one grammatical function to another. This is done here, copying the hub THE-GAZEBO from GOAL to MEDIUM.*

CHOOSER: I'll copy the hub THE-GAZEBO from GOAL to MEDIUM and I put the association between THE-GAZEBO and MEDIUM in Table 5.

CHOOSER: What is the entity which caused or causes GAZEBO-BUILDING (PROCESS)?

ENVIRONMENT: It is SIR-CHRISTOPHER.

CHOOSER: I'll put the association of SIR-CHRISTOPHER with ACTOR in Table 5.

CHOOSER: Is SIR-CHRISTOPHER (CAUSER) identical to SIR-CHRISTOPHER (ACTOR)?

ENVIRONMENT: They are the same.

NARRATOR: *That question does not really contribute anything new. It's just an error check.—The hub for CAUSER was arrived at independently in 4.3 in the Agency chooser.*

CHOOSER: Again we copy a hub from one grammatical function to another. In this case we copy the hub SIR-CHRISTOPHER from ACTOR to AGENT; the resulting new association is in Table 5.

CHOOSER: Then I activate feature GoalInsertedConflated, which is added to the selection expression in Figure 11 . . . and I have finished choosing.

Clauses, Clause, ClauseSimplex;
NoNonDeicticPresent, NoZNonDeicticTense;
Effective, MediumInserted, NonLocation, NonManner, Material;
GoalInsertedConflated, Creative

Figure 11. Selection Expression, stage: (4)

4.4.2 DoingType

GRAMMAR: We now enter the **DoingType** system. The choice options are Creative and Dispositive.

CHOOSER: Did THE-GAZEBO (GOAL) exist before the beginning of GAZEBO-BUILDING (PROCESS)?

ENVIRONMENT: It did not exist.

CHOOSER: OK, I choose feature Creative (added to selection expression in 11).

CHOOSER: . . . and I'm finished in this chooser.

REALIZER: Classify PROCESS Creation

4.5 Clause Voice

4.5.1 EffectiveVoice

GRAMMAR: We now enter the **EffectiveVoice** system—see Figure 12. The choice options are operative (i.e., clause-active) and receptive (i.e., clause-passive).

CHOOSER: Is it preferable to mention SIR-CHRISTOPHER (AGENT) as the agent of GAZEBO-BUILDING (PROCESS)?

ENVIRONMENT: Mention him.

CHOOSER: Is there a paragraph containing WREN-GAZEBO (ONUS) which has a theme?

ENVIRONMENT: It exists.

CHOOSER: What is the theme of the paragraph containing WREN-GAZEBO (ONUS)?

ENVIRONMENT: It's called GREENWICH-REGION.

CHOOSER: I'll put the association of GREENWICH-REGION with PARAGRAPH-THEME in Table 6.

CHOOSER: What symbol represents the most salient chain of relationships in the reader's attention and knowledge between SIR-CHRISTOPHER (AGENT) and GREENWICH-REGION (PARAGRAPH-THEME)?

NARRATOR: *This question is part of some reasoning about conceptual distance—represented by the notion of path—among the agent, the medium and the PARAGRAPH-THEME.*

ENVIRONMENT: It's called WREN-GREENWICH-REGION-PATH.

CHOOSER: I'll put the association of WREN-GREENWICH-REGION-PATH with AGENT-THEMATIC-PATH in Table 6.

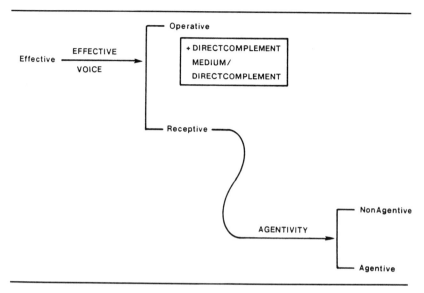

Figure 12. CLAUSE VOICE

Table 6. Function Association Table, Stage: (5)

Hubs	Grammatical Functions
WREN-GAZEBO	ONUS
WREN-GAZEBO-STATEMENT	SPEECH-ACT
NOW	SPEAKING-TIME
GAZEBO-BUILDING	PROCESS
HISTORIC-TIME	EVENT-TIME
HISTORIC-TIME	RELEVANT-TIME
SIR-CHRISTOPHER	CAUSER
GREENWICH	LOCATION
MEDIOCRITY	MANNER
THE-GAZEBO	GOAL
THE-GAZEBO	MEDIUM
SIR-CHRISTOPHER	ACTOR
SIR-CHRISTOPHER	AGENT
GREENWICH-REGION	PARAGRAPH-THEME
WREN-GREENWICH-REGION-PATH	AGENT-THEMATIC-PATH
GAZEBO-GREENWICH-REGION-PATH	MEDIUM-THEMATIC-PATH
THE-GAZEBO	SUBJECT

Clauses, Clause, ClauseSimplex;
NoNonDeicticPresent, NoZNonDeicticTense;
Effective, MediumInserted, NonLocation, NonManner, Material;
GoalInsertedConflated, Creative;
Receptive, Agentive

Figure 13. Selection Expression, stage: (5)

CHOOSER: What symbol represents the most salient chain of relationships in the reader's attention and knowledge between THE-GAZEBO (MEDIUM) and GREENWICH-REGION (PARA-GRAPH-THEME)?

ENVIRONMENT: It's called GAZEBO-GREENWICH-REGION-PATH.

CHOOSER: I'll put the association of GAZEBO-GREENWICH-REGION-PATH with MEDIUM-THEMATIC-PATH in Table 6.

CHOOSER: Does the chain of relationships WREN-GREENWICH-RE-GION-PATH (AGENT-THEMATIC-PATH) contain the chain of relationships GAZEBO-GREENWICH-REGION-PATH (MEDIUM-THEMATIC-PATH) as a proper subpart?

ENVIRONMENT: Yes, it is a part of that one.

CHOOSER: Then I choose feature Receptive, which is added to the selection expression in Figure 13.

NARRATOR: *This means that the chooser has now arrived at the decision that the MEDIUM is more closely related to the PARA-GRAPH-THEME than the AGENT is.*

CHOOSER: I now copy the hub THE-GAZEBO from MEDIUM to SUB-JECT; the new association is in Table 6.

NARRATOR: *We have learned a lot about practical development of the choosers from this particular chooser. It started as just a one-question chooser, asking about whether it was preferable to mention the agent. Later we added the interactions with paragraph theme, and some interactions you didn't see involving the previous clause. All of these changes were based on work by Sandra Thompson. Putting them into the chooser revealed some problems. Those were corrected, and changes from other sources have been added since.*

Developments like this one have shown that the choosers are definable with a wide range of levels of sophistication. It has also been easy to reconcile several people's work in the chooser development process.

CHOOSER: . . . and I'm finished in this chooser.

4.5.2 Agentivity

GRAMMAR: We now enter the **Agentivity** system. The options are Agentive and NonAgentive.

CHOOSER:	Is it preferable to mention SIR-CHRISTOPHER (AGENT) as the agent of GAZEBO-BUILDING (PROCESS)?
ENVIRONMENT:	Mention him.
CHOOSER:	Then I choose Agentive (added to selection expression in 13) . . . and I'm finished choosing.
NARRATOR:	*Several realizations will now appear mysteriously; the entry conditions to a number of gates have been satisfied.*
REALIZER:	Insert AGENT
REALIZER:	Insert ACTOR
REALIZER:	Preselect ACTOR NominalGroup
REALIZER:	Conflate ACTOR AGENT
REALIZER:	Insert AGENTMARKER
REALIZER:	Lexify AGENTMARKER by
REALIZER:	Order AGENTMARKER AGENT
REALIZER:	Insert PASSIVE
REALIZER:	Classify PASSIVE Beaux
REALIZER:	Insert PASSPARTICIPLE
REALIZER:	Classify PASSPARTICIPLE En-participle

4.6 Verbal Voice

GRAMMAR:	We now enter the gate **LexverbPasspart;** see Figure 14.
CHOOSER:	My next job is to determine the intersection of two term sets, which leads to a question that is much too long to read.
ENVIRONMENT:	The answer is also much too long to read. It is a list of all the known en-participles.
CHOOSER:	Then I activate feature LexverbPasspart, which is added to the selection expression; see 16 below in section 4.6.
REALIZER:	Conflate LEXVERB PASSPARTICIPLE
REALIZER:	Conflate MEDIUM SUBJECT
CHOOSER:	. . . and I'm finished in this chooser.

4.7 Mood I

4.7.1 Dependence

| GRAMMAR: | We now enter the **Dependence** system—see Figure 15. The choice options are IndependentClause and DependentClause. |

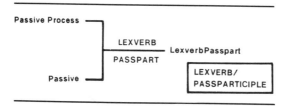

Figure 14. VERBAL VOICE

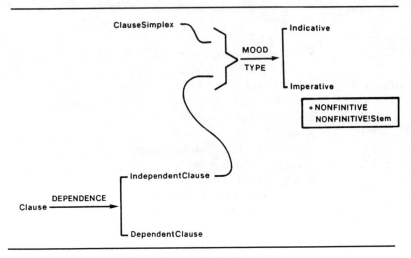

Figure 15. MOOD I

CHOOSER:	Does WREN-GAZEBO-STATEMENT (SPEECH-ACT) represent the entire speech act or is it part of a larger one?
ENVIRONMENT:	It's the whole thing.
CHOOSER:	Then I choose feature IndependentClause, which is added to the selection expression in Figure 16.
CHOOSER:	. . . and I'm finished in this chooser.

4.7.2 MoodType

GRAMMAR:	All right, we now enter the **MoodType** system. The choice options are Indicative and Imperative.
CHOOSER:	Is the illocutionary point of the surface level speech act represented by WREN-GAZEBO-STATEMENT (SPEECH-ACT) a command, i.e., a request of an action by the hearer?
ENVIRONMENT:	It's not intended to command.
CHOOSER:	Then I choose feature Indicative (added to selection expression in 16).
CHOOSER:	. . . and I'm finished in this chooser.

Clauses, Clause, ClauseSimplex;
NoNonDeicticPresent, NoZNonDeicticTense;
Effective, MediumInserted, NonLocation, NonManner, Material;
GoalInsertedConflated, Creative;
Receptive, Agentive;
IndependentClause, Indicative

Figure 16. Selection Expression, stage: (6)

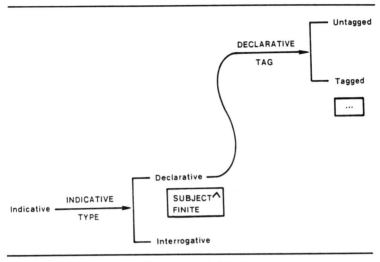

Figure 17. MOOD II

4.8 Mood II

4.8.1 IndicativeType

GRAMMAR: Fine. We now enter the **IndicativeType** system—see Figure 17. The choice options are Declarative and Interrogative.

CHOOSER: Is the illocutionary point of the surface level speech act represented by WREN-GAZEBO-STATEMENT (SPEECH-ACT) to state?

ENVIRONMENT: Yes, it's intended to state.

CHOOSER: Then I choose feature Declarative, which is added to the selection expression in Figure 18.

CHOOSER: . . . and I'm finished in this chooser.

REALIZER: Order SUBJECT FINITE

4.8.2 DeclarativeTag

GRAMMAR: We now enter the **DeclarativeTag** system. The choice options are Untagged and Tagged.

Clauses, Clause, ClauseSimplex;
NoNonDeicticPresent, NoZNonDeicticTense;
Effective, MediumInserted, NonLocation, NonManner, Material;
GoalInsertedConflated, Creative;
Receptive, Agentive;
IndependentClause, Indicative;
Declarative, Untagged

Figure 18. Selection Expression, stage: (7)

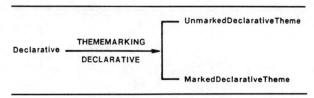

Figure 19. THEMATIZATION

CHOOSER: Should a secondary speech act be performed in conjunction
                    with WREN-GAZEBO (ONUS)?
ENVIRONMENT: There is no need for a secondary speech act.
CHOOSER: Then I choose feature Untagged (added to selection expression
                    in 18).
CHOOSER: . . . and I'm finished in this chooser.

4.9 Thematization

GRAMMAR: We now enter the **ThemeMarkingDeclarative** system; see
                    Figure   19.   The   choice   options   are   UnMarked-
                    DeclarativeTheme and MarkedDeclarativeTheme.
CHOOSER: What concept is specified as the theme of WREN-GAZEBO
                    (ONUS)?
ENVIRONMENT: THE-GAZEBO is.
CHOOSER: I'll put the association of THE-GAZEBO with THEME in
                    Table 7.
CHOOSER: As theme, is THE-GAZEBO (THEME) to be expressed in a
                    marked way?
ENVIRONMENT: No, no special emphasis is needed.
CHOOSER: Then I choose feature UnmarkedDeclarativeTheme, which is
                    added to the selection expression in Figure 20.
CHOOSER: . . . and I'm finished in this chooser.
REALIZER: Insert MOOD
REALIZER: Expand MOOD FINITE

Clauses, Clause, ClauseSimplex;
NoNonDeicticPresent, NoZNonDeicticTense;
Effective, MediumInserted, NonLocation, NonManner, Material;
GoalInsertedConflated, Creative;
Receptive, Agentive;
IndependentClause, Indicative;
Declarative, Untagged;
UnmarkedDeclarativeTheme

Figure 20. Selection Expression, stage: (8)

Table 7. Function Association Table, Stage: (6)

Hubs	Grammatical Functions
WREN-GAZEBO	ONUS
WREN-GAZEBO-STATEMENT	SPEECH-ACT
NOW	SPEAKING-TIME
GAZEBO-BUILDING	PROCESS
HISTORIC-TIME	EVENT-TIME
HISTORIC-TIME	RELEVANT-TIME
SIR-CHRISTOPHER	CAUSER
GREENWICH	LOCATION
MEDIOCRITY	MANNER
THE-GAZEBO	GOAL
THE-GAZEBO	MEDIUM
SIR-CHRISTOPHER	ACTOR
SIR-CHRISTOPHER	AGENT
GREENWICH-REGION	PARAGRAPH-THEME
WREN-GREENWICH-REGION-PATH	AGENT-THEMATIC-PATH
GAZEBO-GREENWICH-REGION-PATH	MEDIUM-SUBJECT-PATH
THE-GAZEBO	SUBJECT
THE-GAZEBO	THEME

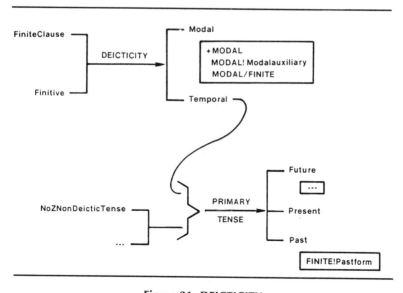

Figure 21. DEICTICITY

75

Clauses, Clause, ClauseSimplex;
NoNonDeicticPresent, NoZNonDeicticTense;
Effective, MediumInserted, NonLocation, NonManner, Material;
GoalInsertedConflated, Creative;
IndependentClause, Indicative;
Declarative, Untagged;
UnmarkedDeclarativeTheme;
Temporal, Past

Figure 22. Selection Expression, stage: (9)

4.10 Deicticity

4.10.1 Deicticity

GRAMMAR: We now enter the **Deicticity** system—see Figure 21. The
                  choice options are Temporal and Modal.

CHOOSER: Does GAZEBO-BUILDING (PROCESS) have a definite exis-
                  tence, possibly hypothetical, in space and time?

ENVIRONMENT: It has a definite existence.

CHOOSER: Then I choose feature Temporal, which is added to the selec-
                  tion expression in Figure 22.

CHOOSER: . . . and I'm finished in this chooser.

4.10.2 PrimaryTense

GRAMMAR: We now enter the **PrimaryTense** system. The choice options
                  are Past, Present, and Future.

CHOOSER: Is GAZEBO-BUILDING (PROCESS) extensional, i.e., con-
                  crete rather than intensional, i.e., generic?

ENVIRONMENT: It's extensional.

CHOOSER: Is the condition or process represented by GAZEBO-BUILD-
                  ING (PROCESS) hypothetical?

ENVIRONMENT: It's real, not hypothetical.

CHOOSER: Does the moment or interval of time HISTORIC-TIME (REL-
                  EVANT-TIME) strictly precede the moment or interval NOW
                  (SPEAKING-TIME)?

ENVIRONMENT: It precedes it.

CHOOSER: Then I choose feature Past (added to selection expression in
                  22).

CHOOSER: . . . and I'm finished in this chooser.

REALIZER: Insert FINITE

REALIZER: Classify FINITE Pastform

REALIZER: Conflate FINITE PASSIVE

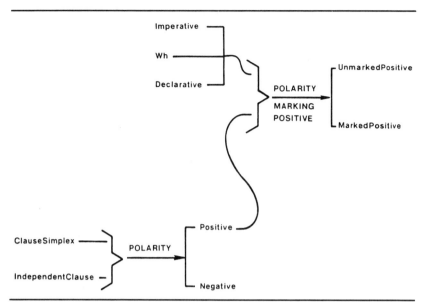

Figure 23. POLARITY

4.11 Polarity

4.11.1 Polarity

GRAMMAR: We now enter the **Polarity** system—see Figure 23. The choice options are Positive and Negative.

CHOOSER: What concept represents the polarity of assertion or occurrence of GAZEBO-BUILDING (PROCESS)?

ENVIRONMENT: It's called GAZEBO-BUILDING-POLARITY.

CHOOSER: I'll put the association of GAZEBO-BUILDING-POLARITY with POLARITY in Table 8.[4]

CHOOSER: What is the value of the polarity of GAZEBO-BUILDING-POLARITY (POLARITY)?

ENVIRONMENT: It's a positive one.

CHOOSER: Then I choose feature Positive, which is added to the selection expression in Figure 24.

CHOOSER: . . . and I'm finished in this chooser.

4.11.2 PolarityMarkingPositive

GRAMMAR: We now enter the **PolarityMarkingPositive** system. The choice options are UnmarkedPositive and MarkedPositive.

---

[4] This table is the final version and appears in full in Table 9 below in section 5.

Clauses, Clause, ClauseSimplex;
NoNonDeicticPresent, NoZNonDeicticTense;
Effective, MediumInserted, NonLocation, NonManner, Material;
GoalInsertedConflated, Creative;
IndependentClause, Indicative;
Declarative, Untagged;
UnmarkedDeclarativeTheme;
Temporal, Past;
Positive, UnmarkedPositive

Figure 24. Selection Expression, stage: (10)

CHOOSER: Should GAZEBO-BUILDING-POLARITY (POLARITY) be given distinguished emphatic or contrastive status?
ENVIRONMENT: No special emphasis is needed.
CHOOSER: Then I choose feature UnmarkedPositive (added to selection expression in Figure 24).
CHOOSER: . . . and I'm finished in this chooser.

4.12 Subject Person

4.12.1 ThingSubject
GRAMMAR: We now enter the **ThingSubject** system—see Figure 25. The choice options are Conscious and NonConscious.
CHOOSER: Is the individual or group represented by THE-GAZEBO (SUBJECT) conscious?
ENVIRONMENT: It's not conscious.
CHOOSER: Then I choose feature NonConsciousSubject, which is added to the selection expression in Figure 26.
CHOOSER: . . . and I'm finished in this chooser.
NARRATOR: *Now several gates that have been waiting do some realization.*
REALIZER: Insert SUBJECT
REALIZER: Expand MOOD SUBJECT
REALIZER: Insert TOPICAL
REALIZER: Expand THEME TOPICAL
REALIZER: OrderAtEnd TOPICAL

Table 8. Function Association Table, Stage: (7)

Hubs	Grammatical Functions
. . .	
GAZEBO-BUILDING-POLARITY	POLARITY

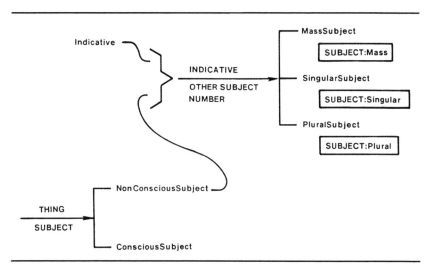

Figure 25. SUBJECT PERSON

REALIZER: OrderAtFront THEME
REALIZER: Preselect SUBJECT Nominative
REALIZER: Conflate TOPICAL SUBJECT

4.12.2 IndicativeOtherSubjectNumber

GRAMMAR: We now enter the **IndicativeOtherSubjectNumber** system. The choice options are MassSubject, SingularSubject and PluralSubject.

CHOOSER: Is THE-GAZEBO (SUBJECT) inherently multiple, i.e., a set or collection of things, or unitary?

ENVIRONMENT: It's unitary.

CHOOSER: Then I choose feature SingularSubject (added to selection expression in Figure 26).

CHOOSER: . . . and I'm finished in this chooser.

Clauses, Clause, ClauseSimplex;
NoNonDeicticPresent, NoZNonDeicticTense;
Effective, MediumInserted, NonLocation, NonManner, Material;
GoalInsertedConflated, Creative;
IndependentClause, Indicative;
Declarative, Untagged;
UnmarkedDeclarativeTheme;
Temporal, Past;
Positive, UnmarkedPositive;
NonConsciousSubject, SingularSubject

Figure 26. Selection Expression, stage: (11)

REALIZER: Preselect SUBJECT Singular
REALIZER: Classify FINITE Singular
REALIZER: Classify FINITE Thirdperson

4.13 LexicalVerbTermResolution

GRAMMAR: We now enter **LexicalVerbTermResolution,** a gate which has
                     a chooser so that it can ask questions about the lexical verb.
CHOOSER: Again I must find the intersection of two term sets, and again it
                     leads to a question too long to read.
ENVIRONMENT: The reply is a list of three en-participles, for build, create and
                     construct.
NARRATOR: *Notice that the result is the set of remaining terms in Figure 5
                     in boldface:* **built, constructed, created.**
CHOOSER: Select one of these terms: (builten createden constructeden)
                     (LEXVERB) to express GAZEBO-BUILDING (PROCESS)?
ENVIRONMENT: I select "built."
REALIZER: I therefore eliminate "created" and "constructed."
CHOOSER: Then I activate feature LexicalVerbTermResolution, which is
                     added to the selection expression in Figure 27.

4.14 Final realization

REALIZER: There are no more systems or gates which can be entered. I do
                     the remaining ordering according to lists of ordered functions.
REALIZER: The resulting ordered set of function bundles is:
                     (TOPICAL SUBJECT GOAL MEDIUM)
                     (FINITE PASSIVE)
                     (PASSPARTICIPLE PREDICATOR LEXVERB PROCESS)
                     AGENTMARKER
                     (ACTOR AGENT)

Clauses, Clause, ClauseSimplex;
NoNonDeicticPresent, NoZNonDeicticTense;
Effective, MediumInserted, NonLocation, NonManner, Material;
GoalInsertedConflated, Creative;
IndependentClause, Indicative;
Declarative, Untagged;
UnmarkedDeclarativeTheme;
Temporal, Past;
Positive, UnmarkedPositive;
NonConsciousSubject, SingularSubject;
LexicalVerbTermResolution

Figure 27. Selection Expression, stage: (12): final expression

Realized as:
TOPICAL + SUBJECT + GOAL + MEDIUM was built by
ACTOR + AGENT
At this point, the hub SIR-CHRISTOPHER is associated
with the function ACTOR. I could realize this by clearing the
Feature Association Table, associating ONUS with SIR-
CHRISTOPHER, and entering the grammar with NominalGroup preselected. However, we won't show this. We
could realize the SUBJECT similarly. Nigel handles both of
these appropriately, but lack of space prevents showing the
details.

5 RESULTS OF THE GENERATION PROCESS

We have now completed one cycle in the process of generating *This gazebo was build by Sir Christopher Wren*. As records of this process, we have accumulated a selection expression—shown above in Figure 27—which is a list of all the features chosen (in systems) or activated (in gates). During generation, feature realizations were applied to the features chosen by the Realizer and he also specified ordering

THEME	(TOPICAL ⌢#) # ⌢ THEME				
MOOD	SUBJECT ⌢ [Singular, Nominative] MOOD	FINITE [Singular, Pastform, Thirdperson]	PREDICATOR		
TRANSI-TIVITY	GOAL [NominalGroup] MEDIUM		PROCESS [Effective, Doverb, Creation] LEXVERB	AGENT-MARKER by	⌢ ACTOR [Nominal Group] AGENT
VERBAL VOICE		PASSIVE [Beaux]	PASSPARTICIPLE [Enparticiple]		
	This Gazebo	was	built	by	Sir Christopher Wren

Figure 28. Clause structure

Table 9. Function Association Table, Complete State

Hubs	Grammatical Functions
WREN-GAZEBO	ONUS
WREN-GAZEBO-STATEMENT	SPEECH-ACT
NOW	SPEAKING-TIME
GAZEBO-BUILDING	PROCESS
HISTORIC-TIME	EVENT-TIME
HISTORIC-TIME	RELEVANT-TIME
SIR-CHRISTOPHER	CAUSER
GREENWICH	LOCATION
MEDIOCRITY	MANNER
THE-GAZEBO	GOAL
THE-GAZEBO	MEDIUM
SIR-CHRISTOPHER	ACTOR
SIR-CHRISTOPHER	AGENT
GREENWICH-REGION	PARAGRAPH-THEME
WREN-GREENWICH-REGION-PATH	AGENT-THEMATIC-PATH
GAZEBO-GREENWICH-REGION-PATH	MEDIUM-THEMATIC-PATH
THE-GAZEBO	SUBJECT
THE-GAZEBO	THEME
GAZEBO-BUILDING-POLARITY	POLARITY

according to ordered lists of functions. The result is the function structure for the clause shown in Figure 28. Here, each column represents one functionally specified constituent, and is the result of the Conflation operation.

Throughout the generation process the Chooser has been keeping track of hub–function associations in the growing function association table. The final version of it is displayed in Table 9.

6 REVIEW

We have seen a detailed example of how text can be generated according to an intention and a plan. Although text generation is not a central concern for most of us, the methods and devices used can be applied in other ways.

1. The chooser framework can serve as a starting point in explorations of the design of a systemic semantics.
2. Choosers also serve as a way of describing the semantics of a given language; the choosers in Nigel constitute the beginnings of a semantics of grammatical choice for English.

3. The chooser and inquiry framework has proven itself very useful as a source of insights and preferences on the grammar itself. It has often been possible to choose between two different systemic representations of a particular grammatical phenomenon, based on the fact that one led to a neat collection of choosers and the other did not. Dependencies among choosers often point to meta-functional organization that is not directly evident from the wiring of the grammar itself.

4. We expect that the choosers will be useful in teaching English, since they give a basis, supported by some research, for explaining the uses of the various grammatical options of the language. Imagine using the EffectiveVoice chooser to help explain the use of the English passive.

5. The choosers also seem useful for discourse studies, since they make it easier to show how particular grammatical options are responsive to discourse information.

6. The set of inquiries of the grammar could be useful in language comparison, in the service both of constrastive analysis and of typological studies. Since each system of the grammar is syntactically motivated, the set of inquiries represents the semantics of grammatical encoding of English. This factors its semantics into an explicit grammatical part and the rest. We expect this factoring to be useful in semantic studies.

REFERENCES

Halliday, M. A. K. (1970). Functional diversity in language, as seen from a consideration of modality and mood in English. *Foundations of Language* **6.3.** 327–351.

An Introduction to the Nigel Text Generation Grammar

4

William C. Mann

USC Information Sciences Institute
Los Angeles, California

One way to develop a functional account of how language is used would be to attempt to specify in detail how texts can be created in response to **text needs**. A text need is the earliest recognition on the part of the speaker[1] that the immediate situation is one in which he would like to produce speech. Text needs arise at the beginning of each turn of a dialogue, before writing personal letters or books, and generally in all kinds of situations in which language use is found. Text needs are logically prior to deciding what to say or how to say it. Research on computer text generation is one way of attempting to say how texts can be created.

Research on the text generation task has led to creation of a large systemic grammar of English, embedded in a computer program and fitted with a semantic stratum. The grammar and program, separately and jointly called Nigel, generates sentences and other units under several kinds of experimental control.

This paper gives an overview of Nigel, emphasizing the ways in which it has augmented various precedents in the systemic framework and indicating the current state of development.

1 A GRAMMAR FOR TEXT GENERATION—THE CHALLENGE

Among the various uses for grammars, text generation at first seems to be relatively new. The organizing goal of text generation, as a research task, is to describe how texts can be created in fulfillment of text needs. Such a description must relate texts to needs, and so must contain a functional account of the use and nature of language, a very old goal. Computational text generation research should be seen as simply a particular way to pursue that goal.

As part of a text generation research project, a grammar of English has been created and embodied in a computer program. This grammar and program, called

---

[1] In this report we will alternate freely between the terms speaker, writer and author, between hearer and reader, and between speech and text. This is simply partial accomodation of prevailing jargon; no differences are intended.

Nigel, is intended as a component of a larger program called Penman. This paper introduces Nigel, with just enough detail about Penman to show Nigel's potential use in a text generation system.

1.1 The Text Generation Task as a Stimulus for Grammar Design

Text generation has been taken up only relatively recently as a computational research task (Mann 1981). It is a research area jointly included in artificial intelligence, computational linguistics and linguistics. Text generation seeks to characterize the use of natural languages by developing processes (computer programs) which can create appropriate, fluent text on demand. A representative research goal would be to create a program which could write a text that serves as a commentary on a game transcript, making the events of the game understandable.[2] Because this kind of research is in a very preliminary stage, text generation serves more as a way of thinking about text and its functions than as an established collection of results.

The guiding aims in the ongoing design of the Penman text generation program are as follows:

1. To learn, in a more specific way than has previously been achieved, how appropriate text can be created in response to text needs.
2. To identify the dominant characteristics which make a text appropriate for meeting its need.
3. To develop a demonstrable capacity to create texts which meet some identifiable practical class of text needs.

Because the relationships between text and need are so important in this research, and because the systemic framework has been developed as a *functional* account of grammar in the service of the speaker, it is an attractive candidate as the framework for Penman's grammar (Berry 1975, 1977, Halliday & Hasan 1976, Halliday 1976, 1981, Hudson 1976, de Joia 1980, Fawcett 1980).[3] For these and other reasons the systemic framework was chosen for Nigel.

In adopting the systemic framework, we have followed the preferences and values which motivate the work, and have used systemic notation. Within these guidelines we have usually followed (or been led by) Halliday.

1.2 Design Goals for the Grammar

Three kinds of goals have guided the work of creating Nigel.

1. To specify in total detail how *the systemic framework* can generate syntactic units, using the computer as the medium of experimentation.

---

[2] This was accomplished in work by Anthony Davey (1979); McKeown (1982) is a comparable more recent study.

[3] This work would not have been possible without the active participation of Christian Matthiessen, and the participation and past contributions of Michael Halliday and other systemicists.

2. To develop a *grammar of English* which is a good representative of the systemic framework and useful for demonstrating text generation on a particular task.

3. To specify how the grammar can be *regulated effectively by the prevailing text need* in its generation activity.

Each of these has led to a different kind of activity in developing Nigel and a different kind of specification in the resulting program, as described below.

The three design goals above have not all been met, and the work continues.

1. Work on the first goal, specifying the framework, is essentially finished (see section 2.2).

2. Very substantial progress has been made on creating the grammar of English; although the existing grammar is apparently adequate for some text generation tasks, some additions are planned (see section 2.3).

3. Progress on the third goal, although gratifying, is seriously incomplete. We have a notation and a design method for relating the grammar to prevailing text needs, and there are worked out examples which illustrate the methods (Mann 1982), but the work so far is far from complete (see section 2.4).

2 A GRAMMAR FOR TEXT GENERATION—THE DESIGN

2.1 Overview of Nigel's Design

The creation of the Nigel program has not required radical revisions in systemic notation nor the reorganization of existing fragments of the grammar of English. The changes have been evolutionary and largely in the direction of making well-precedented ideas more explicit or detailed. The result has unified and extended significant amounts of existing work.

The level of explicitness is set primarily by the desire to incorporate the resulting methods and definitions in autonomous computer programs. Such programs cannot resort to human judgment, to intuitions about favorable cases, to well-known examples or incompletely-specified principles. At each point in the generation process, the method must always specify an appropriate action to take next.

2.2 Programming the Systemic Framework

Systemic notation deals principally with three kinds of entities: 1) systems, 2) realizations of systemic choices (including function structures), and 3) lexical items. These three account for most of the notational devices, and the Nigel program has separate parts for each.

Nigel contains its entire grammar of English as a kind of data inside the program, not "procedurally embedded" as some previous grammars were (Winograd 1972).

It can generate in any of three basic modes of choosing: random choice, manual choice and generation according to a programmed semantics (the Choosers, described in section 2.4). These modes, and the finer controls on each, are part of a flexible set of provisions for testing the generator.[4]

2.2.1 Systems and Gates

Each system has an *input expression,* which encodes the entry conditions for the system.[5] During the generation, the program keeps track of the *selection expression,* the set of features which have been chosen up to that point. Based on the selection expression, the program invokes the realization operations which are associated with each feature chosen. Nigel uses immediate realization rather than delayed realization, invoking each realization as soon as the associated feature is chosen. Systemic notation seems to work equally well whether realizations are performed immediately or in a collection after the grammar has been traversed. However, when the semantic operations are added, as described in section 2.4, it becomes important that realization be immediate.

In addition to the systems there are *Gates.* A gate can be thought of as an input expression which activates a particular grammatical feature, without choice.[6] These grammatical features are used just as those chosen in systems. Gates are most often used to perform realization in response to a collection of features.[7]

2.2.2 Realization Operators

There are three groups of realization operators: those that build structure (in terms of grammatical functions), those that constrain order, and those that associate features with grammatical functions.

1. The realization operators which build structure are *Insert, Conflate,* and *Expand.* By repeated use of the structure building functions, the grammar is able to construct sets of *function bundles,* also called *fundles.*
2. Realization operators which constrain order are *Partition, Order, OrderAtFront* and *OrderAtEnd.* Partition constrains one function (hence one

---

[4] In addition to the parts of the program devoted to generation, there are extensive parts devoted to printing various kinds of entities, representing them graphically, tracing the course of activity during generation, answering various questions about the program's content, and testing the integrity of the definitions as a collection. These together comprise a larger quantity of program than the parts which actually do the generation, but they are not described in this paper. Nigel is programmed in INTERLISP, a dialect of LISP, and so it will run on any computer and operating system which can run INTERLISP, including TOPS-20 and VAX systems.

[5] Input expressions are composed entirely of feature names, together with *And, Or* and parentheses. See the figures in Mann and Matthiessen in this volume for examples.

[6] See the figure entitled Transitivity I (Mann and Matthiessen in this volume) for examples and further discussion of the roles of gates.

[7] Each realization operation is associated with just one feature; there are no realization operations which depend on more than one feature, and no rules corresponding to Hudson's function realization rules. The gates facilitate eliminating this category of rules, with a net effect that the notation is more homogeneous.

fundle) to be realized to the left of another, but does not constrain them to be adjacent. Order constrains just as Partition does, and in addition constrains the two to be realized adjacently. OrderAtFront constrains a function to be realized as the leftmost among the daughters of its mother, and OrderAtEnd symmetrically as rightmost.

3. Some operators associate features with functions. They are *Preselect,* which associates a grammatical feature with a function (and hence with its fundle); *Classify,* which associates a *lexical feature* with a function; *OutClassify,* which associates a lexical feature with a function in a preventive way; and *Lexify,* which forces a particular lexical item to be used to realize a function. Of these, OutClassify and Lexify are new, taking up roles previously filled by Classify. OutClassify restricts the realization of a function (and hence fundle) to be a lexical item which *does not* bear the named feature. This is useful for controlling items in exception categories (e.g. reflexives) in a localized, manageable way. Lexify allows the grammar to force selection of a particular item without having a special lexical feature for that purpose.

In addition to these realization operators, there is a set of *Default Function Order Lists.* These are lists of functions which will be ordered in particular ways by Nigel, provided that the functions on the lists occur in the structure, and that the realization operators have not already ordered those functions. A large proportion of the constraint of order is performed through the use of these lists.

The realization operations of the systemic framework, especially those having to do with order, have not been specified so explicitly before.

2.2.3 The Lexicon
The lexicon is defined as a set of arbitrary symbols, called *word names,* such as "builten", associated with symbols called *spellings,* the lexical items as they appear in text. In order to keep Nigel simple during its early development, there is no formal provision for morphology or for relations between items which arise from the same root.

Each word name has as associated set of *lexical features.* For convenience in managing large numbers of lexical features, there is a tree of lexical categories which can be manipulated by the processes used to enter definitions of lexical items into the program; this tree has no status in the theory.

Lexify selects items by word name; Classify and OutClassify operate on sets of items in terms of the lexical features.

Note that Nigel is not designed according to the view that the lexicon is homogeneous with the grammar, found at the most delicate positions. The semantic parts described below have special provisions for manipulating the lexicon.

2.3 The Grammar and Lexicon of English

Nigel's grammar is partly based on published sources, and is partly new. It has all been expressed in a single homogeneous notation, with consistent naming conventions and much care to avoid reusing names where identity is not intended. The grammar is organized as a single network, whose one entry point is used for generating all kinds of units. As of the summer of 1982, it contains about 220 systems, assigned informally to 28 collections. The relative emphasis on particular phenomena in the grammar can be judged loosely from the populations of the collections, below.

1. ADVERBIAL (1 system)
2. ATTITUDE (1 system)
3. CIRCUMSTANTIAL (14 systems)
4. CLASSIFICATION (3 systems)
5. CLAUSE-COMPLEX (15 systems)
6. CONJUNCTION (3 systems)
7. COUNT/NUMBER (2 systems)
8. CULMINATION (3 systems)
9. DEPENDENCY (18 systems)
10. DETERMINATION (23 systems)
11. ELLIPSIS (1 system)
12. EPITHET (4 systems)
13. MOOD (15 systems)
14. NOUNTYPE (2 systems)
15. POLARITY (6 systems)
16. PRONOUN (7 systems)
17. PP-SPATIOTEMPORAL (8 systems)
18. PP-OTHER (6 systems)
19. QUANTIFICATION (5 systems)
20. QUALIFICATION (6 systems)
21. RANKING (4 systems)
22. TAG (2 systems)
23. TENSE (10 systems)
24. THEME (11 systems)
25. NON-RELATIONAL TRANSITIVITY (19 systems)
26. RELATIONAL TRANSITIVITY (24 systems)
27. VERBALGROUP (2 systems)
28. VOICE (5 systems)

In developing the program, linguistically significant progress has been made in several areas: realization of order has turned out to be a rather complex matter, in which the programming has forced us to add substantially to existing precedents; we have identified a large number of integrity conditions which are applicable to systemic grammars, and programmed them as tests; the grammar has been worked on extensively in the area of tense.

Nigel's lexicon is designed for test purposes rather than coverage of any particular generation task. It currently recognizes 130 lexical features, and it has about 2000 lexical items in about 580 distinct categories (combinations of features).

2.4 Choosers—The Grammar's Semantics

The most novel part of Nigel from a systemicist's point of view is the semantics of the grammar. The goal identified above was to "specify how the grammar can be regulated effectively by the prevailing text need." Just as the grammar and the resulting text are both very complex, so is the text need. In fact, these kinds of complexity actually reflect the complexity of the text need which gave rise to the text. The grammar must respond selectively to those elements of the need which are represented by the unit being generated at the moment.

Except for lexical choice, all variability in Nigel's generated result comes from variability of choice in the grammar. Generating an appropriate structure consists entirely in making the choices in each system appropriately; there is no other locus of variation. The semantics of the grammar must therefore be a semantics of the individual systems. Choices must be made in each system according to the appropriate elements of the prevailing need.

In Nigel this semantic control is localized to the systems themselves. For each system, a procedure is defined which can declare the appropriate choice in the system. When the system is entered, the procedure is followed to discover the appropriate choice. Such a procedure is called a *chooser* (or "choice expert".) The chooser is the semantic account of the system, the description of the circumstances under which each choice is appropriate.

To specify the semantics of the choices, we needed a notation for the choosers as procedures. This paper describes that notation briefly and informally. Its use is exemplified in the Nigel demonstration (Mann and Matthiessen in this volume) and developed in more detail in another report (Mann 1982).

To gain access to the details of the need, the choosers must in some sense ask questions about particular entities. For example, to decide between Singular and Plural in creating a NominalGroup, the Number chooser (the chooser for the Number system) must be able to ask whether a particular entity (already identified elsewhere as the entity the NominalGroup represents) is unitary or multiple. That knowledge resides outside of Nigel, in the *environment.*

The environment is regarded informally as being composed of three disjoint regions:

1. The *Knowledge Base,* consisting of information which existed prior to the text need;
2. The *Text Plan,* consisting of information which was created in response to the text need, but before the grammar was entered;
3. The *Text Services,* consisting of information which is available on demand, without anticipation.

The chooser must have access to a stock of symbols representing entities in the environment. Such symbols are called *hubs.* In the course of generation, hubs are associated with grammatical functions. These associations are kept in a *Function Association Table.* This table is used to reaccess information in the environment. For example, in choosing pronouns the choosers will ask questions about the multiplicity of an entity which is associated with the THING function in the Function Association Table. Later they may ask about the gender of the same entity, again accessing it through its association with THING. This use of grammatical functions is an extension of previous uses. It has several fortunate consequences; relations between referring phrases and the concepts being referred to are captured in the Function Association Table. For example, the function representing the NominalGroup as a whole is associated with the hub which represents the thing being referred to in the environment. Similarly for possessive determiners, the grammatical function for the determiner is associated with the hub for the possessor. In cases of ellipsis, the function which would have expressed the ellipsed element (if it had been inserted into the structure) carries the appropriate hub whether ellipsis takes place or not, so that there is a formal identification of the entity being ellipsed.

It is convenient to define choosers in such a way that they have the form of a tree. For any particular case, a single path of operations is traversed.

Choosers are defined principally in terms of the following operations:

1. *Ask* presents an inquiry to the environment. The inquiry has a fixed predetermined set of possible responses, each corresponding to a branch of the path in the chooser.
2. *Identify* presents an inquiry to the environment. The set of responses is open-ended. The response is put in the Function Association Table, associated with a grammatical function which is given (in addition to the inquiry) as a parameter to the Identify operator.[8]
3. *Choose* declares a choice.
4. *CopyHub* transfers an association of a hub from one grammatical function to another.[9]

An *inquiry* consists of an *inquiry operator* and a sequence of *inquiry parameters*. Each inquiry parameter is a grammatical function, and it represents (via the Function Association Table) the entities in the environment which the grammar is inquiring about. The operators are defined in such a way that they have both formal and informal modes of expression. Informally, each inquiry is a predefined question, in English, which represents the issue that the inquiry is intended to resolve for any chooser that uses it. Formally, the inquiry shows how systemic choices depend on facts about particular grammatical functions, and in particular restricts the account of a particular choice to be responsive to a well-constrained, well-identified collection of facts. Both the informal English form of the inquiry and the corresponding formal expression are regarded as parts of the semantic theory expressed by the choosers which use the inquiry.

---

[8] See Mann and Matthiessen in this volume for an explanation and example of its use.

[9] There are three others which have some linguistic significance: Pledge, TermPledge, and ChoiceError. These are necessary but do not play a central role. They are named here just to indicate that the chooser notation is very simple.

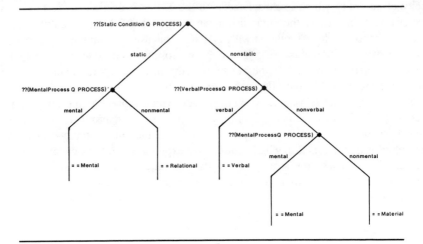

Figure 1. The Chooser of the ProcessType system

The entire collection of inquiries for a grammar is a definition of the semantic scope to which the grammar is responsive at its level of delicacy.

Figure 1 shows the chooser for the ProcessType system, whose grammatical feature alternatives are Relational, Mental, Verbal and Material.

Notice that in the ProcessType chooser, although there are only four possible choices, there are five paths through the chooser, because Mental processes can be identified in two different ways: those which represent states of affairs and those which do not. The number of termination points of a chooser often exceeds the number of choices available.

Figure 2 shows the graphic representational elements which are used to represent choosers.

Table 1 shows the English forms of the questions being asked in the ProcessType chooser.

The sequence of inquiries which the choosers present to the environment, together with its responses, creates a dialogue. The unit generated can be seen as being formed out of a negotiation between the choosers and the environment. This is a particularly instructive way to view the grammar and its semantics, since it identifies clearly what assumptions are being made and what dependencies there are

??	Ask
<?	Identify
==	Choose
<<	CopyHub
!#	Pledge
!*	TermPledge

Figure 2. Graphic representation elements for Choosers

Table 1. English Forms of the Inquiry Operators for the ProcessType Chooser

StaticConditionQ	Does the process PROCESS represent a static condition or state of being?
VerbalProcessQ	Does the process PROCESS represent symbolic communication of a kind which could have an addressee?
MentalProcessQ	Is PROCESS a process of comprehension, recognition, belief, perception, deduction, remembering, evaluation or mental reaction?

between the unit and the environment's representation of the text need. (This is the kind of dialogue represented in Mann and Matthiessen in this volume.)

It also leads to a particularly helpful mode ot testing the choosers, which proceeds as follows:

- From some natural source of text, select a phrase or clause which appears to be within the syntactic capability of the grammar.
- Attempt to generate it using Nigel, in a mode in which the answers to the inquiries come from the user of the program. Answer all of the inquiries straightforwardly according to the selected unit and the context in which it was found.
- See whether the generated result is identical to the original.

This method, which has been called the ''method of honest muddling,'' usually reveals some discrepancy between the way the choosers were intended to work and the way the inquiries are defined. This leads in turn to improved definitions for choosers and their inquiries, and often to a local reconceptualization as well.

The grammar performs the final steps in the generation process. It must complete the surface form of the text, but there is a great deal of preparation necessary before it is appropriate for the grammar to start its work. Penman's design calls for many kinds of activities under the umbrella of ''text planning'' to provide the necessary support. Work on Nigel is proceeding in parallel with other work intended to create text planning processes.

3 USES FOR NIGEL

The activity of defining Nigel, especially its semantic parts, is productive in its own right.[10] It creates interesting descriptions and proposals about the nature of English and the meaning of syntactic alternatives, as well as new notional devices. But given Nigel as a program, containing a full complement of choosers, inquiry operators and related entities, new possibilities for linguistic investigation also arise.

One can run the program to see what it generates. Apart from such a test, there

---

[10] It is our intention eventually to make Nigel available for teaching, research, development and computational application.

seems to be no practical way to find out whether the grammar produces unintended combinations of functions, structures or uses of lexical items.

One can also see how it fails to generate. In the early phases of giving Nigel a grammar of English, many contradictions were found within the grammar. Ordering was sometimes so strong that it produced cycles, so that a constituent was told to precede itself. Incompatible preselections were attached to fundles, requiring that more than one of the options be taken in a subsequently entered system, and so forth. It appears that there is a natural tendency to write the grammar with excessive homogeniety, not allowing for possible exception cases.

One can attempt to replicate text, identifying the semantic conditions which would necessarily have to be present to lead to the particular text at hand. This gives an objective way to assign some rather subtle meanings to text.

On another scale, the whole project can be regarded as a single experiment, a test of the functionalism of the systemic framework, and of its identification of the functions of English.

Nigel accounts for certain kinds of functions and relies on as yet undefined text planning processes for others. This decomposition is significant as a claim about kinds of functions and how they group into logically dependent sequences. The demands for text plan elements challenge future research to create processes which can actually plan texts in a compatible way.

Nigel's grammar, separated from program, choosers and lexicon, is usable in all the traditional ways. Because it is in a consistent notation and has been tested extensively, it has some advantages for educational and linguistic research uses.

In artificial intelligence, there is a need for priorities and guidance in the design of new knowledge representation notations. The inquiry operators of Nigel are a particularly interesting proposal as a set of distinctions already embodied in a mature, evolved knowledge notation, English, and encodable in other knowledge notations as well. For example, the inquiry operators suggest that a notation for knowledge should be able to represent objects and actions, and should be able to distinguish between definite existence, hypothetical existence, conjectural existence and non-existence of actions. These are presently rather high expectations for artificial intelligence knowledge representations.

The choosers seem particularly interesting as an expository device in teaching English to non-native speakers. The procedures document the syntactic devices of the language in a way which avoids the problems of induction from a collection of examples.

There are other practical possibilities. Computer programs with access to complex collections of information may be enabled to express that information in one or more human languages to meet practical human needs for the information.

4 SUMMARY

As part of an effort to define a text generation process, a programmed systemic grammar called Nigel has been created. Systemic notation, a grammar of English, a semantic notation, and a semantics for English are all included as distinct parts of Nigel. When Nigel has been completed it will be useful for a variety of research, educational, and practical purposes.

REFERENCES

Berry, M. (1975). *Introduction to Systemic Linguistics: Structures and Systems,* London: B. T. Batsford.

Berry, M. (1977). *Introduction to Systemic Linguistics: Levels and Links,* London: B. T. Batsford.

Davey, A. (1979). *Discourse Production,* Edinburgh: Edinburgh University Press.

de Joia, A., and A. Stenton. (1980). *Terms in Systemic Linguistics,* London: Batsford Academic and Educational.

Fawcett, R. P. (1980). *Cognitive Linguistics and Social Interaction. (Exeter Linguistic Studies,* **3.**) Heidelberg and Exeter University: Julius Groos Verlag.

Halliday, M. A. K., and R. Hasan. (1976). *Cohesion in English,* London: Longman.

Halliday, M. A. K. (1976). *System and Function in Language.* Ed. Gunther Kress. London: Oxford University Press.

Halliday, M. A. K., and J. R. Martin. (eds.). (1981). *Readings in Systemic Linguistics,* London: Batsford.

Hudson, R. A. (1976). *Arguments for a Non-Transformational Grammar.* Chicago: University of Chicago Press.

Mann, William C., et al. The state of the art of text generation, 1981. To appear in *American Journal of Computational Linguistics.*

Mann, W. C. and Christian M. I. M. Matthiessen. (1983). A Demonstration of the Nigel Text Generation Computer Program. In J. Benson and W. S. Greaves (eds.), *Systemic Perspectives on Discourse: Selected Theoretical Papers from the 9th International Systemic Workshop.* Norwood: Ablex.

Mann, William C. (1982). *The Anatomy of a Systemic Choice.* USC/Information Sciences Institute, RR-82-104.

McKeown, K. R. (1982). *Generating natural language text in response to questions about database structure.* Ph.D. thesis, University of Pennsylvania.

Winograd, T. (1972). *Understanding Natural Language,* Edinburgh, Scotland: Academic Press.

The Systemic Framework in Text Generation: Nigel

5

Christian M. I. M. Matthiessen
USC Information Sciences Institute
Los Angeles, California

A large, systemic grammar has been implemented computationally and a semantic stratum has been developed for it. The grammar and its semantics, called Nigel, are intended as a component in a text generation system. This paper describes the systemic framework as it has been worked out for Nigel in context of the text generation task: Many properties of the systemic framework are justified by the text generation task and this will be indicated. In addition, the task has led to clarifications, revisions and additions to the framework. This paper is independent of Mann and Mann and Matthiessen in this volume, but can usefully be read in the context of those papers as the last in the series.

1 INTRODUCTION

This paper reports on work on systemic grammar and semantics carried out by Mann, Halliday, and Matthiessen, building on previous work by Halliday (Halliday 1961, and onwards, particularly Halliday 1969 for the form of the grammar).[1] In addition to design and theory, the result of the research is a systemic grammar and a corresponding semantics, both of which have been implemented computationally; this component is called Nigel.[2] The present discussion is primarily about the grammar (and semantic) framework and machinery, not about English. It is in some

---

[1] This paper draws on the work carried out by W. Mann, M. A. K. Halliday, and C. Matthiessen in the research on Nigel. I am very grateful to Bill Mann for many comments on drafts of this paper and to Sandy Thompson, David Webber, Jim Melancon, and to participants in the 9th International Systemic Workshop for comments on earlier oral or written versions of the paper. Needless to say, I am solely responsible for all errors.

[2] The grammar is still developing and expanding, but it is by far the largest computational systemic grammar and integrates descriptions of English grammar by Halliday spanning approximately twenty years. The organization of the grammar as presented here reflects the current organization of Nigel. It does not necessarily reflect Halliday's views on what the organization of a systemic grammar and semantics should ideally be like given a particular task.

sense "metalinguistics." Throughout the discussion I will indicate how the design of the grammar relates to the text generation task.

1.1 Grammar: Tasks, Framework and Form

There is a growing awareness in linguistics—certainly not new in systemic linguistics—that the structure and organization of language are influenced by its functions. The same holds true at the metalevel—also an observation with a long history in systemic linguistics, see Halliday 1964; the grammatical framework and the notation should match the task of the grammar.

Any new task for a grammar is a challenge and test for the framework. The task provides us with a working environment in which to develop the framework and a test bed in which to check whether we achieve the goals defined by the task. The systemic grammar to be presented, Nigel, has been developed for a task that is very central in language use, viz. text generation. The task has a number of consequences for the grammar which will be presented after a characterization of text generation.

1.2 The Character of the Text Generation Task

The text generation task can be understood in terms of what a system that deals with that task, a text generation system, must do to generate text.

In a given situation, a need to generate a text may arise. This need will lead to a specification of the goals to be achieved by the generated text (its intent, purpose, functional tenor, or rhetorical mode) and of values for the variables of the communicative situation.

To achieve these goals, a text planning component creates a text plan. The plan terminates in clusters of messages or propositions that can be handled by the grammar. Nigel takes over and starts grammatical encoding. Nigel has to be sensitive to global principles of organization in the text plan as they influence terminal propositional clusters. This is needed to handle, for example, theme selection and conjunction. Nigel must also be sensitive to the locally specified goals and "propositional content." Thus, Nigel's role is defined by the rest of the text generation system, which will be called the Environment. In Nigel, we will distinguish the semantic component, called the Choosers, from the grammatical component, which includes the network representation, called Grammar, and a realizational part, called Realizer.

1.3 Demands on Grammar from the Text Generation Task

The text generation task leads to demands for a grammar that

(I)   in terms of framework and notation:
1.   formalizes grammar in such a way that it can serve the rest of the text generation system. For instance, it should be possible to relate abstractions in the grammar to abstractions in the environment and to control the grammar so as to achieve the desired effects.

2. states the grammar fully explicitly. All aspects of the organization of the grammar have to be "filled in."

(II) In terms of the contents of grammar:

1. is conceived of as a whole and not as a collection of mini-grammars for disconnected areas of grammar.

2. has good overall coverage of communicatively important areas of English grammar rather than just those which test the formalism.

In this presentation of Nigel, I will concentrate on demands (I.1–2); the demands relating to the coverage of the grammar have been dealt with elsewhere (Matthiessen 1982). For the demands under (II), it can just be noted that work done in the systemic framework supports the coverage demands very well. The demands of (I) have been consequential for the framework in a number of ways. Basically, (I.1) has brought out many aspects of the systemic framework that fit the text generation task extremely well. In addition, there have been formal clarifications and new designs.

1.4 Organization of the Paper

It is useful to discuss the organization and processes of Nigel in terms of four dimensions, all of which have a tradition in systemic linguistics. These dimensions are **stratification:** semantics and grammar; **axis:** paradigmatic and syntagmatic; **cycle:**[3] an arbitrary cycle n and the next one $n + 1$, and, finally, **potentiality:** potential and actual. As this list illustrates, each dimension defines two constructs (semantics and grammar, paradigmatic and syntagmatic etc.) The organization within each construct will be called intra-organization (intra-stratal, intra-axis etc.); the relations that relate the two constructs of one dimension will be called inter-relations (inter-stratal, inter-axis etc.) or realizations. The present discussion will concentrate on the first three dimensions, i.e., on stratification, axis, and cycle.

The presentation will be guided by the generation of one particular clause-structure (which can represent for example *This gazebo was built by Sir Christopher Wren*[4]). Each aspect of Nigel will be introduced by a step in the generation of this clause-structure. Section 2 underlines the value of separating the paradigmatic axis from the syntagmatic axis in a text generation grammar and brings in the dimension of stratification as well to show how an explicit paradigmatic organization can be used. Section 3 continues the discussion of the axis dimension, but focuses on inter-axis relations (feature-to-function realization). Section 4 introduces an additional dimension, the cycle, and shows how the problem of inter-cyclic relations has been solved in Nigel. Section 5 ends the generation of the example clause and presents the organization of the syntagmatic axis in Nigel, i.e., of the function structure. There follows, in Section 6, a summary of the three-dimensions introduced.

---

[3] The term and the notion will be explained below.

[4] For a detailed transcript of how Nigel generates this clause, see Mann and Matthiessen in this volume. The illustrations used for this paper have been excerpted from that transcript and edited to fit as examples here.

The example used to illustrate the grammar appears in italics throughout the discussion. The components (Grammar, Chooser, Environment, and Realizer) are as described in section 1.2 above. If read continuously, the illustrative italicized parts constitute a summary of the generation of one clause, presented in detail in the generation drama (Mann and Matthiessen, in this volume).

2 GRAMMAR AND SEMANTICS: PARADIGMATIC AND SYNTAGMATIC STRATIFICATION

This section deals with the issue of relating the Nigel grammar to the rest of the text generation system. This has to be addressed by the systemic principle of stratification, which has been explored in the work on Nigel through the design of a semantic stratum—the so-called chooser framework developed for Nigel—and through a design of the interaction of grammar and semantics. It is argued that two basic systemic functional principles have been instrumental: the separation of the representation of the paradigmatic axis of grammatical organization from the syntagmatic one and the functional representation of syntagmatic organization.

2.1 Separating Paradigmatic from Syntagmatic

In this section we will show how grammar and semantics (the choosers of the grammar) work together and point to how the systemic view and design of grammar make it possible to create a systemic grammar for a text generation system.

We start with the grammar offering a choice.
GRAMMAR: We now enter the **Rank** *system. The choice options are* <u>Clauses</u> *and* <u>GroupsPhrases</u>.

As all systemic grammars from the mid 60s onwards, Nigel is built on the principles that (i) the two axes of organization, the paradigmatic axis and the syntagmatic one, are given separate representations, and (ii) the syntagmatic representation is derived from the paradigmatic one. The primitive of the paradigmatic organization is the **feature,** as for example <u>Clauses</u> in the example above. In Nigel, as in all systemic grammars, features are organized into systems, which, in turn, form a system network.

When the two basic dimensions of linguistic organization are separated, i.e., when we separate paradigmatic and syntagmatic organization, and take the paradigmatic dimension as primary (see Halliday 1966)—to be deep grammar (to use an essentially non-systemic metaphor)—we get a grammar where the paradigmatic organization faces semantics. Or, to put it in another way, the paradigmatic organization is the way into grammar from semantics. The result is a clear separation of grammar as a choice potential (paradigmatic axis) and the means by which the choices are realized (syntagmatic axis). This separation gives us a handle on a systemic grammar as a text generation grammar: It is the choice points in grammar that have to be controlled, and these are stated explicitly as systems. As the characterization of demand (I.1) above indicates, this property of systemic grammars is highly desirable given the text generation task. Let us now move on to how this control can be designed.

2.2 Stratification: The Control of Grammar

The Grammar has offered a choice, a statement of its local resources. The next interactant is the Chooser.
CHOOSER: Does WREN-GAZEBO (ONUS) have its own illocutionary force?
ENVIRONMENT: Yes, it has an illocutionary force.
CHOOSER: Then I choose feature Clauses.

We are at the Rank system in the grammar and the task is now to choose between the two features Clauses and GroupsPhrases. In other words, we need to control the system. This is not a task for the grammar itself, but for the next level (stratum). The device used is a **chooser**.

One clearly defined role for semantics[5] is to be an **interlevel** or **interface**. Halliday (1961) writes that the meaning of an item "is its *relation* to extratextual features." Semantics is, then, an inter-level between grammar and what is outside language; it is "the strategy that is available for entering the language system" (Halliday 1973: 64).

A chooser works as an interface in the way suggested by the example above. It is assigned to a particular system, i.e., it is the chooser of a particular system, and asks the environment questions that will supply it with the information needed to choose appropriately. The Rank chooser (as all choosers) faces both the grammar (through the choice or selection in the grammar) and what is outside the linguistic (Nigel) system (called "environment" in the dialogue). The chooser tests for the distinctions that have to obtain in the environment and when a particular distinction or a particular set of distinctions obtain, the chooser **realizes** these distinctions that are non-grammatical through the grammar by choosing a feature. We will meet other types of realization as we proceed; this type is **inter-stratal realization.**[6]

What is outside language is a highly complex system, as for example Halliday (1978) shows. In the work on text generation systems, it is useful to see what is outside language as the **environment**[7] of semantics and grammar with initially only two parts—a knowledge base and text-plans (from a text-planner).

---

[5] There are currently various kinds of semantics that differ according to what they set out to do. The question is not so much "which semantics is the right one?," but rather "what are the tasks we need to recognize for semantics?."

[6] "Realization" is the general term for a move along one of the three dimensions, stratification, axis, and cycle. We will distinguish inter-stratal realization, inter-axis realization (feature-to-function realization), and inter-cyclic realization (preselection).

[7] There is an obvious correspondence between the term *environment* and the term *context* from Firthian linguistics. However, it is better to use *environment* so as not to make or suggest any implicit assumptions about the nature of what is outside Nigel.

2.3 Associations Between Concepts and Functions

A chooser relates to the grammar by choosing a feature in a system based on information from the environment. This is the paradigmatic interaction with the grammar. In addition, a chooser may create an association between a grammatical function and a concept from the environment. This is the syntagmatic interaction.

The locus in the environment which the choosers can go to to trace information relevant to their questions is called WREN-GAZEBO. Early on in the generation, once it has been established that we're generating a simple clause, the following exchange occurs:
CHOOSER: What concept is the process aspect of WREN-GAZEBO?
ENVIRONMENT: It's called GAZEBO-BUILDING.
CHOOSER: I associate the concept GAZEBO-BUILDING with the grammatical function PROCESS.

Here the chooser creates an association between the GAZEBO-BUILDING concept from the environment and the PROCESS function from the grammar. In Nigel, as in many systemic functional grammars, the primitive of syntagmatic representation is the grammatical function. So grammatical functions rather than classes carry associations. A constituent may be characterized by more than one function.[8] Consequently, a constituent may have more than associations, for example, a constituent may simultaneously be TOPICAL (i.e. topical theme), SUBJECT, and ACTOR.

The type of multi-functional grammar Halliday has developed over the years enables us to manipulate function-to-concept associations in a more sophisticated way than if we simply had one association per constituent. Each constituent may have three functions (at least) in the clause—a transitivity function, a mood function, and a theme function—each one of which may give rise to the concept association carried by this bundle of functions.

If we represent the inter-stratal relations introduced here by ''Choose'' (paradigmatic) and ''Associate'' (syntagmatic), we can summarize the discussion simply, as illustrated in Figure 1.

When we generate, we shunt back and forth between strata, between semantics and grammar. This is the general strategy for all inter-dimension work, as shown below.

3 ASPECTS OF PARADIGMATIC ORGANIZATION

The paradigmatic organization of grammar is the best explored aspect of systemic grammar. This section confines itself to a brief presentation of the **gate** and a few

---

[8] Generally speaking, this is a result of Halliday's meta-functional hypothesis: each meta-function may contribute one or more micro-functions as the characterization of the constituent.

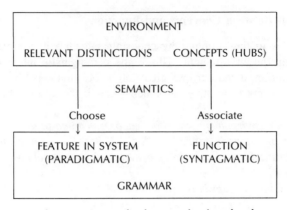

Figure 1. Semantics is an active interlevel

other notions that are not "universal" in systemic grammar. It is also noted how, for example, a disjunctive entry condition is interpreted.

3.1 Paradigmatic Organization as Single Network

The first system entered from Nigel was Rank. The entire system network can be reached from this system. Halliday (1969) has described the grammar of English as one huge network and this is what the fragment represented in the Nigel grammar is.

This means that the notion of rank has been represented as an early system in the grammar; in this respect the Nigel grammar is like Hudson's grammar of English complex clauses in Hudson (1971). There are a number of consequences of treating the grammar formally as a single network.

3.2 Dimensions of the Network: Simultaneity and Dependency

In the system Rank the feature Clauses was chosen. This feature is the input to another system which the grammar now offers:

GRAMMAR: We now enter the ClauseClass system. The choice options are Clause and Clausette.

After appropriate questions to the Environment, the ClauseClass chooser selects Clause, which is the input to yet another system:

GRAMMAR: We now enter the ClauseComplexity system. The choice options are ClauseSimplex and ClauseComplex.

Again after interaction with the Environment, a choice can be made and the

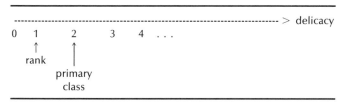

Figure 2. Rank and class in Nigel

ClauseComplexity chooser selects ClauseSimplex, which is the entry condition to (among others) the systems Agency and Manner. In other words, Agency and Manner are simultaneous in the network, both having ClauseSimplex as their entry condition:
GRAMMAR: We now enter the **Agency** *system. The choice options are Middle and Effective.*
And, after some chooser activity:
GRAMMAR: We now enter the **Manner** *system. The choice options are Non-Manner and Manner.*

The move from left to right in a system network is a move in dependency; from a feature or a collection of features to a system whose entry condition they satisfy. In the present example, the move from the system ClauseClass to the system Clause-Complexity is a move in dependency. Each step such as this one increases the **delicacy**[9] (or ''depth''[10]).

Since the grammar is a single network one, the first two steps in delicacy have a special status; the first step is **rank** and the second step is **(primary) classes** at each rank—as shown in Figure 2.

The system ClauseClass was entered above. It represents the two primary classes of clauses, Clause and Clausette (major and minor clauses). If we had chosen GroupsPhrases instead of Clauses in the Rank system, we would have reached the system that specifies primary class at group/phrase rank—see Figure 3.

So, rank and primary class are aspects of delicacy in Nigel. Delicacy is the measure of the horizontal dimension of the network, i.e., of its dependency dimension. The other dimension, the vertical dimension, will simply be called **simultaneity.** The systems Agency and Manner (in the example above) are simultaneous systems in the network.

---

[9] Delicacy, as a technical term, here only applies to the paradigmatic axis—in contrast to, e.g., Halliday (1961) where elements of structure were specified to various degrees of delicacy.
[10] In spatial metaphor terms, the network has breadth (or width) and depth. However, since ''depth'' has already been used as a technical term with another meaning—see, e.g., Huddleston (1965)—and since we already have the term ''delicacy,'' I shall use ''delicacy'' and ''simultaneity'' instead of ''depth'' and ''breadth'' here.

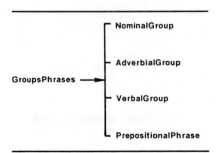

Figure 3. Primary class at group/phrase rank

3.3 The Points of Connection: Systems and Gates

Up to now, we have met only systems in the generation of "This gazebo was built by Sir Christopher Wren." However, once the chooser has chosen the feature Effective, the entry condition to a gate has been satisfied:
GRAMMAR: We now enter the Gate **MediumInsert.**
Here the Grammar does not present a choice option. There is only one output feature.

The gate is a device that is widely used in Nigel, but which has not been standard in systemic grammars before. (For an earlier discussion of various network devices, see a discussion by Fawcett (in press).) Systems and gates both have features as inputs and outputs; they are composed of left-facing (upward, in Stratificational terminology) and right-facing (downwards) disjunctions or conjunctions—or, if they are not feature complexes, their inputs and outputs are single features; see Figure 4.

Feature complexes as inputs can have, for example, a conjunction with a disjunction as one of the conjuncts. In other words, there can be more than one layer.

The disjunction of the output of a system is exclusive; only one of the output features (terms in the system) may be chosen. A disjunction in the input is not

COMPLEXITY / DIRECTION	Single feature:	Feature complex:	
		Conjunction	Disjunction
Right:output	GATE	(Not defined)	SYSTEM
Left:input	All Possible for both GATE and SYSTEM		

Figure 4. System and gate

exclusive, however. If the input to a system is a disjunction of the features Extent and TopicalExtent, both of the disjuncts may be satisfied. However, this only counts as one entry of the system; a feature can only be chosen once in a pass through the grammar. For instance, we may have a specification of the temporal extent (i.e., duration) of the process, either for experiential reasons or for thematic reasons—or for both. So the entry condition of the system specifying the subtypes of extent in English has a disjunction of Extent and TopicalExtent as its input.

3.4 Network Conventions Not Defined in Nigel

A small number of conventions have sometimes been used by systemicists to indicate various restrictions on the selection of feature combinations (symbols include daggers and stars).[11] These conventions have not been defined in Nigel—they do not in fact lend themselves to simple formalizations—but they can be viewed as shorthand for more explicit wiring in the network in Nigel.

Another network convention that has not been formalized in Nigel, but remains informal with respect to the notation used in Nigel is the "loop" of recursive systems (typically found in the logical component). Henrici (1981) observes that "linear recursion is rather more troublesome" than recursion through embedding (which is achieved through preselection in Nigel) and concludes that "much work still remains to be done"; his remarks are still highly relevant.

4 FROM PARADIGMATIC TO SYNTAGMATIC: FEATURE-TO-FUNCTION REALIZATION

Feature-to-function realization has not been as much explored in systemic linguistics as system networks and the nature of syntagmatic representation. This section presents the realization operators that have been specified for Nigel.

4.1 The Step from Paradigmatic to Syntagmatic

One of the systems reachable from the feature ClauseSimplex is ProcessType. The grammar and the chooser work together as before and the chooser makes a choice:
  CHOOSER: Then I choose feature Material . . . and I'm finished in this chooser.
  REALIZER: Classify PROCESS Doverb

It was shown in the previous section how the separation of the representation of the paradigmatic axis and the syntagmatic axis fits well with demands created by the text generation task. Once we have given the two axes separate representations, however, we need to relate them very explicitly. In other words, when we provide

---

[11] Cf. also Hudson's feature addition rules in Daughter Dependency Grammar (Hudson 1976).

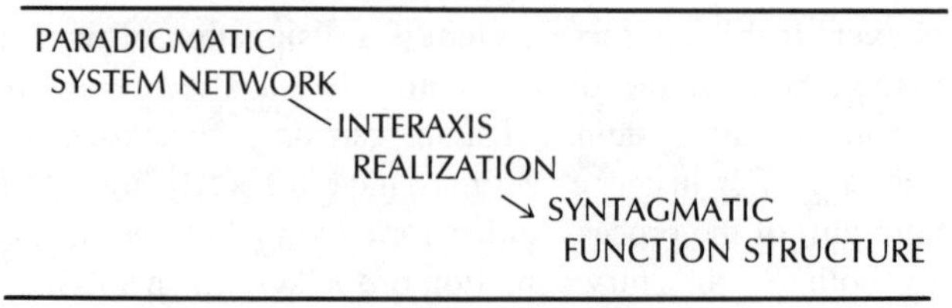

PARADIGMATIC
SYSTEM NETWORK
⟍ INTERAXIS
REALIZATION
⟍ SYNTAGMATIC
FUNCTION STRUCTURE

Figure 5. Inter-axis relations

for separate intra-axis representations, we must also provide an inter-axis representation. In Nigel, this job is handled by feature-to-function realization statements.[12] Given a certain feature or combination of features, these statements, when activated, insert functions into the syntagmatic representation, i.e., into the function structure, and carry out other operations. For each type of realization statement (like insertion) there is a realization operator (like Insert). So, to include feature-to-function realization statements as inter-axis relations into our diagrammatic overview, we can expand the lower box of Figure 1 (leaving out the non-grammatical parts above the lower box) into Figure 5.

4.2 Types of Inter-Axis Realization Operators

The full set of inter-axis realization operators is given below in Figure 6. **Insert** specifies the presence of a function in the function structure being built. The other realization operators specify the syntagmatic relations a function can enter into, i.e., a constituency relation (**Expand**), a simultaneity relation (**Conflate**), and ordering relations (**Partition** and **Order, OrderAtEnd, OrderAtFront**).

Insert and *Conflate* have direct equivalents in Halliday (1969); *Partition* and *Order* correspond to what was called *concatenate* there. *Expand* is Halliday's name for the operator that specifies constituency. For example, both SUBJECT and FINITE can be specified as constituents of MOOD through the Expand operator: (Expand MOOD SUBJECT) and (Expand MOOD FINITE).[13]

The fully specified structure of the functions of the clause being generated is the result of the application of the realization operators. In Figure 11, functions in vertical columns have been conflated. Expansion is indicated by a subscripted parenthesis.

Partition and *Order* both specify orderings of functions, taking a pair of functions as arguments. This first operator just specifies that one function precedes

---

[12] Since the paradigmatic organization is primary, the syntagmatic one is derived from it through realization statements in generation.

[13] The expand operator only specifies constituency within one cycle (see below for this notion); it is used rather sparingly. Inter-cyclic preselection is brought about indirectly through preselection (also discussed below in section 5).

OPERATOR	SYMBOL	EXAMPLE
(Insert X)	+X	+SUBJECT
(Conflate X Y)	X/Y	SUBJECT/AGENT
(Expand X Y)	X(Y)	MOOD(FINITE)
(Order X Y)	X ˆ Y	SUBJECT ˆ FINITE
(Partition X Y)	X|Y	PROCESS|MANNER
(OrderAtEnd X)	X ˆ #	TOPICAL ˆ #
(OrderAtFront X)	# ˆ Y	# ˆ TEXTUAL

Figure 6. Realization operators: symbols

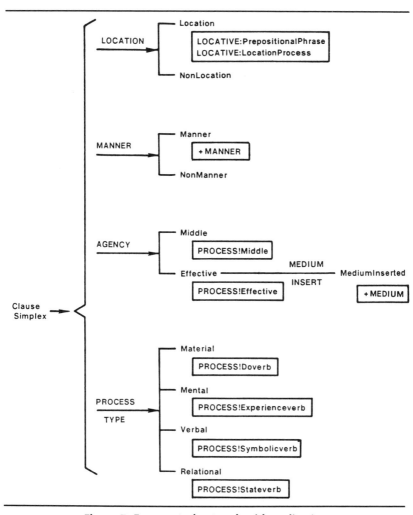

Figure 7. Fragment of network with realizations

another. For example, (Partition SUBJECT FINITE) allows for the possibility of an intervening adjunct,[14] e.g., a conjunctive: SUBJECT CONJUNCTIVE FINITE.

The second ordering operator is Partition plus adjacency: (Order SUBJECT FINITE) means that SUBJECT precedes FINITE and that the two functions are adjacent. (Order TO INFINITIVE) would mean that an infinitive cannot be split from its marker.

The distinction between the two ordering operators thus makes it possible to express the observation that in a structure there are certain places or slots where elements, e.g., adjuncts, may intervene and that in other places they are less likely to.

Realizations are stated in the system network in connection with the features they realize—see the sample below in Figure 7—rather than in a separate list.[15]

5 PARADIGMATIC TO PARADIGMATIC: INTER-CYCLIC REALIZATION

So far we have taken the generation of our clause as far as the paradigmatic representation and realization statements (as summarized in Figure 5 above) can take us. We have not seen the completion of the clause-structure yet, but that is within the capacity of the grammar as presented in the preceding sections (except for some additional ordering information that will be introduced below). It is comparable to the grammar illustrated by Halliday (1969) and the notation defined by Henrici (1981). However, we have neither exhausted the grammar nor reached the lexicon. This section will present how the grammar is re-entered or the lexicon entered to extend beyond one "feature-to-function" cycle. It follows from demand I.2 in section 1.3 that there has to be a fully explicit specification of how the grammar can be re-entered and how the lexicon can be reached. First, let me make clear what is meant by *cycle* in the present context.

5.1 The Notion of Cycle

Huddleston (1965) defines the **depth** of an item in a structure as "the layer at which the item under consideration occurs" and says that it can be "evaluated quite simply, by counting the number of nodes between it and the top of the tree." Given this definition of depth, we can go on to say that the depth of an item is the syntagmatic (structural) reflection of the number of times we have cycled through the grammar to generate the item. One **cycle** can be defined as one complete move from the paradigmatic axis to the syntagmatic axis. Each cycle begins with an entry of the system network and ends with a structure fragment. We will now illustrate how Nigel moves from one cycle to another.

---

[14] The operator corresponds to Martin Kay's SUBJECT . . . FINITE notation.
[15] The separate list display is used for example in Hudson (1971), in Davey (1979), and in Fawcett (1980).

5.2 Preparing for Another Cycle: Preselection

In the previous examples, the Realizer has carried out feature-to-function realiza-tion, i.e., specified the presence of functions and how they are related. In the course of generation, the Realizer also deals with another type of realization (inter-cyclic realization):
    REALIZER: (Preselect ACTOR NominalGroup)
    REALIZER: (Preselect GOAL NominalGroup)

For every functionally characterized constituent there is the possibility either (i) of re-entering the system network to make further choices to determine its internal structure or (ii) of going to the lexicon.

All the function-to-feature operators capture the general systemic notion of pre-selection, the term being used for one of them. The feature associated with a function is either grammatical and the operator is **Preselect** or lexical and the operator is **Classify** or **Outclassify.**

Preselect associates a grammatical feature with a grammatical function, as a realization of one or more grammatical features. For example, in *This gazebo was built by Sir Christopher Wren,* the SUBJECT is determined to be singular in a clause system. This leads to a preselection of the SUBJECT to be a singular nominal group: (Preselect SUBJECT Singular). In this way, Preselect defines an inter-cyclic relation from the cycle in which we make a pass through the clause part of the network to the cycle in which we make a pass through the nominal group part of the network to specify the SUBJECT.

Any feature in the system network has one or more **paths** leading to it, i.e., a set of choices through which it can be reached. As long as there is only one path leading to the feature, it can be preselected and its path computed through redundancy, so-called **path augmentation.** In other words, on a unique path only the most delicate feature need be preselected. When we return to the system network in the next **cycle,** the preselection and the path augmentation make it clear which part of the network to enter.

Classify is like Preselect, the only difference being that the operator associates a lexical feature with a function and not a grammatical one. The lexical features used in Nigel have not been systemicized, so path augmentation is only used for pre-selected grammatical features and not for classified lexical ones.

Outclassify specifies a lexical feature that must *not* be present in the feature set of a lexical item realizing a particular function bundle.[16] For example, (Classify FINITE Reduced) means that the lexical item realizing FINITE is required to have Reduced in its feature set. In contrast, (Outclassify FINITE Reduced) means that the lexical item is required not to have Reduced in its feature set.

There is an additional operator that makes contact with the lexicon, viz. **Lexify.**

---

[16] A **function bundle** or fundle is the result of applying realization operators to single functions. In other words, it is a micro-functionally characterized constituent.

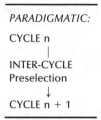

PARADIGMATIC:

CYCLE n
|
INTER-CYCLE
Preselection
↓
CYCLE n + 1

Figure 8. Preselection, the inter-cyclic realization

The two previous operators, Classify and Outclassify, specify lexical items paradigmatically through features that characterize them. Each Classify or Outclassify specifies a set of lexical items. In contrast, Lexify specifies a unique lexical item.[17] (Lexify FINITE will) does not mean that FINITE should be realized by one of the members of the set characterized as "will" items, but that FINITE should be realized by the item *will* itself.[18]

To sum up, preselection serves an inter-role in Nigel just as feature-to-function realization does. In fact, we can define the general notion **realization** as an inter-relation; it is inter-stratal, inter-axis, or inter-cycle. Choose and associate are the inter-stratal relations, the various feature-to-function realizations like Insert and Expand are the inter-axis relations, and Preselection is the inter-cycle relation (see Figure 8).

5.3 The Role of the Gate in Realization

In general, a realization is only stated once, even if there are different paradigmatic conditions under which it applies. This is accomplished by means of the **gate.** For example, there are various conditions under which SUBJECT may be inserted and, instead of repeating (Insert SUBJECT) each time, the following gate is used (see Figure 9).

The gate can also be used for so-called conditional realizations. For instance, we may say "Given feature m, (Insert F), if feature n is also present." Formally, this is equivalent to saying "Given features m and n, (Insert F)" and we can use a gate to do the job for us, without using an additional mechanism; see Figure 10 for this gate.

As presented above, the part of the network with realization statements (Figure 7) is just the display sequence of realizations; it still leaves open different possible application sequences.

---

[17] Actually, to be more precise, Lexify specifies a unique form of a lexical item.

[18] Lexify could be characterized as specifying a form of a lexical item syntagmatically. However, for ease of reference, Preselect, Classify, Outclassify, and Lexify will all be treated as instances of preselection relation between paradigmatic representations at adjacent cycles. For a discussion of a related issue, see Halliday (1963).

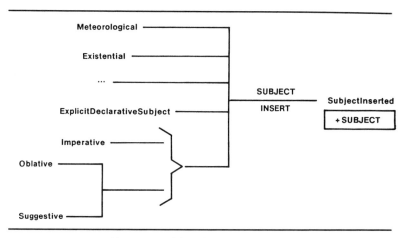

Figure 9. Subject insertion by gate

5.4 The Status of Realization in Systemic Grammar

As already mentioned in the introduction to this section, in systemic linguistics generally realization statement conventions are not in as stable a state as the system network notation. The set of realization operators used in Nigel has been sufficient so far and can be used as the basis for further explorations, for example, of the best way of arriving at the right sequence of constituents.

5.5 Function Realization: An Inter-Cyclic Relation Not Used in Nigel

The type of inter-cyclic realization that has been presented most fully in the literature is **function realization** (see e.g., Hudson 1971). Function realization statements specify features (at cycle n + 1) given a certain function (at cycle n). For instance, Hudson gives the realization [ing-form] (i.e., a feature) for the function GERUND.

Function realization statements are moves along two dimensions: from cycle n to cycle n + 1 (cycle) and from function to feature (axis). In contrast, preselections stay within the paradigmatic axis and only move from one cycle to another.

Often the two realization strategies are fully equivalent. However, there is a drawback with function realization: Whatever information we already have stated paradigmatically at cycle n (for example, the [ing-form] environment) has to be

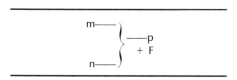

Figure 10. Gate used for conditional realization

(TOPICAL) THEME				
(SUBJECT MOOD	FINITE)			
GOAL MEDIUM		PROCESS	AGENTMARKER	ACTOR AGENT
	PASSIVE	PASSIVE-PARTICIPLE		

Figure 11. Function structure of clause

recoded (via feature-to-function realization) syntagmatically so that function realization can apply and carry the information into the next cycle (via function realization). In the worst case, we have to create specific functions whose purpose is only to carry the information about a particular form in a conjugation or a particular lexical item. This may contribute to the proliferation of grammatical functions that has been noted for the variants of systemic grammar making use of function realization (cf. remarks in Davey 1979).

In Nigel, function realization (as defined and used by Hudson 1971) was first implemented, but was later eliminated, since it has proved possible to do without this type of realization entirely.

6 SYNTAGMATIC REPRESENTATION: FUNCTION STRUCTURE

We have illustrated nearly all the steps that lead to a fully specified and ordered clause-structure. Repeated choosing takes us through the system network. When all feature-to-function realizations have been applied, the result is the full function clause-structure of "This gazebo was built by Sir Christopher Wren." The structure without features specified by the preselection operators is presented in Figure 11. (The subscripted brackets represent expansion and the vertical alignment represents conflation.)

The function structure above is not a fragment; it is the full clause-structure. There is, however, some ordering specification that the realization statements do not give. The so-called function order lists are not "feature realization," but can be viewed as a final set of **ordering constraints** on function structures.

6.1 Function Order Lists

Although making ordering explicit (cf. demand I.2 in section 2) in Nigel required quite a bit of work, the form of the ordering constraints is very simple; it is simply a list of functions—for example, (MANNER TIME LOCATION).

This says that, among the three circumstantials in the list, MANNER precedes TIME, which precedes LOCATION. The ordering is like ''Partition''; no adjacency is required.

These lists will have an effect only if the functional constituents have not been given a conflicting ordering by feature realization, i.e., by Order or Partition. For instance, it would be possible to state the ordering of SUBJECT and FINITE only for yes/no-interrogatives (forgetting about wh-interrogatives), i.e., Interrogative > (Partition FINITE SUBJECT), and have (SUBJECT FINITE) as one of the function order lists. If the clause generated is not Interrogative, no ordering of SUBJECT and FINITE has been specified and the list applies. However, when the clause is Interrogative, an ordering has been specified and the list (SUBJECT FINITE) does not apply.

6.2 Syntagmatic Rules Not Used in Nigel: Structure Building Rules

As was stated above, the function structures generated by Nigel are fully specified by the feature-to-function realizations except for the ordering specifications by the function order lists. In this, Nigel differs from, for example, Hudson's grammar in Hudson (1971) which is more complicated.

Hudson has a category of **structure building rules.** These include rules similar

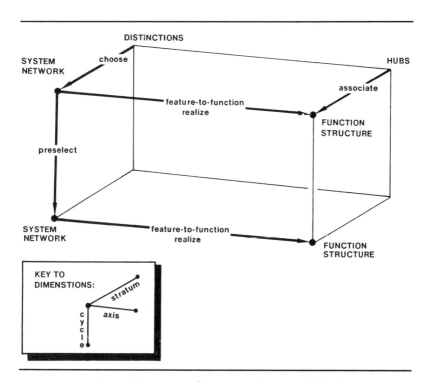

Figure 12. Inter- and intra-organization of Nigel

to Nigel's function order lists, but in addition there are **compatibility rules, addition rules,** and **conflation rules** in Hudson's grammar. It has not been necessary to include any of these rules in Nigel.

7 SUMMARY: ORGANIZATION OF THE NIGEL GRAMMAR

The overall organization and design of the Nigel grammar can be brought out by looking at the two axes of organization, the paradigmatic axis and the syntagmatic axis, and their inter-relations within a cycle and across two cycles. As a result, we can bring Figures 1, 5, and 8 above together here into one figure that summarizes the organization of Nigel diagrammatically (see Figure 12).

I will summarize Nigel in two steps: (i) intra-organization (network and structure); (ii) inter-relations.

7.1 Intra-Axis and Cycle Organization

Within a given cycle n, the system network represents the paradigmatic organization. The function structure represents the syntagmatic organization within a given cycle. These two, the network of systems and the linear structure of functions, are the intra-axis and intra-cycle modes of organization of language. All the other aspects of the Nigel grammar are inter-relations, either inter-axis or inter-cycle.

The primitives of the network and the structure are the feature and the function respectively. Both enter into intra-dimension relations that define the other constructs—systems, function bundles, etc. Figure 13 tabulates the primitives, the relations the primitives enter into, and the resultant complexes of primitives, for both axes. The relations are different for the two axes[19] and this is how we can justify having features distinct from functions in Nigel: the operations performed on features are different from those performed on functions. For example, functions are conflated, but features are not.

There is a difference between the two axes that is not suggested in Figure 13 but which is basic to systemic grammars. The relations that define paradigmatic complexes (systems and gates) are stated at that level. In contrast, the relations that define syntagmatic complexes are not stated as syntagmatic rules (as happens in most current generative grammars) but as feature realizations.

7.2 Inter-Relations

There are theoretically more **inter-relations** than are actually used in the Nigel grammar at present. ''Paradigmatic (at cycle) n to syntagmatic (at cycle) n'' and

---

[19] In this, systemic grammar differs from stratificational grammar where the same relations are used for both axes.

	PARADIGMATIC	SYNTAGMATIC
Primitive	feature	function
Relations among primitives	Conjunction, disjunction, dependency	Conflation, expansion, ordering
Complexes	Systems, gates	Function bundles,* function structures

*A **fundle** or a function bundle is the result of applying realization operators to single functions. In other words, it is a micro-functionally characterized constituent.

Figure 13. Paradigmatic and syntagmatic intra-organization

"paradigmatic at n to paradigmatic at $n + 1$," i.e. feature-to-function realization and preselection respectively are the only ones used at present.

In Figure 14, a complement to Figure 12, inter-relations that have been used in other systemic grammars and many inter-relations that could theoretically be used are shown (indicated by broken lines).

The lines (numbered for reference) are to be interpreted as follows.

Broken line [1] means that a chooser would choose features at cycle n + 1 in addition to choosing features at cycle n. At present, the effect of this is only accomplished indirectly, through preselection. So, for instance, number agreement between SUBJECT and FINITE is accomplished by selecting for subject number in the clause and then preselecting the SUBJECT and classifying the FINITE through

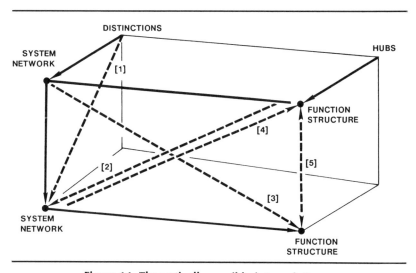

Figure 14. Theoretically possible inter-relations

inter-cyclic (grammatical) realization according to the selection the chooser made in the clause.

In fact, inter-cyclic communication is done only by preselection in the grammar. As was already mentioned in Section 5, function realization (line [2]) is not necessary in Nigel. In addition, there is no inter-cyclic feature-to-function realization (line [3]): if a choice in the clause has effects for the structure of a group, this is handled by preselecting an appropriate feature for the group which, in its turn, will then be realized by an operation of feature-to-function realization.

Line [4] represents inter-cyclic feature-to-function realization where the direction is from one cycle to the preceding cycle. A possible example would be a selection in a group, the realization of which was an ordering of one of the functions of the group-structure with respect to a function in the clause-structure.

Line [5], finally, represents statements that would include functions from say both clause-structure and the nominal group structure realizing the subject constituent of the clause. For example, it is possible to imagine function default ordering lists taking on a role of that kind.

The principles that constrain the Nigel grammar at present can be stated as follows:

1. Within a given cycle, paradigmatic is primary to syntagmatic.
2. Inter-relations never take more than one step at a time; they are either between the two axes keeping within one cycle, or between two adjacent cycles within the same axis—in fact, only within the paradigmatic axis.[20]

Note that the second constraint also states that there is for example no "unbounded" preselection from say cycle n to cycle $n + 5$. The diagram defines what Nigel can do [ability] within the present grammar framework [theoretical possibility]. It may, of course, turn out in future work either that Nigel ought to be able to do more or that the framework itself should be changed. The present set of inter-relations is listed in Figure 15.

7.3 Another Dimension: Potentiality

Figure 12 basically represents the grammar as potential (in Halliday's sense of the term). Any particular example that we generate (such as *This gazebo was built by Sir Christopher Wren*) represents an actual instance of the potential; the generation process itself is an actualization (instantiation) of the potential; cf. Halliday (1973).

The diagram in the figure allows for more than one way of doing actualization; more than one "flow chart" can be derived from it. For instance, the entire system network can be actualized before any structure is built or structure can be built (through feature realization) in tandem with the actualization of the system network.

---

[20] As pointed out above, constituency can be defined as the syntagmatic relation between two adjacent cycles. However, there is no need for special statements to introduce it. The desired effect is achieved by preselection.

[A] SEMANTIC (n) TO GRAMMATICAL (n)

   Choose
   Associate

[B] PARADIGMATIC (n) TO SYNTAGMATIC (n)

   Insert
   Expand
   Conflate
   Order, OrderAtEnd, OrderAtFront, Partition

[C] PARADIGMATIC (n) TO PARADIGMATIC (n + 1)

   Preselect
   Classify, Outclassify; Lexify

Figure 15. Summary of realization types

Issues such as this tend to be more prominent in an implemented grammar such as Nigel's than in a grammar that has not been implemented and is used primarily for description. They are part of the demands of explicitness stemming from the text generation task.

Space constraints prevent me from discussing actualization issues here.

8 CONCLUSION

This paper has presented a "fourth generation" Systemic Grammar that is a continuation of the work reported in Halliday (1969), the Nigel grammar.

The Nigel grammar has been developed for the task of text generation. This task provides both a test for the systemic framework and a research context in which aspects of systemic grammar that have been given less attention than for example the system network can be further explored.

Two major design principles of systemic functional grammars as presented by Halliday (1969) are central to the text generation task. The principles are (i) the separation of the paradigmatic and the syntagmatic organization, giving the former an independent representation, and (ii) a functional approach to grammar with for example structures stated in terms of functions.

The demand for explicitness inherent in the text generation task has given us reason to specify the inter-relations (realizations) in grammar and semantics in detail; the computational implementation has provided an opportunity to test these.

REFERENCES

Davey, A. (1979). *Discourse Production*. Edinburgh, Scotland: Edinburgh University Press.
Fawcett, R. P. (1980). *Cognitive Linguistics and Social Interaction*. (*Exeter Linguistic Studies*, **3.**) Heidelberg and Exeter University: Julius Groos Verlag.

Fawcett, R. P. (1984) System networks, codes and knowledge of the universe: a cognitive perspective on the relationship between language and culture. In Halliday, M. A. K., Lamb, S. M. and Makkai, A. (eds.) *Semiotics of culture and language.*

Halliday, M. A. K. (1961). Categories of the theory of grammar, *Word* **17**, 241–292.

Halliday, M. A. K. (1963). Class in relation to the axes of chain and choice in language. *Linguistics* **2**. 5–15.

Halliday, M. A. K. (1964). Syntax and the consumer. In C. I. J. M. Stuart (ed.), *Monograph Series in Languages & Linguistics.* Volume 17: *Report of the Fifteenth Annual (First International) Round Table Meeting on Linguistics and Language Study.* Washington, DC. Georgetown University Press. 11–24.

Halliday, M. A. K. (1966). Some notes on 'deep' grammar. *Journal of Linguistics* **2.1**. 57–67.

Halliday, M. A. K. (1969). Options and functions in the English clause. *Brno Studies in English* **8**. 81–88.

Halliday, M. A. K. (1973). *Exporations in the Functions of Language.* London: Edward Arnold.

Halliday, M. A. K. (1978). *Language as Social Semiotic.* Baltimore, MD: University Park Press.

Henrici, A. (1981). Some notes on the systemic generation of a paradigm of the English clause. In Halliday, M. A. K. and Martin, J. (eds.), *Readings in Systemic Linguistics.* London: Batsford.

Huddleston, R. (1965). Rank and depth. *Language* **41**. 574–86.

Hudson, R. A. (1971). *English Complex Sentences.* London and Amsterdam: North-Holland.

Hudson, R. A. (1976). *Arguments for a Non-Transformational Grammar.* Chicago, IL: University of Chicago Press.

Mann, W. C. and Christian, M. I. M. Matthiessen. (1985). A Demonstration of the Nigel Text Generation Computer Program. In J. Benson and W. S. Greaves (eds.), *Systemic Perspectives on Discourse: Selected Theoretical Papers from the 9th International Systemic Workshop.* Norwood, NJ: Ablex.

Mann, William C. (1985). An Introduction to the Nigel Text Generation Grammar Computer Program. In J. Benson & W. S. Greaves (eds.), *Systemic Perspectives on Discourse: Selected Theoretical Papers from the 9th International Systemic Workshop.* Norwood, NJ: Ablex.

Matthiessen, Christian M. I. M. (1982). *The Syntactic Coverage of a Text Production Grammar.* USC/Information Sciences Institute, Technical Report.

Towards 'Communication' Linguistics: A Framework   6

Michael Gregory
Glendon College, York University
Toronto, Canada

I

This paper is part of a project I am working on, with Karen Malcolm, to make explicit an encoding-decoding framework for the description of human language behaviour in its social contexts; it will be a stratified, functional, systemic and structural model for the comprehensive description of texts as 'communicative' acts. We see it as a development, within the systemic-functional tradition, in particular of the work of Firth and Halliday, in the light of insights from Fleming's stratified communication model, the tagmemics of Pike and Longacre, and the discourse analysis proposals of Grimes and Gleason.

Our own descriptive work within the framework will be organized on a system, structure, class and unit basis, with due regard to the abstraction scales of delicacy, rank and realization. However, we do recognize that, within the general framework, stratificational methods such as Lamb's relational network organization of description, Fleming's referential, semantic and morphemic trace representation and Pike's tagmemic analysis, by way of trees and formulas within hierarchies and field, wave and particle perspectives, would all likely serve as well, particularly if there is an increased explicitness within these models concerning the multi-functional nature of language's organization. Systemicists, of course, should not think they are the only linguists who recognize a plurality of types of meaning, or 'functions' in language. The Hartford school of stratificational discourse analysis associated with Gleason recognized *meaning, mode,* and *manner* (cf. Cromack 1982); Lockwood (1981), *cognitive, emotive,* and *stylistic* meanings; Beekman, Callow, & Kopesec (1981), *referential, situational,* and *structural* meanings. All these have some correspondence with Halliday's ideational, interpersonal and textual metafunctions (Halliday 1969, 1970, 1973, 1978). Systemicists do not have the monopoly as regards such insights which stretch back a long way, at least to Bühler (1934) and Malinowski (1923, 1935). The major difference is that the functional perspective may more thoroughly permeate our statements as Halliday's 'Modes of meaning and modes of expression' article clearly demonstrates (Halliday 1979).

Malcolm and I bravely hope that our proposed framework, when more fully explicated and exemplified, might serve as a basis for some sort of consensus (for certain purposes such as discourse analysis) amongst linguists of the schools that have been mentioned; theoretically, and, to a great measure, descriptively, we have far more in common than we have that which separates us. For example, we all seem to recognize that discourse or 'text' and the human capacity to produce and understand discourse is what we have to describe and explain; and most of us suspect, if not reject, 'mutation' rules as a dominant, revealing means of description. While acknowledging that there are things to be learnt from the transformationalist school, one must recognize only faint hopes of achieving a consensus with many from that tradition. The scientistic pretensions reflected in their theoretical and descriptive goals, not to mention their obsession with *sentence* as the key unit in description, together with their ignoring of *situation*, the complex of human social behaviour of which linguistic behaviour is a part, at present place a fence between us: not quite an Iron Curtain or even a Glass Wall, but certainly a fence.

II

Some basic positions for 'Communication' Linguistics: firstly, the framework has to be an encoding-decoding one. Chomskyan linguistics has been obsessed with the phenomenon that 'Man talks' and this intra-organism perspective, despite any disclaimers to the contrary, tends towards an encoding emphasis, particularly when linguistic performance is considered uninteresting, but, as Halliday has pointed out (1974), it is more to the point to recognize that *'Men* talk': language is pre-eminently an inter-organism phenomenon, a social, communicative activity, which is why we all 'talk' to ourselves when there is nobody else around; it is also perhaps significant that if we talk to ourselves when there *are* other people around, our fellow men and women begin to suspect that we might be in need of therapy. All this does not mean that we have to take an exclusively decoding stance. Far from it. It seems to me that it is a decoding obsession which vitiates, for example, much New Criticism in the field of literary study and the work of Eugene Winter and some of his associates (cf. Winter 1981, Hoey 1981), and which, in some cases, delayed development in the Descriptivist School (cf. Sampson 1980: 57–80). No, the very fact that language is recognized as an *inter*-organism activity means that a balance has to be kept between the encoding-decoding perspectives; we have to seek to understand the relationships between the user's choices from the language's complex code and from the situation, seen as communication situation, to produce discourse, and the parameters that bound the receiver's interpretation of these choices; we need to regard discourses as the record of exchanges of meaning in Firth's idiom, if we aim to describe language behaviour in its social contexts. This has been, I suggest, recognized in different idiolects by Lamb in the 'The Crooked Path of Progress in Cognitive Linguistics' (1971/73: 14–15) and by Pike in his *Language in relation to A Unified Theory of the Structure of Human Behaviour* (1967), and, of course, it had clear expression in Firth's proposals for the description of *context of situation* in his 1950 paper 'Personality and Language in Society' (reprinted in Firth 1957).

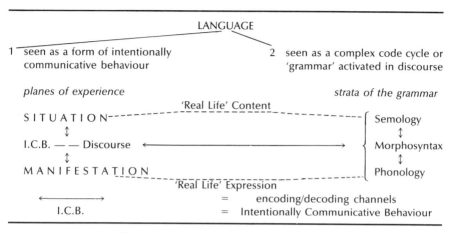

Figure 1. Language as behaviour and code

To summarize the first basic position: if we take exclusively either an 'encoding' or a 'decoding' perspective in description, we are seeing language from only one end. I suggest that the task of the linguist is to see language activity from both ends, and to see it 'sideways-on', to see it in profile as it were. Then the linguist sees it as a mutual activity, a dialectic between user and receiver, rather than as a cause-effect linear sequence (cf. Halliday 1978: 38). It was partly because of this need to avoid an exclusivity of perspective that in 1967 I distinguished situational from contextual categories of language variety distinction, both dialectal and diatypic (Gregory 1967), and in my paper for the Linguistic Association of Canada and the United States in 1981 spelt out the dimensions of *generic situation* as well as those of *register* (Gregory, 1981a, forthcoming). Generic situation is largely shared by user and receiver; register represents the set of meaningful language options the user chooses to select from; the receiver is then often interpreting these not only in terms of the realized registerial choices but also in terms of other linguistic potentialities which could be related to the generic situation. A good part of the meaning of John Donne's poem *The Bait* lies in the contrast between what is linguistically selected and the normal range of expectations of the generic situation from which we get a 'Come live with me and be my love' poem; and many jokes and other kinds of humour depend on this not necessarily isomorphic relationship between register realization and generic situation expectation.

The second basic position is outlined in Figure 1.

Behaviour has been defined as 'the actions or reactions of persons or things under specified conditions' (*American Heritage Dictionary*). In other words, behaviour is manifested in situation. So, in our proposed communication linguistics Malcolm and I view language both as a central form of intentionally communicative behaviour, a form which we call *discourse,* and as the complex code realizatory cycle which such behaviour activates. This is *not* to be understood as a competence-performance dichotomy but as a code *and* behaviour perspective (cf. Halliday, in press). We recognize both *planes of experience* in the behaviour and *strata* in the realizatory code cycle. The three planes of experience in the linguistic communicative event are *situation, discourse* and *manifestation. Discourse* is the linguistic realization of what has been encoded as communicatively relevant to the decoding receiver(s) by a language user or users. The real or imaginary incidents, relations, animate and inanimate objects, and the communicative intents, attitudes, etc. that are relatable to what has been linguistically encoded, and those that might well have been but have not been, i.e. those that can be shown to have been 'at risk', comprise the *situation* of the discourse. *Manifestation* refers to the substance (phonic or graphic in the case of discourse) which transmits what is being communicated. Linguistic behaviour is often accompanied by other forms of more or less intentionally communicative behaviour; in which cases one has to take note of the manifestation of other codes, such as the Kinesic, which encode meaning in situation (see Fig. 2).

As in many contemporary models three strata of language as code are recognized: *semology, morphosyntax* and *phonology.* Adapting Halliday (1979) we maintain that 'meaning' choices in the language's potential at the semological stratum are encoded by 'wording' choices at the morphosyntactic stratum, encoded in turn by 'sounding' choices at the phonological stratum. It is recognized that in some instances, particularly as regards certain features of intonation in English, phonology can be seen directly to realize semological choices. One can also take the decoding path through the stratal cycle.

The third basic position is a decision to hold a balance between paradigmatic and syntagmatic, system and structure statements. Linguistics in the Firthian tradition has taken an increasingly paradigmatic stance over the last dozen years; hence the designation *systemic linguistics.* Certainly, from one very important perspective, 'text', as Halliday puts it, can be seen as 'semantic choice in social contexts' (1977), and it is understandable that system networks are used when there is a strong emphasis on arranging grammars canonically and productively. System network is a good notation with which to characterize the choices facing the encoder, but the decoder meets the choices that have been made in chains of structure carrying units. So in communication linguistics we will pay particular attention to unit and structure, acknowledging the implications of Pike's particle and wave perspectives and Fleming's, and Beekman and Callow's emphasis on the 'packaging' principle in language (cf. Pike 1967, Pike & Pike 1977, Beekman & Callow 1974, Beekman, Callow & Kopesec 1981, Fleming 1978a,b).

This position is related to our fourth and, for the moment, final basic position. I can best characterize it by putting together quotations from Lamb, Halliday and Gleason. Lamb in 'The Crooked Path of Progress in Cognitive Linguistics' (1971–1973: 13–14) wrote: 'Some time ago I rejected as a practical impossibility the goal of generating all the texts of a language and only those, and I proposed that as an alternative we need a relative aim (Lamb, 1966a: 541–543), that is we want a grammar that generates as many texts as possible (rather than all the texts) while generating as few as possible spurious texts. . . . But my current position goes further than this and rejects the generative goal as unrealistic even as a theoretical possibility since that goal presupposes that there is such a thing as the set of grammatical sentences as a well defined set. But such a well defined set does not exist (cf. Hockett 1968). In any real language the boundary between what is grammatical and what is not is constantly shifting.' Halliday in conversation with Parrett about Hymes' communicative competence concept said: 'You say that there is a "sociolinguistic competence" as well as linguistic competence. Or you can do what I would do, which is to reject the distinction altogether on the grounds that we cannot operate with this degree and this kind of idealization. We accept a much lower level of formalization: instead of rejecting what is messy we accept the mess and build it into a theory. . . . There is no need to bring in the question of what the speaker knows: the background to what he does is what he could do—a potential which is objective, not a competence which is subjective.' (Halliday 1978:38). In his Presidential Address to the Seventh Meeting of the Linguistic Association of Canada and the United States Gleason argued, among other things, for interpreting grammars and stressed the importance of residues. He said: 'One reason we have tended to belittle the residue is rooted in the fact that we have been seeking "the correct grammar" and operating in a hyper-Popperian framework, where any single counterexample invalidates a theory. If physicists operated on such a standard we would have no law of gravitation, Newtonian, Einsteinian, or any other. All of them have counter examples of various sorts. . . . If we view grammars not as attempts to capture absolute truth, but as approximations, it might help us take a more healthy relaxed attitude towards residues.' (Gleason 1981: 11). So our programmatic communication linguistics has as its fourth basic position a concern for producing grammars that are weighted towards interpretation rather than generation, prepared to be messy (or 'extravagant' as Halliday says when he's being euphemistic) rather than idealized, and directed towards helping people understand, for a host of practical purposes, the nature of real texts. In doing so it will strive to balance encoding and decoding perspectives, syntagmatic and paradigmatic statements, code and behaviour.

The remainder of this paper will introduce the tentative framework of description by addressing itself to the question of the planal and stratal assignment of categories and features.

III

In Figure 2 the top left hand box is labelled *situation* and is to be understood in terms similar to Fleming's *communication situation* (Fleming, op. cit.) rather than the whole of life's rich pattern. It refers to these extra-textual features of human behaviour and experience which are potentially and/or actually relevant to the production and interpretation of discourses. It is initially glossed as the cultural, social and personal factors which relate to language users' choices and receivers' interpretation of choices from the complex linguistic code-cycle. Four inter-related concepts are at the moment suggested as means by which to 'cage' these factors.

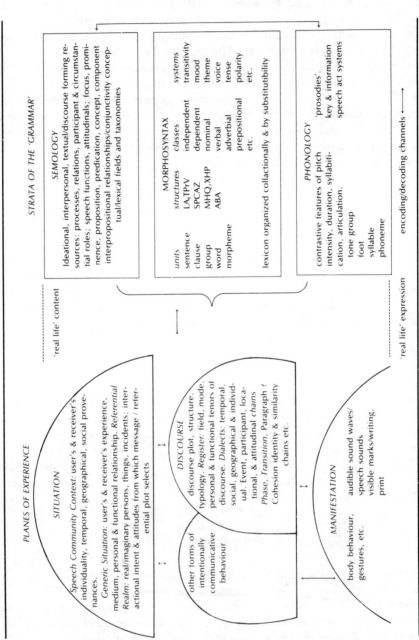

Figure 2. Planal and Stratal Assignment in Communication Linguistics

---

STRATA OF THE 'GRAMMAR'

'real life' content

SEMOLOGY

Ideational, interpersonal, textual/discourse forming resources: processes, relations, participant & circumstantial roles; speech functions, attitudinals; focus, prominence, proposition, predication, concept, component interpropositional relationships/conjunctivity conceptual/lexical fields and taxonomies

MORPHOSYNTAX

units	structures	classes	systems
sentence	LA,TPrV	independent	transitivity
clause	SPCAZ	dependent	mood
group	MHQ,XHP	nominal	theme
word	ABA	verbal	voice
morpheme		adverbial	tense
		prepositional	polarity
		etc.	etc.

lexicon organized collocationally & by substitutibility

PHONOLOGY

contrastive features of pitch intensity, duration, syllabification, articulation.

'prosodies'. key & information speech act systems

tone group
foot
syllable
phoneme

'real life' expression   encoding/decoding channels ⟵

PLANES OF EXPERIENCE

SITUATION

Speech Community Context: user's & receiver's individuality, temporal, geographical, social provenances.

Generic Situation: user's & receiver's experience, medium, personal & functional relationship. *Referential Realm*: real/imaginary persons, things, incidents; interactional intent & attitudes from which message / referential plot selects

DISCOURSE

discourse plot, structure, typology. *Register*: field, mode, personal & functional tenors of discourse. *Dialects*: temporal, social, geographical & individual. Event, participant, locational, & attitudinal *chains*. *Phase, Transition, Paragraph*? Cohesion identity & similarity chains etc.

other forms of intentionally communicative behaviour

MANIFESTATION

body behaviour, gestures, etc.

audible sound waves/ speech sounds visible marks/writing, print

124

Two of them derive from my 1967 'Aspects of Varieties Differentiation' article and my 1978 book (with Susanne Carroll) *Language and Situation,* as modified in my 1981 'Metafunction' article. These are *speech community context* and *generic situation.* The speech community context recognizes that relevant to linguistic communicative acts are the user's and receiver's individualities and temporal, geographical and social provenances, and the degree of awareness of each by each. These dimensions of the speech community context are linguistically reflected in discourse, not necessarily isomorphically, by idiolects, temporal, geographical and social dialects. What is different from previous statements I have made about such matters is the present more explicit recognition that receiver as well as user may be involved and that mutual assessment of these factors can play a crucial part in language events seen as exchanges of meaning, encoding-decoding happenings. John Spencer, my former colleague and collaborator, used to tell of a Scottish labour leader whose habitual dialect was a Scottish variety of Standard English but who never hesitated to lard his discourse with Scots dialect when he was addressing union members north of the English border.

Generic situation is concerned with the user's and receiver's relationships to experience (what is going on, what has gone on, what might go on); particularly important here is whether the experience is part of the immediate, perceivable situation or whether it belongs to what Firth and Malinowski referred to as contexts of experience and memory. It is also concerned with the user's and receiver's relationships to each other, which can be viewed both as a personal relationship (degree of intimacy, etc.) and as a functional relationship (what they are trying to do to or with each other communicatively). Finally it is concerned with their relationship to the medium of transmission, speech, or writing, spontaneous or rehearsed, face to face or not; and this dimension of the situation is important not only as regards what happens in language's two mediums, but also as regards the part that can be played by nonlinguistic and para-linguistic means of communication. Sherzer in his work on Cuna (1980) and Tedlock in his work on Zuni oral narratives (1972) have touched on these matters as I have also in connection with linguistics and theatre (1981b/forthcoming).

The discourse reflection of generic situation is the *registerial* selection described along the dimensions of *field* (linguistic features relatable to the encoding of experience), *personal tenor* and *functional tenor* (linguistic features relatable respectively to the personal and functional relationships between interlocutors) and *mode* (linguistic features relatable to the channel of communication). Generic situation and register are also not necessarily isomorphic as I have indicated elsewhere (Gregory 1967, 1981a,b, Gregory & Carroll 1978, Gregory & Malcolm 1981).

The other two constructs in situation derive from Fleming's static and trace communication model and the use made of it by Larson and Edmiston (Fleming op. cit., Larson 1978, Edmiston 1981). These are *referential realm* and the interconnected concept of *referential plot* now being called *message* or *schema* (Fleming 1982). For Fleming, referential realm refers to the description of the referents and incidents in their time and place from which the communicator selects to form a referential plot. The communicator's and audience's intents, attitudes, beliefs, interests and so on, she handles separately. In this framework the two are not merged but they are yoked together; for us referential realm refers to the real or imagined persons, things, events, *and* the interactional intents and attitudes from which the user selects to form his referential plot or *message* (what is to be communicated) which is in turn encoded in language as what we call *discourse plot*. In other words it is another way of looking at the user's experience and personal and functional relationships with his receiver, and the ideational and interpersonal meanings they give rise to. This is to recognize that from what Halliday calls the semiotic vantage point, language from above, the ideational and interpersonal components go together as being *extrinsic* as opposed to his textual component which is 'enabling' (Halliday 1978:131). It is these two components, the ideational and the interpersonal, which constitute situational *messages*.

In her paper 'Some discrepancies between communication situation and the semantic and/or morphemic data in a text' (8th Lacus Forum 1981), Fleming clearly showed the need for constructs such as these. She argued in her abstract: 'In the referential realm part of the communication situation whether it is factual or nonfactual there are no plurals, collectives or accompaniers: nor are there coordinate, alternative, constrastive or substitute agents, patients, etc. There is also no tense, no quotatives, and no indirect quotations (unless it represents an embedded communication incident). In the referential realm each referent performs individually. There is no dependent versus independent, . . . status of such incidents. The communicator of a message selects from the referential realm what is to be included in the message and omits what he does not wish to include. Certain packaging strategies are then employed to encode the message into the semantic and morphemic strata.'

It is such packaging strategies and their interconnections which I am calling *discourse plot* and this is concerned not only with the packaging of incidents and referents but also with such matters as the semological, morphosyntactic and phonological encoding of, for example, situational anger into discourse irony.

Discourse is used here in the sense in which Halliday and Hasan (1976, 1980) often use *text,* that is for a stretch of language activity which functions as a whole in its environment. It is an activation of the linguistic code potential manifested in situation. *Text* is reserved for the physical record of such activations, whether recorded on paper or tape, and such a record may consist of more than one discourse or only a part of one. As has already been indicated, the meaningful unity of a discourse is seen in terms of its discourse plot which is the semological, morphosyntactic and phonological encoding of referential plot or message. This involves consideration not only of discourse structure (in terms such as beginning, middle and end or whatever is appropriate to the discourse type) but also of event and participant chains (cf. Gleason 1968), locational chains both temporal and spatial, attitudinal chains and lexical chains of identity, co-reference, and similarity, co-class and co-extension (cf. Halliday & Hasan 1980). It also involves overall rationalizable consistancy of register and dialect and inter-sentential cohesive features provided by *reference, ellipsis, substitution, conjunction,* and the *lexical relations* already mentioned (cf. Halliday & Hasan 1976, 1980).

Two concepts are suggested for the description of the linear or dynamic progress of discourse: *phase* and *transition.* Phase I introduced in my paper on aspects of discourse text formation and cohesion in a soliloquy from *Hamlet* (Gregory, 1981b/forthcoming). It characterizes those stretches of text in which there is a significant measure of consistency in what is being selected ideationally, interpersonally, and textually. In our work on children's talk Malcolm and I added the concept *transition* (Gregory & Malcolm 1981). Transitions *in* and *out* of phases are indicated by changes in the kind of choice from one or more functional components. A transition can be anticipated and *included* in the first of two contingent phases and then fully accomplished in the successive phase. Phase can be thought of as a very delicate statement of *register realization* because particular fields, modes, personal and functional tenors of discourse are actualized by particular selections from the functional systems. We suggest, however, that it is perhaps best to reserve *register* for the configuration of the linguistic meaning resources that the members of a culture typically associate with a given generic situation and to use *phase* and *transition* to characterize the dynamic instantiations of registeral choices in a particular discourse (cf. Gregory 1981c, Gregory & Malcolm 1981, and also Halliday 1975:25). What is recognized as a phase in a discourse depends on the delicacy of the analysis which is itself relatable to the purposes of the analyst. If the description is not very delicate the discourse may be seen to consist of only a few phases; as the delicacy of the multi-functional analysis is increased it is often possible to discern phases and transition within the less delicately discerned phases. This flexibility is, I suggest, an advantage rather than a disadvantage, particularly in the analysis of complex discourses. In my paper at the 8th International Systemic Workshop (Gregory 1981c), I advanced the hypothesis that phase and transition may be more useful in the analysis of English discourse than the category of *paragraph* viewed as a constituent structure. Malcolm in her paper to the Ninth LACUS meeting suggested that phasal analysis can be used to test the usefulness of the category of paragraph in spoken as well as written discourse (Malcolm 1982a). Beyond the sentence there is a linear patterning which is describable in terms of phases and transitions. Having discerned that patterning in a discourse we are then, perhaps, in a position to propose a constituent kind of structure for that particular discourse in which phases and transitions play a part. I think I was implicitly doing this in my analyses of John Donne's 'Batter my heart', and Marvell's 'To his Coy Mistress' (Gregory 1974, 1978). Of course there are types of discourse in English, as in any language, which are structurally very clear: knitting patterns, cooking recipes, instruction manuals, for example. In such cases there is a highly predictable relationship between generic situation and registerial realizations and for such discourse it is possible to codify a structure in the semology (cf for discourse structures, Pike & Pike 1977, Longacre 1976). But in languages such as English which are the communicative reflection of complex cultures, there are many discourses in which a structure has to be, as it were, found.

Phasal analysis can help in finding and establishing discourse structures. However the concept of phase is still being tested and is open to further development. Up till now it has been used in the analysis of literary texts which reflect a conscious or 'edited' organization of the discourse realization of message, and on a fifteen minute text of children's talk in which there were obvious changes in what was happening situationally: the presence or absence of an adult, the presence or absence of Lego pieces and the activity associated with them. In such discourses phases could be distinguished solely on the meta-functional criteria and without great delicacy in the analysis (Gregory & Malcolm 1981). In the sample analysis related to this paper, Malcolm (1982b) indicates that in a text she analyzed of conversation between two young women there were problems in discerning phase boundaries. It may be necessary to find criteria for phasal distinctions not only in differences in the selection from the codal resources but also in situational and manifestational factors which may themselves provide sufficient signalling of a significant change in the message. If this is not catered for in the discourse analysis it will have to be dealt with on the other planes of experience in the communicative act.

IV

So far we have been concerned with language as a form of intentionally communicative behaviour, language as discourse. Let us turn our attention to language as code and the stratum called *semology*. And the first question I want to raise and answer is why it is not called *semantics* as in the practice of Halliday and other systemic linguists. I think semantics is a very un-Firthian term for a particular level or stratum of language. Firth always insisted (*vide* his 'Technique of Semantics' and 'Modes of Meaning' papers in Firth 1957), that all of language's patterning is semantic; including how it patterns with situation. He insisted on phonetic meaning, phonoaesthetic meaning, phonological meaning, morphological meaning, syntactic meaning, collocational meaning, and situational meaning. And I think he was not only theoretically wise to do so but also wise in a public relations way. When a layman says something is 'semantic' it can be, in different instances, related to any one of the strata and sometimes to situation and even to manifestation when voice quality, gestures and facial expressions are involved. Semology already exists as a stratal term and can be used more neutrally and specifically.

At the moment this framework operates with a semological 'rank-scale'[1] of *proposition, predication, concept* and *component. Proposition* is the co-occurrence of *predication, speech function* and *organized message,* realized in the morphosyntax of English by independent clauses which select freely from systems of tran-

---

[1] 'Rank-scale' and not *rank-scale* because as both C. Butler and J. Martin have pointed out to me the relations between the 'units' are not the same as those in the morphosyntactic and phonological *rank-scales*. Perhaps this is related to the less language-specific nature of the semological stratum.

sitivity, mood and theme with *new* and *given* possibilities in their phonological tone-groups or groups (cf. Halliday 1973, 1978, Kress 1976). *Predications* can also be realized by dependent clauses, nominal and prepositional groups in the morphosyntax which do not select for mood and have limited organizational possibilities. *Concept,* following Beekman, Callow and Kopesec (1981:18) is seen as 'a referring unit, identifying segments of the referential world of the communication event', with nuclear and delimiting *components.* Concepts are morphosyntactically realized by lexical items which syntactically may be morphemes, words, or groups, which may involve, in the case of a complex concept, embedded clauses. Taxonomic classification of concepts and their lexical and discourse realizations, together with the study of inter-propositional relationships and systems of implicit and explicit conjunctivity such as Martin's (1981) have their place in this stratum.

Very importantly the semology is where we have to work on those systems and structures that underlie morphosyntactic systems of transitivity, mood and theme. I suggest that a transitivity system such as David Young offered in his 1980 *The Structure of English Clauses* and which he presented in a revised and expanded format at the 1981 Systemic Workshop belongs quite properly to the morphosyntax. He dealt well with questions of single and double transitivity, extensivity and intensivity, voice-thorough and voice-blocked, all of which are clearly demonstrable in terms of exponence and distribution in the surface form of English. What the semological stratum has to cope with is the predicational matter of process selection: the many subclasses of action and mental processes, dynamic and static relations, and the range of participant and circumstantial roles which are concomitant with them. These then have to be related to morphosyntactic systems of transitivity, voice and adjunctivization. Keeping the two types of statement separate may not be an advantage in a grammar which aims to be productive with the least number of rules, in which case one may want to allocate all the systems to one stratum as Fawcett (1980) does, but it has distinct favours in interpreting, comparing and contrasting descriptive statements.

Similarly it is proposed that systems of speech function need to be worked out in the semology and then related to the morphosyntactic system of mood. In her 1979 *On the Semantics of Syntax* Eirian Davies has an admirably clear appendix in which she displays what she calls the surface grammar (morphosyntactic in my terms) system of Imperatives, Declaratives and Interrogatives in English. What we still need further work on is how these complexly relate to speech function choices in the semology among different kinds of statement, question or command, or to comment and directive, if that route is preferred. There is also more work to be done on 'modality', on the resources the user has to comment on the experience he is verbalizing.

Theme and information systems are in some respects the least satisfactory part of contemporary systemic descriptions of English. The morphosyntactic realization of theme, and the phonological realizations of 'new' and 'given' have been stated (cf. Halliday 1967a,b, 1968, Kress 1976) but until we tackle matters of focus and prominence (cf. Grimes 1975) beyond the clause and tone group and investigate how these features operate in discourse we won't have completed semologizing this component of the textual function.

In Figures 1 and 2 there is a dotted line linking situation to semology labelled 'real life' content. This is to indicate that users of language, if not linguists, do not make an absolute distinction between experience and language. I take a modified Whorfian view and recognize that language is a part of experience, that is has a shaping role on how we perceive it. Users and receivers do not necessarily make a conscious distinction between the communication situation and what is being organized as language meaning. All of which makes it more important as describers of language that we make distinctions such as those between message and discourse plot, generic situation and register, speech community context and dialect. Similarly at the bottom of the figures there is a dotted line joining phonology and manifestation labelled 'real life' expression. We don't hear or produce sounds but continuums of meaningful sound. Linguists, however, have to distinguish them.

Why do we use *morphosyntax* and not Halliday's and now Lamb's (1982) *lexicogrammar* for the middle stratum? Lexico-grammar I've never liked. For one thing it seems to put the cart before the horse if one takes Halliday's position that lexis is most delicate grammar. Furthermore, the term 'grammar' by itself can be misleading. It has an established use for the whole of the codal description (cf. Lamb 1966b, Fawcett 1980). And when the layman asks a question about 'grammar' the answer he is looking for may be semological, morphosyntactic or phonological or any combination of the three. So, with good precedent 'grammar' is reserved as a term for all that is the concern of the strata of the language's complex code.

At the stratum in question we are concerned with language specific patterns. There is a degree of generality in our semological statements but in the morphosyntax we are concerned with those meaningful internal patterns of a particular language, which can be described in terms of constituency or choice of constituency, so *morpho*, and in terms of sequence or 'order', so *syntax*. The term is not that inappropriate for the formal description of lexis, the lexical inventory organized collocationally and by substitutability; ultimately such a lexicon or thesaurus is an inventory of morphemes.

As Figure 2 indicates this is the stratum at which Halliday's original categories of the theory of grammar really come into their own (1961): system, structure, unit and class. Systems already referred to such as *transitivity, voice, mood* and *theme*, as well as systems of *taxis, polarity modality, aspect, tense, number, person* and *deixis* are related to structures which are carried in English by units such as *sentence, clause, group, word,* and *morpheme*. I discussed in my paper to the 9th LACUS meeting the restoration of the sentence to the systemic description of English. Suffice it to say that I argued that it can be morphosyntactically justified as a distinct unit from clause and that it also has its own semological and discourse implications, enabling communicators to link, topicalize and attitudinalize propositions (Gregory 1982). The units I have mentioned constitute a rank-scale with realizational relationships amongst them, and their structures and systems can be described on a scale of delicacy or progressive differentiation in detail. Units, in English at least, can be usefully classified in familiar terms such as independent and dependent, nominal, verbal, adverbial and prepositional. The morphosyntax is both the surface of the 'grammar' as I use the term, and its heart.

On the left hand side of the phonology box in Figure 2 are Catford's and Halliday's proposals for a rank-scale of units for English phonology: tone group, foot, syllable, and phonematic unit or phoneme, through which features of pitch, intensity, duration, syllabilification and articulation can be seen complexly to realize in the spoken language meaningful contrasts stated in the morphosyntax and semology (Catford 1965, Halliday 1967c). On the right hand side of the box it is suggested that what Firth used to call prosodies of anger, irony, affection and so on, and systems such as 'key' and 'information' (cf. Halliday 1978) as well as speech function systems in which, for example, a certain intonational contour plus morphosyntactic declarative realizes a semological question, can realizatorily by-pass the morphosyntax and be seen as the direct realization of semological choices.

The manifestation box also has two parts to it. The right hand side deals with the substance which carries language: audible sound waves (speech), and visible marks on a surface (writing). The left hand side, which is connected by way of *other forms of intentionally communicative behaviour to situation,* reminds us again, as every actor knows, that language is not the only means by which meanings are exchanged, encoded and decoded in communication situations.[2]

On several occasions I have heard Robin Fawcett say that we must, as linguists, both be obsessed with language but avoid linguo-centricity. One way of doing that is to see language both as code and as one of several forms of behaviour which communicate. The framework Malcolm and I are developing reflects our obsession with language, most particularly with language as activity in the human social context. We hope it will help us, ultimately, to make descriptions of discourses which are demonstrably of practical use and interest not only to linguists but also, and especially, to non-linguists. We want to do this because in the words of the Mexican poet and diplomat, Octavio Paz, ''language is not only a social phenomenon, but at the same time is the foundation of every society and man's most perfect social expression''. (Paz 1970).

REFERENCES

Beekman, J. & J. Callow. (1974). *Translating the Word of God.* Grand Rapids, MI: Zondervan.
Beekman, J., Callow, J. & Kopesec, M. (1981). *The Semantic Structure of Written Communication.* Dallas, TX: Summer Institute of Linguistics.

---

[2] In the light of discussion with J. Martin I would like to suggest that from the perspective of linguistics, *situation* and *manifestation* could be regarded as being essentially areas of *etic* investigation and statement, *discourse, semology, morphosyntax* and *phonology* as *emic*. This is indicated in Figure 2 by the double-headed arrow linking the chain bracket round the strata of the code to the discourse plane.

Bühler, K. (1934). *Sprachtheorie: die Darstellungsfunktion der Sprache*. Jena, Germany: Fischer.
Catford, J. C. (1965). *A Linguistic Theory of Translation*. London: Oxford University Press.
Cromack, R. E. (1982). Meaning, Manner and Mode: Some Early Ideas in Stratificational Text Analysis. *Focus on Discourse Colloquium*. University of Toronto, March 27.
Davies, E. (1979). *On the Semantics of Syntax*. London: Croom Helm.
Edmiston, P. (1981). Kosena paragraph structure. *8th LACUS Forum*. Toronto, Canada.
Fawcett, R. P. (1980). *Cognitive linguistics and social interaction: towards an integrated model of a systemic functional grammar and the other components of a communicating mind*. Heidelberg, Germany: Julius Groos Verlag.
Firth, J. R. (1957). *Papers in Linguistics, 1934–1951*. London: Oxford University Press.
Fleming, I. (1978a). *Field Guide to Communication Situation, Semantic and Morphemic Analysis*. Mimeo. Dallas, TX: Summer Institute of Linguitics.
———. (1978b). Discourse from the perspective of four strata. *The Fifth LACUS Forum*. Columbia, SC: Hornbeam Press.
———. (1981). Some discrepancies between communication situation and the semantic and/or morphemic data in a text. *The 8th LACUS Forum*, Toronto, Canada.
———. (1982). Some implications from Aphasic Data for Linguistic Modelling. *The 9th LACUS Forum*, Evanston, Illinois.
Gleason, H. A., Jr. (1968). Contrastive analysis in discourse structure. *Monograph Series on Languages and Linguistics* **21**. 39–63.
———. (1981). Grammar, Grammars, and Grammarians. *The Seventh LACUS Forum*. Columbia, S.C.: Hornbeam Press.
Gregory, Michael. (1967). Aspects of varieties of differentiation. *Journal of Linguistics* **3**.
———. (1974). A theory for stylistics exemplified: Donne's *Holy Sonnet XIV*. *Language and Style* **VII**, 2.
———. (1978). Marvell's 'To His Coy Mistress': The poem as a linguistic and social event. *Poetics* **7**, 4.
———. (1981a). The Nature and Use of Meta-Functions in Systemic Theory: Current Concerns. *The 8th LACUS Forum*, Toronto, Canada.
———. (1981b/forthcoming). Linguistics and theatre: Hamlet's voice—aspects of text formation and cohesion in a soliloquy. *Linguistics and the Humanities Conference, University of Texas, Arlington* (to be published in *Forum Linguisticum* vol. 7. ed. by Ruth Brend.
———. (1981c). Tagmemics and discourse analysis: a view from systemics. *8th International Systemics Workshop*. Birmingham, England.
———. (1982). Clause and sentence as distinct units in the morphosyntactic analysis of English and their relation to semological propositions and predications. *The 9th LACUS Forum*, Evanston, Illinois.
———. (forthcoming). Meta-functions: aspects of their development, status, and use in systemic linguistics. In Halliday, M. A. K. & Fawcett, R. P. (eds.) *New Developments in Systemic Linguistics*. London: Batsford.
Gregory, Michael & Susanne Carroll (1978). *Language and Situation: language varieties in their social contexts*. London: Routledge & Kegan Paul.
Gregory, Michael & Karen Malcolm. (1981). Generic Situation and Discourse Phase: An Approach to the Analysis of Children's Talk. Mimeograph. Applied Linguistics Research Working Group. Glendon College, York University, Toronto, Canada.
Grimes, J. (1975). *The Thread of Discourse*. The Hague: Mouton.
Halliday, M. A. K. (1961). Categories of the theory of grammar. *Word*. **17**. 3.
———. (1967a&b). Notes on Transitivity and Theme in English, Parts 1 and 2. *Journal of Linguistics*, **3**, 37–81, 199–244.
———. (1967c). *Intonation and Grammar in British English*. The Hague: Mouton.
———. (1968). Notes of transitivity and theme in English, Part 3. *Journal of Linguistics*, **4**, 179–215.

————. (1969). Options and functions in the English clause. *Brno Studies in English*, **8**.
————. (1970). Language Structure and Language Function. In Lyons, J. (ed.), *New Horizons in Linguistics*. Harmondsworth, England: Penguin.
————. (1973). *Explorations in the Functions of Language*. London: Edward Arnold.
————. (1974). *Language and Social Man*. London: Longman (*Schools Council Programme in Linguistics and English Teaching*, Papers, Series **11, 3.**).
————. (1975). Language as Social Semiotic: towards a general sociolinguistic theory. *The First LACUS Forum*. Columbia, SC: Hornbeam Press.
————. (1977). Texts as semantic choice in social contexts. In Van Dijk, T. A. and Petöfi, J. (eds.) *Grammars and Descriptions*, London: Hamish Hamilton.
————. (1978). *Language as Social Semiotic: the social interpretation of language and meaning*. London: Edward Arnold.
————. (1979). Modes of meaning and modes of expression: types of grammatical structure, and their determination by different semantic functions. In Allerton, D. J., Carney, Edward, and Holdcroft, David (eds.), *Function and Context in Linguistic Analysis: Essays offered to William Haas*. Cambridge, England: Cambridge University Press.
————. (in press). Language as code and language as behaviour: a systemic-functional interpretation of the nature and ontogenesis of dialogue. In Makkai, A. Halliday, M. A. K. and Lamb, S. M. (eds.) *Semiotics of Culture and Language*. London: Frances Pinter.
Halliday, M. A. K. & Hasan, R. (1976). *Cohesion in English*. London: Longman.
————. (1980). *Text and Context: aspects of language in a social semiotic perspective*. Tokyo: Sophia University.
Hockett, C. F. (1968). *The State of the Art*. (Janua Linguarum, 73). The Hague: Mouton.
Hoey, M. P. (1981). Discourse-Centred Stylistics: A Way Forward? *The 8th LACUS Forum*, Toronto, Canada.
Kress, G. (1976). *Halliday: System and function in language*. London: Oxford.
Lamb, S. M. (1966a). Epilegomena to a Theory of Language. *Romance Philology*, **19**.
————. (1966b). *Outline of Stratificational Grammar*, Washington, DC: Georgetown University Press.
————. (1971/1973). The Crooked Path of Progress in Cognitive Linguistics. *Monograph Series on Languages and Linguistics* 24. 99–123, 1971. Reprinted in Makkai, A. & Lockwood, D. (eds.) *Readings in Stratificational Linguistics*. Alabama: University of Alabama Press.
————. (1982). On Determining the Number of Strata in Linguistic Structure. *The 9th LACUS Forum*, Evanston, Illinois.
Larson, M. (1978). *The Functions of Reported Speech in Discourse*. Dallas, TX: Summer Institute of Linguistics.
Lockwood, D. G. (1981). Total Accountability in a Theory of Language. *The Seventh Lacus Forum 1980*. Columbia, SC: Hornbeam Press.
Longacre, R. E. (1976). *An Anatomy of Speech Notions*. Lisse: Peter de Ridder Press.
Malcolm, Karen. (1982a). The Paragraph: What is it? Some Traditional and Contemporary Proposals. *The Ninth LACUS Forum*, Evanston, Illinois.
————. (1982b). Communication Linguistics: A Sample Analysis. *9th International Systemics Workshop*, Toronto, Canada.
Malinowski, B. (1923). The Problem of Meaning in Primitive Languages. In Ogden, C. K. and Richards, I. A. (eds.), *The Meaning of Meaning*. London: Routledge and Kegan Paul.
————. (1935). *Coral Gardens and their Magic*, Vol. **2**. London: Allen and Unwin.
Martin, J. R. (1981). Conjunction: The logic of English texts. Mimeo. Dept of Linguistics, University of Sydney.
Paz, O. (1970). *Claude Levi-Strauss: An Introduction*. Trans. J. S. and M. Bernstein. New York: Dell.
Pike, K. L. (1967). *Language in Relation to a Unified Theory of the Structure of Human Behaviour*. The Hague: Mouton.
Pike, K. L. & Pike, E. G. (1977). *Grammatical Analysis*, Dallas, TX: Summer Institute of Linguistics.
Sampson, G. (1980). *Schools of Linguistics*. London: Hutchinson.

134

Sherzer, J. (1980). Verbal and nonverbal deixis: the pointed lip gesture among the San Blas Cuna. *Language in Society*. **2**, 117–131.

Tedlock, D. (1972). *Finding the Center: Narrative Poetry of the Zuni Indians*. Lincoln and London: University of Nebraska Press.

Winter, E. O. (1981). How the Definition of Sentence Might Apply to Context, *The 8th LACUS Forum*, Toronto, Canada.

Young, D. (1980). *The Structure of English Clauses*. London: Hutchinson.

Explanation in English and Korafe   7

Cynthia J. M. Farr
Summer Institute of
Linguistics
Washington, D.C.

Ivan Lowe
Summer Institute of
Linguistics
Dallas, TX

Carl R. Whitehead
Summer Institute of
Linguistics
Washington, D.C.

0 INTRODUCTION

This paper is about explanation, about how people explain actions, attitudes, things, etc. An explanation can be thought of as anything that clarifies—answering the questions how or why. Basically a speaker explains something that needs explaining in terms of things in the culture that he assumes his addressees already understand. There are causal explanations and descriptive explanations. A causal explanation clarifies something by either giving a cause or a reason. A cause is something else in the world related to what is to be explained by a cause-effect relationship. A reason, on the other hand, justifies an action or attitude in terms of a set of beliefs, values or principles. Quite different are the descriptive explanations like elaboration and analogy. Elaboration clarifies something unfamiliar or abstract by spelling out extensive concrete details, whereas analogy clarifies by saying how something unfamiliar is like something familiar.

This paper compares how explanation is done in two widely different languages, Korafe[1] of Papua New Guinea, and English. In section 1 we give a brief sketch of

---

[1] Korafe is a Non-Austronesian language of the Trans-New Guinea phylum and belonging to the Binandere family. It is spoken by the 3000 or so Korafe people living on the headlands of Cape Nelson around the Tufi sub-provincial headquarters and also by those Korafe people living and working in the towns and population centers of Papua New Guinea.

The phonemes of Korafe are /a/, /ạ/, /b/, /d/, /e/, /ẹ/, /f/, /g/, /ḡ/, /i/, /ị/, /j/, /k/, /m/, /n/, /o/, /ọ/, /r/, /s/, /t/, /u/, /ụ/, /v/, and /y/.

The Korafe data for this paper were gathered by James and Cynthia Farr on field trips to Korafe villages between 1972 and 1982.

All the Korafe examples in this paper were taken from native texts, oral or written; none were either elicited or cooked up. A concordance of 61,053 morphemes taken from texts and prepared in the S.I.L. Computer Laboratory at Ukarumpa, Papua New Guinea was used in the analysis. The speaking knowledge of the language is due to Farr and meanings were carefully checked with native Korafe speakers. We would specially like to thank Warrington Isari for his valuable cooperation and insights into Korafe. Many of the initial ideas of this paper were worked out in a field workshop held in 1981 at the Ukarumpa Center of the Summer Institute of Linguistics, Papua New Guinea. We are also grateful to Joe Grimes and Bob Dooley for suggestions on the organization of the paper.

the essentials of the system of explanation in English. Much more could be said of the English system than the space available in this paper would allow—but the object of the English treatment here is to provide a background against which we then present a detailed analysis of the Korafe system in section 2. The special surface structures of Korafe teach us things that those of English might well leave obscure.

The method of analysis for both languages consists in examining the pragmatic relationships signalled by the various connectives commonly thought of as marking either cause or reason. Such pragmatic relationships depend on both the content of the clauses that the connectives link and the linguistic and social context in which the sentence (i.e. clause chain plus connective) is used.

What we find in both English and Korafe are the following:

0.1 A Distinction Between Causes, Reasons, and Descriptive Explanations

A cause explains in terms of certain relationships of cause and effect which are supposed to reflect the way the world is and which have been observed and accepted at large as the way the world is patterned. Causes operate in the world outside the individual and make things happen or mental attitudes arise. They can be physical, social or religious in nature but are always culturally oriented.

A reason, on the other hand, is the individual's way of justifying an action or attitude in terms of a set of beliefs, values, or principles, etc. These beliefs, etc. may be held by the society at large or only by the individual, and a reason can be thought of as an interpretation of an action in terms of such beliefs, etc. giving the action a place in a pattern of such beliefs, etc. (see Davidson 1963). Reasons are again culturally oriented.

One normally separates causes from reasons but at times there can be a fuzzy area between cause and reason where there is no sharp distinction.[2]

0.2 A Distinction Between Public and Private Information

Private information is information provided by the speaker that the addressee is not able to verify, whereas public information is information which is verifiable or potentially verifiable by the addressee. These are like the internal and external information of Halliday and Hasan (1976) but are not the same.

0.3 A Distinction Between Enabling and Sufficient Conditions

An enabling condition is one which is necessary for a certain course of action or state of affairs to take place or for a certain attitude to arise. But the condition does not compel the action or attitude. On the other hand, a sufficient condition (also

---

[2] Concerning the fuzzy area between cause and reason, Anscombe (1957) remarks that in cases of doubt, if an action is described as a mere response to something then that something is a cause, whereas if an action is described as a response to something then that something is cause, whereas if an action is described as a response to something that is thought upon or dwelt upon by the actor then that something is a reason.

EXPLANATION SYSTEM FOR ENGLISH

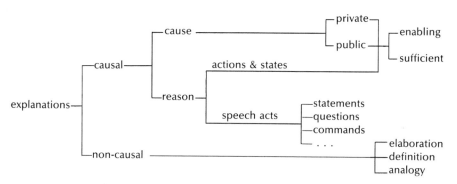

EXPLANATION SYSTEM FOR KORAFE

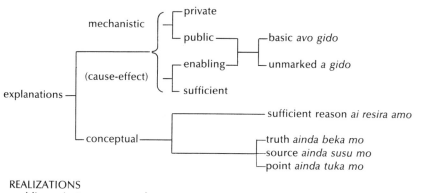

Figure 1.

called a sufficient cause) is one which of itself compels the action, state or attitude. After an enabling condition is fulfilled, there is still a decision open to the participant concerned whether he will or will not go through with the course of action which depends on the condition. There is no such possibility of decision in the case of sufficient causes. Sufficient causes are thought of as being law-like.

The distinction between enabling and sufficient applies to reasons as well as to causes. Some beliefs or values or feelings are held relatively loosely and these simply open up the possibility of action. On the other hand, a belief or value or feeling can be so strong in the mind of the participant concerned that it becomes a compelling or sufficient reason for a certain action or state of affairs to be realised.

It needs to be clearly understood that there are cases where the assignment of private versus public information and of enabling versus sufficient condition is a

question of speaker viewpoint and not merely of an inherent logical relation between two propositions.

At this point we introduce figure 1 which gives the results of our analysis—the
explanation systems for English and for Korafe.

1 EXPLANATION IN ENGLISH

In English we distinguish between causes which describe the world in terms of
cause and effect, reasons which are justifications of actions or attitudes in terms of a
set of beliefs, values or principles, and descriptive explanations which explain by
definition, elaboration or analogy. Such logical distinctions correspond to differences in surface markings.

1.1 Causes

Causes can be sufficient or enabling and either kind can contain either private or
public information.

Examples illustrating these parameters follow. For each sentence, the kind of
cause and the kind of information is given in parentheses following it.

(1)   John got a bellyache because he ate green apples (sufficient cause, public
      information)

(2)   John got a shock because he touched the high tension wire (ditto)

(3)   I got my visa and/so I am going to Brazil (enabling condition, public
      information)

(4)   I went to the beach and/so I went in for a swim (ditto)

(5)   I went to see a specialist because I was getting all sorts of stomach pains
      (sufficient cause, private information)

(5a) I had no choice but to see a specialist because I was getting all sorts of
      stomach pains (ditto)

(6)   I got up because I was feeling stronger (enabling condition, private
      information)

Examples 1 and 2 illustrate sufficient cause with public information. In example
1, the conjunct introduced by *because* tells us that John's eating raw apples was
enough (sufficient) to give him a bellyache—there is a physical law that whoever
eats a number of green apples will get a bellyache and this law isn't broken very
often. Once John has eaten the green apples, he is in no position to decide whether
he'll get a bellyache or not, he simply gets one. Similar considerations apply to
example 2. Thus the distinguishing feature of a sufficient cause is that once the
condition has been satisfied, it compels the effect to take place and the decision is
taken out of the hands of the participant concerned.

Surfacewise, two English clauses one of which expresses an enabling relationship with public information for the other will admit an interclausal *so* but not an
interclausal *because*.

Example 5 illustrates a sufficient cause with private information. First, this is
like example 1 in that the cause expressed in the conjunct introduced by *because*
was so strong that it was sufficient to send the speaker to the specialist. One could
paraphrase 5 by 5a, whereupon it is easy to see that the speaker was forced by
circumstances to do what he did. Second, on the other hand, example 5 is different
from example 1 in that the information in the cause conjunct is private information
since it is known only to the speaker and cannot be verified independently by the
addressee. For why example 5 illustrates sufficient cause rather than sufficient
reason, see the discussion of section 1.2 and especially of section 1.21.

Example 6 illustrates an enabling condition with private information. The condition 'feeling stronger' does not compel one to get up, it does however, make getting
up possible. The condition is also private information, 'feeling stronger' is something difficult for the addressee to verify independently.

1.2 Reasons

A reason explains an action or a state in terms of a set of beliefs, values or
principles. Hence the decision is never taken right out of the hands of the participant
in focus. Reasons are clearly private information.

We distinguish between reasons for states and actions on the one hand and
reasons for speech acts on the other.

1.21 Reasons for States and Actions
Reasons can be either sufficient or enabling just as causes were.

Examples 7 to 9 illustrate sufficient reasons. The reason is given in each case by
the *because* clause. With the same argument as before, a sufficient reason is one
that is sufficient of itself to induce the participant in focus to carry out the action. In
a sentence with sufficient reason, the participant in focus has such a strong mental
committment to the reason proposition that it drives him to a certain line of action as
a consequence, and what choice he has is minimal. The reason proposition itself
may not even be true in the real world; nevertheless it is sufficient in the mind of the
participant in focus to make him act.

(7)   We $\begin{cases} \text{must} \\ \text{have got to} \\ \text{have no choice but to} \end{cases}$ move out of this house because (I believe) there are bad spirits in it

(8)   I $\begin{cases} \text{must} \\ \text{have got to} \\ \text{have no choice but to} \end{cases}$ go to John because (I believe) he's the
only one who can help me

(9)   I $\left\{\begin{array}{l}\text{must} \\ \text{have got to} \\ \text{have no choice but to}\end{array}\right\}$ take my daughter personally by car to

music lessons because (I believe) there are bad characters in the area
who could harm her if she went alone.

Any of the surface alternatives *must, have got to, have no choice but to* within
the braces expresses a sufficient reason relationship; they are diagnostic for sufficient reasons in English.

Examples 10 and 11 illustrate enabling reasons, given again by the *because*
clause in each case. An enabling reason is a reason that will prompt or help the
participant in focus decide to carry out a certain course of action. Enabling reasons,
therefore, are not compelling in the sense that sufficient reasons are, and so a strong
element of decision is still in the hands of the participant in focus. Note that whereas
enabling conditions with public information will admit the surface connective *so* but
not the surface connective *because* (examples 3,4), both enabling conditions with
private information (example 6) and enabling reasons (example 10, 11) are signalled by *because*.

(10)   I $\left\{\begin{array}{l}\text{choose to skip} \\ \text{feel like skipping} \\ \text{am skipping}\end{array}\right\}$ the lecture because I feel sleepy

(11)   I $\left\{\begin{array}{l}\text{choose to go} \\ \text{feel like going} \\ \text{am going}\end{array}\right\}$ to the concert because I like Bach

Either of the surface alternatives *choose to, feel like* within the braces are diagnostic of the enabling reason relationship which always leaves free choice in the
hands of the participant in focus.

1.22 Reasons for Speech Acts

Speakers often append justifying reasons when they make statements, make requests, or ask questions. Thus consider the examples which follow:

(12)   John is home because the lights are on (and so I know)

(13)   Pass your plates up because the stew is very hot (and I don't want anyone
to get burnt)

(14)   Are you leaving soon because I want to talk to you (and so I ask)

In examples 12, 13, 14, the *because* clauses justify the making of the statement,
the making of the request, the asking of the question respectively. More specifically, in example 12, the speaker uses the *because* clause to give his evidence to show
that the statement *John is home* is true, and in this sense justifies his making the
statement.

1.3 Descriptive Explanations

Third we have descriptive explanations. These clarify by describing a phenomenon and the causal component is usually not present although it is not necessarily excluded. Descriptive explanations include definition, elaboration and analogy according to how the description is made and the detail that is put into it.

An explanation by definition (for example a lexicographic definition) gives the most important features of the element to be defined; those features, in fact, that suffice to differentiate it from other elements. Thus a minimum amount of information is involved. Example 15 shows a definition taken from the Longman Modern English Dictionary, Watson (1976).

(15) A carpenter is a workman in wood, a person who makes the wooden frames of house, ships, etc.

An explanation by elaboration clarifies the meaning of a term or proposition by giving a great deal of specific detail on it. Examples 16 and 17 are explanations by elaboration.

(16) A consultant is someone who comes, listens to your problems, asks questions about them in the light of his previous experience which is probably different from yours, and sometimes suggests useful possibilities of solutions.

(17) John discussed things with me last night, he discussed at length the plans for his new house, the cost of the materials, how to get labour, how to get planning permission and when he expected it would be finished.

An explanation by analogy explains something that is unfamiliar or abstract in terms of something else that is concrete and familiar and like the thing to be explained in some essential aspect. Example 18 is an explanation by analogy.

(18) Light is sometimes like particles and sometimes like waves.

2 EXPLANATION IN KORAFE

We pass on now to explanation in Korafe. The various logical relationships between Korafe propositions are very clearly marked by surface connectives—much more clearly than in English. In particular, the following distinctions are marked very explicitly in Korafe (whereas in English the marking is less explicit although still present.):

1. between enabling and sufficient for both causes and reasons,
2. between private and public information,
3. between sufficient causes with private information and sufficient reasons.

There is also a major distinction, again marked by surface forms, between mechanistic or cause-effect explanations on the one hand and conceptual explanations on the other. This is a key distinction in Korafe at the same level as the causal versus descriptive distinction in English but it is not identical with the latter, although there are similarities.

So the treatment for Korafe is divided into two major sections, the mechanistic explanations of section 2.1 and the conceptual explanations of section 2.2. Within each subsection of these, the description will proceed according to the logical relationships signalled by the various connectives. This should not be taken to imply, however, that the Korafe description is more surface oriented; rather it means that the Korafe surface markers fit the categories very neatly. Nor, on the other hand should it be taken to imply that the previous treatment of English is in any sense an etic description—there the surface markings of the various logical relationships are less explicit but they are certainly present.

2.1 Mechanistic or Cause-effect Explanations

A mechanistic explanation in Korafe clarifies something by giving the cause-effect mechanism for it. The cause may vary in strength from an enabling condition which is relatively weak to a sufficient cause which is strong. All causes must be thought of in their cultural context.

As far as the surface forms are concerned, the connectives involved are *aindae, aindae sedo, ava sedo, a gido* and the present description will deal with the use of these forms one by one. In each cause-effect sentence in its unmarked surface form, the cause precedes the effect.

2.11 Sufficient Causes

Sufficient causes in Korafe are marked by *aindae* 'sufficient cause, public information', and *aindae sedo* 'sufficient cause, private information'.

2.111 *aindae* 'sufficient cause, public information' with approximate translation 'therefore'. The morpheme breakdown is *a-i-ndae* 'medial demonstrative-control-purpose', where control has the meaning of agency or instrumentality, something that causes or determines. So in an *aindae* sentence, what precedes *aindae* causes what follows it to be true.

(19) Brothers die (MV) *aindae* (therefore) kinfolk get upset *aindae* (therefore) they roast poisons (MV).

Here the causes are sufficient, the first (in the first conjunct) because people invariably get upset when kinfolk die, the second (in the second conjunct) because there are strong cultural pressures in such situations for people to roast poisons and avenge themselves. The strength and urgency of the causes is further marked by the medial verbs, (MV) in all conjuncts (see appendix on medial verbs). The causes are social and are public information as everything is observable.

(20)   Whatever I have eaten (MV) *aindae* (therefore) I want to defecate (MV)

Clearly there is an almost inevitable cause-effect relationship between what is eaten and what gets defecated. The cause is physical and sufficient. A freer translation would be 'No matter what I eat, I want to defecate it.'

(21)   If you see him you will be thinking of how you should kill him (a very large bird) *aindae* (therefore) you will be startled and quiver all over.

The situation here is that the hunter has seen a very large bird and he is so excited and tense at the possibility of killing such a great prize that he cannot help but be startled and quiver all over. Thus the cause is sufficient.

2.112 *aindae sedo* 'sufficient cause, private information'. This connective differs from its public information counterpart *aindae* just treated by the presence of the verb *sedo* 'say' which marks it as introducing private information, information provided by the speaker and not verifiable by the addressee. Otherwise the same considerations apply as for *aindae*.

(22)   I am feeling (MV) something happening in my body *aindae sedo* (therefore) I am preparing a sleeping mat and a string bag.

Here the first conjunct *I am feeling something happening in my body* is private information; it is information given by a newly pregnant woman to her husband. The addressee cannot independently verify this information so he has to take it on trust. However, once one takes this first conjunct information as true, then it is a sufficient cause for the actions of the second conjunct and the speaker doesn't have much choice but to carry out these actions. Specifically, in the Korafe culture there is a strong necessity for an expectant mother to make a sleeping mat and a string bag for the expected baby.

Note that the verb *feel* in the first conjunct is a medial verb, expressing greater urgency in the cause than the corresponding final verb in the first conjunct of the next example (23).

(23)   Saki's son was born (FV) *aindae sedo* (therefore) he prepared a feast for his wife's male relatives.

Here *aindae sedo* follows a conjunct that is a sufficient cause because of the strong cultural pressure to provide a feast for the wife's male relatives when she has a baby. However, you are allowed to wait up to three years after the baby is born to put on the feast and this lack of urgency is shown by the final verb form of *born*.

The use of the verb *sedo* 'say' to mark the first conjunct as private information may seem strange. In fact, this example comes from a fictional story so that the addressee must depend on the speaker for the information and has no independent means of verifying it.

2.12 Enabling Conditions and Reasons
The connectives which encode enabling (or necessary) relationships are *a gido* 'enabling condition, public information', and *ava sedo* 'enabling reason'. Note there is no surface form which means 'enabling condition, private information'. Such a form would have been a counterpart to *aindae sedo* 'sufficient cause, private information' of section 2.112. In fact, *ava sedo* which also contains the verb *sedo* 'say' and therefore marks private information, is the bridge between enabling conditions (or causes) and enabling reasons. We remember again Anscombe's remark (1957) that there is a fuzzy area between causes and reasons.

2.121 *a gido* 'enabling condition, public information'. In *a gido* sentences, the first conjunct precedes *a gido* and is an enabling (necessary) condition for what follows and the information is public, verifiable by the addressee. The absence of the morpheme *-i-* meaning 'control' in the sense defined in section 2.111 shows that the causal relationship is not as strong as a sufficient cause. The morpheme break-down of the connective is, in fact *a* 'medial demonstrative', *gido* 'see'.

(24) The stars have gone up *a gido* (so) I have called you together to discuss holding a feast.

Here, the first conjunct tells us that a certain season of the year has arrived, the right season for holding feasts. Thus an enabling condition has been fulfilled for the speaker to call a meeting to hold a feast; it was appropriate to discuss the matter at that time of the year but it would not have been appropriate to discuss it at other times of the year. On the other hand, the speaker was not compelled to call a meeting; the decision to do so was still his.

2.213 *ava sedo* 'enabling reason'. The connective *ava sedo* is, in fact, the most common of all the cause-reason connectives in Korafe, and the semantic range of the relationship that it marks is correspondingly wide. Both enabling and weakly sufficient causal relationships are marked by it; however, there is no control morpheme *-i-* (section 2.111) in the connective so it cannot mark a (stronger) sufficient cause. The morpheme break-down is *ava* "contrastive', and *sedo* 'say'. The second part *sedo* marks the preceding conjunct as private information, information that is from the speaker's mind and often related to his personal beliefs, values, principles, etc.,—in fact, the kind of information we would associate with reason. The first part *ava* indicates that the two conjuncts must contrast in content.

(25) We have arrived at my favourite place *ava sedo* (so) we will heave anchors.

The first conjunct *we have arrived at my favourite place* is the speaker's reason for the second conjunct which is an exhortation to heave anchors. The information of the first conjunct is private, and the addressees have to take the speaker's word that the place they've arrived at really is his favourite place. There is also a content contrast between the world of the speaker's personal values in the first conjunct and the world of proposed action of the second conjunct.

(26) She₁ thought the spirit girl₂ was real *ava sedo* (so) she₁ took off and went fishing with her₂.

The private information indicated by the verb *sedo* is the thought world of the girl in focus, i.e., the real girl referred to by *she*₁. (Participant identity is indicated by subscripts.) This thought world of the first conjunct contrasts with the action reported in the second conjunct.

2.2 Conceptual Explanations

The conceptual explanations differ sharply from the mechanistic (cause-effect) ones just treated both in their surface forms and the meaning of the interclausal relationships.

The surface order in conceptual explanations is that the phenomenon to be clarified comes first in the sentence and is followed by the explanation. This is the opposite surface order from that of the mechanistic explanations.

There are four surface connectives used in conceptual explanations. They are *ai resira amo* 'sufficient reason', *ainda beka mo* 'concerning the truth of this', *ainda susu mo* 'concerning the source of this', and *ainda tuka mo* 'concerning the point of this'.

Considerations of both form and meaning divide this group of four connectives into two subgroups, the first subgroup consisting of just the first connective and the second, of the remaining three. The analysis will be presented following this subgrouping and the reasons for the division will become clear as the analysis proceeds.

As far as meaning is concerned, all conceptual explanations involve a mental attitude or a conceptual state.

Thus in section 2.21, a strong belief is invoked as the sufficient reason for an action. In section 2.221 which deals with elaborations and analogies, the explanation changes the conceptual state of the addressee by giving him detailed information about something he is not clear about. Section 2.222 deals with motivations which of themselves involve mental attitudes and in many cases it is a mental attitude which is motivated. Section 2.223 deals with real reasons for evaluations, actions and mental attitudes; and reasons of themselves involve mental attitudes.

2.21 Sufficient Reason

The first group of connectives introducing conceptual explanations consists of just one form *ai resira amo* which encodes 'sufficient reason'. In a sentence so constructed, a mental attitude is expressed in the second conjunct that is strong enough to motivate or even compel the action described in the first conjunct. This sufficient (i.e., strong) reason component is marked as in other connectives by the morpheme *-i-* 'control'. The morpheme *-s-* in *resira* is an allomorph of the verb *say* and tells us that the information is private. Thus the explanation is in terms of a reason rather than of a cause.

In contrast with *ava sedo* (section 2.213) which is the most common of the connectives, *ai resira amo* is the least common. According to informant reaction, however, it is the one explanation connective that cannot be left out of the surface structure of its sentence. If it is, the logical relationship between the conjuncts becomes very obscure.

(27) I have closed down all boat and air traffic *ai resira amo* (my reason is that) people would go down to Tufi and mock the Korafe people in their suffering.

This sentence was reported by a Korafe to have been said by the (foreign) district officer in charge of the area where the Korafe lived. The Korafe people at Tufi were recovering from a recent cyclone and the district officer felt that outsiders might go down to Tufi and be an embarrassment to the Korafe. His feeling was sufficiently strong for him to act upon it and close down all transport.

(28) He (the cassowary) lies down and sleeps in the late afternoon *ai resira amo* (my reason is that) he fears the fireflies (that come out at night).

Here the speaker gives the fear of fireflies as the strongly motivating reason for the cassowary to lie down and sleep in the afternoon.

2.22 Truth, Source and Point
The second group of connectives introducing conceptual explanations are the following three very similar surface forms:

ainda beka mo	'concerning the truth of this'
ainda susu mo	'concerning the source of this'
ainda tuka mo	'concerning the point of this'

The first, *ainda beka mo,* introduces an explanation by elaboration or by analogy. The second, *ainda susu mo* introduces an explanation that gives the source or motivation for an attitude which can lead to an action. The third *ainda tuka mo* introduces an explanation which asserts what the point, i.e., the really important or really relevant idea is behind the statement of the conjunct being explained.

2.221 *ainda beka mo* 'concerning the whole truth or reality of this'. Another way of giving the meaning of this connective is: 'with the information that I am about to give you, you will see the truth or reality or the whole picture behind it all.'

By introducing a conjunct with this connective, the speaker is explaining by giving the whole picture, the whole truth when the previous conjunct has given only part of the truth or the truth in an abstract or condensed form.

Thus this connective has to do with explanations by elaboration or by analogy and these are nearly always noncausal. Of the many examples analysed, only two (32 and 33) have anything that looks like a cause or reason. What distinguishes this connective is the spelling out or elaboration of detail, with the cause-reason component not a distinguishing feature but admissible as an optional extra.

All such explanations are in terms of cultural patterns familiar to the addressee. The information given in the explaining (second) conjunct is public and verifiable by the addressee; however, the logical connection between the conjuncts is supplied by the speaker.

In its basic physical meaning, *beka* is used to refer to the meat in a nut or coconut; in its metaphorical extension here it means 'the whole thing, the total essence'. That is why elaborations and analogies are given by *ainda beka mo*.

2.2211 Explanation by elaboration (expanded paraphrase). In this kind of explanation, the speaker explains a statement by adding specific details. Terms introduced in the first conjunct that are too abstract or too brief, thus have their meaning clarified in the second conjunct as more specific details are added there. In what follows, examples 29, 30, 31 are straight elaborations, and *ainda beka mo* is well translated as 'in detail this means', whereas in examples 32, 33 we have elaborations with a weak reason component and for these *ainda beka mo* is well translated as 'the reason in detail is'.

(29) A man would discuss with his wife and they would then bustle round and go as a travelling trader to some places *ainda beka mo* (in detail this means) he would discuss so that they would have enough loin cloths, laplaps, clay pots and pigs for the trip.

Here the term 'discuss' is introduced briefly in the first conjunct with no details; however, its meaning is made clearer in the second where it is elaborated upon and we are given the purpose of the discussion.

(30) Mourners *ainda beka mo* (in detail they are) those who see a person die, wail, take him, bury him, return him to his place.

Here, the second conjunct explains the meaning of the term 'mourner' introduced in the first by elaborating in detail on what mourners do. The explanatory information is verifiable by the addressee.

(31) There is no tradition behind the keel-angle-headed lizard *ainda beka mo* (in detail this means) we don't eat it, we don't kill it and we don't do anything with it.

Here the speaker elaborates on what the term 'no tradition', introduced in the first conjunct, really means.

(32) They carved up old canoe hulls *ainda beka mo* (the whole reason in detail for this was) they would cook food in these bowls and take it and pass it to the men in the clan house so that they could eat while conducting their business. Or they would use the bowls to send food with guests away from the preparation area.

The second conjunct explains the action of the first in great detail, elaborating on why they carved up the canoe hulls to make bowls.

(33) If you see his (honey eater bird) legs you will laugh *ainda beka mo* (the reason in detail is) you'll see his short legs and you will laugh.

The speaker says that someone seeing the short legs of the honey eater bird will laugh; indeed for the Korafe seeing short legs is a good enough reason to laugh. The second conjunct elaborates on 'legs' of the first conjunct, telling the addressee what kinds of legs he will see.

2.2212 Explanation by analogy. Analogy is another way of explaining or revealing the truth of something that isn't clear. Here, too, *ainda beka mo* is used. It might be translated as 'I mean to say it's just like. . .'

(34) The council gets tax *ainda beka mo* (I mean to say it's just like) when you go to catch fish you take bait and put it on your hook and throw in the line and the fish bites and you pull it in. If you throw in the hook without bait, the fish won't bite and you won't catch it.

This is an example of explanation by analogy. The speaker is explaining a situation where he is trying to raise taxes from the local villagers. If he succeeds in raising a goodly sum, the central government will match it handsomely and the village will get a large sum for its development. He is using a familiar cultural trait, that of using bait to catch fish, to explain by analogy what the situation means to the villagers. In this case, the analogy is the most convenient for the speaker to get the whole truth across.

2.222 *ainda susu mo* 'concerning the source of this' gives the motivation for an action, for a mental attitude or for a mental attitude that leads to an action. Such actions can be either one time actions or customary actions.

The motivation does not of itself determine the action or mental attitude but is rather an enabling condition for it. A sentence with *ainda susu mo* explains by answering the questions, how did this come about? what made this possible? or what helped you decide to do this?

The basic physical meaning of *susu* is 'the base section of the trunk of a tree'. In its metaphorical extension, it means 'basis', or 'motivation' or 'source of'.

In the examples which follow, 35 and 36 deal with motivation (or source) of a mental attitude, 37 and 38 deal with motivation of a mental attitude which then leads to an action, 39 and 40 deal with available resources which motivate an action.

(35) After she spoke, her husband heard, was ashamed and did not answer *ainda susu mo* (what motivated this shame was) since Rina had been married she hadn't eaten fish, she would only eat other food.

The second conjunct gives the motivation (or source) of the husband's shame. He had been a poor provider, in unfavourable contrast to his brothers who had been good providers.

(36) Men desire this bird very much *ainda susu mo* (what motivates this desire is) all men take this bird, tie its feathers together in order to dance.

Here *ainda susu mo* introduces a second conjunct that tells us what motivated the desire, i.e., the mental attitude mentioned in the first conjunct.

(37) She delivered her baby and called her name Dubo (neck) *ainda susu mo* (what motivated this is) she neck gets (loves) her child well.

Here the second conjunct gives her mental attitude of loving the child which led her to act and name the child the way she did.

(38) We raise dogs *ainda susu mo* (what motivates this is) after we raise the dog and it grows up, we take it to the bush and it bites those pigs, bandicoots, cuscus, and rats. We cut them up, parcel them out, cook them, serve them up, and eat them.

The second conjunct gives the advantages which motivate a favourable mental attitude which in turn leads to the action of raising dogs.

(39) Mostly the Wanigela people make clay pots *ainda susu mo* (this comes about since) the clay for making pots is near them.

Here the second conjunct tells about the clay which is an available resource for making the pots mentioned in the first.

(40) After the structure of it is hardened and firm they cook and eat food or they go and dip up water *ainda susu mo* (this comes about since) they make different kinds of clay pots.

Here the second conjunct tells us about the different kinds of clay pots which make it possible for the Korafe to carry out the various activities mentioned in the first conjunct.

2.223 *ainda tuka mo* 'concerning the point of this' gives the most important or really relevant cause or reason. The conjunct that precedes *ainda tuka mo* can describe either an evaluation, a mental attitude or an action whose point in the sense just stated is then given in the second conjunct. Often the point comes out as a sufficient cause.

The point is always expressed very concisely so unlike *ainda tuka mo* (section

2.221) this connective cannot introduce long elaborations or analogies. Also excluded are vague explanations and even enabling relationships; everything must be to the point in fact.

In its purely physical sense, *tuka* is used much more seldom than either *beka* or *susu* but it is found in constructions such as *tuk'aminda* 'there at the point' as you would use if you were telling someone that something was located at the end of the house nearest the sea. In its metaphorical extension, it means 'the really relevant cause or reason or meaning' as stated.

In the examples which follow, 41 and 42 deal with the point behind an evaluation, 43 and 44 deal with the point (as sufficient cause) behind an action implying a mental process such as 'hear', 45 and 46 deal with the one relevant reason (amongst many possible ones) behind an action or mental attitude.

(41) The scorpion is bad *ainda tuka mo* (the point is) it bites and our bodies hurt.

This gives an evaluation that the scorpion is bad in the first conjunct and then, in the second, says very concisely why it is bad, i.e. gives the relevant reason for the evaluation.

(42) I saw but I didn't believe *ainda tuka mo* (the point is) one man is not to marry fifteen women.

In the first conjunct the speaker evaluates something as incredible, and then in the second conjunct he gives very concisely the point he appeals to. He invokes the cultural value that one man does not marry fifteen women and that is sufficient reason for his evaluation.

(43) The leader speaks and the people hear *ainda tuka mo* (the point is that) he is talking about having a feast for his trading partners.

The cultural value invoked here is that a feast for one's trading partners is something very important and so this is a sufficient cause (strong cultural obligation) for the addressees to listen to the speaker.

(44) He lectures and people hear and quit quarrelling and fighting and become peaceful *ainda tuka mo* (the point is that) he has roasted a charm and it remains inside the limegourd.

The charm is the sufficient cause which gives the leader strong mediating powers and influence. When charms are about, people become quiet and stop fighting.

(45) Mother and Dad mostly work *ainda tuka mo* (the real reason is that) they work in order that their children be happy.

The second conjunct here gives the speaker's real (and sufficient) reason why his parents work. Other possible reasons like 'so that everyone can eat' are thereby excluded.

(46) My friends and I were scared to go home *ainda tuka mo* (the real reason was that) we were afraid of our parents.

This was spoken by a child who had been misbehaving with some others. Their mental state of being scared to go home might have been due to several reasons, like evil spirits on the trail, etc., but the speaker says that the real reason in this case was that they were afraid of punishment from their parents.

Both the truth, source, point explanations of this last section 2.22 and the reasons of 2.21 (sufficient reason) and indeed also the enabling reasons of 2.122 involve mental attitudes but they involve them in different ways. The reasons of 2.122 and 2.21 invoke beliefs, values and principles which are clearly all mental attitudes but these are invoked as reasons, i.e. as preconditions. On the other hand, in the conceptual explanations of 2.22, the mental attitude appears in the effect.

3 SUMMARY

This completes the comparison of the explanation systems of English and Korafe. At the highest level, English has a major distinction between causal and descriptive whereas Korafe has a major distinction between mechanistic and conceptual. Within these major distinctions, the contrasts of private versus public information, enabling versus sufficient and cause versus reason are maintained in both languages although Korafe has much clearer surface markings in general than English. Korafe does not have any system corresponding to reasons for speech acts in English; on the other hand, it has a conceptual system which covers much more than the descriptive system of English.

REFERENCES

Anscombe, G. E. M. (1957). Intention. *Proceedings of the Aristotelian Society* 57. 321–332.
Davidson, D. (1963). Actions, reasons and causes. *Journal of Philosophy* 60. 685–700.
Halliday, M. A. K. & Hasan, R. (1976). *Cohesion*. London: Longman.
Watson, O. (ed.) (1976). *Longman Modern English Dictionary*. London: Longman.

APPENDIX I
MEDIAL AND FINAL VERBS IN KORAFE

Korafe verb suffixation falls into two quite distinct types. Final verbs are marked for tense-person-mode while medial verbs are marked only for same versus different referent.

The verb forms in the causal conjunct can take different forms depending on whether a sufficient or an enabling cause is being encoded.

When there is an enabling condition, then *ava sedo* or *avo gido* are the connectives used and the verb in the causal conjunct must be in the final form.

When, however, there is a sufficient cause, then *aindae* or *aindae sedo* are the connectives used and the verb in the causal conjunct may be a final verb or it may be a semifinal or medial verb. The stronger the causal relationship and the more urgent the situation, the more likely is the use of a medial verb.

APPENDIX II
A SAMPLE OF KORAFE SURFACE STRUCTURE

The following is a small sample of Korafe surface structure for those readers who are interested. We give here a morpheme by morpheme gloss and free translation for example 19.

(19)   *nano. namendi*   *amb- earo*
           brothers   die.short process-gnomic aspect.3p.different
                                 referent. sequential

           aindae   *dubo vevera*   *ari*
           therefore   neck hot   do.sequential. irrealis.3p.different
                                 referent

           aindae   *kae*   *bor-earo*
           therefore   poison   roast-gnomic aspect.3p.different
                                 referent.sequential

Brothers die, therefore they (kinfolk) get upset, therefore they prepare sorcery potions.

How to Recognize Systems   **8**

Joseph E. Grimes

Cornell University
Ithaca, New York

MORPHOLOGICAL COMPLEXITY

A theory based on systems is useful as long as we are sure we can recognize the systems. But in morphology, and also in systems realized by function words, various things conspire to make systems hard to recognize.

First there is position: relative orders get fairly tangled, for example when some elements span two or more positions.[1]

The second complication is layering. For instance, a verb sometimes gets inflected, then that inflected verb gets nominalized. The resulting noun may be inflected like a noun, and then perhaps verbalized again, through several layers. The same morphological apparatus may be used in both an inner layer and an outer layer. Sometimes a suffix in an inner layer that would normally come before another there comes after it instead because it is in an outer layer. There is an apparent reversal of order, but only because of the different layers.

The third complication is the dependency pattern. Each affix normally modifies the stem and depends on it. But every so often an affix depends upon another affix. Affix-affix dependencies may mean that a dependent affix can attach itself to any one of several other affixes, and when this happens it seems to float around in the word structure.

Fourth are cooccurrence restrictions. Affixes and function words come in sets. Elements in one set cannot cooccur with each other. In a tense system, for example, if one of the tenses is chosen, the others are locked out of that word. This property of mutual exclusiveness is the basis of our understanding of the semantics of choice in closed systems.

Looking at two such sets, however, we may form the false impression that we should be able to pick any member of one set, put it together with any member of the other, and have something sayable as a result; this leads to interminable footnotes to apologize for the cases where it is not so. We do better to put into the heart of morphological analysis the expectation that not everything in one system occurs with everything in another system.

---

[1] Affixes that precede others of order *j* and follow others of order *k*, where the distance between *j* and *k* is greater than 2, are said to SPAN the orders in between. See Grimes 1967 for a discussion of positional analysis, and Grimes 1964 for a complex example that involves spanning.

Last are semantic anomalies. In lexical idioms like *lower the boom,* even when we know the meaning of the parts, we still do not know the meaning of the whole. In a similar way, in affix systems we sometimes find affix idioms. For example, in Huichol of Mexico the dependent mode prefix cooccurs with the narrative mode prefix, but the meaning of the combination has nothing to do with the meaning of either affix; it constitutes a separate mode in the same set, the evaluative.[2]

METHODS OF ANALYSIS

To sort out morphological complexity there are now three useful tools. The first, positional analysis, puts affixes into partially ordered sets (Grimes 1967). Second, we can also do a complete analysis of complex restrictions on cooccurrence (Grimes, Lowe & Dooley 1978, Grimes 1978). Third, given here for the first time is a new algorithm that is intermediate between the other two in complexity. It identifies the complete subsets of cliques or affixes that are the locus of semantic choices.

REPRESENTATION OF THE DATA

For all three kinds of analysis data must be represented in a consistent way that meets five requirements. First, the forms should be unique. For example, homophones need to be distinguished.

Second, the data should be noncyclical. In the Tucanoan languages of southeastern Colombia there are three suffixes that can occur only two at a time as follows: B follows A, C follows B, but A follows C to form a cycle. The actual forms in Tucano are *-sʔɨi* 'desiderative', which is followed by *ti* 'negative', which is followed by *-kãʔ* 'emphatic', which is followed by *-sɨʔɨi*. For analysis we have to break that cycle. One way is to simply lay aside all the forms in which, say, A and C cooccur; then after we work out the analysis, put them back in.

Data must also be linear in the single dimension of before and after. Our speech organs work in a time-dependent way by moving muscles to shape the sounds we emit, so that speech is basically linear. But there are two kinds of data that need special linearizing. One is things like suprafixes, including tonal affixes and stress patterns; we need to abstract them out and then insert them into the sequence at some definable point, such as just before the segmental morpheme they go with.

The second special linearization is for infixes that interrupt a stem, common in the Austronesian languages of the Philippines: for example, in Kelley-i Kallahan *dumtuk* is a stem, and *dinumtuk* is the same stem with infix *-in-*. (I am indebted to Richard Hohulin for the example.) We simply pull infixes out of the stem and make

---

[2] The evaluative mode was not noted in my earlier work on Huichol, because I had not recognized the combination as a true idiom. Here it appears in Figures 8 to 10 as a single semantic feature.

them look like prefixes as far as order is concerned, and after we finish, tuck them back in where they belong.

Data must be unlayered. We need not worry all at once about things that belong in different layers. In other words, if a verb that takes an inflection is nominalized and that made-up noun is reverbalized, when we are looking at the outer layer of verbalization we should not compare it with anything in the inner layer, and vice versa, because the two taken at the same time may clash. We concentrate on one layer at a time and put the results together afterward.

Data should be morphemically represented; that is, with one representation that includes all allomorphs of each morpheme.

Figure 1 is a subset of the 42 verb prefixes of Huichol, a Uto-Aztecan language of Mexico. The 42 are distributed into 15 relative orders, up to ten of which can occur in a single word. The subset in Figure 1 covers the modal prefixes and the negatives that go with them. Figure 1 contains all possible combinations of these forms in two representations: on the left an ordinary transcription (in which prefixes are separated by hyphens and *i* stands for a high back unrounded vowel [ɯ]), and on the right a data vector. For the prefixes listed across the top, a 1 in the correspond-

	pʔ	ka2	kal	mʔ	ni	ke
pʔ	1	0	0	0	0	0
pʔ-ka2	1	1	0	0	0	0
kal-pʔ	1	0	1	0	0	0
kal-pʔ-ka2	1	1	1	0	0	0
mʔ	0	0	0	1	0	0
mʔ-ka2	0	1	0	1	0	0
ni	0	0	0	0	1	0
kal-ni	0	0	1	0	1	0
kal-ka2-ni	0	1	1	0	1	0
mʔ-ni	0	0	0	1	1	0
mʔ-ka2-ni	0	1	0	1	1	0
-----	0	0	0	0	0	0
ka2	0	1	0	0	0	0
ke	0	0	0	0	0	1
ke-ni	0	0	0	0	1	1

Figure 1. Combinations of selected verb prefixes in Huichol of Mexico

	pʔ	ka2	kal	mʔ	ni	ke
pʔ	0	1	1	0	0	0
ka2	1	0	1	1	1	0
kal	1	1	0	0	1	0
mʔ	0	1	0	0	1	0
ni	0	1	1	1	0	1
ke	0	0	0	0	1	0

Figure 2. Cooccurring pairs of verb prefixes in Huichol of Mexico

ing column means that the prefix is present in the form represented by the row, and a 0 means it is not.

We want to study the things that do not cooccur with each other, but Figure 1 reports the combinations that do occur. To get to noncooccurring forms, first the logical operation of union on the forms that do occur yields a composite in Figure 2 of what pairs of forms cooccur.

For example *pï-* occurs in all the forms reported by the first four rows of Figure 1. Uniting all four rows that have a 1 in the *pï-* column into a single vector that has a 1 in every position where any one of them except *pï-* itself contains a 1 summarizes the cooccurrences of *pï-* in the first row of Figure 2. The same goes for each of the other morphemes: all cooccurrences of each are brought together in the appropriate row of Figure 2. That gives us a square matrix symmetric about the main diagonal. Cooccurrence is not an ordered relation; positional analysis takes care of order separately, but this analysis leaves ordering out of consideration entirely.

Semantic choices are made among alternatives, and alternatives cannot cooccur. Figure 3 highlights this. It is the complement of Figure 2, with every 0 changed to a 1 and vice versa. It includes the identity matrix of 1's along the main diagonal to register the fact that no form cooccurs with itself. In Figure 3 we are ready to look for what are called CLIQUES—maximally connected or complete subsets of the forms in the matrix that are mutually exclusive with each other. These are sets of elements in which every element is unable to cooccur with any other element in the set, and so is an alternative choice to every other element in the set.

ALGORITHM TO IDENTIFY CLIQUES

Figure 3 contains all the basic information that we need, but it does not lay it out in a linguistically useful way. We want to find the linguistically relevant subsets of this

	pï	ka2	kal	mï	ni	ke
pï	1	0	0	1	1	1
ka2	0	1	0	0	0	1
kal	0	0	1	1	0	1
mï	1	0	1	1	0	1
ni	1	0	0	0	1	0
ke	1	1	1	1	0	1

Figure 3. Noncooccurring pairs of verb prefixes in Huichol of Mexico, including the identity matrix

	pï	ka2	kal	mï	ni	ke
pï	1	0	0	1.	1	1
ka2	0	1	0	0	0	1
kal	0	0	1	1	0	1
mï	1	0	1.	1	0	1
ni	1	0	0	0	1	0
ke	1	1.	1.	1	0	1

Figure 4. Noncooccurring pairs of verb prefixes in Huichol of Mexico, with tags (.) for intersecting cliques

list of morphemes—the subsets within which a speaker makes semantic choices. These subsets are what lead to the identification of systems.

Graph theory decomposes any connected graph into a union of COMPLETE subsets or cliques, within which every member is connected to every other member.[3] (Figure 3 represents a graph if we take the 1's in it to represent arcs connecting the form that labels the row with the form that labels the column.) A clique in such a graph is made made up of forms none of which can cooccur with any other member of the clique. Finding linguistically relevant systems can therefore make use of the logic already developed for finding cliques in a graph. The algorithm to do this is given in condensed form in (1).

(1)   For each row i in matrix M,
        If M (i,j) = 1 (untagged), $i \neq j$
        Then compare rows i and j as follows:
        If M (i,k) = 1 (untagged) and
        M (j,k) = 0
        Then tag M (i,k)

We go through Figure 3 row by row. For each 1 in the row we ascertain whether the morpheme the 1 represents could be a member of the same clique as the morpheme the row represents. If it cannot, we tag it. When the process is finished, the 1's that are left untagged represent the cliques directly.

The tagged 1's reflect the fact that cliques overlap with one another. This overlap is common in language, to the point that when all the members of a clique overlap with other cliques, that clique may be hidden from the first pass of the analysis. This condition can be recognized whenever the tagged 1's fall out in a symmetric pattern. To uncover the hidden cliques, we strip away the rows and columns that do not contain any symmetrically tagged 1's and repeat the process. This uncovers the hidden cliques.[4]

For the Huichol data, the first row of Figure 3 tells which forms do and do not cooccur with pï-: it says that mï-, ni-, and ke- cannot cooccur with pï-.

To find a clique with pï- in it, compare the rows for those three forms with the row for pï-. The untagged 1's in a row are like an index that points to other rows that are to be compared against it.

We go through the first row of Figure 3 and compare the fourth row (mï-) against it, because the mï- position of the first row contains a 1. Any columns that have 1's in both rows are candidates for membership in a clique. If, on the contrary, the row we are examining has a 1 in it where the row we are comparing against it has a 0,

[3] Beineke and Wilson 1978. Ivan Lowe and Gary F. Simons independently called this graph-oriented strategy for analysis to my attention, for which I am grateful. The algorithm is my own.

[4] The total set of cliques identified is independent of the order of elements in the rows and columns, and of the order in which they are taken up. Which cliques are hidden from view at any stage of the analysis, however, varies from permutation to permutation.

then the morpheme that other row represents cannot be in the same clique, because the 0 indicates cooccurrence. In the fifth column of the *pï-* row there is a 1 that is matched by a 0 in the *mï-* row. That column, which corresponds to *ni-*, cannot be in the same clique as *pï-* and *mï-*, so the 1 in the *pï-* row is tagged by putting a dot next to it or drawing a circle around it.

Once a 1 is tagged, there is no reason to compare the row it points to with the row it is in, because the tag already shows that those two forms are not in the clique that the row reports. This does not mean, of course, that we throw *ni-* out of the data or that we deny that *pï-* and *ni-* are mutually exclusive; they just don't belong in the same complete subset as *pï-* and *mï-*. The process guarantees that their relationship will be picked up in some other clique.

Finishing the comparison between the *pï-* row and the *mï-* row, *ke-* also fits in the clique because both rows contain 1's in the *ke-* column. The *ni-* row has already been shown to not be part of the same clique, so we skip the tagged 1 in the top row that represents *ni-* and go on to the untagged 1 that represents the noncooccurrence of *pï-* with *ke-* and compare. Wherever there is an untagged 1 in the *pï-* row there is also a 1 in the *ke-* row, so no new tags need be added to the *pï-* row.

Each row in turn is checked against every one of the other rows for which it has an untagged 1 in the corresponding column. As we compare a pair of rows, whenever we find a 1 in the row we are focusing on that is matched by a 0 in the other row, we tag the 1 to show it is outside that clique.

The tagged forms in Figure 4 are asymmetrically distributed, though the matrix itself is symmetric. This means that even though the relationship between *pï-* and *ni-* in the first row does not show membership in the same clique, the *ni-* row shows that they do belong to a different clique. This is because *pï-* enters into two different kinds of relationships; it is here where the complications of systemic grammar begin to emerge. *Pï-* relates to *mï-* and *ke-* in one direction and to *ni-* in another, as Figure 5 shows. In Figure 5 the various maximally connected complete sets or cliques intersect; half of the elements enter into more than one set of relationships each.

In one set of relationships, *ke-* is the normal imperative and *ka$_2$-* is the negative. The fact of the matter is that there are no imperative negatives in Huichol; all imperatives are implicitly positive. *Ke-* is thus tied to the opposition between negative and positive.

In the other set of relationships, *pï-*, *mï-*, and *ke-* are the main modes—indicative, dependent, and imperative, the axis around which verbs revolve. *Pï-* and *ni-* are both indicatives, *pï-* occurring more in conversations, *ni-* more in narratives, but never both in the same word (Grimes 1966). *Mï-*, *ke-*, and *ka$_1$-* all stand in a special relationship to *ni-*; *mï-ni-* is not 'dependent narrative', but is an affix idiom meaning 'evaluation' that has nothing to do with either being grammatically dependent or fitting into a narrative. There is also an idiomatic meaning of 'second person' that arises when *ke-ni-* cooccur, and a special restriction on the cooccurrence of *ka$_1$-ni-*, so these three form a set largely by virtue of their interactions with *ni-*. This does not yet give us the entire analysis, but it does highlight relationships that we do not want to overlook.

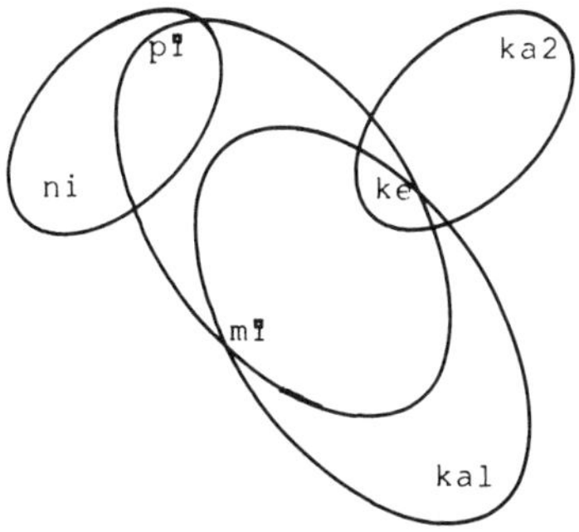

	a	1	chi	la	kil	no	lle
a	1	0	1	0	1.	0	0
1	0	1	1	1	1:	0	0
chi	1	1.	1	1.	0	0	0
la	0	1	1	1	1:	1.	0
ki...1	1	1:	0	1:	1	0	1.
no	0	0	0	1	0	1	0
lle	0	0	0	0	1	0	1

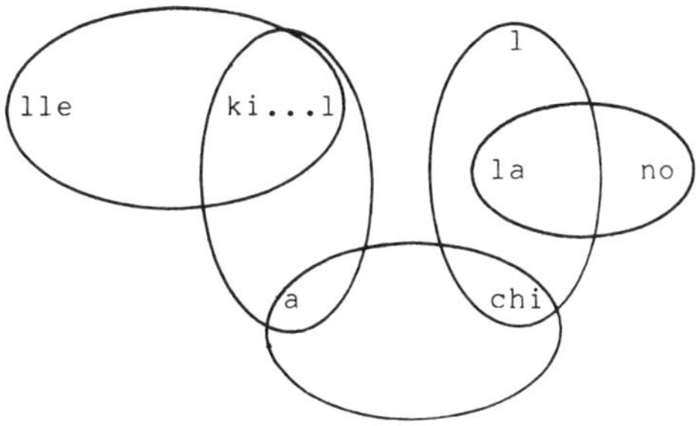

Figure 5. Clique structure of Huichol verb prefixes

Figure 6. Noncooccurring verb suffixes in Mapudungu of Chile, illustrating hidden cliques (:)

HIDDEN CLIQUES

Mapudungu of south central Chile has 61 verb suffixes, of which Figure 6 gives a manageable subset chosen for illustration.[5] Some of the matrix elements tagged by the algorithm are symmetrically placed. These are shown with a colon tagging them rather than a dot. The noncooccurrence of *ki . . . l* and *l*, for example, is not included in any of the cliques that are indicated by untagged 1's.

The symmetrically placed tags in Figure 6 are all places where a clique is masked or hidden by the fact that each of its members are also members of other cliques. To bring hidden cliques to light all that is necessary is to get rid of the information that hides them. Figure 7 is a reduction of Figure 6 to only those rows and columns that in Figure 6 contain symmetric tags. The hidden clique consisting of *l* with *la* and

---

[5] I am indebted to Robert Croese for verifying the Mapudungu data. The morpheme symbolized as *-ki . . . l* 'negative of the imperative' is discontinuous in that *-no* 'negative of the nonreal' and several other suffixes may come between the parts.

	1	lə	ki...l
]	1	1	1
lə	1	1	1
ki...l	1	1	1

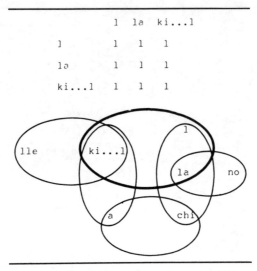

Figure 7. Noncooccurring verb suffixes in Mapudungu of Chile, reduced to uncover hidden cliques

	pos	asr	neg	mod	dep	nər	evl	cnj	imp	dir
positive-assertive	1	1	0	0	0	0	0	0	0	0
asr-negative	0	1	1	0	0	0	0	0	0	0
pos-moderated-asr	1	1	0	1	0	0	0	0	0	0
mod-asr-neg	0	1	1	1	0	0	0	0	0	0
pos-dependent	1	0	0	0	1	0	0	0	0	0
dep-neg	0	0	1	0	1	0	0	0	0	0
pos-narrative	1	0	0	0	0	1	0	0	0	0
pos-mod-nar	1	0	0	1	0	1	0	0	0	0
neg-nar (mod req'd)	0	0	1	0	0	1	0	0	0	0
pos-evaluative (idiom)	1	0	0	0	0	0	1	0	0	0
eval-neg (idiom)	0	0	1	0	0	0	1	0	0	1
pos-conjunct	1	0	0	0	0	0	0	1	0	0
neg-conj	0	0	1	0	0	0	0	1	0	0
pos-imperative	1	0	0	0	0	0	0	0	1	0
pos-imp-direct (idiom)	1	0	0	0	0	0	0	0	1	1

Figure 8. Cooccurring semantic features corresponding to Huichol verb prefixes of Figure 1

	pos	asr	neg	mod	dep	nar	evl	cnj	imp	dir
pos	1	0	1	0	0	0	0	0	0	0
asr	0	1	0	0	1	1	1	1	1	1.
neg	1	0	1	0	0	0	0	0	1:	1:
mod	0	0	0	1	1	0	1	1	1	1:
dep	0	1	0	1.	1	1	1	1	1	1.
nar	0	1	0	0	1	1	1	1	1	1.
evl	0	1	0	1.	1	1	1	1	1	1.
cnj	0	1	0	1.	1	1	1	1	1	1.
imp	0	1	1:	1.	1	1	1	1	1	0
dir	0	1	1:	1:	1	1	1	1	0	1

	neg	mod	imp	dir
neg	1	0	1	1.
mod	0	1	1	1:
imp	1	1.	1	0
dir	1	1:	0	1

	mod	dir
mod	1	1
dir	1	1

Figure 9a. Noncooccurring pairs of semantic features in verb prefixes in Huichol of Mexico, showing intersecting (.) and hidden (:) cliques
Figure 9b. Noncooccurring pairs of semantic features in verb prefixes in Huichol of Mexico, first reduction to identify hidden cliques
Figure 9c. Noncooccuring pairs of semantic features in verb prefixes in Huichol of Mexico, second reduction to identify hidden cliques

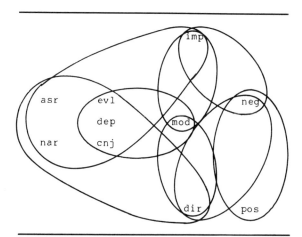

Figure 10. Intersecting cliques of semantic features derived from Figure 9, Huichol of Mexico

ki . . . 1, emerges, and the process terminates because there are no more symmetric tags, hence no more uncovered cliques.

SEMANTIC COUNTERPART

There are further stages in analyzing systems. The stages just described give us the cliques found among the occurring forms. They do not, however, cover the counterparts to categories of meaning that are communicated implicitly by the absence of any of the other forms in a system. Neither do they put things like affix idioms into a systemic perspective.

To do this the most logical maneuver is to replace the original data of affix or function word combinations with the corresponding feature combinations that emerge from ordinary form-meaning analysis. This includes adding in feature values that are assumed by default. It also includes feature values for forms that are expressed idiomatically. The cooccurrence pattern of these features, when plotted in the same way the form cooccurrences were plotted, is the major step toward framing the systemic grammar in semantic terms.

Figure 8 is the feature counterpart of the Huichol forms in Figure 1. It includes the information such as 'positive' that is communicated implicitly by the absence of the overt negative, and the features 'evaluative' and 'direct' (for implicit second person in the imperative) that represent the affix idioms. Figure 9 is the tagged matrices of noncooccurring forms derived from Figure 8 and run through the algorithm with reductions. Figure 10 is the semantic counterpart of the cliques of forms given in Figure 5.

It is still a step from there to displaying the systemic choices within each clique, together with the interactions among these systems; that is the end, and the logical operations I have outlined are the means.

REFERENCES

Beineke, Lowell W. & Wilson, Robin J. (eds.) (1978). *Selected Topics in Graph Theory.* London: Academic Press.
Grimes, Joseph E. (1964). *Huichol Syntax.* The Hague: Mouton and Company.
———. (1966). Some inter-sentence relationships in Huichol. In *Summa Antropológica en homenaje a Roberto J. Weitlaner.* México, DF: Instituto Nacional de Antropología e Historia, pp. 465–470.
———. (1967). Positional analysis. *Lg* **43.** 437–444.
———. (1978). A heuristic for paradigms. *American Journal of Computational Linguistics.* Microfiche no. 80. 232–235.
———, Lowe, Ivan and Dooley, Robert A. (1978). Closed systems with complex restrictions. *Anthropological Linguistics* **20.** 167–183.

Working with Transitivity: System Networks in Semantic-Grammatical Descriptions

9

Erich Steiner
University of the Saarland
West Germany

INTRODUCTION

This article deals with problems that have arisen in the course of descriptive work with TRANSITIVITY system networks. "Descriptive work" here means the analysis and synthesis of clauses in the course of a research project which is currently being carried out in Saarbrücken (West Germany). I shall first try to make clear the status of TRANSITIVITY system networks within linguistic theory. Next, I want to outline the major problems which we encountered in the course of our work with these networks. The third section contains a detailed proposal for a solution of these problems, including our own network for MENTAL PROCESS and a detailed working procedure for assigning semantic structures to clauses occuring in natural (in our case) written, texts. The fourth section deals with the question of independent motivation of semantic system networks from outside linguistics. I shall argue that systemic linguistics offers the opportunity of integrating a theory of action (Handlungstheorie) with a linguistic theory.

1. Transitivity is an aspect of the ideational function of language, which is distinguished, in systemic linguistics, from the interpersonal and textual functions.[1] Within the ideational function, there are other system networks apart from transitivity, such as CIRCUMSTANCE, TIME, VOICE and some others. Transitivity is an area of meaning in which the speaker or hearer chooses and constructs a certain 'type of process' for his clauses. These choices can be expressed in a system network.

The term 'type of process' relates *outward* from language in that it is a reflection of a reality outside language. I would maintain, contrary to all subjective interpretations of the relationship between reality and language, that in the reality of human

---

[1] There has been an interesting discussion recently on the number and nature of functions; cf. Fawcett 1980.

communities there *are* events like relations, actions, mental processes and ver-
balizations. The term 'types of process' relates *into* language insofar as different
types of process are reflected in characteristic patterns of semantic organization and
in grammatical, lexical and phonological form.

In transitivity systems, language encodes extra-linguistic reality in terms of a
finite repertoire of possibilities. In the system networks of systemic theory we use a
variety of labels for the networks and sub-systems, brackets, arrows and straight or
curved lines. Moving along these lines we 'generate' a semantic structure or a
'selection expression', or, in other words, we select according to the options made
available in the networks. Using these processes, we are talking about how we
'*mean*', as we talk about how we 'word' or 'sound' when we talk about grammar,
lexis or phonology; or how we 'do' when we talk about how we act in certain
situations. Linguistics faces the difficulty, in J. R. Firth's words of, "turn language
back upon itself". In systems of transitivity, language symbolizes things, events,
circumstances, qualities etc. of the world around us, and organizes these in characteristic ways.

Within the last fifty years some schools of linguistics have tried to operate
without a semantic level, namely, Taxonomic Structuralists with their emphasis on
analysis and early Transformational grammarians with their emphasis on the *synthesis* of sentences/clauses. Both proved inadequate, but it must be admitted that
linguists have learned a great deal from their work. Taxonomic Structuralists
showed us that while it is possible, to some extent, to set up a purely syntactic
parsing system for sentences, clauses, phrases etc., these parsing systems and the
corresponding grammars have inherent weaknesses as Phrase Structure Grammars
(cf. Chomsky 1957) and miss all those generalizations about language which we
capture in our semantic networks. From transformationalists we have learned that
the goal of generating all grammatically correct sentences in a language cannot be
achieved without, at least, an 'interpretive' semantic component (cf. the line of
development in Katz, Fodor, Postal, Jackendoff). This 'interpretive' semantic component must then interpret the so called 'purely syntactic' structure which contain a
great deal of information one might term 'semantic'.

Accordingly, schools have developed which include, as an essential component,
a (generative) level of "semantics". One of these schools is systemic linguistics.
The semantic level corresponds (more or less closely) to the higher strata of Stratificational Grammar and the generative base of Generative Semantics, to name two
other schools. I have just outlined the motivation for a semantic level which comes
from *inside* linguistics. However, there is much to be said for a semantic level that
is derived from *outside* linguistics, from psychology, sociology etc., as I shall
indicate in the final section of this paper.

While it is relatively easy to motivate networks in general terms, actually setting
up networks and working with them makes for a number of difficulties. Perhaps the
most recent formulation of some of these can be found in Diana Woolard's "A half-
baked review of the 8th International Systemic Workshop" (*NETWORK 3,:* 15).

2. In Saarbrücken we have been investigating, for some time, the semantic-grammatical properties of a type of English verbal group which we call 'Funktionsverbgefüge', an analytical verbal group in which the 'process' is expounded or realized by a verb plus a nominal group:

VG/Verb + NG

The element 'verb' is realized by a certain class of verbs such as "give, make, do, have, get, take. . ." while the 'head' of the NG is realized by a "nominalized process". To give some examples from our corpus:

". . . the cable did its political damage."
". . . women got support from feminists."
". . . we'll just take a look."
"He gives me a quick, hard look."
"The idea has a strong appeal to whites."
"Merry then made his confession."[2]

Our aim is to specify the differences between these analytic verbal groups and synthetic verbal groups. It is relatively easy to do this in the area of syntax. To do it semantically we need a technique of description for the semantics of the verbal group. An example of the kind of question we are asking is: 'What is the difference between saying 'He gives me a quick look.' or 'He looks at me quickly.'?' If we want to show the difference, we need networks for all three of the semantic components. Much could be said about MOOD, MODALITY, INFORMATION, and other such systems, however, here I will concentrate on transitivity. We had much less difficulty with networks from the interpersonal and textual components than with TRANSITIVITY networks from the ideational.

What we needed, then, was a semantically oriented Transitivity-system Network, one that had features such as 'action', 'intended' etc. rather than 'extensive', 'effective'. This is why we chose the classificatory scheme by Michael Halliday (Figure 1) and tried to change it into a real system network by formulating restrictions on combinations of types in the course of our work.[3] Using such a network in the *analysis* of sentences presented certain difficulties: 'How do we unambiguously assign a semantic structure to a clause from a text'? There are some relatively clear cases such as:

'John escaped with the milk can' (action),
'I have read that he escaped' (mental process), and
'John is poor' (relation).

---

[2] For a report on the project cf. Steiner and Burgard, 1981 (mimeo). In the systemic literature the NG's in our verbal groups are usually treated as range - objects, a type of C-element syntactically. We consider these NG's as parts of the predicate, as realizing the semantic process. For the traditional systemic view, cf. Halliday 1967–68, part I, p. 58ff.

[3] The following are publications containing alternative TRANSITIVITY-system networks, not including those of Halliday: Berry 1975, 1977, Davey 1978, Fawcett 1980, Hudson 1974, Sinclair 1972, Monaghan 1979, Muir 1972, Scott et al. 1968, Winograd 1972, Young 1980.

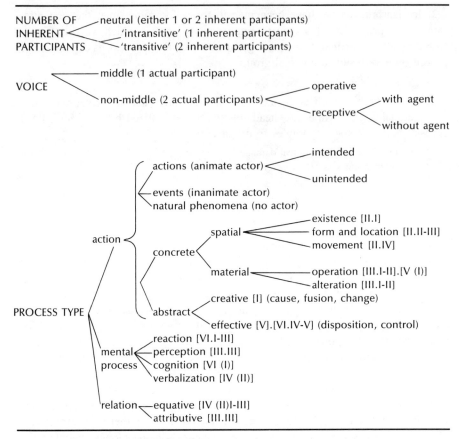

References are sections in *Roget's Thesaurus* in which many verbs occurring in the clause type in question are listed; these are broad correspondences, and there is considerable overlap. Note that the table, although exhaustive, does not show restrictions on combination of types (it is not 'a system network').

Figure 1. Clause Types (Kress 1976)

Our initial criteria were often based on our 'knowledge of the world' as well as some obvious syntactic criteria, such as '*to be*', in the last example above, is a linking verb, which shows that the semantic structure is relation. However, in a number of cases this method does not work. According to our knowledge of the universe, many processes might be called mixed types, depending on which aspect of a process we focus on. In a clause such as 'The car appeared over the hill.' the question arises 'Is this an action process?' In this case it would have to be −intention because of the inanimate subject. Or, 'Might it be mental process?' because it implies someone who perceives this process, in which case it would be a perception process without the processor overtly realized. In the clause 'He gave his consent.', again, this process has characteristics of a verbalization process, but there is no message realized. Instead, we have the function verb 'give', which is a very general action verb, making the whole process resemble a simple action type. Cases such as these are quite frequent.

The problem of metaphor or "incongruence' seems to be without solution as long as we rely predominantly on our 'knowledge of the universe'. From this knowledge, it seems that a certain process remains what it is, regardless of being used as a metaphor by the speaker. In the early stage of our work we had no explicit way of dealing with the dialectics between objective reality and subjective reality (language). To solve our problems we first researched the work of people who had worked with transitivity system networks and published their results in some detail. We surveyed the systemic literature mentioned above and found Fawcett's 1980 work and J. R. Martin's 1979 work the most explicit and helpful. From this work we learned that the search for a formal motivation of features has to be one of two starting points when setting up a network. The second of these, independent motivation, will be dealt with later. Once we had learned this we began to set up networks of our own, modifying them as our ongoing analytical work dictated.

3. First we needed the networks themselves. In the area of TRANSITIVITY quite a number of networks have been published. In the context of our work the network in Fawcett, 1980, p. 137 turned out to be the most suitable because it was a *semantic* network and was explicit insofar as realization rules were formulated and 're-expression tests' were suggested for the inherent participant roles (see Figure 2).

For relational processes we are not yet sure which network to use, but a likely candidate seems to be the one Robin Fawcett recently distributed at the 8th International Systemic Workshop. This decision has not yet been made since relational processes are relatively infrequent in our FVG-corpus. We set up our own networks for mental and verbalization processes (see Appendix I and II). These have yet to be compared to those of Halliday, (1967–68, Part 3, p. 203). We had to develop our own, to combine them with the action process network of Robin Fawcett.

It seems plausible that within our culture(s) a basic distinction is made between processes that are viewed as occuring *outside* our own consciousness and the ones occuring *within*. This would correspond to the ancient debate in our philosophical tradition between objective and subjective reality with the opposing forces of idealism and materialism at either end.

According to the syntax, only MENTAL PROCESS and VERBALIZATION clauses have the potential of having a 'that' clause that functions 'object'. If this potential does not exist a non-finite clause may be in the object position, either with or without subject. If it is an '-ing' participle clause, the subject has the potential of 'nominative' or '-s- genitive'. The type of mental process called 'phenomenon oriented' in our network may have a 'that' clause in subject position. The following cases have to be *excluded:* relational processes (these also can have 'that' clauses as subject, but can by other criteria be relatively easily distinguished from mental process.), causative verbs ('get', 'make' etc. 'that' clauses as subjects, which is a problem as long as these verbs are not listed in a closed class.), and verbs which

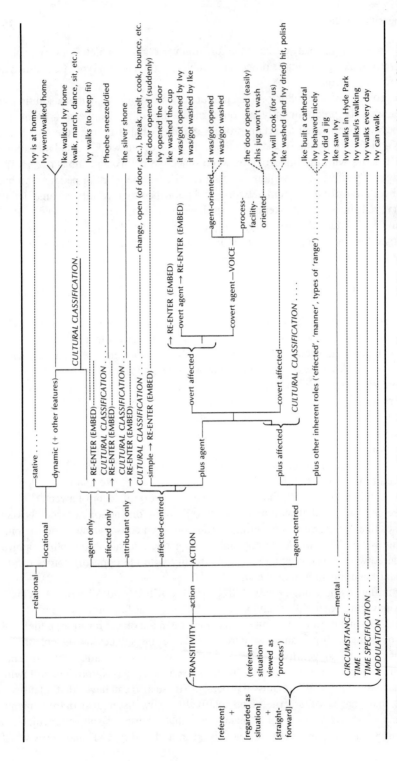

Figure 2. A Transitivity System Network for English Action Processes (Fawcett 1980. Reprinted by permission of the publisher)

refer to the 'stage of process' such as 'stop, begin, continue' which can have non-finite clause objects. Again, as long as we cannot delimit these by other criteria from mental process verbs, they present a problem.

Mental process clauses are formally motivated by the set of verbs by which they are realized. This, however, amounts to a circular definition because the verbs we include in the set of mental process verbs depend partly on how we structure the network itself. Lexical networks can be viewed as continuing transitivity networks to the right, being in that sense 'more delicate'. A mental process network specifies the entry conditions for the lexical networks of mental process.

In my networks (see App. I and II) I have set up the following 'participant roles':

Role	Test
[processor]	what X perceived/thought was . . .
[processor + intention]	normal [processor] − test + [agent] − test (what X did was . . .)
[processor − intention]	normal [processor] − test and NOT [agent] − test
[phenomenon]	what [processor] perceives/thinks about is X
[sender]	what X communicated/uttered was . . .
[message]	what [sender] communicated/uttered was X

We have not extensively dealt with other, non-inherent roles. With verbalization process types participant roles are usually 'receiver/addressee'.

The re-expression tests are a somewhat weak point in the procedure. However, they are not needed for the basic decisions in our procedure. The first decision, whether a clause is action, mental process, or relation can be made on other criteria, as we have seen above.

Roles such as 'processor +intention' and 'processor −intention' are relatively clear at the centre but 'fuzzy' in many borderline cases. In the clauses 'John watched him going' and 'John felt the threat,' we have a clear case of ' +intention' vs. ' −intention'. This decision is more difficult, however, for a pair of clauses like the following: 'People did not respect the regulations' and 'people did not like the regulations'., where I would still argue for the former being ' +intention' and the latter ' −intention'. This problem of 'fuzzy edges' is not a problem unique to semantics. It is the same problem that we face when trying to determine boundaries between features in acoustic phonetics on a sound spectrograph. What has been said here could be called 'formal motivation', because re-expression tests of this form are nothing but different options of the respective clauses in the "clefting" of clause constituents.

Realizational rules, formulated along the lines of Fawcett (1980) are given together with our networks in App. I and II. I have not formulated rules for every possible combination of features, which could, however, easily be done for the others. Note that there is an option in the network of mental process which is not formally motivated in our context, the ' +intention/−intention' splitting after 'processor' oriented. In other words, both have the same realization rules. In a more comprehensive network, though, they would be motivated because both features present an entry condition for different networks if we let them lead into different sets of lexical items and if we let the '+intention' type be the entry condition for the 'do-clefting' in the textual component.

The network developed thus far will still, when used as a generative device, generate ungrammatical sentences such as '*I watched that he came' and '*I desire you coming'. The reason is that mental process *as a class* can operate the way our network states it, but not every verb realizing mental process has all these options. This is the same problem any grammar faces with finite/non-finite clause verb complementation (cf. Quirk et al. 1972; 832 ff.). As long as we cannot specify these restrictions within our system network we have to add a marker for the potential syntactic framework of every verb in our CULTURAL CLASSIFICATION networks and have to filter out already generated structures by matching these with the individual verbs. This reformulates the old problem with the boundaries between syntax and lexicon, and grammar and lexis, to use Firth's and Halliday's terms. Syntactic markers such as the ones we have just mentioned can be found in the *Dictionary of Contemporary English* (Proctor 1978), the *Advanced Learner's Dictionary* (Hornby 1948) and in H. E. Palmer (1938), *A Grammar of English Words*.

Figure 3 indicates the procedure, used to assign semantic structures to clauses from our corpus. It is not a 'flow-chart' in that there are points which are merely *labels* and not directly points of decision; no 'yes', or 'no' lines lead directly out of them. These are only mnemonic devices and may be dropped. At some points the procedure leads into sub-programmes. These are part of the transitivity system network. As these programmes, with the exception of relation, are well specified elsewhere, I won't list them in detail here. Note that we switch between potential and actual at some points. This is theoretically important and will be taken up later.

Lexical networks present a particular problem in systemic linguistics (cf. Fawcett 1980: 151 ff., Berry 1977: 62 ff.). The general assumption is that lexical networks, or CULTURAL CLASSIFICATION networks, have as entry conditions certain features of the transitivity network. Basically, two solutions seem to be possible: either having as entry conditions features to the left of our network, that is, less delicate features which will give us relatively few cultural classification networks with a complicated internal structure, or having as entry conditions features to the right of our transitivity network which will give us a number of cultural classification networks with a less complicated internal structure and a lot of overlap in membership, in terms of lexical items. The most important question in this connection is that of the *internal structure* of these cultural networks and of the *motivation of their features*. At present we think of these networks as consisting of features which resemble the entries in the table of contents in Roget's *Thesaurus* or in Longman's *Lexicon of Contemporary English*. The Thesaurus would have to have a well defined and thorough taxonomic build-up, which is a problematic goal. The features could be connected by the usual lines of systemic networks. Paths through the networks would lead to or have as exponents, either lexical items or groups of items. We would have realizations such as 'house, door, woman, idea, go, run,

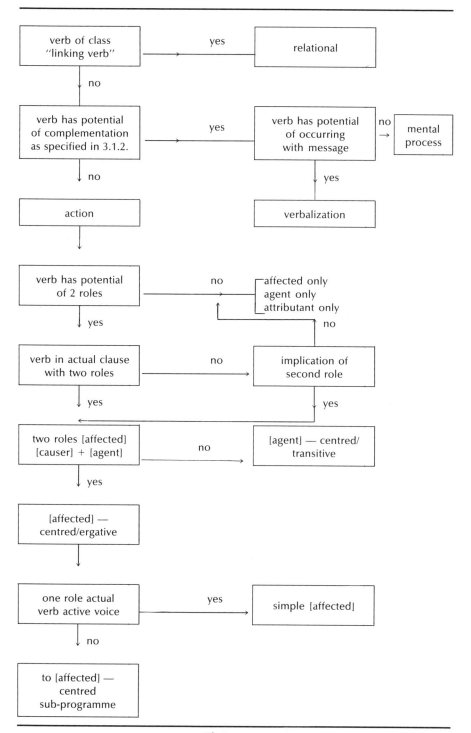

Figure 3.

black, round. . .', but also 'to make an effort, to kick the bucket. . .'. All lexical items, especially verbs, will have an index specifying their role framework (potential). Accordingly, these lexical items could only be 'inserted in' (realize) semantic structures with which they yield acceptable sentences. Again, this is nothing new if we think of subcategorization and selectional restrictions in transformational grammar or of 'values' in dependency grammar or else simply of H. E. Palmer's early dictionaries (cf. Palmer 1938).

There are difficulties, however, inherent in this approach. I have tried it out with students and we found that the decision as to *where* to put features (nodes) in such a network and *how to label* them is difficult. Labels of nodes can themselves be terminal features. My suggestion does not amount to very much more than turning Katz, Fodor and Postal's taxonomies of semantic features around and calling them a 'network'. The general framework of systemic linguistics, of course, is different from theirs.We gave the formal motivation for the mental process network above. The few unclear cases have been located and can be dealt with in the future. The same applies to verbalization. The motivation of the relational network, or at least its demarcation from action, mental process and verbalization, seems to be clear (class of verbs, syntactic structure). The proposals in Fawcett (1980: 137) would introduce some difficulties by having a number of verbs as realizations of relational processes which have hitherto been treated as action verbs. Using our procedure we shall analyze all other processes as action.

At the points in our procedure where we have to refer to 'participant roles' such as 'agent', 'affected', 'message' etc., we encounter difficulties in the borderline areas. Our re-expression tests, as well as those in Fawcett (1980) should not create the illusion that we are deciding using anything other than the faculty mind/language that we want to explain.

The same is true for our use of the test for 'implication of second role'. This is the well known question of 'inherent roles', or, to use the terminology of dependency grammars, of 'facultative vs. obligatory constituents' (fakultative vs. obligatorische Aktanten). Let us, on the other hand, make it clear that, for the task 'at hand', this question is answered as soon as we have a lexicon giving definitive role frames for verbs. In this case we simply consult the information attached to the entries in the lexicon (culture classification networks). The question of polysemy seems difficult to solve, for the present at least. What we do in our analysis is rely on an intuitive understanding of whether we have in an actual case *one* verb with slightly different shades of meaning realized in different actual contexts, or, one form which is the phonological realization of completely *different* paths through the network. For example, the clause 'We called last night but nobody was at home' would, according to our procedure, be classified as verbalization without the message being overtly realized. However, the obvious interpretation of this clause is, 'we tried to visit you. . .'. The interpretation 'We stood outside your house shouting. . .' does not seem very likely. Such examples are quite numerous in our corpus but, as our example indicates, the context will, as a rule, decide which meaning is intended. Nevertheless, the problem remains that we'd like to assign to this clause the structure 'action', rather than 'verbalization', whereas our procedure so far forces us to call it 'verbalization'. The only solution we can think of at present is to have different entries for one phonological form in our lexicon (CULTURAL CLASSIFICATION-networks). Let us admit, though, that this only means relegating to the lexicon the problem of deciding where to draw the lines between different actualized meanings of *one* lexical item and different lexical items with one phonological form.

Despite certain difficulties, our procedure in our descriptive work does achieve important goals. I have outlined our task in the research project earlier. To check on the 'sameness' or 'difference' of meaning between our analytical and corresponding synthetic verb forms we had to have a system of semantic description such as the one previously outlined. Using this technique it has been possible to make comparisons in a way that indicates the systematic and regular differences between such structures. We have furthermore been able to identify the unresolved difficulties more precisely than before. Appendix III provides further illustrations of our method.

Finally, a word on those disturbing 'fuzzy edges' that remain. What about the participant roles in this clause 'I cannot help admiring you'? Are they 'actor - goal', or 'agent - affected', or 'processor - phenomenon', or 'processor - goal'? What is it that makes a participant role what it is? It is its *place in the system*. In fact, I cannot tell what a given role is unless I know the system of roles from which I can choose for a given structure. Setting up such systems is precisely what we have been doing all the time. If I know that for a given clause under certain conditions (cf. our procedure) I can only choose, say, between 'processor' and 'phenomenon', I shall be able to do so. Something may not be unquestionably an agent, affected or phenomenon, but rather to a greater extent than something else. In the following clauses:

'I walked down the stairs'. and
'I fell down the stairs'.

I could call 'I' a number of roles depending on the kind of abstraction I am making. If, however, for certain explicit reasons I know that it must either be 'agent' or else 'affected' there will be little doubt.

One may shudder at this lack of 'absoluteness' in delimiting our categories, but let us look at the most 'clear-cut' area of the linguistic sciences, the one whose terms can 'easily' be reduced to physical phenomena, *phonology*. One of the most interesting approaches in this field is, in my opinion, the one exemplified in Jakobson and Halle's *Fundamentals of language* (1956). In this book, the features of the phoneme are related to physical events, articulatory and acoustic. To summarize the method for determining phonemes given by Jakobson and Halle: The string of speech is segmented into units, which are realizations of choices from a system (Jakobson's famous universal-feature-matrix) that consist of articulatory/acoustic features. Each of these features is a *process* (plosion/friction or frequency/amplitude of cycles) between which boundaries have to be drawn with *respect to the system*.

Now, if you look at a sound spectrogram you will realize that these boundaries may be relatively clear-cut in one area (say, between consonants and vowels or between bilabial voiced-plosives and velar voiceless plosives), but may not be in other areas (say, for a compact vs. diffuse pair, in which the extreme positions of bilabial vs. velar are not involved but rather, for example, dental vs. palatal). Remember that the acoustic criterion for the 'compact vs. diffuse' decision is that of the 'concentration of energy in a relatively narrow, central region of the spectrum vs. absence of this concentration' or, for the 'tense/lax' opposition that of 'relative spread of energy in the spectrum and in time' (Jakobson and Halle 1956: 29 ff.). In other words, we can only assign the feature 'lax' to a sound if I know that my only other choice in this area is 'tense'. The same holds true for most of the other phonetic features in Jakobson's feature matrix.

Secondly, for an untrained person the boundaries are very difficult to draw in many cases, although he may be perfectly able to *understand* and *speak* the language. This is the same problem of 'fuzzy edges' that we face in semantics.[4]

4. I began in section 1 with a general statement of the problem of the ideational function of language. Section 2 re-stated the problem within the field of our work in Saarbrücken. Section 3 contains our proposal for a solution that rests on the formal motivation of features and an explicit statement of how we assign semantic structures to clauses from a text.

Let us now go back to the more general question of the independent motivation of networks. Surely, if our only purpose was to analyze clauses just for the sake of analyzing them, and if we were not convinced that the way systemic linguistics states semantic structures was founded in, and gives us insight into other fields of scientific and social activity, we might as well choose some other method of formalization. It is in the field of independent motivation that we find the only basis for defending what we are doing (cf. Steiner 1983: 327 ff.).

In the following we shall look at the processes where we can best 'observe' our networks, or rather what is symbolized by our system networks, at various *processes of change*. Where in the course of the development of systemic linguistics have semantic systems been independently motivated? It was, so far as I know, in the collaboration between linguists and sociologists that socio-semantic networks symbolizing behaviour as meaning were first developed and set up (cf. Halliday 1973, forthcoming, Turner 1973). An example of such a network, reproduced from Turner (1973:155) is shown in Figure 4.

This approach reflects the intuitive notion that speaking, meaning and doing are interrelated as modes of action and meaning in certain important ways. This as-

---

[4] For sound spectrograms which can serve as an illustration, cf. O'Connor 1973: 160 ff. For research concerning the question of psychological reality of semantic structures in TRANSITIVITY, see Engelkamp 1980 and the literature referred to therein.

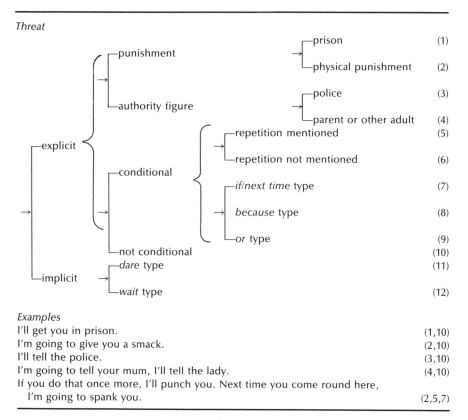

Threat

Figure 4.

sumption follows the tradition of the 'London School of Linguistics'. It suggests that we should try to formulate socio-semantic, semantic and grammatical networks with 'pre-selection' from the socio-semantic to the grammatical level. The main theoretical problem is that the few socio-semantic networks set up thus far, are specific to a certain type of situation (education) and it is not easy to see, initially, how we can arrive at more general networks which are still specific enough to allow the formulation of realization rules to semantic and grammatical networks. I shall make a suggestion in that direction shortly.

The second major direction of research in this area is the one exemplified in Halliday's *Learning How to Mean*. Watching the systems as they develop in child-parent (and, of course, in child-child) interaction is a rich source for the investigation of independent motivation for our networks (Halliday forthcoming b).

Psychology is a motivation from outside systemic linguistics. Here I would strongly advocate a look at Russian studies in language and cognitive development. There is a tradition beginning with Pavlov and continuing with Vygotsky, Luria, Leont'ev and some others in which a wealth of empirical facts about the development of the cognitive system in interaction has been collected and evaluated Pavlov, (1955), Vygotsky (1977, 1978), Luria (1966), Leont'ev (1975, 1975b, 1978). This has also led to a close investigation of the *destruction* of the same system in aphasia. Similarly, the work of Roman Jakobson in this area should be mentioned, although he dealt predominantly with the *phonological* aspect of language development and its destruction (Jakobson 1969).

Sociology or *Anthropology* is another major area of motivation. The ideas of Sapir and Whorf and their empirical investigations certainly belong here, as well as those of Dell Hymes and of Levi-Strauss (Levi-Strauss 1958). The tradition of Bernstein, Halliday and Turner has already been mentioned (cf. esp. Bernstein 1980). But there seems to be the problem of how we link up *actions* as described by other social sciences with those *semantic* actions which we as linguists focus on. This lies behind the question of 'situational specificity' of networks. In the Firthian and Neo-Firthian tradition this problem is well known as that of formulating the descriptive categories of the context of situation. Malinowski had a single, concrete and situationally specific context for every interaction he described (cf. Malinowski 1935). Firth saw that this was not what was needed if one wanted a description of linguistic action and non-linguistic action in terms of system and structure. Firth suggested that: "A context of situation for linguistic work brings into relation the following categories: the relevant features of participants: persons, personalities including their verbal and non-verbal action, relevant objects, and the effect of the verbal action. Contexts of situation and types of language function can then be grouped and classified" (cf. Firth 1950:182).

In this we have a general framework for all situation types, but somehow the categories do not seem wholly satisfactory; they seem obvious on one hand, and superficial or positivistic from a sociological point of view. This may have been one of the reasons why people like Bernstein, Halliday and Turner returned to more restricted, specific contexts. What, then, could be a framework for the context of the situation? What is the basic type of situation that best characterizes modern societies and which influences the systems and structures, linguistic and non-linguistic meaning? It is, in my view, the situation in which the process of material and cultural reproduction of a society is taking place. It is the working process with its basic elements as defined by Karl Marx and as elaborated, from a more linguistic point of view, by Ferrucio Rossi-Landi (Marx 1974: Vol. 1, ch. 5, Rossi-Landi 1974:1821ff). I propose that if we state as our consensus view that as systemic linguists we regard *language* as a meaning potential which is realized/actualized in processes (speaking/meaning) which in turn are integral parts of situations, and if we state that *action* in general has in common with language that it rests on a potential of actions which is realized or actualized in a society, cultural community and in situations therein (language as a social semiotic), and if we state that both are the essential components of the process of cultural (re-) production, then we ought to look for a general type of situation that specifies its elements as elements of exactly that process of (re-) production.

The elements of this situation-type are: the materials on which one works, the instruments, the worker, the working operations, the end for which one works and the product. I propose that we regard this as the basic, underlying type of situation in which 'doing, meaning and saying' take place, the categories of which are reflected on and, at the same time, 'worked upon' by language. M. A. K. Halliday in a well known passage once said that ''the nature of language is closely related to the demands that we make on it, the functions it has to serve'' (Halliday 1970:141). To this, I'd like to add: ''The demands in the generalized *working* situation, the functions in the generalized *working* situation.'' The situation-type 'working pro-cess' is a generalized type of situation in the same way that the linguistic metafunc-tions (the ideational, interpersonal and textual) are generalized functions of all the single, concrete functions that language has to serve in single, particular contexts of situation.[5]

Finally, I suggest that we have a close look at the process where interaction is being imitated, on a very modest level, as ''Artificial Intelligence'' (cf. Winograd 1972, Davey 1978). Within this area, there are, from a certain point of view, two major directions: one trying to simulate intelligent behaviour *without* trying to model the organism-internal processes and psychological processes in humans; the other more ambitious aim is the simulation of psychological and cognitive processes (storing and retrieving of information, problem solving etc.). Of these two, the second seems more interesting for linguistics. Artificial Intelligence is a much disputed field for several reasons, and rightly so. (Cf. Joseph Weizenbaum's *Com-puter power and human reason. From judgement to calculation* (1976)).

I have been advocating in this paper what I'd like to call a *dialectical view* of language. Dialectical here means that language is not an isolated phenomenon but instead is dependent on (i.e. is materially and functionally a product of) something else. This 'something else' is *society*, with the process of production and re-production as its structuring base. Language is often said to be a mirror of this social reality; this is the anti-mentalistic, materialistic part of the argument. This *product of* social reality, and this is the dialectical part, acquires the power of influencing, maintaining or changing this very same reality. In short, language *is* not only a mirror of reality, it *does* actively structure social reality. This general property of language confronts us in the problem of 'congruence'. If language was just a mirror there should be a one-way-determination from socio-semantic via semantic to gram-matical networks.[6] That is, the structure of processes outside language, in the context of situation would determine the structure of linguistic units strictly. As we all know, this is not the case.

What is language about, what does it mirror? As far as transitivity systems are concerned, language is about agents, affected entities, processes, phenomena, rela-tionships in the context of situation. This is nothing but an abstract way of referring

---

[5] Let me refer here to two authors who put forward a theory of how language developed in this general type of situation, a literary critic in the first case and a historian in the second: Caudwell 1937, and Thompson 1949, 1955, 1975.

[6] The problem remains in a one-level-network approach like Fawcett's.

	Realizations	Situation	Congruent Realization	Incongruent Realization
THEME	order of constituents	I am angry about s.o. else's behaviour.	Your behaviour last night was terrible.	My mother did not like your behaviour last night.
INFORMATION	Intonation	I want to know *where* s.o. went. There is no doubt about *who* went.	Where did you go last night? I went to the cinema.	Where did you go last night? I went to the cinema.
MOOD	presence vs. absence of certain clause elements, order of constituents intonation	I order s.o. to do s. th.	Open the window!	Will you please be so kind as to open the window?
MODALITY	modals adverbials intonation	I doubt that Jack went home.	Probably, Jack did not go home.	Jack actually went home? (You're not trying to tell me . . .)

Figure 5.

178

to the elements of the basic working process. In MOOD selections, it indicates the speaker's role towards the addressee. In MODALITY, it shows the speaker's attitude towards his/her message. As far as INFORMATION systems are concerned language reveals what is 'given' and 'new' in an information unit. A linguistic THEME tells what you are talking about. Yet, language does not mirror the corresponding states of affairs passively. Instead, language presents these states according to *the view of the speaker.* A speaker may very well choose to present something which is 'objectively there' in the context of situation in a way that is entirely his own. So, language mirrors what is objectively there through the active, structure-changing medium of the speaker. To illustrate this see Figure 5.

In this table I left out TRANSITIVITY, which brings us back to a question of method already touched upon in Section 3. If, say, a verb is *potentially* the realization of a process of verbalization, does this mean that it is so in every actual case?[7] In the following clauses:

'She said that dinner was ready'.,
'She admitted her mistake'. and
'President Meier regularly makes formal statements'.

according to our procedure, all these sentences would be assigned the feature verbalization. There seems to be a difference, though, between these sentences: The first is clearly verbalization, but the second has properties of verbalization, only by implication. The focus seems to have shifted in the direction of action. The final clause of this group would also be classified as verbalization according to our procedure, and yet there is not even a hint of any message realized. The focus seems to be more on what President Meier *does* than on what he *communicates.* So this last clause seems to have shifted even more in the direction of action.

How are we to proceed in such cases? Which are the rules rather than the exceptions which, superficially, seem to be somehow "cutting across the lines"? I suggest that we first put emphasis on the *potential,* the process realized in the verb. Having done this, however, we examine the *actual* syntactic structure. This may lead us to modify the interpretation in the following manner.

The first clause was *potentially* verbalization. Its *actual* semantic structure was 'speaker, message'; its actual syntactic structure

The actual in this case is a relatively straighforward realization of the potential of the VERBALIZATION system network. The syntax is unique to mental process

---

[7] Cf. Gonda 1951, *Remarks on the Sanskrit Passive,* pp. 1 ff for a very illustrative treatment of the question whether a "passive, active, middle" process, as it is actualized, is always a "passive, active, middle" process in terms of the semantic system of a language and objective reality.

and verbalization clauses. This is the reason why we have the 'intuitive feeling' that this sentence is a clear case of verbalization. In the second clause we might begin with the categorization 'verbalization, sender, overt message, other'. The semantic structure is verbalization as well, and we know that the formal item 'admit' is in the verbalization part of the Cultural Classification networks. The *syntactic* structure, however, is one that is also found in the syntax of action clauses:

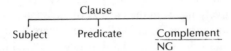

The message, as it were, is 'reified'. This means that in the interpretation the clause, while being potentially clearly verbalization, slightly shifts in the direction of action. Other factors, such as the animacy and intention of the first participant role contribute to this interpretation as well. In the final clause, we assign the semantic structure 'verbalization, sender + message, covert message'. In this case, provided we regard 'makes statements' as the realization of the 'process' rather than as 'process + range', which we argue for (Steiner & Burgard 1981), we still have a 'verbalization' process (*to state*), but its most characteristic semantic and syntactic constituent 'message' is not actualized at all. In addition, the process is realized in two constituents one is a semantically very general 'action' verb. All this shifts the interpretation of the actual sentence considerably towards the direction of action while still retaining the implication of verbalization.

This means that we have to account for the interplay or the dialectical relationship between *actual* and *potential* in our method, ultimately by extending our original procedure (Section 3) to actual surface structure and having paths leading back to earlier points of selection. We are at present working on this.[8]

CONCLUSIONS

In my field of research I needed a method of semantic description. Systemic linguistics fulfilled my need to a certain extent although some difficulties became apparent, as I have tried to indicate. In this paper I have tried to arrive at some solutions to various 'problem spots' as well as further exploring the area of interconnection between linguistics and other sciences from my point of view. In this, I offer nothing more than an outline. For me, however, they suggest directions which our work has to take, if we want to give our science the status it deserves, that of a theory which makes substantial contributions to the explanation of humanity's ability to interact, to maintain or change social structures, the ability to mean.

---

[8] I think that this is what people of the "Funktionale Grammatik" in the GDR mean when they write about "potentielle und aktuelle Bedeutung", cf. Schmidt 1963. A more general survey of the dialectics between systems and their realization is given in Pawelzig 1970.

ACKNOWLEDGEMENTS

I am very grateful to Professor Peter Erdmann (Saarbrücken) for permitting me to use his corpus of written American and British English and for discussing several aspects of my work with me during the last two years. My special thanks are due to Dr. R. P. Fawcett (Cardiff, Treforest, GB) for discussing various aspects of his work in semantics with me, which is closely related to the contents of this paper. Several of my colleagues in Saarbrücken have helped me by reading a draft of this paper and critically commenting on it; for this I am grateful to Roger Charlton, Karin Ebermann, Birgit Kellner and Mark P. Line. I wish to stress that I alone am responsible for any weaknesses in form and content that remain.

REFERENCES

Bernstein, B. (1980). Codes, modalities and the process of cultural reproduction: a model. In *Pedagogical Bulletin* **7,** Department of Education. Lund, Sweden: University of Lund.

Berry, M. (1975). *An Introduction to Systemic Linguistics[1]: Structures and Systems*. London: Batsford.

———. (1977). *An Introduction to Systemic Linguistics[2]: Levels and Links*. London: Batsford.

Caudwell, C. (1937). *Illusion and Reality*. Reprint, 1973. London: Lawrence & Wishart.

Chomsky, N. (1957). *Syntactic Structures*. The Hague, Netherlands: Mouton.

Davey, A. (1978). *Discourse Production: A Computer Model of Some Aspects of a Speaker*. Edinburgh, Scotland: Edinburgh University Press.

Engelkamp, J. (1980). Some studies on the internal structure of propositions. In *Psychological Research: An International Journal of Perception, Learning and Communication*, **41.** Berlin and Heidelberg: Springer Verlag, pp. 355–371.

Fawcett, R. P. (1980). *Cognitive Linguistics and Social Interaction*. Heidelberg and University of Exeter: Julius Groos Verlag.

Firth, J. R. (1950). Personality and language in society. In J. R. Firth (ed.), 1957, *Papers in Linguistics 1934–1951*. London: Oxford University Press.

Gonda, J. (1951). *Remarks on the Sanskrit Passive*. Leiden Netherlands: E. J. Brill.

Halliday, M. A. K. (1967–68). Notes on transitivity and theme in English, Parts I and II: In *Journal of Linguistics* **3.1;** Part II in *Journal of Linguistics* **4.2.**

———. (1970). Language structure and language function. In Lyons, J. (ed.), 1970. *New Horizons in Linguistics*. Harmondsworth, England: Penguin.

———. (1973). *Explorations in the functions of language*. London: Edward Arnold.

———. (1975). *Learning How to Mean*. London: Edward Arnold.

———. (forthcoming). *The Meaning of Modern English*. London: Oxford University Press.

———. forthcoming b. Language as Code and Language as Behaviour: A Systemic Functional Interpretation of the Nature and Ontogenesis of Dialogue. In Fawcett, R. P.; Halliday, M. A. K.; Lamb, S. & Makkai, A. (eds.), forthcoming. *Semiotics of Culture and Language*. London: Frances Pinter.

Hornby, A. S. (ed.). (1948). *Advanced Learner's Dictionary*. London: Oxford University Press.

Hudson, R. A. (1974). English Complex Sentences: An introduction to systemic grammar. Amsterdam: North-Holland Publishing Company.

Ikegami, Y. (1981). *"Activity," "Accomplishment", "Achievement", A language that can't say "I burned it but it didn't burn" and one that can*. Trier, Germany: Linguistic Agency University of Trier (L.A.U.T.).

Jackendoff, R. S. (1972). *Semantic Interpretation in Generative Grammar*. Cambridge, MA: MIT Press.

Jakobson, R. & Halle, M. (1956). *Fundamentals of Language*. The Hague: Mouton.

Jakobson, R. (1969). *Kindersprache, Aphasie und allegemeine Lautgesetze.* Frankfurt/Main, Germany: Suhrkamp (First published 1944).

Katz, J. J. & Fodor, J. (1963). The structure of a semantic theory. *Language* **39:2.**

Katz, J. J. & Postal, P. M. (1964). *An Integrated Theory of Linguistic Description.* Cambridge, MA: MIT Press.

Kress, G. (ed.). (1976). *Halliday: System and function in language.* London: OUP.

Leont'ev, A. A. The hueristic principle in the perception, emergence and assimilation of speech. In Lenneberg, E. H. & Lenneberg, E. (eds), 1975, *Foundations of Language Development,* **1.** New York: Academic Press.

————. (1975 b). *Psycholinguistische Einheiten und die Erzeugung sprachlicher Aussagen.* Berlin: Akademie-Verlag.

Leont'ev, A. N. (1978). *Activity, Consciousness and Personality.* Englewood Cliffs, NJ: Prentice Hall.

Levi-Strauss, C. (1958). *Anthropologie Structurale.* Paris: Plon. (English translation, 1963). New York: Basic Books.

Luria, A. R. (1966). *Higher Cortical Functions in Man.* New York: Basic Books.

Malinowski, B. (1935). *Coral Gardens and Their Magic.* New York: American Book Company.

Martin, J. R. (1979). *The Meaning of Features in Systemic Linguistics.* Mimeo: University of Sydney.

Marx, K. (1974). *Das Kapital.* Berlin: Dietz Verlag. (Karl Marx, Friedrich Engels Werke Bd. 23 ff). (English translation, 1962). London: J. M. Dent & Sons.

McArthur, Tom. (1981). *Longman Lexicon of Contemporary English.* Harlow England: Longman.

Monaghan, J. (1979). *The Neo-Firthian Tradition and its Contribution to General Linguistics.* Tübingen, Germany: Max Niemeyer Verlag.

Muir, J. (1972). *A Modern Approach to English Grammar.* London: Batsford. (R. P. Fawcett, ed.). *Network: News, Views and Reviews in Systemic Linguistics and Related Areas.* Cardiff, Wales: The Polytechnic of Wales.

O'Connor, J. D. (1973). *Phonetics.* Harmondsworth, England: Penguin.

Palmer, H. E. (1938). *A Grammar of English Words.* Harlow, England: Longman, Green & Co. Ltd.

Pavlov, I. (1955). *Selected Works.* Moscow: Foreign Language Publishing House.

Pawelzig, G. (1970). *Dialektik der Entwicklung objectiver Systeme.* Verlin: VEB Deutscher Verlag der Wissenschaften.

Proctor, P. (ed.). (1978). *Dictionary of Contemporary English.* London: Longman.

Quirk, R., Greenbaum, S., Leech, G. & Svartvik, J. (1972). *A grammar of contemporary English.* London: Longman.

Roget, P. M. (1852–1953). *Thesaurus of English Words and Phrases.* Harmondsworth, England: Penguin.

Rossi-Landi, F. (1974). Linguistics and economics. In Sebeok, Th. A. (ed.), *Current trends in linguistics,* **12.3.** The Hague, Netherlands: Mouton.

Schmidt, W. (1963). *Lexikalische und aktuelle Bedeutung.* Verlin: Akademie Verlag.

Scott, F. S., Bowley, C. C. Brockett, C. S. Brown J. G. & Goddard, P. R. (1968). *English Grammar.* London: Heinemann.

Sinclair, J. McH. (1972). *A Course in Spoken English: Grammar.* London: Oxford University Press.

Starosta, St. (1982). Case relations, perspective, and patient centrality. In *Working Papers in Linguistics.* **14,** No. 1. Honolulu, HI: Department of Linguistics, University of Hawaii at Manoa.

Steiner, E. & Burgard, J. (1981). *Bericht: Funktionsverbgefüge, Amerikanisches Korpus.* (Mimeo). Universität d. Saarlandes, Anglistik.

Steiner, E. & Schmitz, W. (1982). Review: "Language and control" (Fowler, Hodge, Kress and Trew), and "Language as ideology" (Kress and Hodge). In *Network* **3.**

Steiner. E. (1983). *Die Entwicklung des Britischen Kontextualismus.* Heidelberg: Julius Groos Verlag.

Thompson, G. (1949). *Studies in Ancient Greek Society, Vol. 1.* London: Lawrence & Wishart.

————. (1955). *Studies in Ancient Greek Society, Vol. 2.* London: Lawrence & Wishart.

————. (1975). *Marxism and Poetry.* London: Lawrence & Wishart.

Turner, G. (1973). Class and childrens' languages of control. In Bernstein, B. (ed.) *Class, Codes and Control, Vol. 2.* London: Routledge & Kegan Paul.

Vendler, Z. (1967). *Linguistics and Philosophy.* Ithaca, NY: Cornell University Press.

Vygotsky. L. S. (1977). *Denken und Sprechen*. Frankfurt/Main: Fischer Taschenbuch Verlag. (First published 1934.)

——. (1978). *Mind in Society*. Cambridge, MA: Harvard University Press.

Weizenbaum, J. (1976). *Computer Power and Human Reason: From Judgement to Calculation*. Reading, England: W. H. Freeman.

Winograd, T. (1972). *Understanding Natural Language*. Edinburgh, Scotland: Edinburgh University Press.

Young, D. J. (1980). *The Structure of English Clauses*. London: Hutchinson.

APPENDIX I

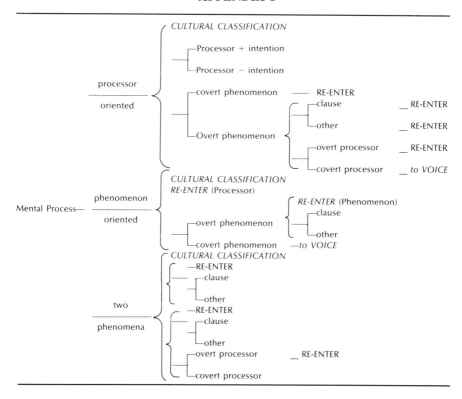

Feature	Conditional Features	Realizations
[sender + message]	[overt sender]	sender r S
[covert message]	NOT [+other roles]	O at C
[overt message]	NOT [+other roles]	message r C
[−message]	[+other roles] $\wedge$ [overt sender]	other role r C
[+message]	[+other roles] $\wedge$ [overt sender]	other role r C_1
		message r C_2
[RE ENTER CLAUSE]	NOT [other roles]	clause r C
[RE ENTER CLAUSE]	[+other roles]	clause r C_2

(continued)

Feature	Conditional Features	Realizations
[covert sender]		message OR other role r S
[covert sender]	[+message] ∧ NOT [+other roles]	message r S
[processor oriented]	NOT [receptive]	processor r S
[processor oriented]	[overt phenomenon] ∧ [overt processor]	phenomenon r C
[processor – intention]	NOT [covert processor]	processor r S
[phenomenon oriented]	[overt phenomenon]	phenomenon r S processor r C
[phenomenon oriented]	[covert phenomenon]	processor r S
[RE ENTER CLAUSE]	after [processor oriented]	clause r C*
[RE ENTER CLAUSE]	after [phenomenon oriented]	clause r S*

*Motivation for "receptive" VOICE will have to come from THEME-system.

APPENDIX II

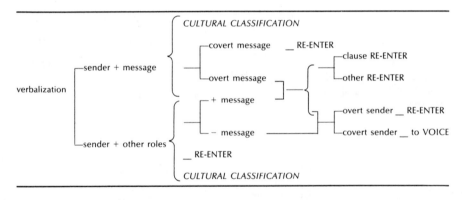

Features	Sample Realizations
[processor oriented, CULT. CLASS]	look, read, recognize, think, accept, dream, fear, know . . .
[processor oriented, processor + intent. covert phenomenon]	I stood and watched I had a closer look
[processor oriented, processor + intent. overt phenomenon, RE-ENTER clause]	We discovered that she was a good cook
[processor oriented, processor + intent. overt phenomenon, RE-ENTER other]	I discovered a fly in my coffee
[processor oriented, processor + intent. overt phenomenon, RE-ENTER other, receptive]	The fly in my coffee was discovered (by me)
[processor oriented, processor – intent. covert phenomenon]	I had a strange feeling (It was very dark) and we couldn't see
[processor oriented, processor – intent. overt phenomenon, RE-ENTER other]	Daddy knew her well enough
[phenomenon oriented, CULT-CLASS]	terrify, horrify, please, shock, impress, influence, surprise . . .

Features	Sample Realizations
[phenomenon oriented, overt phenomenon, clause]	That she really went away surprised us all
[phenomenon oriented, overt phenomenon, other]	The mere look of it shocked me
[phenomenon oriented, covert phenomenon]	Everybody was shocked
[two phenomena, clause, clause, covert processor]	That he said it means that he will do it.
[verbalization, CULT-CLASS]	say, answer, stammer, cry, comment, complain, demand . . .
[sender + message, covert message]	He never complained. She made no answer
[sender + message, overt message, RE-ENTER clause, overt sender]	Peter replied that this had been our last chance
[sender + message, overt message, RE-ENTER other, overt sender]	The government conceded defeat immediately afterwards
[sender + other roles, – message]	Nobody ever answered him
[sender + other roles, + message, RE-ENTER clause, covert sender, VOICE receptive]	He was told that he had to leave
[sender + other roles + message, RE-ENTER other, overt sender]	I told everybody the whole truth about my accident

APPENDIX III

Sample: The warden *gave his personal assurance* that
                                     the food would be perfectly healthy
TRANS.   [verbalization, sender + message, overt message, clause, overt sender]
CIRCUMST.   [manner]
THEME   [unmarked, 1st role]
INF. FOCUS   [unmarked, on process + manner (IF 2 information units)] → FVG
TYPE X[9]   [accomplishment]
synthetic version: The warden assured (s.o.) personally, that the
                                     food would be perfectly healthy
TRANS.   [verbalization, sender + other role, + message, overt message, clause, overt sender]
CIRCUMST.   [manner]
THEME   [unmarked, 1st role]
INF. FOCUS   [unmarked, on manner OR on process]

---

[9] We are at present working on the incorporation of a system network into TRANSITIVITY, which will reflect a categorization of verbs developed in Vendler 1967, and in Ikegami 1981. This categorization states that every verb is one of 4 types: Activity, Accomplishment, Achievement, State. We employ this distinction in our descriptive work, extending it to clauses instead of merely to verbs.

TYPE X^9	[accomplishment]
Sample:	Brereton *made his final announcement.*
TRANS.	[verbalization, sender + message, covert message] $\rightarrow$ FVG
CIRCUMST.	[manner]
THEME	[unmarked, 1st role]
INF. FOCUS	[unmarked, on process + manner]
TYPE X^9	[NOT activity]
synthetic version:	BRERETON *announced* something finally.
TRANS.	[verbalization, sender + message, overt message]
CIRCUMST.	[temp.]
THEME	[unmarked, 1st role]
INF. FOCUS	[unmarked, on temp.]
TYPE X^9	[achievement]

Comparison and Intensification: 10
An Ideal but Problematic Domain
for Systemic-Functional Theory

Robert Veltman
University of Kent
England

The aim of this study has been to investigate why so many instances of comparison in English are meant and taken as acts of intensification and to show that this investigation is best accomplished within the framework of Systemic-functional theory. Confusions and the scattering of intuitions largely arise from not working within a Systemic-functional framework. At the same time, the nature of the framework has to be constrained and the goals of the theory outlined so that the demands of an area of investigation are met and theory and domain suited in an 'ideal' manner. Finally, although the domain of description lies within what is traditionally known as 'grammar', the effect is to involve crucially 'discourse' characteristics in the description, namely 'phoricity' and 'entailment'. This minimizes the need to separate out grammatical and semantic perspectives.

I. The poet Dylan Thomas complained of a type of Christmas present he would receive, a book 'that told you everything about the wasp except why'. I sometimes have an analogous reaction to linguistic descriptions, especially those that purport to explain phenomena on exclusively formal bases. Systemic - functional grammar, as far as I can see, has the virtue of setting itself the more realistic and stronger goal of accounting for the properties of language in terms of their meaning potential and contexts of use.

There are two statements of intent in the literature which most characterize the aims and hence might serve as exploratory guidelines: one by Hasan (1973) to the effect that linguistic creativity is not a question of new sentences but of new meanings, and the other by Halliday that "the internal organization of language is not arbitrary but embodies a positive reflection of the functions that language has evolved to serve in the life of social man". (Halliday, in Kress 1976:25).

Assuming that these statements are valid in their own right and that they characterize the model, then non-phonological stratification in a systemic-functional grammar can only be regarded as expedient and provisional, pending some intuitive breakthrough. Thus, Halliday, in conversation with Parrett, suggests that a separate semantic structure is necessary except for "certain limited purposes" where "it has been possible to bypass the level of semantic structure and go straight into lexico-grammatical structure, as in Turner's work with children". (Halliday 1978:41).

Which approach is *theoretically* the more sound? In the light of the statements of intent quoted above, it would appear to be the approach which did not offer separate semantic and lexico-grammatical networks. I suggest therefore that there are certain 'ideal domains' for systemic-functional analysis, which are amenable to being treated semantically in the widest sense, and whose associated networks relate meanings to discourse and lexico-grammar in a relatively economical way.

The existence of 'ideal domains' presupposes the existence of 'non-ideal domains' for the theory. It seems that areas concerned with speech act (cf. Martin 1981:52), where non-biuniqueness and non-phonological stratification are routine characteristics of description, enforcing the setting up of quite distinctive sociose-mantic and lexico-grammatical networks with relatively arbitrary feature tie-ups, are examples of non-ideal domains. Here, little of interest can be captured in a unitary, unstratified network. While this mode of organization reflects and supports the important distinction to be made in adult as opposed to child's language between speech events or uses and metafunctional abstraction, it fails to meet the maximal demands embodied in Halliday's criterion of non-arbitrariness cited above.

Comparison, and its relation with intensification, at least as far as English is concerned, is for a number of reasons an 'ideal domain'. Firstly, there is an element of non-arbitrariness in the names 'comparison' and 'intensification' in contrast with other well-known grammatical terms such as 'mood' or 'subject', although even these as Halliday suggests (in Kress 1976:16) are "clearly relatable to language use" . . "the notion of a 'purely grammatical' function being absurd". Secondly, they have long been recognised as definable areas of human behaviour realized as language behaviour. Thirdly, they are associated with typical lexical and structural realizations. On these grounds alone, these areas, particularly comparison, should have merited closer attention in contemporary literature than they have received. However, their particular appeal for systemic-functional grammar is enhanced by further considerations. They each appear to have distinct metafunctional origins, comparison in the ideational component and intensification in the interpersonal component, which have their reflexes in form as well as in meaning as far as these areas are concerned. Moreover, their interrelationship seems to arise out of meta-functional contiguity and interplay, along the lines displayed between modality and modulation conceived as "the same options in different functional environments". (Halliday 1970:350). Lastly, an investigation of them reveals possibly interesting consequences for the form of a systemic-functional grammar.

I shall resume discussion with a consideration of the last-mentioned issue, raising once more the question of 'bi-uniqueness'. The functional aspects of comparison and intensification will be treated later in a description of the networks associated with comparison in particular. Comparison will serve as the focus of this study.

It would be wrong to suggest that either comparison or intensification is immune to non-biuniqueness. The notion of 'ideal domain' is a relative one and ultimately depends on the extent to which semantic options, including textual ones, and lexico-grammatical choices can be conflated and captured in single networks. Nevertheless, a contrast made between comparison, on the one hand, and, on the other, speech acts (questions, exclamations etc.) and mood (interrogative, exclamative etc.) reveals qualitative differences in the respectively associated types of non-biuniqueness. It is well known that there is no typical way of asking questions, making commands, for instance: declaratives may be used to ask questions as well as interrogatives; and to make commands as well as imperatives. Hudson, following Austin, explains this by asserting that declaratives are in a maximal sense 'illocutionarily equivocal' (Hudson 1975:3). Thus, as far as speech act/mood networks are concerned, speakers resort to different choices in the *same* network for the performance of similar acts. Now, it is a fact that comparison may, in a typical way, as the name implies, be effected by a grammatical structure known as the 'comparative' (this terminological distinction bearing superficially a close resemblance to the '-tion/-ive' oppositions in the speech act/mood networks), as well as other means: primarily of conjunction, epithet and juxtaposition of antonymous or partially synonymous lexical items or propositions. However, these choices in comparison are, for the most part, choices in *distinct* networks, or at *differing* ranks. It could be argued, therefore, that the various realizations of comparison are not bound by a narrow range of meaning potential as the realizations of the speech act/mood networks are. In respect of comparison then, the paradox brought about by absence of biuniqueness needs less urgently a stratified solution.

In English, as Halliday and Hasan show (Halliday & Hasan 1976:76–87), comparison is effected by 'general' systems, realized in 'deictic' networks, and 'particular' systems, realised in 'non-deictic' networks, if the nominal group is selected. Another illustration of the separation of meaning potentials in comparison is implicit in Martin's description of Tagalog (Martin 1981a:325–327). Martin demonstrates how Tagalog speakers may use conjunction networks for purposes of comparison, without indicating whether more specialized networks are used. Conversely, while English has a primary means of conveying comparison known as the 'comparative', comparison in English may be implicit in certain uses of conjunction. Nevertheless, implicit, conjunction-marked comparison is not comparison, as far as the semantic system of English is concerned. Halliday and Hasan (1976:323) classify comparison in English as an aspect of 'reference' but not of 'conjunction', even though they assign to conjunction an 'adversative' subcategory, which, according to Martin, is a (perhaps) defining feature of comparison in Tagalog. In many languages conjunction is indeed a major means of effecting comparison. However, as Milner suggests in his 'Fijian Grammar', processes of inference may be involved in interpreting conjunction-marked expressions conveying comparison, in that the 'bases' or contrasted propositions are "used figuratively". On the Fijian sentence 'E qase ko Malakai ka gone ko Eroni', glossed as 'Malakai is old and Eroni is young', but translated as 'Malakai is older than Eroni', Milner

---

remarks: "Malakai may in fact be a child of ten and Eroni a few months younger" (Milner 1956:29).[1] Martin, on the other hand, takes a similar structure in Tagalog, which, although he refers to it as 'comparative', he refrains from translating as the English comparative. He exemplifies the structure in the following way:

(1a) mataas si Fred   samatalang   maliit si Juan
     'tall'   'whereas'   'small'

(1b) Fred is tall whereas John is small   (Martin 1981a:326)

The English gloss/translation does not mean but may only provide grounds for inferring 2:

(2)   Fred is taller than John.

since 2 does not entail either that Fred is tall or that John is small. Although the use of adjectives as 'implicit comparatives' (cf. Ross 1970) might offer a basis for understanding 1a and b as acts of comparison (where 'tall' = 'taller than average'), Milner's remark quoted above discounts the possibility that such a mode of interpretation could have any *direct* relation to the comparative interpretation of 1a and b. It may be more strongly argued that if Tagalog has no special lexical or grammatical means for effecting comparison, then 1a may be understood in the same way as 2 is; but if 1b and 2 derive from quite separate networks, a fact that is reflected though it need not be, in their contrasting structure, then 1b cannot count in the first place as an act of comparison. While 1b could be offered status as a periphrastic form of comparison, I would hesitate to assign 'will you buy me a sandwich' the status of periphrastic request.

Halliday and Hasan's general/particular distinction is satisfactory but only within the textual perspective of reference. If other metafunctional perspectives are adopted, as will be done later, more complex relationships are perceived that cast

---

[1] Milner's main entry on 'Comparison' is on page 29:
70. COMPARISON
(a) Comparison is often indicated by using two bases which are opposites (i.e. hot and cold, big and small) in the following way:

E levu ko Suva ka lailai ko Lautoka	Suva is large and Lautoka is small (i.e. Suva is larger than Lautoka)
E qase ko Malakai ka gone ko Eroni	Malakai is old and Eroni is young (i.e. Malakai is older than Eroni).
E katakata ko Viti ka batabatā ko Toga	Fiji is hot and Tonga is cold (i.e. Fiji is hotter than Tonga).

It should be noted that in the last three examples the bases are used figuratively: Malakai may in fact be a child of ten and Eroni a few months younger.
Taken from Milner, G. B. (1956) *Fijian Grammar*. Suva.

doubt on the status of 'general' as a possible, let alone major, subcategory of comparative.

I am arguing therefore for a non-stratified approach to comparison in particular, in terms of Martin (1978), where it is suggested that "contextually neutral networks" are justified in that "stratification is motivated in the light of certain descriptive goals, and that non-formally motivated features will reflect these goals. The more general the goals, the less non-formally motivated features will be bound by situation" (Martin 1978:30). Within Martin's framework of 'first-level networks' (features formally motivated), 'second-level networks' (features non-formally motivated) and 'mediated networks' (both types of feature motivation), the last type is considered to typify 'ideal domains', since stratification is thereby minimized.

Mediated networks, however, would seem to be subject to a lack of constraint compared with first- and second- level ones. In a review of Kress (1976), I critically observed that the networks displayed in the book were inconsistent in respect of the linguistic strata to which parallel features belonged (Veltman 1979:40). This difficulty may have arisen because of a failure to distinguish between the features themselves, the criteria for their motivation, and their output. Since the primary task of networks is to generate meanings (cf. Hasan's statement on creativity), then all features are fundamentally semantic, including those features that are metalingual by nature, e.g. phoricity features. The criteria for motivating them may be either semantic or distributional, wherever these are distinguishable.

For instance, in the transitivity network (see Figs. 1 and 2), 'reciprocal' clauses are distinguished from 'non-reciprocal' clauses in that the former set has a plural or conjoined subject and *each other* as object: *They kicked each other* versus *They kicked my friend.* 'Reciprocal'/'non-reciprocal' are non-formal features but the criteria for their motivation are formal. At a more delicate stage in the same network, clauses marked 'symmetrical' are differentiated according to whether they convey an abstract notion of 'relation' or a concrete one of 'contact': *Ronnie is different from Pierre* versus *Ronnie clashed with Pierre.* This quite justifiable semantic motivation also has its reflex in form, in that if these clauses are restructured with the complement nominal group conjoining with the subject to form a thematically undifferentiated phrase (cf. Huddleston 1971:75), as in: *Ronnie and Pierre are different* and *Ronnie and Pierre clashed,* the former but not the latter is ambiguous: both have reciprocal meanings, but only the former may have as its complement an element that occurs previously in the text or extra-textually in the situation: *Maggie enjoys banquets but Ronnie and Pierre are different.*

This example of 'covert' motivation (cf. Whorf 1956, Quirk 1972) has some interesting consequences for the grammar. Firstly, it may be that when features are non-formally motivated, this motivation is supported by covert criteria of a formal character. Secondly, covert criteria are, in a sense, 'deep', relating superficially disparate items and differentiating between those that are superficially similar; they therefore have their own, peculiar semantic import. Thirdly, as Fig. 1 shows, they may be obtained through cross-referencing within the network.

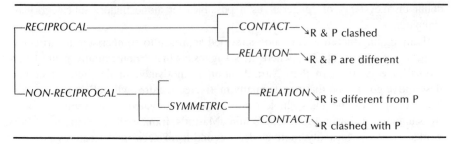

Figure 1.

Fourthly, the role of covert criteria becomes especially significant when intra-network *cross-referencing* trails lead not *across* the network between descendent nodes but *back* to a common 'root node' to which a 'root feature' is tied (cf. McCord 1975). Such *back-referencing* characterises the comparative network, where elements participating in the realization of all terminal features of the network may be traced back to the root feature 'COMPARATIVE' via a single, covert formal criterion, which will be called here 'Predeterminer Adjective Position' (henceforth PDAP) and is exemplified in 3:

(3a)   For a while the Falklands will remain *too serious a matter* to be left to Sir Bernard. (The Guardian 16.6.82)

(3b)   *For a while the Falklands will remain a too serious matter to be left to Sir Bernard.

The following items may appear in PDAP, grouping them as elements that characterize in a coextensive way the feature 'comparative': *more, -er, less, as, too, enough, sufficiently, so, that, how?,* and *however*. This characterization of the comparative seems to be less desultory and vague than descriptions I am familiar with, although grammarians' intuitions have often tended in this direction.

Fifthly, and finally, if the above items, on the grounds of PDAP, fully typify the network, does PDAP provide a basis for contrasting the whole comparative network with one or more others? The set of items known as 'intensifiers', e.g. *very, quite, somewhat, a little,* have in some respects a similar distribution to the comparative

---

[2] In Turkish, indefinite nominal groups with adjectival modification take PDAP shape. 'A hard-working man' is *çalişkan bir adam* ('hard-working - a - man'). When *bir* precedes the adjective, as in *bir çalişkan adam*, it has only a numeral function, meaning 'one' or 'a single'. I am grateful to Zsuzsa Ronay of the University of Szeged for pointing out that in colloquial, non-prescribed Hungarian PDAP is, as in Turkish, a feature of indefinite nominal groups: (olyan) erös egy ember '(so) strong a man' '(such) a strong man'. It seems that further investigation of PDAP on a cross-linguistic basis would be valuable for understanding of language typology and possibly language universals. The 'sortal' theory discussed in section V could well serve as a departure point for such an investigation.

elements listed above e.g. *John is too/very serious* and *?This carpet is too/very hexagonal* but differ in two crucial ways:
(i) They are not associated with a phrase (here called 'specification') that follows the item they *focus* on; thus: **John is serious to laugh/*John is very serious to laugh/John is too serious to laugh*. This feature does not in an obvious way cover the PDAP defined comparative elements, *that, how?* and *however;* though, as will be shown, it does cover them if considered from a 'less obvious' discourse oriented perspective.
(ii) They are never associated with PDAP, as the following versions of the text in 3 show:

(4a) For a while the Falklands will remain a very serious matter. .

(4b) *For a while the Falklands will remain very serious a matter. .

(4c) *For a while the Falklands will remain a very serious matter to be left to Sir Bernard. (confirming i)

Hence, PDAP serves to distinguish comparative expressions from intensifying ones and in so doing to distinguish the output of one network from that of the other. But if, as is about to be argued, comparison is ideational in origin and intensification interpersonal, PDAP could be assigned a theoretically enhanced role in as much as it reflects the metafunctional affiliations of two particular networks and thus contributes in an abstract way to the definition of their meaning potential. Therefore, the role of PDAP might be described as supporting the 'metafunctional integrity' of comparison and intensification, come what may in terms of context and speech event. We have, then, an initial set of reasons for regarding comparison and its relation with intensification an 'ideal domain' for the theory.

II. Intensification, then, is interpersonal in origin. It has affinities with the non-verbal, communicative dimension (cf. Abercrombie 1968:59, Lyons 1972:55) and is functionally 'expressive' rather than 'conative' (cf. Halliday 1978:48). Like comparison, it is capable of being effected by a whole variety of linguistic realizations (cf. Bolinger 1972), and is typically associated with a number of closed system items, called 'intensifiers'. As was shown above, intensifiers differ from their comparative counterparts in two fundamental ways: they do not occur in PDAP nor are they associated intrinsically with a specifying expression, since they specify self-sufficiently.
Intensification is scalar, unidimensional, relying on self-sufficient specifying devices, i.e. intensifiers, that are semantically conventional and predictable in that the 'degrees of intensity' they refer to have a predetermined sense for users of a language. Intensification includes exclamatives, such as *How tall he is!* and *How short he is!*, while for their interrogative counterparts, *How tall is he?* and *How short is he?*, only the former is decontextually acceptable, *tall* being the 'unmarked' choice in an antonymous pair. This formal distinction directly reflects a semantic

one, in that the exclamative pair entail respectively, 'he is tall'/ 'he is short', while the acceptable interrogative sentence entails no such meaning. This explains why items serving as focus of How interrogatives and comparatives refer to positive, semantically neutral, undirectional notions of size, seriousness, energy etc. Quirk et al. (1972) consider that How? interrogatives underlie comparison. Paradoxically, How exclamatives constitute a problem for the PDAP theory of comparison and intensification, since they may adopt PDAP patterning. This important issue is treated in greater detail in the final section of this paper.

Comparison is notional, rather than scalar, bidimensional and characteristically uses unconventional specifying devices. As will be shown, when specifying devices in comparison are conventional or predictable in meaning, intensification results rather than comparison.

Intensification and comparison are often confused in the literature; for instance, *too* and *so* are regularly classed as intensifiers, e.g. in Quirk et al. (1972). The intuition that confuses them is understandable, since commentators have largely been working outside the metafunctional framework of systemic-functional theory. A shared but, as shown above, limited type of environment (e.g. *He is too/very serious*) and shared restrictions on gradability of focus (e.g.? *This carpet is too/very hexagonal*) are important factors in confusing the two classes. It should be borne in mind that for speakers, from the perspective of what they want to mean in some situations, no crucial semantic distinction is discernible between comparison and intensification. Sections III and IV of this paper are concerned with this convergence. The crux of the problem seems however to be a neglect of the significance of PDAP. Whenever PDAP has been observed, its role has been looked upon as inconsequential.[3]

Campbell and Wales, criticising transformational treatments of comparison for their indifference to the semantics of the area, find comparison interesting: firstly, because it is a domain permitting access to the study of the correspondence between linguistic, logical and intellectual operations; and secondly, because comparison is essential to the classification and perception of similarities and differences between situations (Campbell & Wales 1969:215).

It would appear, then, that comparison has ideational affiliations, being con-

---

[3] For example, Lees introduces illustrates PDAP at the very end of his study, as an exceptional, surface phenomenon, as a feature of "the 'equative' (as) form of the comparative construction". (Lees 1961:184). Similarly, Huddleston (1967:101) and Campbell and Wales (1969:fn. 226) introduce examples of PDAP without examining their particular consequences. Bresnan (1973) regards PDAP as the structure underlying the comparative construction, but ignores the relationship that PDAP bears witness to, between comparison and intensification, restricting herself to the former. Moreover, her scheme, which relies heavily on *much* as a pivotal element, fails to offer a radical distinction between comparative and intensifying items, since they often have in respect of *much* similar distribution: too much (of) a coward: very much (of) a coward, *too of a coward: *very (of) a coward, enough of a coward: somewhat of a coward, *but* *enough a coward: somewhat a coward. Studies by Seuren (1973), Kuno (1981) and Klein (1982) pay virtually no attention to the PDAP phenomenon.

cerned with the speaker's representation of reality. The problem is that representation of reality itself is ultimately subjective and is open to manipulation, whether conscious or subconscious. However, while intensification is uni-dimensional, concerned with a speaker's or logical subject's feelings, impressions and immediate reactions, comparison requires, on the whole, reflection and an ability to balance one dimension of reality against another. Both intensification and comparison involve acts of specification, but intensifier specification is largely conventional and predictable in that speaker and hearer share a knowledge of a particular scale's semantic subdivisions[4] whereas comparative specification allows for *novel allocation of values*. 'Novel allocation of values' is an option in the system of Entailment, represented by the feature 'non-conventional', and if rejected the consequences are significant. For this reason, 'implicit' comparatives, such as *he is tall* (cf. Ross 1970) are not semantic comparatives, since the undeclared specification 'than average' is entirely conventional and predictable in application, hence its ellipsis. They are intensifying expressions rather.

The semantic justification, just presented, for characterizing comparison as ideational is supported by a more formal analysis.

Table 1 and the accompanying network in Fig. 2 demonstrate that Comparative clauses share features on the one hand with Relation clauses, which encode the notions of likeness and difference between entities and situations and share features with Reciprocal clauses, and with Transitive clauses on the other. Comparative clauses themselves encode, non-coextensively, the features associated with Relation clauses such as the non-acceptance of reflexives (in sentences like EV and VI, but not in sentences like *John knows someone older than himself*) and anaphoric reference when their second arguments are not realized (GIV-VI and HIV-VI).

There are other compelling reasons for associating comparison generally with transitivity and more particularly with transitive clauses. Some of the clauses in column D in Table 1 have *voice*, in the sense of having two thematically differentiated arguments that can be interchanged, moreover. This alternation of arguments may or may not result in a morphologically variant structure. With Symmetric clauses (see Table 1 col. F) there is no morphological variation: *X is similar to Y* entails and is entailed by *Y is similar to X*. With Asymmetric clauses morphological variation does occur: just as *X was seen by Y* entails and is entailed by *Y saw X*, so DVI, *John is older than Mary* entails and is entailed by *Mary is younger than John* or *Mary is not as old as John*. The comparative structure is thus seen as being

---

[4] This may not, however, always be the case. A recent discussion on school reports by James Redek (The Guardian 20.7.82), shows that it is only assumed that there exists a common manner of interpretation of conventional values attached to particular scales: "Reports . . are largely valueless because, when sent home, schools do not provide the necessary do-it-yourself seismograph which would allow parents to measure the significance to be attached to a comment in relation to whoever makes it. The word "satisfactory" is two-edged. Written by an average teacher it might mean what it says. Written by Miss Jean Brodie it would be a calculated insult, meant to provoke and offend."

Table 1. TRANSITIVITY System Network: Features (F) and Their Motivation (m). (A Selection)

A.

F. RECIPROCAL
m. arg_{-12} Thematically Undiff. $arg_{-12} \searrow$ *each other*

I	John and Mary kicked each other
II	John and Mary kissed each other
III	John and Mary talked with each other
IV	John and Mary are similar to each other
V	John and Mary are as old as each other
VI	*John and Mary are older than each other
VI!	John and Mary tried to be braver than each other.
VIII	John and Mary are opposite each other

B.

F. INHERENT
m. X *each other* $\rightarrow$ X

	↛John and Mary kicked	
	→John and Mary kissed	
	→John and Mary talked	
	→John and Mary are similar	
	↛John and Mary are as old	
	↛John and Mary are older	
	↛(see B VI)	
	↛John and Mary are opposite	

C.

F. CONTACT/RELATION
m. if F(B) and if anaphoric reading available then RELATION; if not, then CONTACT

—
CONTACT
CONTACT
RELATION
—
—
—

D.

F. NON-RECIPROCAL
m. args. 1 & 2 Thematically Diff.

I	John kicked Mary
II	John kissed Mary
III	John talked with Mary
IV	John is similar to Mary
V	John is as old as Mary
VI	John is older than Mary
VII	John is opposite Mary

E.

F. REFLEXIVE
m. arg_{-2} reflexive

I	John kicked himself
II	?John kissed himself
III	?John talked with himself
IV	*John is similar to himself
V	*John is as old as himself
VI	*John is older than himself
VII	*John is opposite himself

F.

F. SYMMETRIC
m. if F(D) (then GOALTRANSITIVE) & if not F(E) & if arg_1 X $arg_2 \rightarrow arg_2$ X arg_1, then SYMMETRIC

DI↛Mary kicked John
DII↛Mary kissed John
DIII→Mary talked with John
DIV→Mary is similar to John
DV↛Mary is as old as John
DVI↛Mary is older than John
DVII↛Mary is opposite John

	G. F. GOAL-INTRANSITIVE m. arg₂ not realised	H. F. LOGICAL m. if F(G) & anaphoric**	Terminal Features
I	John kicked	John saw Mary. ?He kicked.	The following terminal features appeal directly to the Lexicon: CONTACT, RELATION, POSITION, TRANSITIVE, NORMAL, ABNORMAL, GROOMING.
II	John kissed	John saw Mary. ?He kissed.	
III	John talked	John saw Mary. ?He talked.	COMPARATIVE appeals directly to the Lexicon if realised as 'dominate', 'outplay', 'outrun' etc.; otherwise to the Grammar, specifically 'The COMPARATIVE System Network'.
IV	John is similar	Mary likes tennis. John is similar.	
V	John is as old	Mary is thirty-two. John is as old.	
VI	John is older	Mary is thirty-two. John is older.	
VII	John dressed	John saw Mary ?He dressed.	
VIII	John is opposite	Where's John?/Mary is by the wall. John is opposite.	

**i.e., in discourse and not via arg₁.

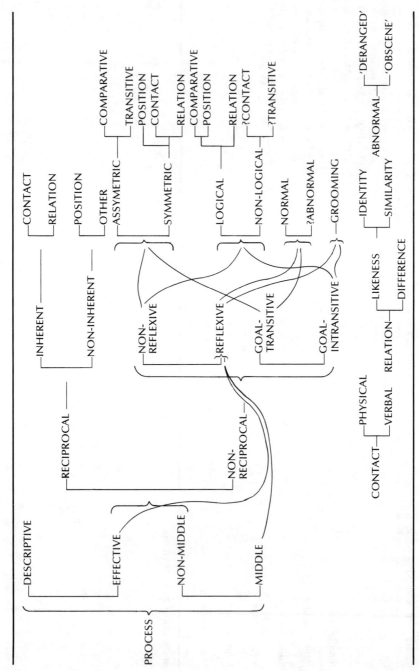

Figure 2. *TRANSITIVITY System Network*

mapped onto both operative and receptive clauses, marked respectively by active and passive verbal groups. Justification for this view is available from three sources, which are not, however, fully compatible with each other; first, it is possible that the 'unmarked'/'marked' choice between antonymous adjectival pairs, which is highlighted in comparison, including How? questions, is a reflection of the active (unmarked)/passive (marked) distinction, which the following snippet from a radio interview illustrates: ' . . . My husband is much older than I am . . (pause for reflection) . . I am much younger than my husband . . ', where *older* is unmarked. The opposition between the marked and unmarked perspectives emphasizes the condition of asymmetry that characterizes comparatives. It is, however, argued by Campbell and Wales (1969:229) that comparatives are fully analogous with clauses containing passive verbal groups, and not at all with those containing active verb forms, in that the comparative minus the specifying expression (e.g. *than John*) is equivalent to a 'short' passive. That comparatives do not readily occur with reflexives that are coreferential with a comparative topic element (c.f.col.E) lends support to this view of comparatives as short or long passives, owing to the long recognized, clause-internal incompatibility of passives and reflexives. The comparative-as-passive argument is vitiated, however, by the fact that the unrealized element in short passives is not anaphoric as the unrealized element in short comparatives is; it is rather an indefinite, quantified expression as with some goal intransitives, such as *John is eating.*

A further way of motivating the relationship between comparative structures and those of other transitive ones is prompted by Miller and Johnson-Laird's observation that $F(x,y)$ relations cannot be expanded to include three or more or n-tuple arguments (Miller & Johnson-Laird 1976:25). It was pointed out above that the comparative construction is at odds with conceptualisation, in the sense that the latter can envisage a comparison of any number of individuals, situations or entities in terms of a single common property. But the number of terms permitted in comparison is two and only two. This strange restriction is reflected more generally in transitivity patterns, and more particularly in causative constructions. It is sometimes supposed, for instance by learners, that languages with morphological causative constructions, such as Turkish and Swahili, can have three-place clauses of the following kind: *Fred caused-to-kick the donkey the wall* meaning 'Fred caused/got the donkey to kick the wall', where 'the donkey' and 'the wall' are directly represented and not obliquely, via prepositions or case-markings other than accusative. It is probable that no such language exists. . Languages like Turkish and Swahili, either use a periphrasis for three place causation, as English does, or allow the second agent, in this case 'the donkey' to appear obliquely in the equivalent of a by-phrase or an instrumental. The reason for this is that causative morphemes in such languages are built over and semantically entail stative constructions and meanings, which for the most part are one-place: the addition of the causative morpheme simply makes the construction a two-place one. Thus, in Swahili we have *punda anakimbia* 'the donkey runs' (one-place, stative) and, with the addition of the causative morpheme 'j', *Fred anamkimbiza punda* 'Fred makes the donkey run'; however two-place transitive, non-causative predicators never become three-place when made causative: *Fred amefuta alama* 'Fred erased the mark' (two-place, transitive, non-causative), *alama imefutika* 'the mark is erased' (one-place, stative) and *Fred amefutisha alama* 'Fred had the mark erased' (two-place, causative). A very small number of stative constructions are inherently two-place: e.g. *eat, see, know, have* and may occur in three-place causative constructions, having however only a 'benefactive' meaning, in which the direct object is not agentive, but affected. The construal of comparatives as two-place transitives is therefore in keeping with this apparently universal restriction on causatives.

To say that comparison is ideational in origin is not simply to state that comparative clauses encode this metafunction - that goes without saying. At clause level, where the manifestation of ideational meaning is in the system of transitivity, we find that one of the major varieties of transitive patterning is to be found in the comparative construction, just as it is to be found in reflexive clauses, and so on. Traditionally, a clause, such as 5:

(5)   John drinks more tea than coffee.

would be analyzed as: Actor *John;* Process *drinks;* Goal *more tea than coffee* (Nominal Group of mHq structure with *tea* at Head) The present perspective argues for an analysis in which *John* and *coffee* are the major clause participants and *drinks more tea than* is the process.

This constituency formula might well be described as the *semantic structure* of the clause in question, not in opposition to any putative 'syntactic' structure, such as the previous formula outlined, which would be a rather negative approach, but in recognition of the fact that networks ideally generate meanings. Nor should it be forgotten that such a semantic structure is, at least partially, formally motivated.

III. There are two sectors in the Comparative Clause network illustrated in Fig. 3 that directly concern the relation between comparison and intensification: realization, which through phoricity is derived from the textual component of language, and entailment.

A brief discussion of the less delicate features of the network is followed by a number of short texts and examples for the most part illustrative of the way choices in realization and orientation affect the relation between the network itself and intensification.

Halliday and Hasan (1976:76–87) emphasize the close links between comparison and reference (here 'phoricity'): "Likeness is a referential property . . hence comparison is a form of reference" since it encodes likeness (1976:78). What Halliday and Hasan call 'standard of reference' and I call 'specifying expression' or 'specification' is the key to the understanding of the reference system of the comparative: " . . there must be a standard of reference by which one thing is said to be superior,

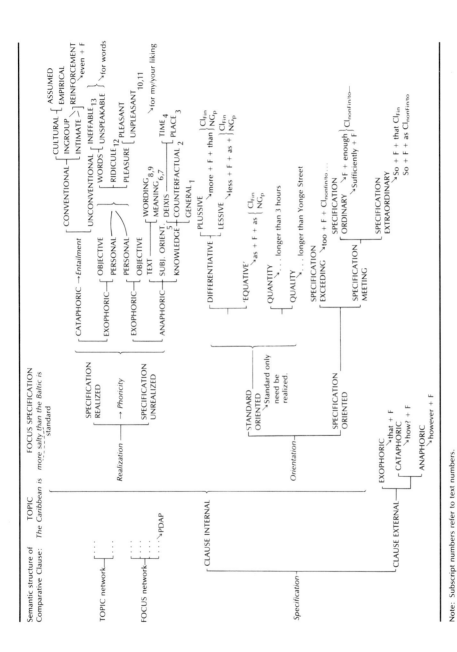

Figure 3. The COMPARATIVE System Network: 'Specification' sector.

Note: Subscript numbers refer to text numbers.

201

equal or inferior in quality or quantity'' (1976:81). Comparative reference may be 'explicit' (here, 'specification realized') as in 5 above, or 'implicit' (here, 'specification unrealized') as in 6:

(6)   We are demanding higher living standards.

The main differences between Halliday and Hasan's treatment of comparison and this one are:

a. 'general' comparison here is not comparison but a separate option of 'relation' in the Transitivity network;
b. PDAP here is introduced as a criterial formal reflex of comparison;
c. Halliday and Hasan restrict themselves to the textual characteristics of comparison. Ideational and interpersonal factors are equally important and are often highlighted by the textual component in its 'enabling' role;
d. Entailment systems are emphasized here, particularly with respect to their role in distinguishing between comparison and intensification.

A notable feature of comparison are what transformational grammarians call 'deleted' elements. These from a systemic-functional point of view are not regarded in such a negative light. As Halliday and Hasan show, absence of an element may actually perform a linguistically central, cohesive role. Hence an element, such as the specifying expression in comparatives, may or may not be realized, but should it not be realized its phoric or referential properties may well be different from those it would have were it realized. The terms *how?*, *however* and *that*, which are subject to PDAP and therefore comparative (viz. *how brilliant a scientist is she?*, *however brilliant a scientist she is, I won't marry her* and *she was that brilliant a scientist*) never occur clause internally with a specifying expression; their specification is 'clause external' and is recovered in discourse, in the form of knowledge, '*required*' in the case of *how?* and '*not required*' in the case of *however* and *that*[5] All other comparative items are associated with the potential for explicit specification. These are organized in a system of '*orientation*', depending on whether orientation is towards a '*standard*' of comparison included in the specifying expression or towards the specifying expression as a whole. Thus we may contrast 7 with 8:

(7)   John is more talkative than his sister.

(8)   John is too talkative to warrant trust.

With '*specification orientation*', the specifying expression is either fully realized or fully unrealized, while with '*standard orientation*' (7 above), partial explicitness is possible, the explicit item being the 'standard.'

---

[5] In some dialects of English *that* may be associated with a specifying expression: 'He's that much in love-he can't sleep'.

When specification is unrealized, discourse controlled anaphoric reference as well as exophoric reference dominates. When specification *is* realized, clause internal cataphoric reference as well as exophoric reference dominates.

With unrealized specification, anaphoric reference tends to be linked with standard orientation, (though not exclusively), while exophoric reference tends to go with specification orientation (manifested by such items as *too* & *so*). This particular area i.e. exophoric reference combined with specification orientation in unrealized specification, is particularly associated with intensification.

The following texts illustrate some of these relationships. The texts are numbered and correspond with the terminal features in Fig. 3 through the numbering.

TEXTS

1. Whitehall has backed subsidies for coal, acted to stop the import of *cheaper coal*, and encouraged state sector business to turn to coal for their energy needs. (The Observer 11.7.82)
2. Some of Arafat's critics within the PLO accuse him of being too much of a politician and not enough of a statesman. They think he should have been *bolder* and cut away ruthlessly from the rejectionists like Habash. (The Guardian 11.7.82)
3. It is *more advisable* to pitch the tent under the trees.
4. Women are getting *stronger*. But we're still in a transitional state, rather like the trades unions. (The Observer 11.7.82)
5. She (Severine) belatedly took up the offer of an impoverished feminist paper 'La Fronde', later going on with them to campaign for the vote for women. But it was a vicious circle. She was seen as *too committed* to the feminist cause. (The Guardian 21.7.82)
6. There is no way I would have supported the closure of the nursery - their work is *too valuable* (Adscene 17.6.82)
7. And politically? Labour has lost out. It gave *too wholehearted support* to ASLEF at the national executive. (Daily Mirror 19.6.82)
8. The Croquet association would be very happy to have you come along and watch, even *happier* to lend you a mallet so you can take part. (The Observer 18.7.82)
9. Its fascination lies with the strategy, like snooker, though there are probably *more tactical possibilities in croquet.* (The Observer 18.7.82)
10. It's all right for Mr. Benn's "bedsit brigade" to infiltrate local parties with Trotskyists; it is respectable for a far left dominating the Hemel Hempstead executive deliberately to flout the majority votes of its branches. . . But it is an evil plot for Mr. Golding to suggest that local Trade unionists turn up and vote against Mr. Benn at Bristol. If it were not *so tragic,* it would be funny. (The Times 23.7.82)
11. It's *too darn hot.* (Cole Porter)

12. Mr. Heston told delegates that Mr. Lang's "implication that the United
    States is somehow engaged in a scheme to export its culture on a planned
    basis is *so naive as to be laughable.*" (The Times 30.7.82)
13. You are *too kind.*

Examples 10-13 are cases of intensification taking a comparative form. They are
all exophoric in the sense that reference is made to the speaker's, or if interrogative,
the hearer's feelings. Example 12, where specification is realized, specification
takes the form of a relatively predictable 'print-out', expressing ridicule. Exophoric
reference is normally predictable from the circumstances prevailing at the moment
of utterance. However, the exophoric reference exemplified in 10-13 is predictable
from the feelings of the speaker, which being unuttered are categorizable over a
limited range only: specification here may relate to pleasure or displeasure, ridicule
or simply the inability to utter words, 'ineffable' for something impressive, 'un-
speakable' for something disturbing. Thus 11 could be expanded as 'It's too darn
hot *for my liking*' and 13 as 'You're too kind *for words!* . As was previously
mentioned, these expansions are recoverable in virtue of their predictability and
predictability in relation to a scale is characteristic of intensification. Furthermore,
when specification is unrealized, items such as *so, too* and *enough* are often dis-
tributionally indistinguishable from intensifiers such as *very.*

IV. When specification is realised, the cataphoric function of comparison comes
into its own, but with more interesting consequences than previous transforma-
tionally oriented treatments have revealed.

The problem of entailment in comparison was raised early on by Lees (1961) and
reconsidered by Chomsky (1965), Huddleston (1967) and Campbell and Wales
(1969) as well as others, particularly in relation to the interpretation of sentences
like:

(9)   I know a more successful lawyer than Bill.

which would obligatorily entail that Bill was a lawyer. Chomsky also noticed in this
respect the oddity of

(10)   John is sadder than this book.

where John's sadness cannot be equated with a book's sadness.

Transformational grammar (though see Campbell & Wales 1969, Hankamer
1973) has tended to represent all specifying expressions in comparatives as having
an underlying propositional structure, involving elements in the focus. Seuren
(1973) inserted a degree element and a negative element coming within the scope of
the negative one, to the effect that *John is taller Bill* is derived from' John is tall to
an extent to which Bill is NOT tall.' Seuren justifies this reading on the grounds that

in some foreign languages, e.g. French, the negative element is overt, that, diachronically, the English 'than' is 'that not' and that comparative clauses obey
similar restrictions to negative clauses; thus we have 11 but not 12:

(11) John is happier than he has ever been.

(12) *John is happier than he has never been.

But this is a general restriction affecting questions as well as negatives and comparatives. Rather than say that questions and comparatives are both underlyingly
negatives, we might say that what negatives, questions and comparatives all share is
non-entailment. *John is not tall, Is John tall?, How tall is John?* and *Mike is taller
than John,* simply, do not entail that John is tall.
    Certainly, Seuren's negative is an improvement on representations which did not
include one, thus suggesting positive entailment. It was remarked above, in criticism of a Tagalog-type treatment of comparison in English, that 1b. Fred is tall
whereas John is small is not equivalent to 2. Fred is taller than John, since the latter
does not entail that Fred is tall, nor that John is tall, nor for that matter, that John is
small or that Fred is not small. The hearer could reply to 2:

(13) . . . but neither is (what you would call) tall.

This conversational possibility is interesting because through the adversative element *but* it admits the possibility of entailing that Fred and John . . are tall. The
first speaker could of course retort:

(14) I didn't say that either of them was tall.

However, there exists a degree of asymmetry between the Topic of the comparison
in 2, *Fred,* and the Standard, *John.* Another possible rejoinder to 2 is:

(15) . . but while Fred is tall, John is not (tall).

but not:

(16) . . but while Fred is not tall, John is (tall).

This means that entailment on the topic side is rather more vague than on the
specification side. Therefore, what should be reflected in the system network, at
least initially, is the more systematic distinction to be made between the entailment
types of the standard-focus relation. Seen from this perspective, comparison is
either *'unconventional'*, the unmarked choice or *'conventional'*, the marked one. It
has already been shown that intensification has a conventional, predictable char-

acter, based on a speaker-hearer shared knowledge of points on a scale, a knowledge that covers so-called 'implicit' comparatives and, in addition, unrealized comparative specification, where a personal, exophoric element is concerned e.g. Text 11 'It's too darn hot'. This factor of convention in intensification is systematically present in certain quite common uses of comparison, where specification is realized.

The 'normal' utterance of 2 is unconventional and ideational in the sense of 'representational' or having no 'expressive' element, there being no entailment that John is tall. But if John were a well known basket-ball star, it would be entailed that John is tall and consequently that Fred is very tall. *Even* 'reinforces' this entailment:

(17)   Fred is even taller than John.

When a standard-focus relation is entailed, the specifying expression functions as an intensifier and is thus interpersonal in origin. Convention, the feature motivated by standard-focus entailment, relies on a shared reality and shared reality is the basis for social solidarity and intimacy, essentially reflected in the social system by interpersonal meaning. This intimacy could be one shared by only two individuals, the speaker and the hearer, where for 2. John is not a basket-ball star but merely a two-metre giant, the two participants happen to know. Here, *John* is not really a 'by-word' for height; but in other contexts, where John is a basket-ball player, *John* may be. For instance, among systemicists a certain scholar's networks may be a by-word for complexity, another's for simplicity, yet another's for obscurity. Thus a statement such as:

(18)   Your networks are as complex as Robin's.

could be not only a statement of fact, where it is not entailed that Robin's networks are complex, but also an 'in-group' utterance entailing that Robin's networks are indeed complex (meaning, of course, more complex than the average systemicist's), which is another way of saying in an out-group fashion 'Your networks are very complex'.

Therefore, an initial distinction may be made between intensifier-like *conventional* comparison on an *intimate,* speaker-hearer only basis and on a wider *in-group* basis, the group extending to whole linguistic or cultural communities, provided some common cultural element or element of knowledge or belief is shared.

However, these examples of intensification relying on specific types of entailment relations made available by the structure of the comparative clause, depend on 'extensive' reference or made-to-measure knowledge; that 'John is tall' or that 'Robin's networks are complex' is not either part of English or part of the cultural knowledge that many speakers of English share. . Many conventional comparisons reflect the knowledge a native speaker has of his language—not in a structural, generative sense, but in a more clearly cultural sense. In the first place, a speaker knows the attributes of institutions, artifacts and figures celebrated in the culture. Sometimes, the relationship between the institutions, artifacts and figures, and their attributes is *empirically* postulable by the speaker; at other times it is *assumed*. An example of an empirically testable convention is:

(19) He's old enough to have met Conan Doyle.

entailing that anyone who met Conan Doyle and is alive in 1985 must be ancient. Bolinger (1972:27), quoting Spitzbardt, offers the following as an example of "the free-wheeling manufacture of outlandish comparisons": 'as surely as that ewe over there will have twins this year'. The hearer will understand that a full-bellied ewe will probably have twin lambs. Tyler's example (Tyler 1978)

(20) He's as worthless as tits on a boar.

requires the hearer to know that a boar is a male pig and that male breasts have no known-to-the-layman function. Having made this series of deductions, the hearer interprets 20. as an entertaining means of saying 'he's utterly worthless'.

But what if 20 were spoken by someone who was simply repeating something he had heard, perhaps as a child, and had not the foundation of cultural knowledge to make these deductions? The worthlessness of the boar's breasts will be assumed only, the speaker knowing 20 only as a figure of speech whose impact is an intensifying one. Note that differential comparison is as effective as equative here:

(21) He's more worthless than tits on a boar.

Many similes and metaphors never achieve empirical status in the speaker-hearer's knowledge: such expressions as 'It's as plain as a pikestaff' or 'I was as pleased as Punch' or 'He's as happy as a sandboy' rely for their interpretation on unquestioned assumptions that pikestaffs are plain or that sandboys are happy without speaker-hearers' knowing what sandboys are or about their propensity for happiness. If such knowledge is or becomes available, such locutions aid and abet the construction of reality, often of an unpalatable sort, by creating stereotypes. Assumed, conventional entailments made available by the structure of comparative clauses are the essential ingredient for this. The entailment system, as 20 and 21 demonstrate, lends itself to hyperbole and hence, if the entailment is not empirically decodable, to a false view of reality. Hyperbole, of course, is a vehicle for intensification and is thus interpersonal in content.

On the other hand, 'unconventional' comparison, free as it is from entailment, permits what was referred to in Section II as 'the novel allocation of values.'

Thus theories of comparison that exclusively imply that comparison entails a standard-focus relation or that it does not are false. Both positive and non-entailment are regular characteristics of the comparative construction, their distinctiveness and analysis being best approached from a systemic-functional perspective.[6]

V. So far I have attempted to explain why comparison and its relation with intensification is an ideal domain for investigation in systemic-functional theory: both areas of meaning have distinctive metafunctional loyalties yet study of context reveals functional interplay which is reflected both formally and non-formally. I have also suggested that it may be possible to dispense with a separation of socio-semantic and lexico-grammatical networks.

It was emphasized that the key to the understanding of the relationship is PDAP, in that items typically associated with the comparative construction have a PDAP distribution that those characterizing intensifying expressions do not. It was claimed that the feature/+PDAP or/−PDAP maintained the 'metafunctional integrity' of the domains of meaning in question. Nevertheless, there are residual problems that at the moment elude solution or for which only the most tentative solutions can be offered. First, not all comparative items are automatically associated with PDAP in the appropriate environment of nominal groups with singular noun heads, introduced by the indefinite article: those that do not automatically are *enough, sufficiently; more, -er* and *less;* and *too* when negated, as in 22a–f:

(22a) a happy enough ending. .

(22b) a sufficiently effective cure. .

(22c) a more disappointing result. .

(22d) a tougher disposition. .

(22e) a less elegant proof. .

(22f) a not too ambitious plan. .

---

[6] Not all discourse approaches to comparison reach acceptable conclusions. For instance, Peter Fries (1980), in his interesting treatment of comparison from the point of view of Eugene Winter's 'comparative denial'. Fries is critical of the 'Ross-Seuren analysis', which posits a negative element in 'than' clauses, on the grounds that comparisons of 'equality' with 'as . . . . as' do not intuitively encode negation. Fries explains this by asserting that "comparisons of equality focus on similarity while comparisons of inequality focus on difference" (1980:130). I suggest that there is no deep difference between comparatives of 'inequality' with 'more . . . than' and comparatives of 'equality' with 'as . . . . as'. Fries himself points out that 'as . . . as' comparatives are restricted for negation in the specifying expression, as are 'more . . than' comparatives:

    9(ii)   Bill ran as fast as I couldn't. etc. (1980:125) Rather, the difference they encode cuts across the
          two structural types, which is one of 'entailment' versus 'non-entailment'.

Moreover, Fries' analysis tends to support a 'universal' approach to comparison, adumbrated by Martin (1981a) in his treatment of Tagalog, and pre-emptively criticised by me in Section I above, as opposed to a 'language-specific' or more properly a 'language type-specific' approach, espoused in this account, which avoids gross non-phonological stratification due to non-biuniqueness.

Secondly, *more, -er* and *less* tend to be associated with PDAP, and then not obligatorily, under negation, as 23a–d exemplify:

(23a) I have never heard a more eloquent speech than the one you gave.

(23b) I have never heard more eloquent a speech than the one you gave.

(23c) ?I have heard more eloquent a speech than the one you gave.

(23d) I have heard a more eloquent speech than the one you gave.

While a direct explanation for the data in 22 is not forthcoming, the data of 23 could be explained in terms of the equivocation of the indefinite article: in 23d it clearly has a numerative function as 'one', whereas, in 23a and b it has a 'sortal' meaning. Not only is PDAP unambiguously 'sortal' as far as the interpretation of the indefinite article is concerned, but comparison, in its unconventional, ideational, unmarked mode, is intrinsically 'sortal'. For Lyons, "A sortal classifier is one which individuates whatever it refers to in terms of the kind of entity it is." (Lyons, J. 1977:463); the article in 23d is not sortal but 'mensural'[7] Thus,

(24) This painting is expensive.

is ambiguous between the readings of 25 and 26.

(25) This painting is an expensive thing.

(26) This painting is an expensive one.

In 26 the predicated nominalization can be, further, glossed as 'expensive for a/as a/qua painting (and not relatively to all items)'. Therefore, 24 under its sortal reading 26 encodes a limitation to the relationship of entailment between the subject and its predicate. Any limitation to entailment is non-entailment, or, more accurately *suspension of entailment,* which is exactly the situation with unconventional comparative clauses, as in 27.

(27) This painting is more expensive than that one.

where neither painting is entailed as being unlimitedly expensive. Similarly, no unrestricted entailment is available in 28, which is PDAP structured and, hence sortal:

(28) This is too expensive a painting for the museum to purchase.

---

[7] The Turkish phenomenon outlined in note 2 above reflects this distinction:
article - adjective - noun head is *mensural* (bir çalişkan adam)
adjective - article - noun head is *sortal* (çalişkan bir adam)

(the museum having enough funds to buy a different sort of object for the same price as that at which the painting was being offered)

This attempt at a semantic explanation of PDAP has, once again, involved the notion of entailment, which as a factor in identifying and interrelating comparison and intensification, seems to be a worthy semantic counterpart to PDAP itself. *How?* interrogative clauses and *How!* exclamative clauses are ultimately distinguished in the clause mood system, the latter sharing SP structure with declarative clauses. They also contrast in terms of entailment: the former suspends entailment, since 'knowledge is required'; the latter depends on entailment for interpretation. Contrast 29 with 30:

(29)   How long was the journey?

(30)   How long the journey was!

Another point of contrast, which raises problems, is that while interrogative and exclamative clauses encode an interpersonal element through membership of the mood system, this description emphasizes the ideational nature of interrogatives in that these are a type of comparative and hence ultimately associated with the transitivity network. Provisionally, it may be suggested that How? interrogatives are 'relatively' ideational compared to How! exclamatives. This is one problem that I will not treat here. However, the fact remains that How! exclamatives are associated with PDAP, as in 31 and 32:

(31)   How long a journey it was!

(32)   John told me how long a journey it was.

Note that 32 is ambiguous between an exclamative meaning ('John was impressed at the great length of the journey') and a declarative meaning ('John told me the length of the journey'). 33 is not ambiguous:

(33)   John asked me how long a journey it was.

where, despite the SP structure characteristic of subordinate clauses, only an interrogative meaning is available.

Two lines of argument are available. The first is that both independent and dependent How! exclamative PDAP clauses are somehow marked and unusual in comparison with their what! exclamative counterparts, whereas How non-exclamatives are quite natural and have no unmarked 'rival'. Therefore, How! exclamative PDAP clauses are to be excluded from the data and do not constitute counterevidence to the theory. But this is a rather arbitrary and negative approach, out of keeping with the spirit of systemic-functional grammar. A more consistent approach is to make the following observations.

Since comparison may serve as a vehicle for intensification when a standard-focus relation is entailed, then it comes as no surprise that a particular comparative form *How,* if involved positively in the system of entailment should function as an intensifier. The difference though between interrogative and exclamative manifestations of How clauses, on the one hand, and unconventional comparatives, on the other, is that for the latter the entailment-suspension of entailment contrast was largely a covert one (apart from 'even' reinforcement), while for *How* clauses it is overt, except in certain subordinate clauses, where depending on the main predicator, the distinction is neutralized in declarative order. Thus, the association of How! exclamatives with PDAP is not prejudicial to the theory and, in fact, can be absorbed by it. The reason why *very,* and other intensifiers apart from *How!* do not appear in PDAP, is that they lack the polysemous properties of *How* that straddle the boundaries of entailment and metafunction.

CONCLUSION

If a model of language is to be interpreted in the way suggested by Malinowski and others (see Kress 1976:vii-xxi) as a 'mode of action', as a system that generates meanings (Hasan 1973) and as a non-arbitrary reflection of human social development (Kress 1976), then there is every case for integrating meanings and the forms they correspond with in single networks; features being semantic and their motivation semantic or distributional. The analogue of stratification in systemic-functional theory is a more interesting and dynamic mode of organization, that of metafunctional discreteness and interplay: the superficially apparent finiteness of a language's resources allows for the human attribute of equivocation, attainable when metafunctions interact in similar domains.

The investigation of comparison and its relation with intensification in English is able to interpret this view of systemic-functional linguistics in a relatively uncomplicated, 'ideal' way, provided the representation respects metafunctional discreteness and integrity, characterized at root or least delicate level by PDAP and, more delicately, by metafunctional interplay involving discourse typifying systems of phoricity and entailment.

REFERENCES

Abcrcrombie, D. (1968). Paralanguage. *British Journal of Disorders of Communication* 3. 55–59.
Bolinger, D. (1972). *Degree Words.* The Hague: Mouton.
Bresnan, J. (1973). Syntax of the comparative clause construction in English. *Linguistic Inquiry* 4. 275–343.
Campbell, R. N. & Wales, R. J. (1969). Comparative structures in English *Journal of Linguistics* 5. 215–251.
Chomsky, N. (1965). *Aspects of the Theory of Syntax.* Cambridge, MA: MIT Press.
Fries, P. H. (1980). On negation in comparative constructions. In Blansitt, E. L. & Teschner, R. (eds.), *Festschrift for Jacob Ornstein: Studies in General Linguistics and Sociolinguistics.* Rowley, MA: Newbury House Publishers, pp. 120–133.

Halliday, M. A. K. (1970). Functional diversity in language, as seen from a consideration of modality and mood in English. *Foundations of Language* **6**. 323–361.

Halliday, M. A. K. (1976). The form of a functional grammar. In Kress, G. R. (ed.), *Halliday: System and Function in Language*. London: Oxford University Press. pp. 7–25.

Halliday, M. A. K. (1978). *Language as Social Semiotic*. London: Edward Arnold.

Halliday, M. A. K. & Hasan, R. (1976). *Cohesion in English*. London: Longman.

Halliday, M. A. K. & Martin, J. R. (eds.) (1981). *Readings in Systemic Linguistics*. London: Batsford.

Hankamer, J. (1973). Why there are two than's in English. *Papers of the Chicago Linguistic Society* **9**. 179–192.

Hasan, R. (1973). Code, register and social dialect. In Bernstein, B. (ed.) *Class, Codes and Control* **2**. London: Routledge & Kegan Paul.

Hinde, R. A. (ed.) (1972). *Non-Verbal Communication*. London & New York: Cambridge University Press.

Huddleston, R. (1967). More on the English comparative. *Journal of Linguistics* **3**. 91–102.

Huddleston, R. (1971). *The Sentence in Written English*. London & New York: C.U.P.

Hudson, R. A. (1975). The meaning of questions. *Language* **51**. 1–31.

Klein, E. (1982). The interpretation of adjectival comparatives. *Journal of Linguistics* 113–136.

Kress, G. R. (ed.). (1976). *Halliday: System and Function in Language*. London: Oxford University Press.

Kuno, S. (1981). The Syntax of comparative clauses. *Papers of the Chicago Linguistics Society* **17**. 136–155.

Lees, R. B. (1961). The grammatical analysis of the English comparative construction. *Word* **17**. 171–185.

Lyons, J. (1972). Human language. In Hinde, R. A. (ed.), *Non-Verbal Communication*. London & New York: Cambridge University Press. pp. 49–85.

Lyons, J. (1977). *Semantics* **Vol. II**. London, New York & Melbourne: Cambridge University Press.

Martin, J. R. (1978). The meaning of features in systemic linguistics. University of Sydney mimeograph.

Martin, J. R. (1981a). Conjunction and continuity in Tagalog. In Halliday, M. A. K. & Martin, J. R. (eds.), *Readings in Systemic Linguistics*. London: Batsford. pp. 310–336.

Martin, J. R. (1981b). How many speech acts? *University of East Anglia Papers in Linguistics*, **15–16**, 52–77.

McCord, M. C. (1975). On the form of a systemic grammar. *Journal of Linguistics* **11**, 195–212.

Milner, G. B. (1956). *Fijian Grammar*. Suva: Fiji Government Printing Department.

Miller, G. A. and Johnson-Laird, P. N. (1976). *Language and Perception*. Cambridge, MA: Harvard University Press; London: Cambridge University Press.

Quirk, R. Greenbaum, S., Leech, G., & Svartvik, J. (1972). *A Grammar of Contemporary English*. London: Longman.

Ross, J. R. (1970). A note on implicit comparatives. *Linguistic Inquiry* **1**. 363–366.

Seuren, P. A. M. (1973). The comparative. In Kiefer, F. & Ruwet, N. (eds.), *Generative Grammar in Europe*, Dordrecht, Netherlands: Reidel.

Tyler, S. A. (1978). *The Said and the Unsaid*. New York: Academic Press.

Veltman, R. (1979). Review of Kress. *Journal of Literary Semantics*. **8.1**. 36–41.

Whorf, B. L. (1956). Grammatical categories. In Carroll, J. B. (ed.), *Language, Thought and Reality: Selected Writings of Benjamin Lee Whorf*. New York: Wiley. 87–101.

Discourse Systems and Structures and their Place within an Overall Systemic Model

11

Christopher S. Butler
University of Nottingham
England

1. INTRODUCTION

Since the publication of Sinclair & Coulthard's important work on classroom discourse (Sinclair & Coulthard 1975), there has been a remarkable upsurge of interest in the analysis of spoken discourse. Sinclair & Coulthard's model was explicitly Hallidayan in orientation, taking as its organizational basis the Scale and Category model proposed by Halliday for the grammatical level (Halliday 1961). It is therefore perhaps not surprising that much of the work which has flowed from Sinclair & Coulthard's original proposals has been carried out by linguists working within, or sympathetic to, a systemic framework (see, for example, the papers in Coulthard & Montgomery 1981, especially the contribution by Berry (1981a)).

The purpose of the present paper is to re-examine work carried out within the Sinclair & Coulthard framework, concentrating on two issues which seem to me not to have received the detailed attention they deserve.

The first section will present a view of the place of discourse within an overall systemic model: more specifically, I shall deal with the relationship between discourse and semantics, syntax and speech acts. Since I have discussed this area in detail elsewhere (Butler 1982, forthcoming), only a brief summary, without full argumentation, will be presented here.

The second, and major, part of the paper starts out from the observation that although discourse analysts have provided stimulating accounts of syntagmatic patterning in discourse, work on paradigmatic aspects is scanty. Such work would, however, allow us to see the discourse features of particular stretches of language against the background of contrasting features, an approach which is especially useful if we wish to compare the use made of discourse resources in different social contexts. I outline a model, based on the daughter dependency model proposed for syntax by Hudson (1976, 1978), in which systemic features are linked to discourse structure by means of explicit realization rules. The work of Sinclair & Coulthard (1975), and of Burton (1978, 1980, 1981) on dramatic and conversational texts, is then amended, extended and formalized in terms of the model proposed.

213

Because of the limitations of space, I shall not attempt a full account of discourse systems and structures here, but shall illustrate from the area of directive interactions, viz. those whose communicative function is to secure non-verbal action on the part of the addressee.

2. THE PLACE OF DISCOURSE WITHIN AN OVERALL SYSTEMIC MODEL

2.1 Communicative Function and Semantics

A crucial question for the discourse analyst is whether the communicative function of an utterance can be accounted for within the familiar domain of syntax and semantics, or whether instead a new level of linguistic description is needed. (I shall use the purposely vague term 'communicative function' for the time being: its nature will, I hope, become clear later.) Sinclair & Coulthard (1975:23) assume provisionally that a separate level is indeed necessary. Elsewhere (Butler 1982, forthcoming) I have argued in detail for the correctness of this position. Briefly, there is a considerable weight of evidence in favour of the view that the only aspects of communicative function which should be accounted for within the semantics are those which are interpretable directly from the form of the sentence uttered. Thus 1 below is, semantically, a question, and 2 a statement, irrespective of whether they are actually being used, in a discourse context, to ask a question and make a statement, or as indirect requests.

    (1)   Can you move that table?

    (2)   That table's in the way.

Among other systemic linguists who have published in this area, only Hudson (1975) takes this position. Fawcett (1980) takes the view espoused in the (non-systemic) work of Sadock (1974), namely that 1 can be semantically a request, whereas 2 is always a statement, however used. Martin (1981) also regards the potentially requestive nature of 1 as a semantic matter, but claims that directive uses of sentences such as 2 are too rare in texts to warrant setting up a separate level. The position of Halliday (1984) is rather unclear: he presents a model in which 'social-contextual' categories such as 'demanding/ goods and services' are reinterpreted in terms of 'semantic' categories including 'command', 'question' and 'statement', but since his categories are not defined, it is difficult to know how 1 and 2 would be analyzed. A full critique of these approaches can be found in Butler (1982, forthcoming): in what follows, I shall assume the correctness of the view that the semantics contains a specification of only those properties of sentences which can be related in a direct (though not always one-to-one) way to syntactic properties such as mood, modalization, etc. As we shall see later, such a view allows us to propose just one set of mechanisms for the interpretation of indirect speech acts.

2.2 Discourse Analysis and Speech Act Theory

The question which now arises is how, if at all, the nonsemantic aspects of communicative function can be accounted for within a linguistic theory. When serious work on discourse structure began in the 1970s, one framework for the analysis of communicative function was already available: speech act theory, as propounded by Austin (1962) and Searle (1969) provided a model which stimulated a number of important attempts to deal with communicative function, and especially the problem of indirect speech acts, within an extension of the current syntactic and semantic models (see, for example, Gordon & Lakoff 1971, Heringer 1972, Davison 1975, Green 1973, Lee 1974, Sadock 1974). And yet Sinclair & Coulthard saw little in this considerable body of work which was of relevance to their concerns. The reason was that speech act accounts of communicative function dealt largely in terms of utterances isolated from their discourse context, and so paid little or no attention to the ways in which utterances fit together to form a coherent discourse. Putting it another way, most speech act accounts fail to make any predictions about the possible co-occurrence and sequencing restrictions which are shown in discourse. The work of Sinclair & Coulthard and their colleagues, and also that of Labov (Labov 1970/1972a, Labov & Fanshel 1977) can be seen as an attempt to specify these syntagmatic relations. In the words of Labov (1970/1972a, p. 252 in the 1972 version), "the fundamental problem of discourse analysis is to show how one utterance follows another in a rational, rule-governed manner - in other words, how we understand coherent discourse".

Despite Sinclair & Coulthard's rejection of the speech act approach, (see also Coulthard 1975:75) certain of the categories they propose do, in fact, correspond closely to the illocutionary properties of speech acts discussed by Austin (1962). Sinclair & Coulthard distinguish three types of category: discourse (e.g. informative, elicitation, directive), situational (e.g. statement, question, command) and grammatical (e.g. declarative, interrogative, imperative). Discourse categories are defined in terms of the expectations set up in the structure of discourse: for instance, a directive predicts a following non-verbal action. Since grammatical information is not, by itself, sufficient to determine the discourse function of a given utterance, the utterance must first be tagged with situational information. Although Sinclair & Coulthard do not themselves relate their categories to speech act theory, their discussion of 'situational' categories such as 'command' makes it clear that they are basically illocutionary, in that they relate to what Searle (1976) has called 'illocutionary point', e.g. to get the hearer to do something. However, an utterance with given illocutionary properties may serve any of several discourse functions: for instance, a 'command' is, in discourse terms, a 'directive' only if it is acting as the head of a move whose primary function is to get the hearer to perform a non-verbal action; commands can also be put to other discourse uses, for instance as 'clues' to help pupils in the classroom towards an appropriate response to a teacher's elicitation. A full discussion, with exemplification, can be found in Butler (1982). Edmondson (1981), working towards a rather different framework, comes to a similar conclusion.

2.3 The Interpretation of Utterances in Discourse

We saw above that illocutionary categories (Sinclair & Coulthard's 'situational' categories) are more general than discourse categories, in that one illocutionary category can correspond to a number of different classes of discourse act, defined by their positional and predictive properties. I now wish to propose that the illocutionary properties of utterances form an intermediate stage in the interpretation of connected discourse. This interpretation mechanism is viewed as part of the linguistic system: it is not, at least at this stage, being claimed that it represents the actual sequence of psycholinguistic operations performed by the hearer.

Part of the input to the interpretation device is a semantic specification of the sentence uttered, which is in turn derived from the lexicosyntactic form of the sentence. Note that this is an important departure from the account given by Sinclair & Coulthard: the latter attempt to relate discourse, via situational categories, directly to form, without going through any semantic specification. Consider the following rule of interpretation, proposed by Sinclair & Coulthard to account for the potential mismatching of formal and situational categorization:

> An interrogative clause is to be interpreted as a *command to do* if it fulfils all the following conditions:
>
> (i) it contains one of the modals *can, could, will, would* (and sometimes *going to*);
> (ii) if the subject of the clause is also the addressee;
> (iii) the predicate describes an action which is physically possible at the time of the utterance. (Sinclair & Coulthard 1975:32)

Such a rule, however, fails to explain why *can, could, will, would,* but not, for example, *may* or *might,* can signal that the utterance is to be interpreted directively. In order to do this, we must examine the meanings of the modals concerned. Further, Sinclair & Coulthard's correlation of function with lexicosyntactic categories is unable to account for the ways in which various modalized directives pattern with respect to the social context. As I have shown elsewhere (Butler 1982), the acceptability of certain combinations of modal verb and mood, and the unacceptability of others, also the relative politeness of acceptable modalized directives in a particular social context, are predictable, not from the form of the directives, but from the meanings associated with particular modals and mood categories. The rules of interpretation given by Labov (Labov 1970/1972a, 1972b; Labov & Fanshel 1977) are superior to Sinclair & Coulthard's rules in this respect, since they make reference to semantic categories such as ability and willingness, rather than to forms as such.

Unfortunately, neither Sinclair & Coulthard nor Labov discuss a mechanism by which formal or semantic information can be reinterpreted in 'situational' or illocutionary terms. This is, of course, precisely what can be achieved by means of general conversational rules of the type proposed by Grice (1975, 1978), extended to cover the deduction of one apparent illocutionary force from another, rather than simply the deduction of an implied propositional content. The application of such an extension of Grice's rules to the interpretation of an indirect speech act is discussed in detail by Searle (1975).

As will be apparent from our earlier discussion, however, the deduction of illocutionary force (or, more realistically, of a probabilistically weighted range of possible illocutionary forces) for an utterance is not the end of the interpretation process. The final stage consists of an examination of the position of the utterance in the discourse: if, for instance, a 'command' or 'request' is the only act in its move, or if it is accompanied only by acts with subsidiary function, and if it is followed by a non-verbal action, or a stretch of discourse which makes it clear that such a response was expected, then the 'command' is acting as a discourse directive.

3. SYSTEM AND STRUCTURE AT THE DISCOURSE LEVEL: A REINTERPRETATION AND FORMALIZATION OF THE SINCLAIR & COULTHARD APPROACH

3.1 Syntagmatic and Paradigmatic Relations

Sinclair & Coulthard's model concentrates on syntagmatic relations is discourse, and this is understandable, for two reasons. Firstly, as we have seen, the main drawback of speech act theory was precisely its failure to predict restrictions on the syntagmatic patterning of discourse. Secondly, Halliday's Scale and Category model, on which Sinclair & Coulthard's work was based, in fact paid more attention to syntagmatic than to paradigmatic relations, although 'system' was theoretically held to be just as important a category as 'structure'. In later versions of systemic theory, however, paradigmatic relations, as formalized in system networks, have assumed a more prominent position (see e.g. Halliday 1978:40). The systemic features of any given stretch of language at a particular linguistic level can be viewed against the background of the features which contrast with those actually selected. Such a perspective is particularly useful if we wish to compare different varieties of a language, which may make statistically selective use of particular features or sets of features. The often quoted high proportion of passive, as against active, clauses in some kinds of technical English is one elementary illustration. The selection of certain kinds of semantic feature correlating with the degree of politeness being signalled in an interaction is another example, with which my own work has been concerned.

What I am suggesting, then, is that it may be desirable and useful to develop a model of discourse, parallel to, and realizationally related to, models of semantic and syntactic organization, in which paradigmatic relations, formulated as system networks, are the generative base, and are related, by explicit realization rules, to structures representing the permissible syntagmatic relationships between discourse items.

A concern with the paradigmatic relations of discourse would seem to underlie Halliday's (1984) proposal for a 'social-contextual' network: we have seen, however, that this account is unsatisfactory in a number of important ways. Berry (1981b) has also presented a preliminary sketch of networks and realization rules for the structure of directive exchanges. Her account, however, is intended merely as a pointer to possible developments, and does not claim, at this stage, to generate full discourse structures in terms of the component acts, or to account for all possible types of directive exchange. Furthermore, the specific goals of Berry's inquiry (to relate co-occurrence and sequencing restrictions in discourse, not only to formal properties, but also to the roles taken up by participants in the discourse) make it fruitless to compare her work with any proposal which does not have these particular aims in view.

The model I shall propose here arose out of my attempts to account for the interpretation of certain types of utterance as potentially directive in function, and for the correlation of meaning (and ultimately form) with social properties of directives, and in particular with their relative politeness in a given social situation (see Butler 1982). This attempt necessitated the construction of a model in which systemic and structural relations at the syntactic, semantic and discourse levels could all be specified, the levels being linked by mapping rules sensitive to social contextual features. Hudson's daughter dependency grammar (Hudson 1976, 1978) was chosen as the most comprehensive and explicit account of systemic syntax to date; further, it was found that patterning at the levels of semantics and discourse could also be described in terms of the theory, with only minor modifications. In the remainder of this paper I shall show how, for the area of directive discourse function, a model of the Sinclair & Coulthard type can be improved upon and formalized within a daughter dependency framework.

3.2 The Model: A Brief Sketch

As in Hudson's proposals for daughter dependency syntax, discourse items are sub- and cross-classified by means of a set of 'classification rules', which can be represented in the form of a system network, with no formal distinction between 'categories' such as act, move, etc., and 'features' such as directive.

A selection expression for the highest discourse unit is built up from the network, and acts as input to a set of realization rules. Only three of the six types of rule proposed by Hudson for syntax are needed at the discourse level: daughter dependency, sister dependency and sequence rules. Daughter dependency rules are used to introduce those daughters (constituents) which have features depending directly on those of the mother (constitute): they generate all 'head' elements, and those non-head elements whose features are determined by those of the mother. Any non-head constituents whose properties depend on those of the head, rather than those of the mother, are introduced by means of sister dependency rules. (For further discussion of the use of daughter and sister dependency rules see Schachter 1980:282.) Between them, these two kinds of dependency rule introduce features of each constituent of the unit whose selection expression is being realized. They do not, however, specify the ordering of the features: this is the function of the sequence rules.

Not all of the features of the constituents will have been specified by the dependency rules: we therefore return to the system network, entering it at the point corresponding to the constituent concerned. The process of classification and realization is repeated, in a cyclic fashion, until the whole structure, consisting of discourse acts in a particular configuration, has been generated.

This is the end-product of the discourse rules; discourse/semantics mapping rules (not discussed here, but see Butler 1982) then specify the possible mappings of discourse acts on to their semantic realizations, these being differentiated in social contextual terms.

3.3 Partial Networks for Directive Discourse Function

The networks presented here are based on an amended and extended version of Burton's (1978, 1980, 1981) account of discourse patterning in dramatic and conversational texts, which, although keeping quite closely to Sinclair & Coulthard's original proposals, is of more general application than the original classroom-based work.

3.3.1 Primary Classification
The least delicate classes of discourse item are the unit labels act, move, exchange, transaction and interaction:

3.3.2 The Classification of Exchanges
Burton recognises two classes of exchange: boundary exchanges mark the transition points between transactions, and will not be considered further here, since they cannot contain directives; conversational exchanges form the main body of a transaction. We thus have a simple system:

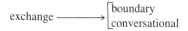

3.3.3 The Classification of Moves
Burton proposes seven classes of move. Framing and focusing moves are constituents of boundary exchanges, and will not be discussed further here. Normal opening

moves constitute the first speaker's contribution to a conversational exchange; bound-opening moves expand the original opening by means of additional, closely bound material; re-opening moves occur after a preceding opening (normal, bound- or re-opening) has been challenged. Supporting moves fulfil the expectations of the preceding opening move by, for example, giving a reply in response to an elicitation, or performing a non-verbal action in response to a directive. Challenging moves present a disruption to the discourse, in that they fail to fulfil the expectations set up by the preceding opening. These five classes of move, which we shall need to discuss below in relation to directive function, are illustrated below by part of a transaction in Burton's data from Pinter's *The Dumb Waiter:*

(3)	Ben:	A child of 8 killed a cat.	Opening
	Gus:	Get away.	Supporting
	Ben:	It's a fact. What about that eh? A child of 8 killing a cat.	Supporting
	Gus:	How did he do it?	Bound-opening
	Ben:	It was a girl.	Challenge
	Gus:	How did she do it?	Re-opening
	Ben:	She—	Supporting
		It doesn't say.	Challenging
	Gus:	Why not?	Challenging
	Ben:	Wait a minute.	Challenging

Both Sinclair & Coulthard (1975:36) and Burton (1980:149) recognize that there is a predictive relationship between the kind of opening (including bound- and re-opening) or (in the case of Burton's analysis) challenging move, and the kind of supporting move which may follow. For instance, if the first speaker produces an opening move with a directive as its head act, the second speaker is expected to provide a supporting move with a non-verbal reaction to that directive as its own head. Other pairings are: informative/acknowledge, elicitation/reply, and (in Burton's analysis) accuse/excuse. The 'rules' given by Sinclair & Coulthard and by Burton, however, make no provision for the formal specification of such pairings. This problem can be overcome by cross-classifying opening and challenging moves as informing, eliciting, directing or accusing, and supporting moves as acknowledging, replying, reacting or excusing, and then ensuring that the realization rules give the correct sister dependency relations in generating the structure of the exchange. Since normal openings, bound-openings, re-openings and challenging moves all need to be cross-classified in the same way, we are justified in setting up a cover feature, [initiating], to include them all. Summarizing the position with respect to directives, then, we may say that [directing] is a sub-class of [initiating] move, contrasting with [informing], [eliciting] and [accusing]. [Directing] moves can be cross-classified as [normal opening], [bound-opening], [re-opening] or [challenging]. These relationships are shown in network form below.

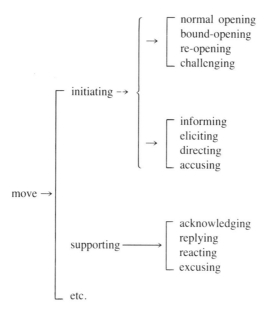

3.3.4 The Classification of Acts

Burton proposes 19 individual classes of act, many of which are taken over from Sinclair & Coulthard's account. In formulating a description of the paradigmatic relations among these act classes, one question which arises is whether we can justifiably group the 19 act types into larger classes. It would seem that such a grouping is justified, on two grounds: firstly, certain sets of acts will need to be referred to together in the realization rules; and secondly, the members of these sets of acts show functional similarities. For instance, we shall need to say that the act classes [directive], [informative], [elicitation] and [accuse] behave as a single set in the sequence rule which generates the correct ordering of acts in move structure. Furthermore, these four act classes show a functional similarity in that they carry the main topic of the exchange. We therefore recognize a super-class of act, [topic-bearing], covering the four types. Similarly, we recognize a class [responsive], which subsumes [react], [acknowledge], [reply] and [excuse]. Further groupings of acts which can be justified in a similar way, and which we shall need to refer to in discussing the structure of directing and reacting moves in Section 3.4.2, are as follows:

[preparatory] ⎡ [starter]— directing attention towards some area in order to fa-
               cilitate the hearer's response to a coming initiation.
           ⎣ [preface]— signalling reintroduction of a diverted topic, or an
               interruption, or a personal viewpoint on what is to
               come.

[reinforcing]   [comment]—expands, justifies or provides additional information
                          to, a preceding informative or comment.
                [prompt]—   reinforces a preceding directive or elicitation.
[pre-topic]   [marker]—   signals a discourse boundary, and shows speaker has
                          a topic to introduce.
                [summons]—indicates speaker wants to get hearer's attention in
                          order to introduce a topic.

We shall also need to refer to two classes of act which do not form part of any larger
sub-group:

[accept]—   indicates understanding of the previous utterance, and willingness to
            comply with discourse expectations.
[evaluate]—comments on appropriateness of preceding utterance.

Examples of the various classes of act mentioned above, as found in association
with directives, are given below. The examples are constructed, unless otherwise
specified.

(4)	(from Sinclair & Coulthard 1975:76)		
	Teacher:	These three then are for you to sort out for yourselves.	(starter)
		Can you translate can you be an Egyptologist and translate the names from this chart.	(directive)
(5)	Committee member:	My position is this.	(preface)
		Let's decide right now what we're going to do.	(directive)
(6)	(from Burton 1980:164)		
	Ben:	Well make the tea then will you.	(directive)
		Time's getting on.	(comment)
(7)	A.	Pass me that chisel, will you.	(directive)
		Come on!	(prompt)
	B.	OK.	(accept)
		(passes chisel)	(react)
(8)	A.	Now,	(marker)
		can you just pass me that chisel?	(directive)
	B.	(passes chisel)	(react)
(9)	A.	John,	(summons)
		can you just pass me that chisel?	(directive)
	B.	(passes chisel)	(react)
(10)	A.	Close the window, will you.	(directive)
	B.	You're right, it is a bit cold.	(evaluate)
		(closes window)	(react)

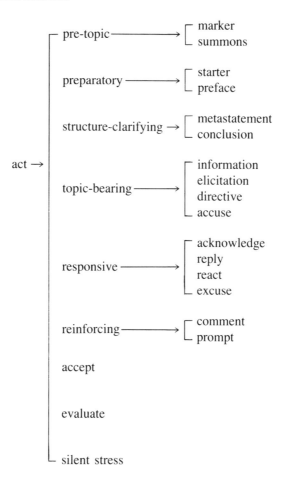

3.4 From System to Structure: Realization Rules

I shall now illustrate, from the area of directive function, the three types of realization rule which take us from the system network to well-formed discourse structures. Since Sinclair & Coulthard, and also Burton, were working within an essentially Scale and Category model, the structures they proposed consist of 'elements', which are distinct from the classes of item which can realize these elements. Within a daughter dependency framework, our structures will consist merely of sets of features on nodes with particular relations of constituency, dependency and sequence. We shall start with the 'largest' discourse unit to be considered here, the exchange, and work 'downwards'.

3.4.1 Generating the Structure of Conversational Exchanges

Burton's structural formula for a conversational exchange is $I(R(I^r(R)^n)^n)^n$: there is an obligatory I element, realized by an opening, re-opening or challenging move, followed optionally by one or more supporting moves realizing the R element(s). An optional I^r element, realized by a bound-opening move, may follow, and may be further supported. We may introduce the obligatory daughter of a conversational exchange by the following daughter dependency rule:

DD1

conversational $\longrightarrow$ $\left\{ \begin{array}{l} \text{normal opening} \\ \text{re-opening} \\ \text{challenging} \end{array} \right\}$

where $\longrightarrow$ (*on* the line) shows a daughter dependency relation, and curly braces enclose alternatives. When rules for transaction structure have been properly worked out, it will have to be shown that the first conversational exchange in a transaction must start with a [normal opening] move.

The supporting move which may follow an initiating move must be introduced by a sister dependency rule, since the subclass of supporting move permitted depends on the sub-class of initiating move, not on the mother feature [conversational]. The relevant rule for a [directing] initiating move is as follows ($\longrightarrow$, *above* the line, indicates a sister dependency rule):

SD1$_{optional}$ directing $\overset{\rightarrow}{}$ reacting

A bound-opening move can be present only if there is a supporting move as sister. We therefore introduce it by means of an optional sister dependency rule:

SD2$_{optional}$ supporting $\overset{\rightarrow}{}$ bound-opening

The following rule, which can provide support for the bound-opening, forms a loop with SD2:

SD3$_{optional}$ bound-opening $\overset{\rightarrow}{}$ supporting

The sequence of moves in a conversational exchange is given by the following sequence rules:

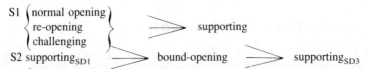

S1 $\left\{ \begin{array}{l} \text{normal opening} \\ \text{re-opening} \\ \text{challenging} \end{array} \right\}$ $\Longrightarrow$ supporting

S2 supporting$_{SD1}$ $\Longrightarrow$ bound-opening $\Longrightarrow$ supporting$_{SD3}$

Here, $\Longrightarrow$ means 'precedes', and the subscript differentiates between two occurrences of [supporting], according to which rule they are mentioned in.

3.4.2 Generating the Structure of Directing and Reacting Moves
Amending Burton's scheme slightly to allow for the intuitively correct possibility of prefaces in normal opening moves, as well as in bound- and re-opening moves and challenges, we may state the structure of directing moves, in Burton's terms, as follows:

(pre-head)	head	(post-head)
starter *or* preface	directive	comment *or* prompt

Additionally, a normal opening move may have an optional 'signal' element, realized by a marker or summons (that is, by our [pre-topic] class).

The presence of a [directive] depends on the feature [directing] on the mother move; we therefore introduce it by means of a daughter dependency rule (parallel rules apply to informing, eliciting and accusing moves).

DD2 directing $\rightarrow$ directive

Directives, like other sub-classes of [topic-bearing] act, can be optionally preceded by a [preparatory] act, and followed by a [reinforcing] act. Since there is no other class of move in which *either* [marker] *or* [summons] can occur, and similarly no other class in which *either* [comment] *or* [prompt] can occur, we introduce these by means of optional daughter dependency rules triggered by the feature [initiating].

DD3$_{optional}$ initiating $\rightarrow$ preparatory
DD4$_{optional}$ initiating $\rightarrow$ reinforcing

We introduce the optional pre-topic act in a normal opening move by a daughter dependency rule, since topic-bearing acts can occur without pre-topic acts in other types of initiating move.

DD5$_{optional}$ normal opening $\rightarrow$ pre-topic

Let us now turn to the structure of the [reacting] subclass of supporting move. Burton's structure is:

(pre-head)	head	(post-head)
accept	react	comment

It would seem, however, that [evaluate] can co-occur with [accept], as in, for example, the following adaptation of our earlier Example 10:

(11) A. Close the window, will you.   (directive)
      B. OK.   (accept)
      You're right, it is a bit cold.   (evaluate)
      (closes window)   (react)

We introduce the obligatory [react] by a daughter dependency rule:

DD6   reacting $\rightarrow$ react

The presence of [accept] as an optional sister depends on the presence of a [responsive] act as follows:

SD4$_{optional}$ responsive $\rightarrow$ accept

[Evaluate] occurs only in supporting moves, and so is introduced by a daughter dependency rule:

DD7$_{optional}$ supporting $\rightarrow$ evaluate

[Comment], however, is not specific to supporting moves, and so is introduced by a sister dependency rule:

SD5$_{optional}$ responsive $\overset{\rightarrow}{}$ comment

The sequence of acts in a directing move is specified by the following general rule covering other types of initiating move as well:

S3 $\Longrightarrow$ pre-topic $\Longrightarrow$ preparatory   topic-bearing $\Longrightarrow$ reinforcing

For reacting moves, the sequence is given by the following general rule:

S4   accept $\rightarrow$ evaluate $\rightarrow$ responsive $\rightarrow$ reinforcing

These two rules can be collapsed into a single rule, in which the 'choices' in brackets relate to act classes, only one of which is possible in any given class of move:

S5   pre-topic $\Longrightarrow$ $\begin{Bmatrix} \text{preparatory} \\ \text{accept} \end{Bmatrix}$ $\Longrightarrow$ evaluate $\Longrightarrow$ $\begin{Bmatrix} \text{topic-bearing} \\ \text{responsive} \end{Bmatrix}$

$\Longrightarrow$ reinforcing

3.5 An Exemplificatory Derivation

I shall now go through the derivation of the structure of a single conversational exchange with overall directive function.

(12)   A.   John,   (summons) ⌐ directing
                 could you just hold this spanner for me
                 a minute?   (directive)
                 I seem to need three hands.   (comment) ⌐ reacting
          B.   Sure.   (accept)
                 (takes spanner)   (react)

The whole exchange has the feature [conversational], so that DD1 operates, and we introduce a daughter marked as [normal opening] (and therefore, from the network, also having the less delicate feature [initiating]). The feature [directing] is added by free choice from the network for moves. SD1 now applies to give [reacting] (and, less delicately, [responding]) as a sister, and S1 places the opening move before the supporting move. So far, then, we have:

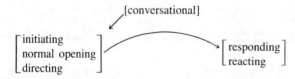

DD2 gives [directive] (less delicately, [topic-bearing]) as a daughter of the first move. DD5 introduces [pre-topic], and we choose from the network the additional feature [summons] for this act. DD4 gives a further daughter labelled as [reinforcing], and we choose [comment] from the network to accompany this feature. DD6 gives [react] (and less delicately, [responsive]) as an obligatory daughter of the second move, and SD4 gives [accept] as a sister. S5 gives the sequence [summons] ≫[directive]≫ [comment] for the first move, and [accept]≫ [react] for the second. The complete structure is as follows:

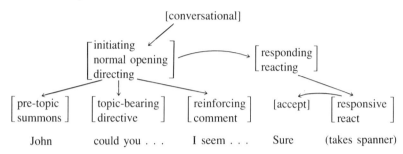

4. CONCLUDING REMARKS

Discourse is seen, in the model described here, as a level separate from semantics and syntax, but related to these levels by realization in the following way:

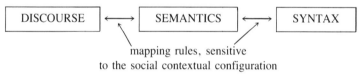

mapping rules, sensitive
to the social contextual configuration

Although work within the Sinclair & Coulthard type of framework has provided stimulating accounts of syntagmatic patterning in discourse, paradigmatic relations have been neglected. The present paper has attempted to restore the balance by proposing a model for the description of discourse, based on Hudson's daughter dependency theory of syntax, in which system networks are linked to structures by explicit realization rules.

REFERENCES

Austin, J. L. (1962). *How to Do Things with Words*. Oxford: Clarendon Press.

Berry, M. (1981a). Systemic linguistics and discourse analysis: a multi-layered approach to exchange structure. In Coulthard, M. & Montgomery, M. (eds.) *Studies in Discourse Analysis*, pp. 120–45.

—————— (1981b). Towards layers of exchange structure for directive exchanges. *Network*, **2**, 23–32.

Burton, D. (1978). Towards an analysis of casual conversation. *Nottingham Linguistic Circular*, 7/2, 131–64.

—————— (1980). *Dialogue and Discourse*. London: Routledge & Kegan Paul.

—————— (1981). Analysing spoken discourse. In Coulthard, M. & Montgomery, M. (eds.) *Studies in Discourse Analysis* pp. 61–81.

Butler, C. S. (1982). *The Directive Function of the English Modals*. Unpublished Ph.D. thesis, University of Nottingham.

_____ (forthcoming). Communicative function and semantics. To appear in Halliday, M. A. K. & Fawcett, R. P. (eds.), *New Developments in Systemic Linguistics*. London: Batsford.

Coulthard, M. (1975). Discourse analysis in English—a short review of the literature. *Language Teaching and Linguistics: Abstracts*, **8**, 73–89.

Coulthard, M. & Montgomery, M. (1981). *Studies in Discourse Analysis*. London, Boston & Henley: Routledge & Kegan Paul.

Davison, A. (1975). Indirect speech acts and what to do with them. In Cole, P. & Morgan, J. L. (eds.), *Syntax and Semantics, 3 (Speech Acts)*. New York & London: Academic Press, pp. 143–85.

Edmondson, W. (1981). *Spoken Discourse: A Model for Analysis*. London & New York: Longman.

Fawcett, R. P. (1980). *Cognitive Linguistics and Social Interaction: Towards an Integrated Model of a Systemic Functional Grammar and the Other Components of a Communicating Mind*. Heidelberg, Germany: Julius Groos Verlag, and Exeter, England: University of Exeter.

Gordon, D. & Lakoff, G. (1971). Conversational postulates. *Papers from the Seventh Regional Meeting, Chicago Linguistic Society*. Chicago, IL: Department of Linguistics, University of Chicago.

Green, G. M. (1973). How to get people to do things with words. In Shuy, R. W. (ed.) *Some New Directions in Sociolinguistics*. Washington, DC: Georgetown University Press.

Grice, H. P. (1975). Logic and conversation (Harvard William Jones Lectures, 1967). In Cole, P. & Morgan, J. L. (eds.), *Syntax and Semantics, 3 (Speech Acts)*. New York & London: Academic Press, pp. 41–58.

_____. (1978). Further notes on logic and conversation. In Cole, P. (ed.), *Syntax and Semantics, 9 (Pragmatics)*. New York & London: Academic Press, pp. 113–27.

Halliday, M. A. K. (1961). Categories of the theory of grammar. *Word*, **17**. 241–92.

_____ (1978). *Language as Social Semiotic*. London: Edward Arnold.

_____ (1984). Language as code and language as behaviour: a systemic-functional interpretation of the nature and ontogenesis of dialogue. In Fawcett, R. P., Halliday, M. A. K., Lamb, S. M. & Makkai, A. (eds.), *The Semiotics of Culture and Language Vol. 1: Language as Social Semiotic*. London, Frances Pinter, pp. 3–35.

Heringer, J. (1972). Some grammatical correlates of felicity conditions. *Working Papers in Linguistics*, Ohio State University. **11**. 1–110.

Hudson, R. A. (1975). The meaning of questions. *Language*, **51**. 1–31.

_____ (1976). *Arguments for a Non-transformational Grammar*. Chicago, IL, & London: Chicago University Press.

_____ (1978). Daughter dependency grammar and systemic grammar. *UEA Papers in Linguistics*, **6**. 1–14.

Labov, W. (1970/1972a). The study of language in its social context. *Studium Generale*, **23**. 30–87. Revised version in Labov, W. *Sociolinguistic Patterns*. Philadelphia, PA: University of Pennsylvania Press, 1972.

_____ (1972b). Rules for ritual insults. In Sudnow, D. (ed.) *Studies in Social Interaction*. New York: The Free Press, 120–69.

Labov, W. & Fanshel, D. (1977). *Therapeutic Discourse: Psychotherapy as Conversation*. New York, San Francisco, CA & London: Academic Press.

Lee, P. (1974). Perlocution and illocution. *Journal of English Linguistics*, **8**. 32–40.

Martin, J. R. (1981). How many speech acts? *UEA Papers in Linguistics*, **14/15**. 52–57.

Sadock, J. M. (1974). *Towards a Linguistic Theory of Speech Acts*. New York: Academic Press.

Schachter, P. (1980). Daughter dependency grammar. In Moravcsik, E. A. & Wirth, J. R. (eds.), *Syntax and Semantics, 13 (Current Approaches to Syntax)*. New York & London: Academic Press.

Searle, J. R. (1969). *Speech Acts: An Essay in the Philosophy of Language*. Cambridge, England: Cambridge University Press.

_____ (1975). Indirect speech acts. In Cole, P. & Morgan, J. L. (eds.), *Syntax and Semantics, 3 (Speech Acts)*. New York & London: Academic Press, pp. 60–82.

_____ (1976). A classification of illocutionary acts. *Language in Society*, **5**. 1–23.

Sinclair, J. McH. & Coulthard, R. M. (1975). *Towards an Analysis of Discourse: the English Used by Teachers and Pupils*. London: Oxford University Press.

On Types of Meaningfulness in Discourse

12

Eirian C. Davies
University of London
England

This paper is concerned with the boundary between semantics and pragmatics, and with the nature of the 'interface' where they meet. It seeks to develop an approach (previously proposed in Davies 1979:19–42) for distinguishing between literal syntactic meaning and non-literal meaning ('significance'), and for attempting to relate them systematically.

The basic premises on which this approach rests are as follows:

(i) That syntactic organization in English is itself meaningful.

(ii) That each construction type (CT) which is formally distinguishable in terms of surface syntax has associated with it a unique semantic specification. Each semantic specification (SeS) is a set of semantic features. Any SeS assigns one distinct interpretation, in terms of (non-referential) syntactic meaning, to the single CT with which it is associated.[1]

---

[1] The claim in (ii) could be modified to allow for syntactic ambiguity (one syntactic form and more than one semantic specification: 'syntactic homonymy') by formulating it in terms of 'sets of semantic specifications', as follows:

(iiA) Each construction type which is formally distinguishable in surface syntax has associated with it a unique set of semantic specifications.

There are two forms of (iiA), as follows:

a. A 'strong' version: namely, that no SeS which is a member of the set of SeSs associated with one CT can be a member of a set of SeSs associated with any other CT.

b. A 'weak' version: namely, that no set of SeSs associated with one CT will have exactly the same membership as that of any other set of SeSs associated with any other CT.

The weak version contravenes the further claim in (ii) that any SeS is associated with only one CT, and so allows for partial syntactic synonymy (except, accidentally, between CTs with one member sets of SeSs). I would want to reject it on those grounds.

Any SeS is itself a set of semantic features. We have allowed, in the formulation of (ii) for any distinction in surface syntax to be meaningful. That is, any 'syntactic specification' (SyS) which differs in only one feature from any other SyS will be distinguished. This allows for a high degree of overlap between distinct SySs (i.e. for major areas of intersection between the two sets of syntactic features). We can expect the case to be similar in relation to SeSs. That is, where one SeS has all but one feature in common with another SeS we should recognise two distinct SeSs.

(footnote continued)

(iii) That the SeS will give just those features of syntactic meaning which attach to a given CT in all its uses, contexts and co-texts. That is, it will specify the common denominator (CmD) of semantic features. Any SeS is context-independent.

(iv) That this context-free CmD semantic specification will be derived from a semantic component which has the following characteristics:

a. It is a separate level independently motivated, and established and organized in its own terms. Divisions within it need not, therefore, correspond with areas of syntactic form such as transitivity or mood, established in terms of syntactic criteria.

b. It is based on a small number of semantic primes.

The exact character of this semantic component,—the type of independent motivation, and the nature and identity of the semantic primes involved—, is not an issue in what follows. I have made one proposal (Davies 1976, 1979), but the discussion below is unaffected by whether or not this is found acceptable. All that is required is the postulation of the existence of some semantic theory underlying a semantic component with the two characteristics just given, which is capable of yielding a specification of the distinctive meaning of each construction type distinguished in surface syntax (cf. (ii)).

(v) That the CmD semantic specification (SeS) associated with any given surface syntax construction type gives the 'literal (syntactic) meaning' of that CT.

(vi) That although an SeS may be complex (involving combinations of semantic primes, typically from different areas within the semantics, and of attributes on primes), the complexity involved in relating a single syntactic construction type to a variety of different speech act 'functions' is to be accounted for elsewhere: namely, in the area of relations between the literal syntactic meaning (given in the CmD SeS) and contextual factors. That is, the functional multivalency of syntactic categories will be accounted for at the interface between syntactic semantics and pragmatics.

(vii) That the traditional speech functions, and other related 'functions' such as 'request' etc., are categories of non-literal meaning (which I shall call 'significance'), and lie within the pragmatics.

(viii) That any linguistic category such as 'imperative', may be related to any pragmatic category such as 'command' by means of a single rule. The general form of this claim, and the rule proposed, were given in Davies 1979 (27–28) as follows:

Full syntactic homonymy can be defined in terms of (iiA) as follows: 'Where each SeS which is a member of set,L,of SeSs is such that it constitutes a disjoint set of semantic features in relation to every other SeS which is a member of L, the CT with which L is associated is fully syntactically homonymous'. Partial homonymy would involve intersection between two (or more) SeSs as members of the same set L. I would take apparent homonymy of either kind as prima facie evidence that syntactic distinctions had not been exhausted.

In this paper, I make the unmodified claim (ii), as given in the text, and find it not to be disproved in the cases considered.

. . . First order significance is a value of an 'expression'. The expression has the form 'X+C', where X is a variable whose values 'α, β . . . ν,' represent different combinations of surface grammar construction type and L(iteral) M(ood) M(eaning), and C is a variable whose values 'a,b, . . , n', represent different contextual features. (The expression, (E)) 'X+C=V' states a first-order significance, V, whose value may be worked out where the values of X and C are known.

It may be useful in what follows to amplify this statement using the following abbreviations:

Syntactic Specification: 'SyS'
Semantic Specification: 'SeS'
Linguistic Specification: 'CoS'
First order significance: 'FOSg'

Then, (where, SyS + SeS = LgS) we have the formula:
(F) LgS + CoS = FOSg. That is, for any sentence, α,

$$LgS_\alpha + CoS_a = FOSg_1$$
$$LgS_\alpha + CoS_b = FOSg_2$$

(cf. Davies 1979: 180–1, 187–8).

The general statement of this theoretical position includes intonation with syntax as aspects of surface linguistic form and can be summarized as follows (using 'InS' for 'Intonational Specification', 'SeS$_s$' for the semantic specification of the syntactic category and 'SeS$_i$' for the semantic specification of intonational features):

$$\{ (SyS + SeS_s) + (InS + SeS_i) \} = LgS,$$

then, as before,

(F) LgS + CoS = FOSg.

(ix) That it is not a property of any element of extra-linguistic 'reality' as such, that it should be accounted for in the semantics as opposed to the pragmatics, or conversely. Part of the total effect made by a given utterance on a given occasion will result exactly from the 'placing' of such factors: within the semantics, where they will be realized in syntactic form, or within the context, where they will not be so realized. The questions of 'placing' in this way may be seen as a 'discourse strategy' in its widest sense (cf. Gregory 1985).

(x) That there is more than one level or 'order' of non-literal meaning. This notion provides a means of accounting for the fact that a given construction type may have two or more functions simultaneously. For example, a jussive imperative such as *Go away* may function in the same given context both as a command, at the first 'order of significance', and as a warning at some higher order of significance. This involves the claim that a device of the form of (E) above may apply recursively, further contextual factors entering in at each application or 'stage' (cf. Davies 1979: 37–8). Categories of significance are only automatically mutually exclusive if they are of the same order of significance. A second stage might be shown as follows:

$$X' + C^2 = V'$$

where X' is the variable whose values are categories of first order significance, C^2 is a variable whose values represent a second set of contextual features and V' is a category of second order significance (2OSg).

As with a first stage application of (E), as shown in (F),

$$X'_{(i)} + C^2_a = V'_1$$
$$X'_{(i)} + C^2_b = V'_2$$

The input for a third stage would be a category of second order significance combined with features from a third set of contextual factors. That is:

$$X'' + C^3 = V''$$

Where X'' is the variable whose values are categories of second order significance, C^3 is a variable whose values represent a third set of contextual features and V'' is a category of third order significance.

The upper limit to the number of orders of significance appears, at present, indeterminate. I shall refer to orders of significance above the first as 'Higher orders of significance'.

It can be seen from this outline that the extent to which features of linguistic form determine the final value of the equation diminishes steadily at each higher 'stage'. This, I believe, helps to provide some explanation for the fact that certain categories of 'function' such as 'warning', may be conveyed by a wide variety of different construction types in surface syntax (cf. Austin 1962: 62; Davies 1979: 26–7). In principle, this notion provides a framework in terms of which the phenomenon of indirect speech acts may be accounted for (cf., e.g., Searle 1975).

(xi) That it is not a property of any element of extra-linguistic reality as such that it should enter into a Contextual Specification at any one particular stage rather than another, anymore than that it should be accounted for in the pragmatics as opposed to the semantics, or vice versa (cf. (ix)).

(xii) That there are different aspects of syntactic organization. This is to follow Halliday in his (1970) establishment of different components of the grammar, at least in relation to surface syntax.

(xiii) That there are different kinds of literal syntactic meaning (LSM) associated with the different aspects of surface syntactic organisation. This again is to follow Halliday's approach to multiple components of the grammar. But it should be noted that, if the semantics associated with syntactic distinctions is seen as an independent level (as in (iva) above), the different kinds of LSM need not, and probably will not, correspond with particular areas of semantic organization. On such an approach, any given kind of LSM, such as the literal meaning of the mood system, represents only an area of inter-connection between the 'free-standing' dimensions of syntactic organization and semantic organization.[2] To call such an area of interconnection

[2] 'Mood' is used here, throughout, as by Halliday (e.g., 1970) to include distinctions between (and within) declarative and interrogative within indicative.

'literal meaning' is to view it from the perspective of linguistic form. But it is equally possible to view the connecting area from the semantic perspective. If one chooses to use the term 'planes' for divisions/areas within the organization of the semantics, then one can distinguish an area of interconnection between semantics and syntax associated with 'plane x'. For example, in my own (Davies 1979) proposals drawn up within this framework, the area of interconnection which I called 'literal mood meaning' drew on primes from three different 'planes' within the semantics in assigning 'interpretations' (semantic specifications) to the different construction types distinguished in terms of a surface syntax of mood. Conversely, it was possible, within that framework, to think of various features of surface linguistic form associated with one particular semantic plane. For example, the plane (proposed there) of 'telling' was associated with surface syntax features, not only of finiteness and mood of the verb, but also with clause dependency (which falls outside the mood system in surface syntax), and with features of intonation.

(xiv) That, as we have approached it so far, the notion of 'categories of significance' rests on linguistic form in the sense that this is what is said to 'have significance'; but that such a formulation states a special case only. Significance may attach either to verbal acts or to non-verbal acts such as gestures (cf. Davies 1979: 23). Like meaning, significance is a relational concept; so that to say 'V is the significance of X in C' is to assign an interpretation to X in terms of a set of independently established variables within a different area of the analysis of experience, of which V is a category. That is, 'significance' is always the significance *of* something in terms of something else. A category such as 'command' is most usefully seen as a category of behaviour, a social act. To say that 'X has the first order significance of 'command' in context C' is not to say, on this view, that X itself (the linguistic CT) *is* a command; it is only to say that, in the given circumstances (context C) X is being used to make a command; that is, that the act of uttering X in C is included within the set of social acts which can be labelled 'making a command'. This is merely to stress the point that a category of social acts such as 'command' should be thought of as established in principle independently of linguistic form.

(xv) That, in the first instance, it is possible to isolate different kinds of non-literal meaning/significance, in addition to the different levels or orders of significance sketched in (x). These are seen as related to different kinds of literal meaning, which allows a distinction at least between an 'interactional significance', related to literal mood meaning, and an 'interpretational significance' related to a literal transitivity meaning. It may seem reasonable also to postulate a third type of significance, one related to the literal meaning of features of surface form within the areas of theme and cohesion as described by Halliday (1967, 1970) and Halliday and Hasan (1976).

The notion of such different kinds of significance is a theoretical abstraction. It allows the convenience of initially giving individual consideration to different kinds of literal meaning in relation to the contextual factors relevant to each separately, so that the import or 'effect' of a given CT used in a particular context may be analysed from one point of view at a time. But, just as it is difficult to discover items which have only one kind of literal meaning (cf. Davies 1979: 51–2), so cases of 'single significance' in context are extremely rare, if not theoretically precluded. Even an item such as *Hi,* which may be assigned a literal mood meaning and an interactional significance in context, can also be distinguished in terms of a second kind of literal meaning from which is derived another aspect of its significance in use. For example, the distinction between *Hi* and *Oi* is not accounted for within literal mood meaning, or indeed by any type of literal syntactic meaning. I, therefore, follow Halliday (1966) in distinguishing initially between lexical and grammatical meaning; (although I refer only to the syntactic aspect of the latter), and extend this distinction to related types of significance (Davies 1979: 15–16, 31–2). A statement of the 'full significance' of any sentence item in use will generally be 'mixed' in the sense of involving more than one type of significance (i.e. more than one type of literal meaning with its associated set of relevant contextual factors).

(xvi) That categories of significance are categories of meaningfulness in discourse. They can be established only by reference to the surrounding co-text and context in which the linguistic item which 'has significance' occurs.

Within this general framework, let us now explore the possible usefulness of the formula (F) as out-lined in (viii) above. For this purpose, I restrict myself to the syntax and semantics of mood, and shall illustrate initially with the 'plain' jussive imperative without tag (and with falling intonation).

First, let me outline a possible list of semantic features, postulated as common to all uses of the jussive imperative, qua jussive imperative, which would constitute a 'common denominator' of syntactic meaning for that construction type, to be formulated within the terms of whatever semantic theory is adopted to give the SeS element in the LgS:

a. The one envisaged as carrying out the action is the Addressee. (Second person actor).
b. There are grounds for assuming that the Addressee will not carry out the action without some encouragement to do so. ('Negative inertia').
c. There are grounds for assuming that the action concerned is not being, and has not been, carried out at the time of utterance.
d. There are grounds for assuming that the Addressee is capable of carrying out the action.
e. The Speaker has the right to decide whether or not the Addressee carries out the action.
f. The Speaker has the right to tell the Addressee his (Speaker's) decision concerning the Addressee's action.

There are grounds for arguing that this list is too semantically 'rich' (cf. Bolinger 1967, 1977). Item (e) causes some problems as a CmD element, and so, in relation to one particular set of examples, does item (b); but I reserve discussion for the examples concerned.

Let us now examine some cases of jussive imperatives which may have more than one function in use, and see if such 'multivalency' can be accounted for in terms of variation in contextual features (the SeS content outlined above remains constant in all cases). If so, we will need to specify such contextual features, and to ask whether or not such multiple functions are themselves mutually exclusive.

To say, (1) *Come in,* in response to a polite knock on the door, seems to be to give a permission, rather than in any sense to issue a command. On the other hand, in circumstances where S and A meet just outside S's room and A clearly wants to talk for some time, to say the same thing might be thought of more as an invitation. Again, if a group of students were making a lot of noise in the corridor outside the head of department's room and the latter opened his door and said *Come in,* this might count more as a command than as either an invitation or a permission, given that it was clear to all concerned that the students would much prefer to disappear quickly in the opposite direction.

Similarly, (2) *Have a drink* might be an invitation to a guest, or an instruction to someone who was choking on a piece of food; and (3) *Tell me all about it* might function as a command, an invitation, or possibly a permission; also as a request.

I have not attempted to give an exhaustive list of the possible functions of these examples. But there is enough here to establish the point that a single sentence item, not merely a single surface syntax construction type, may have more than one function in use. Such functional multivalency of the item does not depend on lexical or grammatical ambiguity in the examples sketched.

I would claim that this variability of function can be accounted for in terms of contextual factors, and propose one such factor in an attempt to do so: namely, that of 'Addressee's wishes'.

The first context outlined for (1), contains an indication that the Addressee has a positive wish to perform the act of 'coming in': his knock on the door. We could label this 'A's wish: Actually yes'. In the second context there are some grounds for thinking that the Addressee might want to perform that act (a long conversation is probably more comfortably carried out while sitting down and with less likelihood of interruptions). We can say here, perhaps, that although there is no clear indication of A's wish in context, there is some basis in context for assuming that it might be positive, and label this 'A's wish: Potentially yes'. In the third context there are indications that the (group) Addressee has a negative wish, a wish not to perform the act; 'A's wish: Actually no'.

In the contexts sketched for (2), the first is rather like the second one above for (1) in that there are grounds in it (based on social conventions) for assuming that the Addressee as a guest might wish to 'have a drink'. Here again, then, we might label the context as containing the feature: 'A's wish: Potentially yes'. In the second context for (2) where the Addressee is choking, his wishes with respect to 'having a drink' can be considered as beside the issue. That is, the wishes which he could be conventionally assumed to have would relate to an act ('stopping choking') which is other than that conveyed in the imperative. We might label this feature, 'A's wish: neutral'.

It is not difficult to suggest contexts in which (3) would function as a command, by virtue of the fact that there was some definite indication in context that the Addressee wished to keep silent on the given topic (A's wish: Actually no'-'not to tell'). Examples might be a suspect under police interrogation, or a child caught guiltily trying to hide some broken china, etc. Similarly, in a context such as casual conversation between two friends, in which one suddenly makes some major disclosure (of more importance to himself than to the other) and adds, 'but that's a long story, and I'm still chewing it over', for the other to say *Tell me all about it* might function as an invitation, by virtue of the fact that there was enough indication in context (including co-text) that the Addressee might wish to confide further (A's wish: Potentially yes'). On the other hand, if there was clear indication of a positive wish 'to tell all about it', some preceding remark such as 'I'm bursting to talk about . . . .' , then (3) in reply would surely count as a permission by virtue of this clear indication of 'A's wish: Actually yes'. (3) might also count as a request without the rising intonation which would alter its LgS and thereby take it into a different category of surface form. I would suggest that, for (3) to have this 'effect', there would need to be some indication in context that the Addressee might be reluctant to tell; for example, if he had conveyed that the topic concerned was highly confidential. We could label this: 'A's wish: Potentially no'.

We can now summarize this discussion as follows. We have postulated a dimension of contextual analysis, namely that of 'Addressee's wishes in relation to performing act 'x''. This we can treat as a variable, 'AW'. We have suggested 'values' (mutually exclusive options in terms of this dimension of contrast) for AW as follows:

AW_1 Actually yes
AW_2 Potentially yes
AW_3 Potentially no
AW_4 Actually no
AW_5 Neutral.

Associated with each different AW value we have a different 'function', which we can state using our formula (F) by virtue of the fact that a different value for the contextual variable AW gives a different value for the contextual specification, and so for that of FOSg in (F).

LgS		+ CoS	= FOSg 'Permission'.
J(ussive) I(mperative)		(AW1)	
"		+ CoS	= FOSg 'Invitation'.
		(AW2)	
"		+ CoS	= FOSg 'Request'.
		(AW3)	
"		+ CoS	= FOSg 'Command'.
		(AW4)	
"		+ CoS	= FOSg 'Instruction'.
		(AW5)	

The value AW_5: 'Neutral', represents one device for indicating that, in certain cases, the AW variable may not be relevant; but that this in itself is meaningful. This allows a distinction between a variable which is potentially relevant in the CoS specification of a given CT, but fails to be so in certain instances, and one which is never relevant, in principle (non-applicable). The AW variable, as we have it above, clearly falls into the first category in relation to imperatives, but into the second category in relation to, for example, epistemic modal declaratives.

Any CoS element in an application of (F) will typically involve more than one variable, so that our sketch above represents only a partial picture for imperatives. A full CoS is seen as assigned in terms of the set of all potentially relevant variables for a given CT, of which one (or more) may have the value 'neutral' in certain instances. Such instances may correspond with a division within register. For example, the neutral value of AW_5 could be typically associated with imperatives in the register of instruction manuals, including cookery books.

I use 'context' throughout as a general term, to include co-text. Features given in a CoS may be partly derived from surrounding co-text which, for example, may supply a clear indication of the Addressee's wishes with respect to performing a given action.

On the basis of the above discussion, there seem to be some grounds for saying that (F) is useful in accounting for the functional multivalency of the 'plain' jussive imperative. But (at least) two points which the general treatment raises require further discussion.

Firstly, the question of problems to do with the CmD approach to the semantic specification element in LgS. In the suggested list of features (above), (b) the 'inertia' component, and (e) the Speaker's right of decision, both raise difficulties. Bolinger (1977: 165) also points out problems that relate to (d), 'the Addressee's ability to carry out the action', instancing *Tell it to the Marines*. All three cases raise the same general problem; namely, that of a feature postulated as belonging to a CmD semantic specification being found to be contravened in context in particular cases. In what follows I shall deal only with (b): 'there are grounds for assuming that the Addressee will not carry out the action without some encouragement to do so. (Negative Inertia)'. But the general proposal made below for accounting for such conflicts in relation to (b) is held to apply equally to any other CmD SeS feature.

The main group of examples involving difficulties to do with (b) are those of the type of, (4) *Move and I'll shoot*. Two points immediately arise about examples of this type: (i) they involve a relation between two clauses, the second of which is non-imperative, and (ii) many of them (including (4)) may have either a 'threat' or 'non-threat' significance.

At first sight, this functional multivalency appears to be related to CoS. Let us suppose two different types of context for (4), one in which (b) is contravened, and another in which it is not. We can illustrate the first type, I, by an example in which a burglar, surprised in the act of helping himself to the family silver by an armed and irate householder, shows every sign of being about to make for an open window and escape. For the householder to utter (4) in such circumstances would amount to issuing a (preventive) threat. Such a context provides grounds for assuming that the Addressee is likely to carry out the action of the imperative clause unless actively discouraged ('Positive Inertia', the opposite inertia value to that given in (b)); and this is part of the reason for the Speaker to say what he does.

For the second type of context, II, we could illustrate with the scenario of a two-man hunting expedition. Let us suppose that one of the two men was armed and the other not, and that they encountered their quarry suddenly in such a way that the armed man saw it first, and the unarmed man had stationed himself in an observation position directly in the former's line of fire. For the man with the gun to say (4) in such circumstances to his unarmed companion would not count as a threat. Further, the factor of the latter's apparently settled immobility provides grounds in context for assuming (b) (negative inertia) in relation to *Move;* and this is part of the reason for the Speaker to say what he does.[3]

But let us also consider variations of both I and II. Suppose, in context I, that the burglar (an amateur) seemed rooted to the spot with fright, and gave no indication of being about to move. In such circumstances (context Ia), (4) would remain a threat, although perhaps a redundant one, and so rather overbearing in effect; it would not seem a particularly apposite thing to say. That is, the difference between (4) in contexts I and Ia, which is a question of inertia assumption in context, chiefly affects its degree of relevancy. But (4) could only be less revelant in Ia than in I if it is assumed to 'mean' the same thing in both contexts. That is, the relative 'oddness' of (4) in Ia is explicable by postulating a feature of 'positive inertia' in the SeS of its first clause. On the basis of our argument above, this conclusion implies that the first clause in (4) is not an imperative.

Suppose, in context II, both men saw their quarry at the same time, and the unarmed man gave every indication of being about to scramble out of the way (context IIa). For the other to say (4) in such circumstances would be redundant, and perhaps officious in effect, but would not be a threat any more than in II. Here again we can account for the difference in effect between (4) in II and IIa by postulating a constant SeS feature (of negative inertia) which is paralleled/reinforced in II, but contravened in context IIa. That is, it is only by virtue of a constant SeS feature that (4) can have two different effects according to contextual variation. On this reading, clause 1 in (4) qualifies as a (positive) imperative.

I suggest, on this basis, that two different CTs can be distinguished for (4), according to the imperative/non-imperative distinction in clause 1. I would argue that the formal identity of this clause in both readings is not a matter of 'syntactic homonymy' (one CT(/SyS) and more than one SeS) but of 'morphological homonymy' (one morphological form: 'plain stem of verb', and more than one syntactic

---

[3] The point at issue does not depend on the dual possibilities for the object of *shoot (you/it).* cf. *Shut the door and I'll scream:* (a) 'If you shut the door (which I don't want you to do) I'll scream (which you don't want me to do)' vs. (b) 'If you shut the door (which I do want you to do, to keep out that madman who is pursuing us both with a knife) I'll scream (which you do want me to do as it would bring help). That is, constructions with an intransitive clause 2 behave in the same way: (a) is a threat, and (b) is not.

function: imperative,/non-imperative).[4] The CTs may be distinguished by two tests, used in combination: namely, the possibility of inserting (i) *If you do,* and (ii) *Please* before the verb of the first clause (with omission of *and* between the two clauses in the first casc). If (i) can be added without involving more than a minimal change of meaning and (ii) cannot, the first clause is non-imperative.

If the change of meaning which results from adding (i) is major, or perhaps debatable, but that involved in adding (ii) is slight (i.e. consists only in a modification of feature (e) 'Speaker's right to decide' in our SeS for imperatives) then the first clause is imperative.[5]

The distinction can be illustrated more clearly with examples where lexical content predisposes to interpretation in one direction or the other, such as

(5)   *Break that vase and I'll break your neck* and

(6)   *Give me that nail and I'll bang it in*

(cf. Bolinger 1977: 158–65). (5) takes (i) with minimal change of meaning, but (ii), the addition of *please,* produces a meaning which differs in major respects, including the inertia value. (6) takes (i) without becoming unacceptable, but the change of meaning seems greater than in (5) on this test, involving an element of equally weighted possibilities perhaps, not present in the original. On the other hand, (6) takes *please* with minimal change of meaning. In terms of these tests, 4) behaves like (5) when it has threat significance, and like (6) when it does not.[6]

On this basis, we seem to have co-variation as follows for (4): (i) the SyS feature of first clause 'non-imperative', associated with the SeS feature 'positive inertia', giving a significance of 'threat'; and (ii) SyS: first clause 'imperative', associated with SeS: 'negative inertia', giving a 'non-threat' significance. It should not be surprising, given (F), that associated differences in SyS and SeS, giving different LgSs, yield different categories of significance. But it may seem from this that we do not need both SeS and significance, since they co-vary here. However, we have already shown that a distinction between SeS and CoS may provide a useful means of accounting for the difference in full significance between (4), with non-imper-

---

[4] Except in the verb *to be,* the stem form of the verb also realizes 'plain' present tense (apart from third person singular). I do not see any strong arguments against accounting for its different syntactic functions at the same 'stage', rather than, say, distinguishing '+/− finite indicative' as a matter of 'morphological homonymy' and '+/− imperative' as a matter of 'syntactic homonymy'.

[5] The absence/presence of *please* is taken as a distinction in SyS correlating with a distinction in SeS: namely that between feature (e) and a feature (e') 'Speaker wishes the Addressee to carry out the action', features (a) − (d) inclusive remaining constant. ('Decision' in (f) also varies to 'wish' in a feature of (f'), but this is an automatic result of variation from (e) to (e').) The argument used in test (ii) is that if the change in SeS associated with adding *please* can be fully accounted for in the terms just given, this is evidence that the clause tested is imperative. If, on the other hand, (e') and (f') are newly added to the SeS (rather than being modified from (e) and (f) respectively), and inertia value is reversed, then that clause is non-imperative.

[6] *If you do move I'll shoot (you)/*Please move and I'll shoot (you);* as opposed to, (?)*If you do move I'll shoot (it)/Please move and I'll shoot (it).*

ative clause 1, in context I as opposed to Ia, and between (4), with imperative clause 1, in context II as opposed to IIa. Cases with non-imperative clause 1 which had non-threat significance would help to confirm the motivation for separating SeS and CoS. These are not hard to find. For example, (7) *Lose that job and you'll find another just as good* has a non-imperative first clause on the two tests above, but does not function as a threat. In fact, the threat vs. non-threat distinction in significance is, I believe, associated principally with the AW value in CoS as related to the second (*'ll: shall/will*) clause. Where this can be assumed to be positive the CT functions as a 'promise' of some kind, or at least as a reassuring prediction as in (7); where negative, the significance is some variety of 'threat', as in (7') *Lose that job and you'll be unemployed for life.* (cf. Davies 1979:97 on *shall*).[7] (Both (7) and (7') have positive inertia as an SeS feature for clause 1).

Several points emerge from this discussion, which makes no pretence of offering an adequate survey of the CT concerned, since the limited focus is essentially on one feature in the SeS proposed for imperatives (together with contextual factors). The most important, for the purposes of this paper, are as follows: (i) the idea, implicit in our discussion of (4) in different contexts, that the same variable (here 'inertia') may enter into both the SeS and the CoS of, not only the same CT but the same example, in a single occurrence; and, (ii) that this same variable may have opposing values in SeS and CoS on the same occasion. These notions constitute one proposal for an answer to the general question of what weighting to give to, and how to interpret, the contravention in context of features proposed for an SeS.

Two main approaches to establishing a CmD SeS for any given construction type seem possible. The first would give equal weighting to all instances of the given CT in use, and accept for the SeS only those features of meaningfulness common to it in all the different contexts in which it could be observed to occur. I shall call this a 'factorizing out' approach. The second would proceed from a different theoretical basis which allowed a distinction between constant, 'inherent' features of meaning and varying concomitants in use. I shall call this a 'predictive' approach.

One problem with the former approach is the possibility of arriving at an 'empty' SeS (one with no semantic features), and so, at the conclusion that the CT in question had no syntactic meaning.

If we apply that approach to 'imperatives', I am persuaded by Bolinger's rigorous analysis (1967, 1977: 152–82) that we are left with no feature of meaning in a distinctive 'imperative SeS'. He concludes (1977: 177–9) that imperatives may be seen as 'the bare infinitive used for commands', and that the one common, and constant, element of meaning associated with the bare infinitive is that of 'hypotheticalness'. The category 'imperative' is shown to be distinct neither in form nor meaning, and so is rejected from the syntax.[8]

---

[7] The distinction in type of threat between (7') and non-imperative (4) hinges on features in SeS and SyS to do with 'voluntary/involuntary' in the verb, and the person of subject in the second clause. (7) and imperative (4) can be compared in the same respects in relation to 'non-threats'.

[8] Bolinger's analysis of constructions such as (4) − (7) (1977: 158–65) gives the difference between the

But, even here, we might need to reduce further; for it is possible to find instances where the bare infinitive used as command occurs in contexts in which that one remaining feature of 'hypotheticalness' is contravened. Domestic squabbles provide recognizable instances such as (8) *All right blame me,* when it is only too clear from context that this is exactly what the Addressee is, and has been, doing; or (9) *(That's right) give him the rotten pear* said when this has already been done (perhaps by mistake). (The effect of this construction used in these circumstances has a 'non-standard' significance which is often sarcastic, although not necessarily so. Compare (10) *Run* shouted to encourage a child already doing so.) If we factorize out 'hypotheticalness' on the basis of such examples, we are left with no positive features of meaning associated with the bare infinitive. This approach then may lead us to admit a progressively larger amount of 'syntactic homonymy'.[9]

On the other hand, if we do not 'factorize out', and if we abandon the goal of establishing a CmD statement of meaning for 'imperative', we are faced with a large number of different meanings for it. Sometimes (often) it relates to hypothetical action, but sometimes not; sometimes it is used when the Addressee is capable of carrying out the action, but not always; its use may be associated with cases where the Speaker has some right (by virtue of his social role as parent perhaps) to decide on whether or not the Addressee performs the action, but this is not necessarily so (cf. the language of advertising), and so on. What this amounts to, in terms of our framework, is that we would be unable to specify an SeS for 'imperative' in terms of semantic features; it would have to be done at best in terms of listing applicable semantic variables, without being able to specify values on them. In such a case one might expect another construction type, such as modal declaratives with *will,* to have associated with it the same list of applicable variables. Here again, we stand to lose 'imperative' as a separate category, since although it is distinct in form in this case, it is not distinct in meaning. We are, in fact, having to admit 'syntactic synonymy'.

What appears to be at issue is the question of the proper weighting to give to context. I would claim that a distinction between meaning and use is essential here. If we can specify certain features, even though they are values on situational variables, as belonging to a CmD context-free semantic specification, then we derive two advantages. When such features are contravened in particular contexts,

---

bare infinitive as used in (5), as opposed to (6), as a difference between condition and command. Later he writes (1977: 179), 'The bare infinitives constitute a single system that derives its variety from intersections with other systems. They have a relatively invariant meaning that is variously colored in different contexts; but it is the contexts that differ, not the verbs.'

That is, in our terms, Bolinger would treat the different 'readings' of clause 1 in (4) as being a matter of significance, and recognize the formal identity of that clause in both readings in his syntax, and its associated semantics. I have suggested that the different readings are a matter of syntactic semantics, corresponding to two different CTs, and would recognize the formal identity of *move* in both readings only in the morphology.

[9] We may, in fact, be led to consider the bare infinitive as non-distinct from the present tense, once 'hypotheticalness' is lost. That would take us to the 'stem form of the verb' as 'CT', and so into morphology.

first we need not factorize them out, which enables us to avoid the empty set for SeS; and, second, by holding them constant, we can 'explain' the difference in effect produced by such contravention as compared with other cases where the same features are reinforced in context.

I shall devote the rest of this paper to attempting to illustrate and substantiate the second advantage claimed. Let us take (11) *Shut the door* said in a context in which it is clear that the Addressee is on the point of doing just that. Here, if we keep (b), 'negative inertia', as a feature in the SeS for the imperative, we have a case where it is contravened in context, (similar to that of (4) in context IIa). Suppose further that the context were such that it was a bitterly cold day with snow blowing in from outside and only an idiot would leave the door open. To say (11) in such circumstances would convey an implicit reproach by virtue of having (b) as one element in imperative SeS. That is, only if the mere selection of the imperative construction can be interpreted to mean (among other things) 'There are grounds for me to assume that the Addressee will not carry out the action unless encouraged (told) to do so' is it possible to account for the reproachful/rebuking effect of saying (11) in this case. The implication of using the imperative here is that this Addressee is a person who never shuts doors unless told to, despite looking as if about to do so. The clash between the feature of 'negative inertia' in SeS and the feature of 'positive inertia' in context can be used to account for the irritating effect of saying (11) in such a context, and to explain why it might well provoke a spirited retort.

Without some notion of a context-independent set of constant features in the SeS of the imperative, contexts such as that just sketched for (11) would force us to exclude from it the feature of negative inertia, and there would be no mechanism to account for the reproachful 'non-straightforward' import of (11) in such a case. Similarly, without some such notion, in (12) *Give me an ice-cream* (with falling intonation) said by a child to his mother, we would probably have to jettison (e) in the list for imperative SeS (Speaker's right to decide) and would not be able to explain why the Addressee might reply by telling him to add 'please'. Again, if we took (13) *Sign your name here* we would be hard put to explain, without such a notion, why it might embarrass an Addressee who couldn't write his name. To put this another way: why, if the context is such that it is clear to all that the Addressee is incapable of signing his name, would the use of (13) be in some sense inappropriate? Without some notion of a constant SeS I believe there is no answer. All that could be done would be to note this context of occurrence and exclude (d) 'Addressee assumed to be capable of carrying out the action' from the SeS of imperatives.

In practice, perhaps no one would want to allow equal weighting for the feature in context to cancel out the opposite value in SeS in a case such as this last. But, I would argue, the same principle is at issue in less obvious instances, such as (11) above.

That is, a 'predictive' approach would allow us to interpret (11), in the context sketched above, as conveying an implicit reproach and (12) as lacking in marks of respect. It would also enable us to explain why the use of (13), given contemporary expectations and attitudes on literacy, might, in the context sketched, embarrass the Addressee.

The theoretical point at issue relates to the assumption listed as (ix): namely, the claim that it is not an inherent characteristic of any situational factor, per se, that it should be accounted for within the semantics as opposed to the pragmatics, or vice versa. What is involved is the status of situational and contextual factors in the model. It is, I believe, misleading to equate them. That is, dimensions of contrast involving such situational variables as the Addressee's apparent intentions with respect to carrying out a given act, or his wishes in relation to doing so, or his ability to do so, are not, in themselves, either specifically elements in the syntactic semantics or in the contextual specification used in (F) to give categories of significance in the pragmatics. To say that variable N involves a factor of a 'situational' type is not, in itself, to say anything about whether N enters into SeS or CoS in applications of (F). (I have suggested elsewhere (1979:30), for example, that the AW variable, which we have used above as one element in CoS for jussive imperatives, forms part of the SeS for modal declaratives with *can*. So that it is part of what the latter construction type always means, but not so for the former.)

Now if this is the case, it allows us to propose that a 'predictive' approach, in relation to examples such as (11)–(13) above, involves the further claim that the same dimension of situational analysis may be an element both in the SeS element in LgS and in the CoS of a single application of (F) in relation to one particular example; and moreover, that this single situational variable may have mutually exclusive values in SeS and CoS in this one application of (F).

That is, not only may the one dimension of situational contrast be an element in either the syntactic semantics or in the contextual specification, but it may be an element in both simultaneously, and with opposing values as between the two in a single instance.

This may appear at first sight to be a somewhat startling and counter-intuitive proposal. But it rests on the claim, accepted as orthodox in Systemic linguistics, that context is an independent level. I understand this to mean that different principles of organisation are involved in context, and not that the raw material itself is different from that which enters into the semantics. This distinction is somewhat parallel to that often made between the levels of phonology and phonetics.

For example, the dimension of contrast 'fortis'/'lenis' enters into both the phonetics and phonology of English. If we take the English alveolar plosives in weakly accented intervocalic positions, as in *water/warder, latter/ladder*, phonological /t/, in the first member of each pair of words, is 'realized as a lenis rapid tap resembling a /d/ or one tap [ɾ], (Gimson, 1980: 163–5). Here we have a case where the consonant is both phonologically 'fortis' and, in that given 'co-text', phonetically 'lenis'. Further, this contrast could itself be said to be in some sense 'meaningful', since it occurs generally in American English, but not so widely in British R.P. In our terms, then, a contrast between opposing values on the same variable in relation to the same item (in the same instance), but at different levels, is both allowed for here and seen as meaningful (in as far as it indicates one accent of English rather than another).

In view of this analogy, the notions that an item such as (11) may simultaneously have the feature 'negative inertia' in its (syntactic) semantics and 'positive inertia' in its contextual specification for a given occurrence, and that this contrast is itself in some way meaningful, do not, perhaps, seem intrinsically strange. If the analogy is pursued, the (syntactic) semantics would rate with phonology as '-emic', and the contextual level with phonetics as '-etic', for, in the CoS, analysis returns to the particular occasion and specific event. As with phonetics and phonology, so with (syntactic) semantics and context: the same raw material is involved (sound waves/situational factors) but different principles of organization apply in its ordering and analysis.

I have illustrated, so far, with jussive imperatives, but the approach above is of general application and relates equally to indicative constructions, both declarative and interrogative. It enables us to explain, for example, cases such as those discussed in Berry (1981) in which interrogatives in a quiz programme have a particular effect by virtue of the fact that it is clear to all concerned that the Speaker (= quizmaster) already knows (more authoritatively than any other participant) whether or not the given proposition is the case (in a polar interrogative) or exactly which fully specified proposition is the case (with a non-polar interrogative). If we specify a feature: 'Addressee is presented as knowing whether or not p is the case' as an element in the SeS of indicative (non-modal) polar interrogatives (whether or not our syntactic semantics is seen as organized in terms of roles and operations as semantic primes), then we can specify CoS features in terms of the same variable. This enables us to account for the particular significance of 'unreal' (quiz/exam) questions in terms of 'value clash' on the same variable seen as occurring in both SeS and CoS, (cf. Davies 1979: 187–8). This is exactly parallel to our treatment of (11) in relation to the inertia variable.

If we postulate such a 'knowledge variable', values on it for SeS (as realized in syntax) may be assigned in terms of which participant (as defined by speech role: Speaker/Addressee) is presented as knowing 'whether or not p is the case'; and for CoS in terms of which participant (defined in the same way) is generally accepted as knowing (the same thing) in the given context. We might, over-simplifying, propose two values initially as follows (I use literal subscripts to avoid confusion with Berry's use of K_1, K_2 for a different purpose):

Knowledge variable: KN
  KN_a: Speaker knows)
)—whether or not p is the case.
  KN_b: Addressee knows)

Then:

$$SyS_{I(ndicative)\ D(eclarative)} + SeS_{KN_a} = LgS_{ID.}$$
$$SyS_{I(ndicative)\ P(olar)\text{-}I(nterrogative)} + SeS_{KN_b} = LgS_{I_{P\text{-}I.}}$$

(Assuming falling intonation in LgS_{ID} and rising intonation in $LgS_{I\ P\text{-}I}$).

Applying (F) we have:

(i)LgS_{ID} + CoS_{KN_a} = FOSg 'statement' (KN value identity in SeS & CoS).

(ii)LgS_{ID} + CoS_{KN_b} = FOSg (?)'answer'(KN value opposition between SeS & CoS).

(iii)$LgS_{I\ P\text{-}I}$ + CoS_{KN_a} = FOSg 'unreal question' (KN value opposition between SeS & CoS).

(iv)$LgS_{I\ P\text{-}I}$ + CoS_{KN_b} = FOSg 'open question' (KN value identity in SeS & CoS)

In (ii) on this basis we perhaps come near to specifying one sufficient condition for 'reply' significance in discourse structure. At any rate, we can account, in this way, for the rather different significance attached to a declarative indicative used as an answer to an all-knowing quiz master, as opposed to that which attaches to one used 'in its own right', where the KN value applies in CoS as well as in SeS, for example as a conversation opener.

By allowing a third value on the KN variable we may further account for constructions of epistemic modality in this respect, giving:

KN_c : Neither Speaker nor Addressee knows (e.g. (14) *It may be raining in London now*).

As before, this feature may be either reinforced or contravened in CoS.

$SyS_{E(pistemic)\ M(odal)\ D(eclarative)}$ + SeS_{KN_c} = LgS_{EMD}

Applying (F) we may derive:

(v)LgS_{EMD} + CoS_{KN_c} = FOSg 'hypothesis'.
(vi)LgS_{EMD} + CoS_{KN_a} = FOSg 'hedge'.
(vii)LgS_{EMD} + CoS_{KN_b} = FOSg 'trailer'.

(Names for categories of FOSg are purely mnemonics; the substantive point is that such categories can be systematically distinguished on this basis.)

This analysis has no difficulty in meeting Huddleston's objection (1981:122) involving the example (15) *There may be* in a context where it is used as a reply to an enquiry whether there is a question on modality in an examination set by the Speaker of (15). In such a context, where it is accepted by all concerned that the Speaker does know, using an epistemic modal declarative has a different significance from that which it has where its SeS feature, KN_c, 'neither knows', is reinforced, as opposed to contravened, in context. Cases of this kind are accounted for in (vi).[10] Having added the value 'c' on the KN variable, we can now also provide for:

---

[10] Huddleston's other example *You may have seen 'Iolanthe' when the D'oyly Carte were here last year* of which he notes that in saying it 'I do not imply that you don't know whether or not you did' is accounted for by (vii).

(viii) $LgS_{ID} + CoS_{KN_c} = FOSg$ 'claim'.
(ix) $LgS_{I\,P-I} + CoS_{KN_c} = FOSg$ 'poser'.

That is, such an approach allows us to predict categories of significance which might not arise for some time from textual analysis.

The three values suggested above for KN are, in fact, inadequate to account for the subtle distinctions in this area which are realized in the surface syntax of English. For example, we should certainly add a fourth value, KN_d: 'Both Speaker and Addressee know' which in turn will lead us to refine our specifications of KN_a and KN_b. Further, we will need to subdivide KN_d in terms of relative authority for Speaker and Addressee (cf. Davies 1976: 318, 324–339, 351; 1979: 125–8, 131, where a 'telling' variable is also invoked in this connection, and Berry (1981), who employs a distinction between 'primary' and 'secondary' knower, but, in the present terms, in relation to CoS only, and not to SeS, with which she is not dealing.

Lack of space prevents the necessary elaboration here, but perhaps enough has been out-lined to indicate the potential usefulness of (F) in accounting for the functional multivalency of CTs in this area of the surface syntax also. That is, (F) appears to state a relation between linguistic and pragmatic categories in such a way that it can be used to account for several types of meaningfulness in discourse.

The exact number and identity of the features I have suggested above, and elsewhere (Davies 1976, 1979), for inclusion in the SeSs of CTs within the mood system, require more testing, and may well need further revision. But the basic principles that: (i) some such list of semantic features for each syntactically distinct construction type is discoverable, and, (ii) that features in such a (SeS) list are always realized by the CT concerned, irrespective of whether or not any of them may also be contravened in context (to particular effect) on particular occasions, seem to be essential. They provide a theoretical basis by means of which a relatively small number of syntactic categories and their associated semantic specifications (the latter distinguished in terms of a small number of semantic primes) may be related, via recursive applications of (E), to an indefinitely large number of pragmatic categories of significance.

REFERENCES

Austin, J. L. (1962). *How to Do Things with Words*. Oxford: Clarendon Press.
Berry, M. (1981). Systemic linguistics and discourse analysis: a multi-layered approach to exchange structure. In Coulthard M. and Montgomery M. (eds.), *Studies in Discourse Analysis*. London: Routledge and Kegan Paul.), 120–145.
Bolinger, D. L. (1967). Imperatives in English. In *To Honor Roman Jakobson: Essays on the Occasion of his Seventieth Birthday*. The Hague and Paris: Mouton, 335–62.
——— (1977). *Meaning and Form*. London: Longman.
Davies, E. C. (1976). A study of Conditional, Causal and Interrogative Construction in English, with Reference to Situational Factors. Ph.D. dissertation, University of London.
——— (1979). *On the Semantics of Syntax: Mood and Condition in English*. London: Croom Helm.

Gimson, A. C. (1980). *An Introduction to the Pronunciation of English,* 3rd ed. London: Edward Arnold.

Gregory, M. (1985). Towards "Communication" Linguistics: a Framework. Paper given at the Ninth International Systemic Workshop, Toronto, August 1982. (This volume.)

Halliday, M. A. K. (1966). Lexis as a linguistic level. In Bazell, C. E. Catford, J. C. Halliday, M. A. K. and Robins R. H. (eds.), *In Memory of J. R. Firth* London: Longman, 148–62.

——— (1967). Notes on transitivity and theme in English, Part 2. *Journal of Linguistics* **3,2.** 199–244.

——— (1970). Language structure and language function. In Lyons J. (ed.), *New Horizons in Linguistics.* Harmondsworth, England: Penguin, 140–65.

Halliday, M. A. K. & Hasan, R. (1976). *Cohesion in English.* London: Longman.

Huddleston, R. (1981). Review of Davies, 1979, *Journal of Linguistics* **17,1.** 121–4.

Searle, J. R. (1975). Indirect speech acts. In Cole, P. and Morgan, J. L. (eds.), *Syntax and Semantics* **Vol 3.** New York: Academic Press, 19–82.

Process and Text: Two Aspects of Human Semiosis 13

J. R. Martin

University of Sydney
Australia

1. INTRODUCTION: PROCESS VS. TEXT

In the *Prolegomena* (1961) Hjelmslev uses two sets of terminology in resolving Saussure's dichotomy of *langue* and *parole*. Wh∍n discussing semiotic systems in general, Hjelmslev refers to a semiotic's meaning potential as *system,* and the realization of this potential as *process*. But when focusing on one of these semiotic systems, language, he uses the corresponding terms *language* and *text*. Hjelmslev may not have intended anything in particular by this particular choice of terms. But his selection of terms for the actual, at least in their English renditions, is intriguing. *Process* is much more the 'active' member of the pair: it connotes what at first strikes one as an interactive dynamic perspective on manifestation. *Text* is on the other hand more 'static': it calls to mind a product whole, complete, a kind of *fait accompli*. So little is accidental in Hjelmslev that one cannot help speculating on his use of these terms to distinguish language from the semiotic systems which in general comprise our culture. Is there a sense in which linguistic manifestations are products rather than processes while the realization of other semiotics is action rather than a thing? Is it just our oldest method of recording language, our writing systems, which make us think in this way? Whatever the case (we may never in fact know just what seeds Hjelmslev was sowing here), there is a sense in which process and text do reflect rather different perspectives on the actual and its relation to potential. In this paper the difference between these two perspectives, and the need for both of them in a complete account of human semiosis, will be considered.

2. LANGUAGE, REGISTER AND GENRE

The difference between the product and process perspectives is unfortunately not easy to illustrate with reference to grammar or phonology. Neither of the terms, as they are being looked at here, refers to the 'process' of manifestation, or *realization,* as it is conceived on these strata. This is presumably why linguists have been so happy to live without the distinction considered here for so long. Rather, to

CONVERSATIONAL STRUCTURE CONJUNCTION REFERENCE LEXICAL COHESION	TRANSITIVITY THEME MOOD group LEXIS & word systems	TONALITY TONICITY TONE foot & syllable prosodies phoneme systems
discourse	*lexicogrammar*	*phonology*

Figure 1. Outline of a tri-stratal systemic functional grammar with central systems on each stratum noted

clearly illustrate the product/process complementarity one has to look at text. There, once any attempt at an exhaustive description is made, the need for both perspectives becomes clear. This means that in order to discuss the question at all one needs a model of text in context - of discourse in relation to grammar and lexis and to those semiotic systems which language itself realizes. This takes us far beyond anything we can be sure of, into the realms of wild speculation perhaps. Nevertheless, some kind of model has to be set up if we are to progress; so here, with apologies, is my current best guess at how it all fits together.

To begin, let us assume a tri-stratal model of language such as that sketched out in Fig. 1. The strata are named, abstracting away from phonic substance, phonology, lexicogrammar and discourse. The fundamental unit on each stratum (where the action is in terms of the number of choices made) is the phoneme, the clause and the text, respectively. The lexicogrammar assumed is a very rich systemic-functional one. Following Halliday (1967 forthcoming) it includes descriptions of TRANSITIVITY, MOOD and THEME, group and word rank systems, and a yet to be accomplished collocational approach to lexis (Halliday 1961, 1966, Sinclair 1966). Such a rich 'semantax' leaves the next stratum free to handle inter-clause relations: REFERENCE, CONJUNCTION and LEXICAL COHESION as outlined in Halliday and Hasan (1976) along with CONVERSATIONAL STRUC-TURE (based on the work of Sinclair & Coulthard 1975, and Berry 1981a, b, c). Two of the three examples of the need for both a product and a process perspective will be taken from this stratum: from REFERENCE in section 4.1 and from CON-VERSATIONAL STRUCTURE in 4.2.

In addition to this semiotic system, which has so far been the special preoccupation of most linguists, it is necessary to consider two further semiotic systems, which will be referred to here as register and genre. These two systems are what Hjelmslev referred to as *connotative semiotics:* semiotics whose expression plane is another semiotic system. Linguists, especially those with an interest in why language is the way it is, have probably been remiss in ignoring these semiotics; since it is the function of language to realize them, both of these parasites, register and genre, have profoundly affected the structure of language itself (see Halliday 1973, 1975, 1978 for discussion). These connotative semiotics are stacked up against language in Fig. 2. There language is treated as the phonology of register and

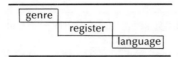

Figure 2. Language in relation to its connotative semiotics: register and genre

register the phonology of genre. The 'level' occupied by each of these semiotics will be referred to as a communication *plane* (note that this is *not* Hjelmslev's usage; he used the term *plane* for what is now generally referred to as a *stratum*). The third example of the need for a product/process opposition will be taken from the most abstract of these semiotics, genre, and will in fact be discussed before the others in section 3 below.

Register will be briefly considered in section 4. It comprises the traditional Firthian contextual categories of *field, mode* and *tenor* with field covering the institutional focus of a text (see Benson and Greaves, 1981), mode the medium through which it is realized, and tenor the social distance between speaker and addressee. Halliday's rhetorical genre (for him an aspect of mode; 1978:143), Gregory's (1967) functional tenor and Ure and Ellis's (1977) role have been more or less abstracted away from this plane and set up as a further underlying semiotic, genre, of which more in section 3. All this takes us far beyond what is at present testable, arguable or even mildly convincing; so it is perhaps best to stop at this point, leaving the problems of ideology, code and foregrounding for best guesses at another time.

3. GENRE

Genres are how things get done, when language is used to accomplish them. They range from literary to far from literary forms: poems, narratives, expositions, lectures, seminars, recipes, manuals, appointment making, service encounters, news broadcasts and so on. The term genre is used here to embrace each of the linguistically realized activity types which comprise so much of our culture. Its meaning extends far beyond its use in literary studies to refer to different kinds of verbal art, though each of these does remain a genre in the usage here.

Set up as a semiotic system underlying register as it is, one of the principal descriptive responsibilities of genre is to constrain the possible combinations of field, mode and tenor variables used by a given culture. No culture makes use of all possible combinations. In western culture for example, one does not lecture about typing, bicycle maintenance or house cleaning. There is no real reason why one couldn't (it is easy to imagine a comedian doing just this - but to make us laugh). But these fields simply do not combine with power (tenor) and abstract reflective monologue (mode) in our culture. When people are being socialized into these institutions genres other than lectures are used.

Some of the holes in a culture's register paradigms, such as those just discussed, appear at a first glance somewhat arbitrary. Others are more obviously highly functional. Some fields do not combine with particular tenor and mode values because of taboo. Sex for example does not readily combine with power (tenor) and spontaneous dialogue (mode). It is not always 'polite' in our culture to talk about sex to our inferiors; if one does so, it may be construed as a rather threatening, often sexist, demand for sexual favours. Similarly there is a general constraint against talking about sex while doing it, regardless of the tenor involved. There are however er genres which legitimize this field. Sex is fine as a topic among peers (realizing solidarity tenor) providing the mode is reflective; and sex is acceptable in lectures and seminars where there is bound to be a differentiated power relationship of some kind but the mode is reflective monologue (where children are involved this is only just becoming a legitimate combination in our culture).

At other times, functional holes in a culture's register paradigms seem to exist for the purpose of ensuring that culture's survival. Semioticians for example, especially those intent on revolution, quickly discover that they are not allowed to discuss their work in casual conversation. Most people feel threatened by the idea that there are rules, abstract invisible ones, of various kinds, which explain a lot of the behaviour they treasure as thoughts and feelings of a personal kind. Semioticians threaten freedom! When semioticians do break through this barrier and attack the arbitrariness of one or another of these rules, most people start to feel threatened by a loss of security - sacred truths become banal. Semioticians threaten security! The result of all this is that the people who are trained to recognize invisible semiotic repression of many kinds have to shut up about it. Romantic liberalism gags them. This is immensely useful to those benefiting from this repression. Jay Lemke refers to holes of this kind as *disjunctions* (cf. Lemke 1982). If holes like this are filled, a culture is bound to change, quickly and radically.

The second reason for setting up genre as an underlying semiotic is a more positive one. Genre does more than legitimize combinations of field, mode and tenor in a culture. As well it represents at an abtract level the verbal strategies used to accomplish social purposes of many kinds. These strategies can be thought of in terms of stages through which one moves in order to realize a genre. In narrative of personal experience, for example, (cf. Labov & Waletzky 1967) one begins with an Abstract (a synoptic summary of sorts of the story to be told), continues with an Orientation (introducing protagonists and setting them in time and space), follows on with a Complication (a series of events leading up to something going wrong), inserts an optional Evaluation (suspending the action for a moment to comment on and thereby highlight the crisis), carries on with a Resolution (solving the crisis for better or worse) and ends with a Coda (a brief comment on why the story was worth telling). All genres have a beginning-middle-end structure of some kind; these structures will be referred to here as *schematic structures* (equivalent to Hasan's 1977; 1980 generalized text structures). Schematic structure represents the positive contribution genre makes to a text: a way of getting from A to B in the way a given culture accomplishes whatever the genre in question is functioning to do in that culture.

In order to illustrate the concept of genre in detail, consider now one genre, or rather one set of related genres, which might be referred to as service encounters (see Hasan 1979). This genre has been studied in some depth by Ventola (1982) following up some suggestions of Hasan (1979, and Halliday and Hasan, 1980). Ventola has focused her attention on the following service encounters: post office, travel agency and small shop. Her proposal for the schematic structure of these service encounters is as follows:

> Greeting (an exchange of *hello*'s)
> Attendance Allocation (selection of the next customer: *Next please.*)
> Service Bid (offer of service: *Can I help you? -Yes/no.*)
> Service (statement of needs and their provision: *Yes, I'm looking for . . .*)
> Resolution (decision to or not to buy: *Yes, I'll have those . . .*)
> Pay (exchange of payment)
> Goods Handover (exchange of goods)
> Closing (exchange of thanks)
> Good-bye (an exchange of *bye-bye*'s)

The elements of schematic structure for this genre are listed here in their unmarked order of occurrence; the actual sequence of realization is somewhat variable.

The question that schematic structures of this kind immediately poses is: where do they come from? Hasan (1980) suggests that they are determined by particular values of field, mode and tenor. Schematic structures are in other words generated by register. This formulation will be inverted here where elements of schematic structure will be interpreted as determining particular values of field, mode and tenor. The elements themselves will be generated by genre networks. This follows from the discussion presented above concerning the use of genre to constrain a culture's legitimate combinations of field, mode and tenor variables. It should perhaps be pointed out here that there is really nothing descriptively at stake in this inversion. What is descriptively important is the way in which values of register and schematic structure correlate. This direction of determination is a moot point as far as this correlation is concerned. Direction of determination stops being a moot point only when relations between genres and sub-genres are taken into account. What then of genre agnation - of genre as system?

Here one is on very shaky ground indeed. There do not appear to exist descriptions of different kinds of service encounters which would make it possible to formalize genre agnation in a principled way. What follows by way of formalization is intended only as an illustration of what genre as system might entail. The network itself will no doubt prove something of an embarrassment as the study of genre unfolds.

A tentative formalization of service encounter agnation is presented in Fig. 3. Realization rules are presented in Table 1 next to features which determine the presence or absence of particular elements of service encounter schematic structure. No attempt is made to specify the sequence of elements at this stage. Terminology is definitely a problem: there is no 'traditional grammar' of genres to draw on. So-

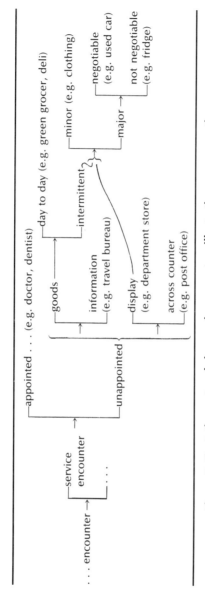

Figure 3. Tentative network for service enounters illustrating genre agnation

Table 1. Realization Statements for Service Encounter Features

[encounter]	+Greeting; +Good-bye
[service encounter]	+Service; +Resolution; +Closing
[appointed]	+Wait (*Won't you have a seat; the doctor will be with you in a moment.*)
[not appointed]	+Service Bid
[goods]	+Pay; +Goods Handover
[across counter]	+Attendance Allocation
[intermittent]	+Sales Pitch (persuasion to buy); +Reassurance (assertion of goods goodness if bought)
[major]	+Delivery (arrangement of transportation or pick-up)
[negotiable]	+Bargain (negotiation of price)

ciology and social anthropology will no doubt turn out to have a great deal to offer semiotics in this area.

The network in Fig. 3 and the corresponding realization rules in Table 1 would, if anywhere near correct, go some way towards distinguishing one genre from another and showing the relations between them. But they are still a long way from generating well-formed schematic structures for service encounters in our culture. First of all, nothing has been said about the sequence of elements. Ventola's elements have been listed in their unmarked sequence above. But as her work has shown, one does not have to collect very many service encounter texts before one comes across departures from this norm in what are still felt to be well-formed texts. Greetings for example are found initially, after Attendance Allocations and after Service Bids as well; Services may occur after Goods Handovers, if the client remembers something else that is needed. Clearly getting elements in the right order is not straight-forward. Second, some of the elements in a service encounter can occur more than once; there may be more than one Service and Resolution in the structure - a customer may have more than one need. So recursion has to be built into the description at some point. Third, there are at least three places in the schematic structure where client or server may opt out: clients may refuse the Service Bid, saying that they are just looking; servers may have to opt out in the Service because they do not have what the client is looking for; and clients may opt out in the Resolution because the goods or information offered are not what they want. Each of these departures has the effect of aborting the service encounter as client and server skip forward to the Closing (alternatively a client may skip back to the Turn Allocation if he has genuinely refused the Service Bid to look around with the intent of purchasing something when he finds it).

None of these problems are intractable. But they do raise serious questions about generating well-formed schematic structures with a network such as that in Fig. 3. This is perhaps not too surprising. Taking grammar as his model a systemicist might at first expect that if he works out the relations between genres and sub-genres of related kinds and formalizes these in a network, then it will be a simply matter to formulate realization rules generating well-formed schematic structures. After all, it works for clauses; why wouldn't it work here? Schematic structures are however different in kind from clause structures, and this procedure turns out to be naive. For one thing in clauses the sequence of elements tells you what kind of clause it is; but with schematic structure sequence is more variable - what matters is that a Greeting is accomplished, not so much when it is. For another, recursion works differently in clauses then in schematic structures. In principle, only ranking units, clause, group or word can be recursive in grammar. One does not find recursion of inherent elements of clause structure (eg. recursive Actors or Ranges or recursive Subjects or Finites). It is only by passing recursion down the rank-scale that one can get more than one Actor or Subject in a clause (*John and Mary arrived.* has one Actor, not two, which is realized by a nominal group complex). But with schematic structure there does seem to be genuine recursion of elements that are not ranking units. There may be several Services and Resolutions in an service encounter; but these elements are not elements of a different rank from Greeting, Closings or Good-byes. Finally, in grammar, once one begins a clause, one finishes (leaving false starts and other hesitation and interruption phenomena aside). There is not in clause

Notational conventions for the interpretation of Fig. 4:

Flow chart notation:

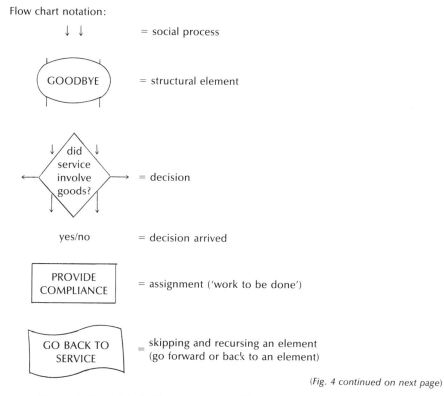

(*Fig. 4 continued on next page*)

Figure 4. Ventola's tactic pattern for initial elements in service encounter

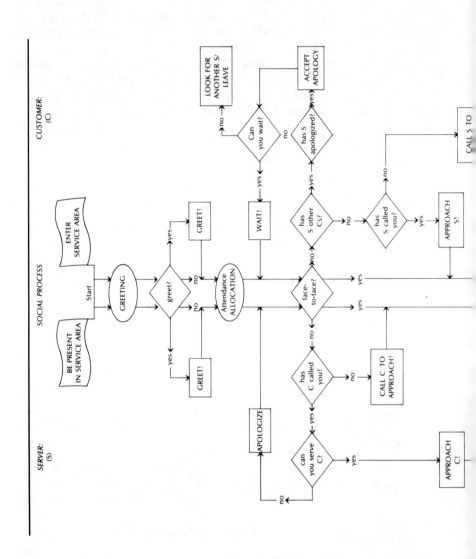

SERVER:
(S)

SOCIAL PROCESS

CUSTOMER:
(C)

BE PRESENT
IN SERVICE AREA

ENTER
SERVICE AREA

Start

GREETING

greet?

GREET!

GREET!

Attendance
ALLOCATION

APOLOGIZE

WAIT!

Can
you wait?

LOOK FOR
ANOTHER S/
LEAVE

has S
apologized?

ACCEPT
APOLOGY

has
S other
Cs?

face-
to-face?

has
C called
you?

CALL C TO
APPROACH!

has
S called
you?

APPROACH
S!

CALL S TO

can
you serve
C?

APPROACH
C!

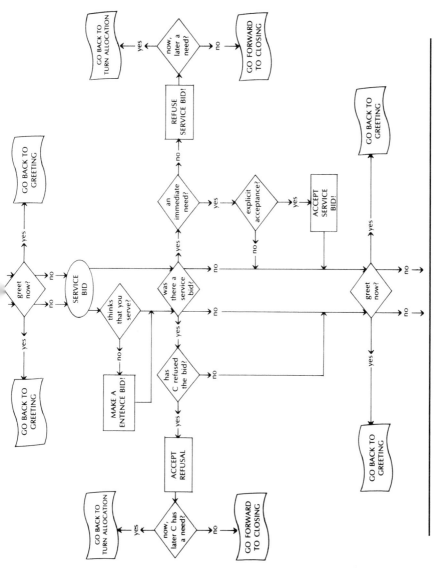

Figure 4. Ventola's tactic pattern for initial elements in service encounter (*cont'd*)

257

structure a set of elements which permit a speaker to stop talking or a listener to stop listening, with the clause remaining well-formed regardless. But with schematic structure there are elements which, depending on how they are negotiated, allow the interlocutors to abort the encounter: one *can* escape! Again, this is not to argue that clause structures are principled in a way schematic structures are not. But it is to point out that the mechanisms for formulating these principles are bound to be different in kind; system networks and realization rules are not going to be equipped for the job.

What *will* work? Ventola's suggestion is that the way to generate well-formed schematic structures for service encounters is to make use of an elaborated decision tree or flow chart (cf. Fawcett 1975). The first part of her analysis of the tactics pattern necessary for the service encounters she was investigating is presented in Fig. 4. This deals only with the first three elements in her service encounters (for the complete tactic pattern see Ventola 1982). Interpreted in light of the notational conventions included in this figure, this kind of notation appears much closer to what is necessary that system networks and realization rules. Options are included permitting different sequences of the elements required by the genre. Choices are formalized which permit speakers to abort the encounter. And opportunities are provided for backward loops in the flow chart so that recursive elements can be generated. It seems certain that future work on genre and schematic structure which adopts any kind of generative focus will have to include analyses of this kind.

In terms of its generative power the flow chart has three crucial advantages over system networks and realization rules: 1. it allows realization to take place over time —it is not necessary that every decision be taken before the realization of a unit starts; 2. it allows for the recursion of elements which are not ranking units; and 3. it allows for the structure to be aborted at various places during its realization. Interestingly enough the power of a flow chart tells us something about the weakness of system networks and realizations rules which should prove of interest to those concerned with constraints on generative power as far as grammar is concerned.

Now, in terms of the product/process dichotomy, where does this take us? In order to answer this question it is necessary to elaborate the terminology so that the opposition in question in interpreted from the point of view of system/language as well as that of process/text. This is accomplished in Fig. 5, where potential and actual are taken as cross-classifying the active and static perspectives. Potential as seen from the static perspective is termed a *synoptic system;* viewed actively it is termed a *dynamic system.* Actual, when viewed statically will be termed *text;* when viewed dynamically it will be referred to as *process.* Thus synoptic systems generate texts; dynamic systems generate process. The synoptic/dynamic opposition is at the root of Bourdieu's (1977) critique of social anthropology; the term *synoptic* is taken from his work. Lemke (1979) introduces the same opposition, making use of the term *dynamic* for the 'active' perspective.

Interpreted in terms of this terminology, Fig. 3 represents genre potential as a synoptic system. There genres are viewed objectively, after the fact, as things, with particular relations to each other in our culture. Fig. 4 on the other hand represents

	potential	actual
static	synoptic system	text
active	dynamic system	process

Figure 5. Static and active perspectives cross-classifying potential and actual

genre potential interpreted as a dynamic system. There genre is viewed subjectively, in the process of manifestation, full of interacting decisions, dependencies, choices and the like. Ironically, as one moves from potential to actual in the process of realization, each of these radically different systems turns out to amount to the same thing - a schematic structure which is simultaneously a text and a process (cf. Halliday and Hasan, 1980:11 where a somewhat different distinction is made between text and process; process, in the sense used here does not really seem to be distinguished from realization in Halliday's discussion). In a sense, the dynamic system somehow disappears: it is etic, enabling, lurking between the lines as it were rather than emic, enabled, and manifest in the final result (for this reason writing systems transcribe text, not process, and semioticians, at least linguist ones, tend to get distracted from dynamic potential, especially if their approach to potential has a strong syntagmatic bias as in transformation theory). It appears then that while one can live without a strict process/text distinction in our models of semiotic systems, the dynamic/synoptic opposition is critical. We will never be in a position to make predictions about well-formed schematic structures unless the systems which generate these process/texts are viewed as two distinct but symbiotically interacting potentials.

In passing, to further illustrate the points made here, consider for a moment a completely different semiotic system: the game of bridge. Here only the bidding will be considered, not the actual playing of the hands. Fries (1981) has attempted to formalize the options open to bidders in this card game as outlined in Fig. 6. This network represents the synoptic potential relevant to bidding moves which form the text/process in the first part of a bridge game. Of course, as Fries points out, not all of the options in this network are open to a bidder at any one time. An actual bid must be selected from a much more restricted potential which depends on whether the bid is an opening bid or not, on whether one's partner has bid, on what one's partner has bid and on what conventions partners are using to bid in the game. Obviously the only way to generate well-formed bidding sequences in bridge is to formulate bidding dynamically as well as synoptically. While it is true that the bid a player makes at any point in the game is synoptically related to all other bids as outlined in Fig. 6, the range of options open at any one time is in fact very limited (especially for a skilled player) and must itself be determined by a dynamic system which treats bidding as a process rather than a text. Once again, a transcription of the actual bidding, such as that found in bridge columns in newspapers and magazines, does not distinguish process from text. The synoptic potential underlying the bidding will be familiar to most readers. But what is not so readily accessible is the dynamic potential which has generated just this bidding sequence. This is of course

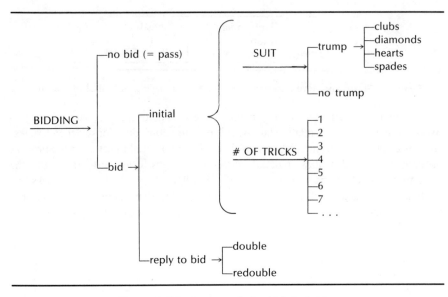

Figure 6. Fries's network for bids in bridge

what the 'expert' bridge columnist seeks to elucidate in his commentary. In order to teach a computer to play bridge this dynamic potential would have to be formalized. Interestingly enough it seems to be part of the raison d'etre of complicated games such as bridge that such a dynamic formalization is not easy to accomplish. By nature, such games have a relatively simple synoptic system (when compared to language and its connotative semiotics) and a comparatively complicated (though not as complicated as for a game like chess) dynamic system. For some reason humans find this kind of semiotic fun. One cannot help wondering whether this is simply because games are a pleasant change from language or because humans would in fact be happier if genres and registers and languages were synoptically simpler systems and dynamically more open ones (cf. Lemke 1982, who appears to suggest just this). Of course humans might have to give up a large part of their culture to attain this (this is presumably why heavens of various kinds, fieldless, tenorless, modeless and genreless as they often seem to be, are so attractive, particularly to the oppressed).

4. SYNOPTIC AND DYNAMIC SYSTEMS IN LANGUAGE

Having argued for the importance of both a synoptic and dynamic perspective on two very different semiotic systems, genre and bridge, the question naturally arises as to whether these two perspectives are relevant to language as well. The answer that most linguists have implicitly given since Saussure is *no;* a synoptic perspectives has almost exclusively dominated linguists' work on phonemes and clauses.

Now that linguists have begun to turn their attention to texts, however, the answer is no longer so simple. Certainly there are linguists who approach discourse synoptically and attempt to model discourse structure on that of grammar (e.g., Longacre, 1976). Recently on the other hand, post-variationists such as Lavandera have argued for a more dynamic approach: 'I approach texts as dynamic processes taking place in time rather than as finished products with a static structure.' writes Lavandera in the introduction to an article on the motivation for choices between indicative and subjunctive in Spanish discourse ([n.d.]:1). In this section two major aspects of discourse structure, CONVERSATIONAL STRUCTURE and REFERENCE will be briefly reviewed in order to demonstrate the necessity of both a synoptic and a dynamic perspective as far as generating well-formed discourse structures is concerned.

4.1 Conversational Structure

Consider first exchange structure. The best synoptic description of the structure of exchanges to date is that being developed by Margaret Berry at the University of Nottingham (see Berry 1981a, b, c). The analysis of exchange structure presented here is taken from her work, which is itself an extension of earlier work by Sinclair and Coulthard (1975). Berry's network for exchange structure is presented in Fig. 7 (Berry 1981c:29). It generates exchange structures such as those illustrated in text 1 and 2. Text 1 is a four move [action oriented] exchange, text 2 a four move [proposition oriented] one.

(1)	A.a. Who is the most boring Canadian in the world?	dk1
	B.b. - Margaret Trudeau?	k2
	A.c. - Right.	k1
	B.d. - Oh.	k2f
(2)	A.a. Have a beer.	da1
	B.b. - Okay.	a2
	A.c. - Here you go.	a1
	B.d. - Thanks.	a2f

Text 1 is a kind of quiz. The primary knower, A, who is acting as an authority on the topic at hand, asks B a question. B responds, somewhat tentatively using a tone 2 (there are, after all, so many boring Canadians, especially from the point of view of Canadians) with an answer. The primary knower then confirms this proposition, now completed, to be the case and finally B, the secondary knower comments in relief. In Berry's terms, 1.a is a dk1 (delayed k1) move by the primary knower, 1.b is an elicited k2 move by the secondary knower, 1.c is the actual k1 move by the primary knower (the obligatory element in information exchanges) asserting the proposition as developed in 1.a and 1.b to be correct, and 1.d is a follow up move by the secondary knower commenting on the proposition. Information exchanges may begin with k2 or k1 moves as well as in texts 3 and 4, but these variations will not be further discussed here.

(3)   A.a. Who is the most boring person in the world?   k2
      B.b. - Margaret Trudeau.   k1
      A.c. - Oh.   k2f

(4)   A.a. Margaret Trudeau is the most boring person.   k1
      B.b. - Too true.   k2f

Text 2 is parallel is structure, but is oriented to an exchange of goods rather than of information. The primary actor, A, delays giving B a drink by first inquiring if he wants one; B replies that he does, then A gives him the drink and B thanks him. In Berry's terms in 2.a the primary actor delays acting by making an offer; in 2.b B accepts the offer, telling A to in fact get him a drink; in 2.c A replies with a verbalized a1 move; and in 2.d B follows up with an expression of gratitude. Like information exchanges, action exchanges can begin with any of a dx1, x2 or x1 move. Action exchanges beginning with a2 and a1 moves are illustrated in texts 5 and 6 respectively but will not be further discussed here.

(5)   A.a. Could you get me a drink.   a2
      B.b. - Sure.   a1
      A.c. - Thanks.   a2f

(6)   A.a. Have a drink.   a1
      B.b. - Thanks.   a2f

This brief presentation does not really do justice to the complexities involved. Hopefully it will suffice to show what can be accomplished from a synoptic perspective. Berry's analysis, once the realization of the features in Fig. 7 is made explicit, does make predictions about well-formed exchanges in English; and it does show how exchanges are alike and different from each other. As such the analysis far surpasses in descriptive adequacy anything presented in speech act theory or ethnomethodology. But is this perspective enough? It will be suggested here that it is not, for reasons very similar to those developed for the schematic structures considered in section 3.

Consider text 7. In this text A rejects B's first and second k2 move, waiting for the right answer. The completion of the exchange is in effect suspended until the proposition A has in mind is correctly completed. When it is A plays the k1 move and B completes the exchange:

7.A.a.   Who is the most boring person in Canada?   dk1
  B.b.   — Joe Clark?   k2
  A.c.   — No.   —
  B.d.   — Pierre Trudeau?   k2

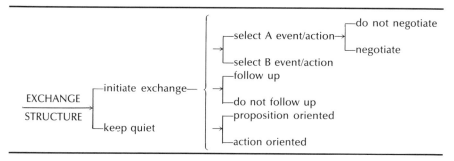

Figure 7. Berry's 1981c Network for Exchange Structure

A.e.	— No.	—
B.f.	— Um, Margaret Trudeau?	k2
A.g.	— Right.	k1
B.h.	— Oh.	k2f

Text 7 raises two problems for the synoptic description outlined above. First of all, there are 3 k2 moves, not just 1 as predicted. And in principle there might be many more in a longer such guessing game. Second, it is not clear what roles in the exchange moves 3.c and 3.e are playing. They might be coded as k1 moves, but would then have to be distinguished somehow from 3.g since 3.g predicts a following k2f move whereas 3.c and 3.e precede a k2 move. The same phenomenon is found in action exchanges as illustrated in 8.

8.A.a.	Can I get you a drink?	da1
B.b.	—//2 scotch//	a2
A.c.	—No.	—
B.d.	—//2 gin//	a2
A.e.	—No.	—
B.f.	—//2 beer//	a2
A.g.	—Okay.	a1
B.h.	—Thanks.	a2f

Texts 7 and 8 illustrate one of the dynamic phenomena discussed with respect to schematic structures above: namely, recursion of elements of structure where this recursion cannot be interpreted in terms of the recursion of ranking units. Neither texts 7 or 8 are in any sense exchange complexes. And in both texts, moves b, d and f are neither move complexes nor clause complexes (there is no natural place for a recursive loop in Fig. 7). One of the elements of exchange structure is simply repeated until the exchange can be resolved. Note in passing that this need not be the x2 move:

(9)   A.a. Margaret Trudeau is the most boring person in the world.   k1
       B.b. - No, she isn't.   -
       A.c. - Yes, she is.   k1
       B.d. - She is not.   -
       A.e. - She is.   k1
       B.f. - Oh, alright.   k2f

(10)   A.a. Can I get you a beer?   da1
       B.b. - No.   -
       A.c. - C'mon.   da1
       B.D. - Nope.   -
       A.e. - Have one.   da1
       B.f. - Oh, alright.   a2
       A.g. - Here.   a1
       B.h. - Thanks a lot.   a2f

Consider now texts 11 and 12. These texts illustrate another dynamic aspect of exchange structure which has parallels in schematic structure. In 11 the exchange is interrupted while A makes sure he has heard B correctly:

(11)   A.a. Who is the most boring person in Canada?   dk1
       B.b. - Margaret Trudeau.   k2
       A.c. - //2 Margaret//   -
       B.d. - Yes.   -
       A.e. - Right.   k1
       B.f. - Obviously.   k2f

In 12 the exchange is interrupted while B queries A's reasons for negotiating the exchange. Note that if B had not been satisfied by A's explanation he might have aborted the exchange completely:

(12)   A.a. Can I get you a drink?   da1
       B.b. - Why?   -
       A.c. - I'm trying to get you drunk.   -
       B.d. - Okay.   a2
       A.e. - Here we go then.   a1
       B.f. - Thanks.   a2f

Texts 11 and 12 show that exchanges can be interrupted or even aborted entirely. The synoptic account given above makes no provision for moves such as c in 11 or b in 12. This feature of exchange structure resembles the problem of exit options in schematic structure. As noted above clients may if they wish refuse a service bid, either to interrupt the development of the schematic structure while they look around a little longer, or to abort the encounter entirely if they are genuinely just window shopping. It is part of the dynamic structure of both schematic structures and exchanges that they can be interrupted in this way.

Note at this point that although it was suggested earlier that dynamic systems are invisible, disappearing as text is formed, they may in fact appear to repair a process which is breaking down. This is what is going on in texts like 9 through 12 where confirmations and queries are used to get the exchange back on the right track. So in a sense it is only when something goes wrong that process can be distinguished from text. One can perhaps draw an analogy here between language and games such as ice hockey or rugby. There referees supervise the formation of text, intervening with stoppages in play and penalties when ungrammatical texts are formed. These interventions are like confirmations and queries in exchange structure: text and process for a moment become distinguishable. One of the more interesting developments over the past few years in both these sports has been the co-option of violence into the synoptic system of these games. Physical intimidation has proved a successful means of winning a game - what was once an illegitimate process has become an integral part of a team's strategy. This means that violence which was once viewed as an aberration must now be treated as text: process and text have fused. Upsetting as it is to many fans, the games have changed. It may be that interaction of this kind between text and process will contribute something to our understanding of semiotic change, which means a change in the synoptic system of a semiotic as change is now conceived. The future of semiotic systems in other words lies in their dynamic systems, lurking between the lines. Violence has always been part of ice hockey, but it has not always been a way to win.

To date Berry's proposals for exchange structure have not attempted to synoptically control the recursion and interruptions in texts like 7 through 12. The network in Fig. 7 has not been extended to generate text with such structures. Berry has discussed related structures (1981a:135–139, 1981b), making reference to embedded exchanges, and has hinted that transformational rules might be used to embed them. The fact that alternative descriptive strategies (alternative to system networks and realization rules) have to be used to generate such structures in her approach appears to support the synoptic/dynamic opposition drawn here. In Fig. 8 the flow chart notation introduced in section 3 is used to tentatively formalize just a part of the dynamic system underlying information exchanges. Whether or not the flow chart is simply a notational variant of the strategies used by Berry to handle such phenomena is an important question which will not be answered here.

The flow chart is a preliminary one and deals only with the first move in a negotiated information exchange and possible reactions to it by the secondary knower. These reactions include first of all confirmation sequences such as that illustrated in 11. These may be requests for the whole of the dk1 move to be repeated as in 13, wh echo questions focusing on one of the dk1 moves MOOD functions as in 14, or simple repetitions of part of the content of the dk1 move as in 15. The flowchart then allows for challenges to the relevance of the dk1 move as illustrated in 12 above. All this apparatus takes us only as far as the k2 move.

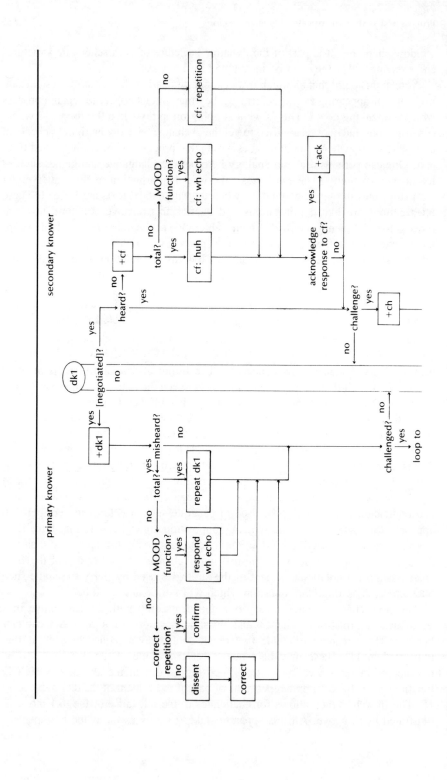

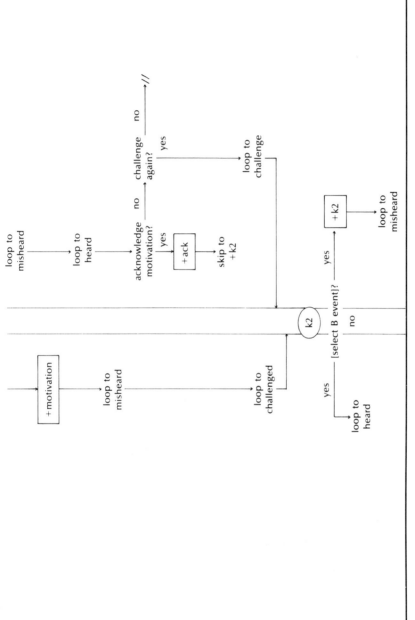

Figure 8. Tentative formalization of the dynamic system underlying the dk1 move in an information exchange (notation as for Fig. 4 except decision diamonds and looping/skipping notation omitted)

(13) A.a. Who is the most boring person in Canada?
      B.b. - What?
      A.c. - Who is the most boring person in Canada?
      B.d. - Oh.
         e. - Um, Margaret Trudeau?
            ...

(14) A.a. Who is the most boring person in Canada?
      B.b. - Where?
      A.c. - In Canada.
      B.d. - Oh.
         e. Um, Margaret Trudeau?
            ...

(15) A.a. Who is the most boring person in Canada?
      B.b. - //2 Canada//
      A.c. - Yeah.
      B.d. - Oh.
         e. - Um, Margaret Trudeau?
            ...

4.2 Reference

A second example of the need for synoptic and dynamic systems at the level of
discourse can be illustrated with respect to English's participant identification system, REFERENCE. A synoptic account of some of the central options in this
system is presented in Fig. 9. Systems 1, 2 and 3 crossclassify participants in a text
as [generic] (eg. *Tigers have stripes.*) or [specific] (eg. *That tiger has dark stripes.*),
[presenting] (eg. *There's a tiger over there.*) or [presuming] (eg. *That tiger looks
dangerous.*), and as [comparative] (eg. *I've never seen a fiercer tiger.*) or not.
Systems 4, 5 and 6 subclassify phoric nominal groups into pronouns ([reduced]),
demonstratives ([directed]) and the definite article ([undirected]). And system 7
allows for the presumption of a superset, realized through superlative modification
(eg. *That's the biggest tiger I've ever seen.*).

When phoric nominal groups presume information located elsewhere in the same
text, a cohesive tie is formed (see Halliday and Hasan, 1976). These ties are in fact
a kind of discourse structure. In text 16, *it* cannot be understood until the listener
connects it to the previous mention of the tiger. Once the connection is made, *it* and
a tiger constitute a referential structure:

(16) There's *a tiger* over there and *it* looks like attacking.

Note that the synoptic account of REFERENCE given in Fig. 7 makes no attempt to
generate structures of this kind. The network subclassifies and crossclassifies participants, not participant structures. There have been, as far as I know, no attempts
to set up systems at some rank larger than and realized through participants to

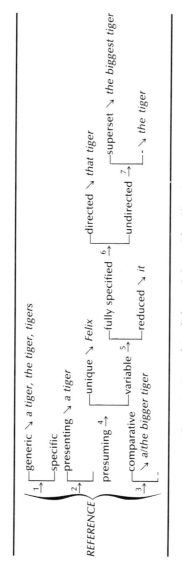

Figure 9. Central English participant identification systems

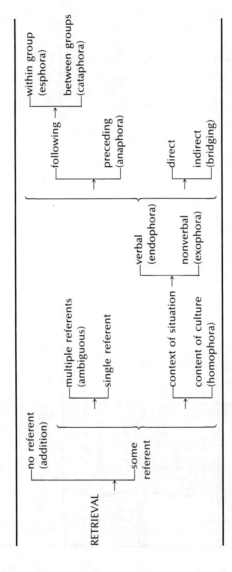

Figure 10. RETRIEVAL processes for phoric reference

account for these structures. Indeed it is not at all clear what kind of unit this would be how an attempt at mother control of these structures could succeed.

What linguists have attempted to do is outline the ways in which speakers decide what options to choose from Fig. 7 and how listeners recover information when phoric items are used. One such account of this process is presented in Fig. 10. There an account is given of the RETRIEVAL processes speakers and listeners assume when identifying participants in text: Fig. 10 treats these processes as a system network, making use of a typical synoptic formalization strategy. But is this network really synoptic in its orientation? Clearly it is not. It is not really classifying either participants or participant structures. Rather, it describes in what will probably turn out to be only a crude and partial way the operations a listener might perform in locating the referent of a phoric nominal group. Even taken to this point the RETRIEVAL options refer only to some of what goes on when reference structures are formed; considerable elaboration would be necessary before it could be implemented in say a text generation project where computers, not linguists, generate discourse structures. Again, the flowchart notation developed by Ventola seems applicable. This will not be pursued here; but some kind of dynamic formalization is necessary if participant structures are to be generated.

As with conversational structure, process is most clearly distinguished from text where participant identification breaks down. In 17 B's query focuses attention for a moment on the retrieval process:

(17) A.a. . . . and then he came up
      B.b. - Who?
      A.c. - John
         d. - he came up and . . .

Another angle on process is found when speakers use experiential structures to instantially identify participants as in 18:

(18) A.a. . . . and then John came up,
         b. that's my boy-friend,
         c. and said . . .

A further perspective is provided by the work of Clark and his colleagues on the time it appears to take listeners to track down information when it is implied by the co-text rather than explicitly present (Clark and Haviland, 1974). Their work indicates that it takes listeners longer to build the reference structure in 19 where the presumed information is implied than in 20 where it is explicitly available.

(19) John got the picnic basket out of the car.
      The beer was warm.

(20) John got some beer out of the car.
      The beer was warm.

The difference between REFERENCE and CONVERSATIONAL STRUCTURE
when approached from both a synoptic and dynamic perspective is of some interest.
CONVERSATIONAL STRUCTURE seems to have a more developed synoptic
system than REFERENCE. It is possible to set up a system network at exchange
rank which makes testable predications about the sequence of moves in conversation. A good deal of conversational structure can be predicted from this approach.
There remain however a number of conversational gambits open to interlocutors
which are not netted in. For these, a dynamic tactic pattern of some kind will have
to be worked out. With REFERENCE on the other hand, it appears that next to
nothing can be predicted about well-formed participant structures (= REFERENCE
chains) via mother control. There is simply no mother around to act as a point of
origin for systems which would make predictions about well-formed reference
structures. REFERENCE thus appears a less prominently synoptic system than
CONVERSATIONAL STRUCTURE. Its structures will have to be generated almost entirely through dynamic systems. This is not to argue that either of these
discourse systems can be approached from just one or the other perspective. Both
types of discourse structure have dynamic and synoptic systems underlying them.
But it does appear that one or the other perspective may be more prominent when it
comes to generating well-formed text.

    Indeed, much of the difficulty linguists have experienced in text generation
probably stems from the importance of dynamic systems in this enterprise. Linguists come to discourse equipped with synoptic generative models, not dynamic
ones. With the aid of these models they either proceed, with some embarrassment,
apologizing for their lack of success as if only time stood in the way of progress; or
they back off, confidently declaring that discourse has no structure, is not part of
language anyway, and can be left to psychologists and philosophers who are better
equipped to deal with 'thoughts' and 'feelings'. Moving from one stratum or plane
to the next is never easy. But distinguishing between synoptic and dynamic systems
will make the going a bit smoother, at least until we stumble over something else
which although manifestly present, is invisible and not netted in by the descriptive
strategies we import from what we have already done.

    Nothing will be said here about register dynamics; only discourse and genre have
been considered. Certainly some of the register variation that one finds in a single
text will be accounted for by schematic structure: different elements of schematic
structure can be used to preselect different values of field, mode and tenor in
different parts of a text. But it will be true as well that not all register variation can
be handled synoptically in this way. The genres that linguists are presently working
on are just those with a relatively clear schematic structure (ie. those most amenable
to synoptic analysis). But genres which are closer in their structure to casual conversation will have much more prominent dynamic than synoptic systems involved in

their generation. Clearly some kind of powerful and relatively open-ended formalization of register dynamics will be needed for such texts.

5. CONCLUSION

The moral of all this (to borrow a closing element of schematic structure from another genre) seems to be that as long as we have as our goal the explicit generation of text in context, something will eventually come along and save us from ourselves. The panacea offered in this paper is the distinction between synoptic and dynamic systems. This distinction is of course not without its problems. For one thing, linguists have next to no experience in dealing with dynamic systems. It is not clear what counts as a significant generalization. It is not altogether clear what kind of formalism is best adapted to capturing these generalizations. It is not clear how such a formalism can be constrained. It is not clear what the best heuristic strategies will be for investigating dynamic systems. And it is not clear how linguists will distribute the responsibilities of heuistics and theory as far as dynamic systems are concerned: what for example will count as evidence in an argument about the structure of a dynamic system. Finally the way in which synoptic and dynamic systems interact, synchronically in a derivation, ontogenetically in language learning, and diachronically and phylogenetically in language change is not at all understood.

On the other hand, looking at the synoptic/dynamic distinction in less cowardly terms, working on dynamic systems may well get linguists out of the syntactic shell they once erected to cut themselves off from the other semiotic systems which comprise our culture. This could only be a positive development, leading to a truly integrated science of signs - a semiotics in which language turns out not to be so special after all. Linguistics for the last 25 years has been led by a group of people whose main concern has been to show how language is different from everything else. The results of this vast and research consuming enterprise, centering around the question of constraints on left movement out of constituents in clause structure (cf. Newmeyer 1980, Radford 1981) are hardly inspiring. One cannot help thinking that if this is what linguistics is about, then it is truly time that semiotics took over. This is certainly what Saussure, Hjelmslev, Sapir, Firth, Pike and Halliday have always had in mind. There is no real reason at this stage of development why linguistics cannot embrace social science, accepting its challenge.

REFERENCES

Benson, J. D. & Greaves, W. S. (1981). Field of discourse: theory and application. *Applied Linguistics* **2.1**. 45–55.

Berry, Margaret. (1981a). Systemic linguistics and discourse analysis: a multi-layered approach to exchange structure. In Coulthard, M. and Montgomery, M. (eds.), *Studies in Discourse Analysis*. London: Routledge and Kegan Paul, 120–145.

_____ (1981b). Polarity, ellipticity, elicitation and propositional development, their relevance to the well-formedness of an exchange. (a discussion of Coulthard and Brazil's classes of move). *Nottingham Linguistic Circular* **10.1.**

———— (1981c). Towards layers of exchange structure for directive exchanges. *Network* **2,** 23–32.

Bourdieu, P. (1977), *Outline of a theory of Practice.* London and New York: Cambridge University Press.

Clark, H. H. & Haviland, S. E. (1974). Psychological processes as linguistic explanation. In Cohen D. (ed.) *Explaining Linguistic Phenomena.* Washington, DC: Hemisphere.

Fawcett, R. P. (1975). System networks, codes and knowledge of the universe. Paper read to the Burg Wartenstein Symposium on the Semiotics of Culture and Language.

Fries, P. H. (1982). Language and interactive behaviours: the language of bridge. Central Michigan University. Mimeo.

Gregory, M. J. (1967). Aspects of varieties differentiation. *Journal of Linguistics* **3.** 177–198.

Halliday, M. A. K. (1961). Categories of the theory of grammar. *Word* **17.3.** 241–292.

———— (1966). Lexis as a linguistic level. In Bazell, C. E. Catford, J. C. Halliday M. A. K. and Robins, R. H. (eds.) *In Memory of J. R. Firth.* London: Longman (Longman Linguistics Library). 148–162.

———— (1967). Notes on transitivity and theme in English (Parts 1–3). *Journal of Linguistics* **3.1,** 37–81; **3.2,** 199–244; **4.2,** 179–215.

———— (1973). *Explorations in the Functions of Language.* London: Edward Arnold (Explorations in Language Study).

———— (1975). *Learning How to Mean: Explorations in the Development of Language.* London: Edward Arnold (Explorations in Language Study).

———— (1978). *Language as a Social Semiotic: The Social Interpretation of Language and Meaning.* London: Edward Arnold.

———— (forthcoming) *A Short Introduction to Functional Grammar.* London: Edward Arnold.

Halliday, M. A. K. & Hasan, R. (1976). *Cohesion in English.* London: Longman (English Language Series **9**).

———— (1980). *Text and Context (Sophia Linguistica VI).* Tokyo: Sophia University.

Hasan, R. (1977). Text in the systemic-functional model. In Dressler W. (ed.), *Current Trends in Text Linguistics.* Berlin: de Gruyter (Research in Text Theory).

———— (1979). On the notion of text. In Petofi J. S. (ed.), *Text vs. Sentence.* Hamburg, Germany: Buske.

Hjelmslev, L. (1961). *Prolegomena to a Theory of Language* (translated by F. J. Whitfield). Madison WI: University of Wisconsin Press.

Labov, W. & Waletzky J. (1967). Narrative analysis: oral versions of personal experience. In Helm J. (ed.). *Essays on the Verbal and Visual Arts.* Seattle, WA: University of Washington Press. pp. 12–44.

Lavandera, B. R. Shifting moods in Spanish discourse. CIAFIC-CONICET. Mimeo.

Lemke, J. (1979). Action, context and meaning. City University, New York. Mimeo.

———— (1982). Making trouble. City University, New York. Mimeo.

Longacre, R. E. (1976). *An Anatomy of Speech Notions.* Lisse, Netherlands: Peter de Ridder Press.

Newmeyer, F. T.(1980). *Linguistic Theory in America: The First Quarter-Century of Transformational Generative Grammar.* New York: Academic Press.

Radford, A. (1981). *Transformational Syntax: a student's guide to Chomsky's extended standard theory.* Cambridge, England: Cambridge University Press (Cambridge Textbooks in Linguistics).

Sinclair, J. (1966). Beginning the study of lexis. In Bazell, C. E. Catford, J. C. Halliday M. A. K. Robins R. H. (eds.) *In Memory of J. R. Firth.* London: Longman (Longman Linguistics Library).

Sinclair, J. & Coulthard R. M. (1975). *Towards an Analysis of Discourse: The English Used by Teachers and Pupils.* London: Oxford University Press.

Ure, J. & Ellis J. (1977). Register in descriptive linguistics and linguistics sociology. In Uribe-Villegas O. (ed.) *Issues in Sociolinguistics.* The Hague: Mouton. 197–243.

Ventola, E. (1982). Contrasting schematic structures in service encounters. University of Sydney: Mimeo.

Ideology, Intertextuality, and the Notion of Register

14

J. L. Lemke
City University of New York

WHY INTERTEXTUALITY?

If we look at words isolated from the utterances in which they occur, we create a special 'dictionary context' in which we are not likely to learn either how their meanings depend on the other words with which they combine or how we make utterance meanings that go beyond the dictionary meanings of the words. And if we were to look at utterances (or written sentences) in isolation, restricting ourselves to a special 'grammar book context', we would not expect to learn much about how their uses depend on the rest of what is being said and the situation as a whole, nor about how we can use these bits of talk together to do more than we can do with them separately. But if we study a discourse, a whole situated text by itself and apart from other texts or occasions of discourse with which it may have definite relationships, do we not likewise still run the risk of learning nothing about how we build every text upon and out of other texts? or about the social functions of the system of texts we build—and do not build?

*Inter*textuality is an important characteristic of the use of language in communities. The meanings we make through texts, and the ways we make them, always depend on the currency in our communities of other texts we recognize as having certain definite kinds of relationships with them: generic, thematic, structural, and functional. Every text, the discourse of every occasion, makes sense in part through implicit and explicit relationships of particular kinds to other texts, to the discourse of other occasions. A story may be heard as a fable in the manner of Aesop, belonging to a genre which among other features has a characteristic internal organizational structure (in the manner of Propp 1968, Colby 1973, Hasan 1979). It may be functioning at the time as a rejoinder to yesterday's argument and so be part of a larger structure of action over time, and it may echo and develop the themes of that argument or of other story-tellings with which it has no recognized structural relations. The discourse practices of a community both build systems of texts related in these ways and establish the recognized kinds of relationships there may be between texts or the discourse of different occasions. Any system of practices that can do this can also insure that some kinds of texts are seen as *not* related to one another (in particular ways, or at all), thus providing a powerful means for the maintenance of ideologies that serve wider social functions.

When yesterday's argument is resumed today, we are inclined to speak in terms of the relationships of two discourses, two texts; but when the argument of ten minutes ago is renewed, we may talk in terms of two episodes of a single discourse, two parts of one text. It may well be that the same kinds of relationships exist both across stretches of 'a' text and between 'distinct' texts. If so, then this provides a third reason for an intertextual approach to the study of discourse. Such an approach enables us to analyze what goes on in a discourse in terms of its functions in relation to other discourses, its contribution to systems of discourse relationships (and non-relationships) that may sustain significant social ideologies, and its use of text-forming devices that can be characterized in general terms that unite them with the ways we tie texts to one another.

THE NOTION OF REGISTER

The notion of *register* as it has been used by Michael Halliday and others (e.g., Halliday 1978, Gregory 1967, Ure 1971, Ure & Ellis 1974) provides one way to describe how a community differentiates among the texts it produces according to how it defines the situational context and how it uses language in various *types* of situation. It gives one kind of answer to the basic questions of intertextuality: *which* texts go together, and *how?* That texts 'go together' means that there is some sense in which they are relevant contexts for each other's interpretation, that socially significant meanings are being made by the community through the interrelations of these texts. To say *how* they go together is to specify what kinds of relationships between them help make these meanings. The kinds of relationships made between texts and the sets of texts related in these ways together define the system of intertextuality in the language use of a community.

The notion of register is usefully protean, and we can look at it for present purposes in at least five rather different ways, each of which has something to say about the problem of intertextuality. In one basic sense Register can be regarded as the paradigmatic system of discourse, providing a systematic typology of texts. If two texts belong to the same register they are expected to share certain linguistic features, to have made the same kinds of choices in the networks for transitivity, mood and modality, theme and information focus, logical complexing of clauses, etc. We can use such linguistic criteria to specify how the various texts of a register are related to one another. Other texts will not share these features and will be assigned to other registers; the register system tells us how registers differ from one another, and so separates texts. A system network for register, like a system network for the clause, imposes a topology on the set of texts like that on the set of agnate clauses, such that some texts or clauses can be said to be more alike, to share more features selected at the front (least delicate) end of the network, while others are less alike.

Even looking at the notion of register purely in terms of the linguistic forms appearing in texts (and we may wish to include the cohesive devices and structure-organizing patterns of a text among its linguistic forms; cf. Halliday & Hasan 1976, Hasan 1980), it is possible to ask whether there are 'missing registers'' in a community. For while it may be convenient to describe the system of language in terms of relatively independent selection in the families of system networks Halliday has labeled as those serving the Ideational, Interpersonal, and Textual functions of language, in a particular human community one will not necessarily find that there are registers in use in which all possible, potentially 'free' combinations of such selections actually occur. Such 'gaps' in the community's use of language would presumably reflect constraints on language use that derive from what is and is not conceivable to say and do in a particular community, from the meanings that are and are not made there, among all that could be made with the full meaning potential of the language system. Some such gaps may well play a role in maintaining the stability of the social order of that community.

We can in fact also regard the notion of register as precisely a restriction of the total meaning potential of a language. In any particular register only a portion of that meaning potential, and in each text of the register, the *same* restricted portion, is being actualized. We may say of texts in the same register not just that they share certain formal linguistic features, but that they make only certain kinds of meaning with language. Now the separation of texts into different registers implies that they make quite different kinds of meanings and we can begin to question what the social function in a particular community may be of its particular way of insulating some kinds of discourse from others in this way. Missing registers correspond to kinds of meaning that simply are not made, or at least not made with language, and here certainly would be a powerful stabilizing mechanism for a community's social order and, at the same time, a system of critical points of potential change should these meanings come to be made and recognized in a community where they formerly were not. But it is still something of an oversimplification merely to speak of forms being used or not, meanings being made or not. A missing register, or an occuring register, implies a certain *combination* of meaningful selections in the ideational, interpersonal, and textual families of networks. Why some combinations rather than others? Or more specifically, *which* selections in one family are expected to combine with which selections in the others? *When* are certain meanings made or not made?

A third way of looking at the notion of register is as a typology of situational contexts: the contexts in which language is being used to make particular kinds of meanings that are characteristic of a particular situation type. Halliday's notion of register would classify context types in terms of three simultaneous systems: that of Field, which characterizes the kind of activity in which language is used, with topic seen as part of that characterization; that of Tenor, distinguishing situations by the role relationships given and constituted by social interaction; and that of Mode, characterizing the ways in which language is being used in the situation, including the medium of communication and the rhetorical and genre patterns in use. When texts are said to belong to the same or different registers in this sense, the relationships between them are viewed as relationships between the activities in which they occurred and which they helped make happen, but only the formal (paradigmatic) relationships of the activites are captured by these systems. Two instances of a particular activity may be quite similar, especially as regards the kind of discourse that occurs in them, but they may also have other kinds of relationships *as activities* (rather than as kinds of discourse), such as temporal sequence and proximity, participation of the same persons, etc. Moreover, register gives us a linguist's typology of human activities-with-language, the view from language, and foregrounds especially those differences in the activity context which are most relevant to differences in the choice of linguistic forms. Obviously there may be other typologies of human social practices which emphasize similarities and differences which are not necessarily as critical for linguistic choices (i.e. which matter only for relatively more delicate choices in the linguistic networks) but which are quite important for adequate description of people's responses to talk, for describing the progress of a social interaction, or for characterizing how types of social activities contribute to the structure of the community's overall social system.

The separation of texts which do not share the same field, tenor, and mode assigns them to what the community may regard as completely different and unrelated activities, a kind of disjunction of domains of human social practice which we know can well support the kinds of unnoticed contradictions that help stabilize a social order (e.g. our own habits of separating politics from art from science from religion, etc.) In this view missing registers are kinds of situations for language use that simply do not occur in a community, and more precisely, combinations of topics and activities, personal relationships, and modes of discourse that do not occur, again reflecting and contributing to the stability of the social system of a community.

The fourth notion of register is that of the register system of a speech community as its systematic practices of deploying certain of the resources of its language system for particular purposes in some situational contexts and other linguistic resources in other situations. It is on the basis of this notion of register as a sort of 'interface' between the system of social activity types and the system of language that we might hope to be able to predict the linguistic features of texts produced on particular occasions, or to reconstruct the kind of occasion from the text. Indeed it is this notion of register that would enable us to tell newcomers how to produce situation-specific use of our language. We will have more to say shortly about this notion of register in relation to issues of intertextuality and social stability and change. A similar, fifth notion of register is that being developed by Jim Martin (1982), which situates Register as a full semiotic system in its own right between the semiotic of Genre, which tries to capture the typology of meaningful kinds of social action in the community, and the semiotic of Language proper, which includes phonology, lexicogrammar, and the discourse systems of cohesion and rhetorical structure. In Martin's formulation, following Hjelmslev's (1961) usage, there are *connotative* relations among these semiotics, such that Register is the expression plane of Genre at the same time that it is the content plane for which Language provides the expression. But in Martin's view as well, Language is the anchor of the entire meaning system, and Register and even Genre are to be mapped primarily in terms of their relations to Language. This is a very important task for linguistics, but perhaps a more difficult if not an impossible one without simultaneous efforts to describe the semiotic systems of social action as such, and to map language in relation to them as well. For the problems of intertextuality and social dynamics a more symmetrical approach seems essential.

REGISTER AND INTERTEXTUALITY

Is it necessary and sufficient for two texts to be socially recognized as relevant contexts for each other's interpretation that they belong to the same register? Do the relations defined by the register system suffice to characterize their intertextual relations?

Imagine two texts which are each the record of separate instances of the same kind of situation. In New York and Toronto on the same night, in two different but generally similar kitchens, two otherwise unrelated pairs of husbands and wives argue face-to-face about whether the husband's mother should be invited for the long holiday weekend. Grant similarity of field, of tenor, and of mode, and expect that these texts will share many linguistic features. In what sense are these texts an intertextual pair? In what circumstances in our community might they be used or presented as a pair? Are there meanings being made through the relations of these texts above and beyond the meanings that are being made in each of them? Probably only through the metadiscourse practices of people like us, linguists and social analysts. This *is* a quite legitimate practice of our community, and it *does* provide a possible *third* text in terms of which the three will form an intertextual set (cf. Riffaterre's *mediated type* of intertextuality, 1980), but it is quite different as a mode of intertextual relation between the two original texts from other pairs we might imagine. What of the relation between the New Yorkers' argument of that night and their argument on the same theme the night before? or two hours before? or a year ago? What of the relation of that night's argument text to the discourse of a phone call between the husband and his mother the day before, or the day after? or to a letter from the wife to her sister discussing family problems and written later that evening? or to the poem the husband wrote to his mistress the next morning about love and understanding? or to the text of their wedding ceremony? In all these cases, and in ways quite different from the relations of the New York to the Toronto argument texts, certainly across differences of medium and genre (Mode), of role relationships and interactional ploys (Tenor), and to some degree across activity type and overt topic (Field), intertextual relations can be and often are built in our community. These texts may overtly cite one another in ways the New York and Toronto texts will not, and short of overt citation, they may allude to or implicitly invoke one another in ways that, after the murder, may certainly be of interest to the police detective, the court psychiatrist, the biographer, and the historian. The participants themselves, in making these texts, may make them in relation to each other, may make meanings through the relations they construe among them that penetrate into and go beyond the isolated meanings of the texts by themselves. The cohesion of social life is largely made through such intertextuality, not just in the relations of activities and events to one another, but in the ways in which the resources of language are deployed in those activities to create the relationships between them. The notion of register, even in its language-relevant typology of situational contexts, does not capture many of the socially most important kinds of relationship among the texts made in a community, though it does contain elements of a useful theoretical framework for doing so.

When we make meaning with a text, by writing or speaking it, by reading or hearing it, by participating in the activities of which it is a part, we do not do so apart from other texts. We operate the system of language and the cultural semiotic of social action through the whole set of texts (and action-texts) through which we interact in our community. In this widest sense the meanings made in *any* arbitrary pair of texts, and the forms through which those meanings are made, will have many specifiable relations for the linguist and social analyst, whether or not they are recognized by most members of the community. But in a narrower sense, not *every* other text that has even one word in common with 'this' text, however relevant for the diligent lexicographer, is equally likely to be a relevant intertext for the participants, or to be cited within 'this' text. But if a text shares a particular 'key word' with our text, or even a close synonym of that key word, it is more likely to be a relevant intertext. What makes some words 'key words' for a text? Key words or their synonyms are likely to turn up in titles, summaries, abstracts, and classifications for information-retrieval purposes. Two texts that shared not just the same few key words, but the same title, or summary sentence, or abstract might be even more likely to be relevant intertexts. But such a characterization of texts must be relatively subtle, subtle enough to recognize shared themes even across the stylistic and metaphoric transformations of different genres, media, and role relationships of participants. For very often it is not a specific text or set of texts that is relevant, in the sense that these would be identifiable by participants, but an abstract thematic field or system of thematic relationships, which may be encountered in many texts, any sufficient subset of which enables participants, each with a different textual experience, to share meanings in terms of such a common thematic system.

Imagine two texts which do share a common thematic system. Apart from meanings made between them by the analyst, as in the case of the mother-in-law arguments in different cities on the same night, not all texts with the same thematic systems are equally likely to be relevant intertexts: some are foregrounded by participants (or analysts) not in terms of thematic commonality, but in terms of the relations of the activities of which the texts were a part. In many cases of course those activity relations have been realized by specific features in the texts themselves: citations, allusions, quotations, paraphrases, metastatements citing other activities as well as other texts, etc. Again what may be shared among the participants is not the specific event whose text is relevant, but only an abstract system of related activity-types from which one can reconstruct the kind of event that is relevant and, in terms of a register system, the kind of text made in that kind of event.

I have given so far what I believe to be the basic, interlocking modes of intertextual connection: relating (1) texts which share a common thematic system, the more so if that system is otherwise foregrounded in the texts, and the more so if the texts occurred in events which belong to the same regular activity pattern or sequence in the community and if that pattern is otherwise foregrounded in the overall flow of social activity which includes the events and their texts; and (2) texts whose events belong to such a sequence, and the more so if they also share a common thematic system.

One can recognize in this intertextual principle a fundamental mechanism also seen to be at work over short stretches of text. In her work on cohesion and textual coherence, Ruqaiya Hasan (1980, 1981) concludes that two kinds of cohesive devices normally support one another in the production of coherent text: lexical cohesive ties between clauses by virtue of taxonomic 'semantic' relations among them (e.g. synonymy, whole-part relations, etc.)—cf. thematic relations—and the grammatical cohesive relations such as the use of pronouns, definite articles, conjunctions, etc.—ties which create a more 'syntactic' structural relationship between clauses, more like the activity-pattern syntax of social action.

But beyond this basic mode of (inter)textual connection which I will describe more carefully later, the real problem of intertextual analysis is that *any* similarity of two texts, any principle by which they may be classed as belonging to the same abstract paradigmatic system, and *any* difference of two texts in terms of which they may be assigned to distinct roles in some syntagmatic structure, either of language or of social action generally, *may* be the basis for an intertextual relation between them. The same problem is perhaps more easily recognized over longer stretches of what we take as being 'one' text. In Joyce's *Ulysses* or Nabokov's *Ada,* two clauses or two paragraphs or quasi-sentences, even if many pages apart, may be read in relation to one another not just thematically or actionally, but by virtue of the language, dialect, register, or script they seem to be in; the sounds and rhythms we make when reading them aloud; shared words, phrases; similar but transformed words and phrases, or whole sentences; shared or similar locations, participants, sub-genres (e.g. poems within the novel), rhetorical ploys, situation-types, narrative sequencing devices, large-scale discourse structure patterns other than those that directly represent relations of the actions narrated, etc. etc. And of course we may look to similar grammatical choices in the segments as well. These possibilities occur across longer stretches of situated dialogue (not just in the constructed texts of modern novels), where the analogue of 'one text' is the social recognition of a single bounded activity (e.g. one two-hour seminar or dinner conversation), and becomes more problematic as we treat as 'one text' all the things said by the same participants to one another across the varied activities of a day, or all the things said by different participants in differing or similar activities in the same room on that day. *Which* textual connections should we pay more attention to, *when?* How do we tell, or argue, which of all the *possible* relations between two stretches of text are the ones in terms of which, in this case, the participants, including ourselves (even as analysts) are making the most significant inter/intratextual meanings?

If our concern is with *which* stretches of text are to be read in relation to a given one, then obviously the more possible kinds of relations we can construct between two passages the better, but more connections are useless unless they in some sense support one another; that is, unless the meanings we make through them somehow contribute to a coherent overall system of meaning relations between the passages. (After constructing such 'stable' relations in a text, of course, one has to go one to analyze its inherently 'unstable' readings as well, but that is a problem best left to another discussion.)

If our concern, on the other hand, is focussed on *how* some particular stretches of text are related; that is, on which kinds of relationships between them are important, then in addition to the criterion that the meanings made possible through these relationships support one another, a particular kind of relationship between two passages becomes more useful to us if it can also guide us to find important relationships between other passages.

An isolated, *possible* relationship between stretches of text will be termed a *weak* relation, and the passages weakly related, until we find either, and hopefully both, that there are other relationships between the passages that support a coherent or stable meaning relation between them, making them *strongly* related, and/or that this same kind of relationship recurs between other passages in the text(s), so that we can consider it a strong or *foregrounded* kind of relationship in/between the text(s).

On the shorter scale of clause-to-clause relations in normally cohesive text, this same principle lies behind Hasan's (1980, 1981) notion of cohesive harmony and its 'principle of two-ness', the recurrence or 'echoing' that defines chain interactions. Two chains are said to interact, contributing to textual coherence, when the same kind of syntactic relation (in functional terms) is created two or more times between these sequences of referentially or semantically related lexical items running through a passage. A difference between Hasan's formulation and the effect of the principle I have just described is that for her the chains are given by text-independent semantic relationships among their members, and not constituted (even in part) by the syntactic interactions between them, but her model does single out those chains or members of chains that do participate in the syntactic interactions as 'central' to the coherence of the text and recognizes under the heading of 'instantial lexical cohesion' that texts do use their syntactic resources to create text-specific semantic ties. As newly creative metaphors may become cliches and finally end as synonyms in the lexicon, so a thematic relation constructed in one stretch of a text may then be taken for granted in other parts of what, partly thereby, are taken to be other passages of the same text, and then also in other texts of the same author, period, or style, and end as indexical not of some particular set of texts, but of a speech community, a dialect, or a language. All meaning relations among forms are characteristic of some definite, perhaps very wide set of social contexts; dictionary and taxonomic semantic relations, in this view, are specific to minimally specified (secondary) contexts, which often occur in the primary context of metalinguistic discussion, or when usually available contextual information is missing. We should not ask *whether* two items are synonyms (or antonyms, etc.) or not, but *when* they are. Looked at in this way, we can construct an essential unity among the principles of short and long scale coherence in a text, foregrounded meaning relations between texts, and the short and long term coherence of the flow of social activity.

In the sections that follow I will try to formulate more explicitly how two general classes of relationships between texts and events co-operate within and between the semiotic systems of language and social action to weave global patterns across texts and events that (1) foreground certain kinds of relationships within those classes as the ones in terms of which coherent meanings are made in a particular community, and (2) by the same processes 'background' other possible relationships in particular contexts, creating 'gaps' that can help stabilize the social system of meaning and action in a community while preserving reserve adaptive potential for future system change.

STRUCTURING RELATIONS ACROSS TEXTS

The notions of register that we have discussed provide some key elements for the analysis of the kinds of meanings that are made not locally in short stretches of a text like clauses or intonation units, nor even, ordinarily, through clause-complexes or short discourse units, but which are made over longer stretches of discourse and especially through the relations between occasions of discourse regarded as activities and as texts. We are concerned with these relatively *global* rather than local patternings of language use and social action.

Let us take for granted a linguistic semiotic system (LgS) representable by the relations within and between available choices in the system networks for the phonology, grammar, and language-specific text-forming resources of a language. Our concern now will not be with these resources as such, but with their deployment in relation to two other semiotic systems (and secondarily the deployment of some of their subsystems in relation to others).

Clearly we need a semiotic system defining the meaning relations within and between the various recognized kinds of social practice in a community, which specifies the interactional situational contexts within which we deploy the resources of LgS. Call this the social action semiotic (AcS). A particular interactional *situation-type* within the AcS system is enacted by interactional *strategies*, whose likelihood of use in particular contexts is also specified by the AcS. Every episode of social interaction is analyzable and typable (often multiply) within the AcS just as every stretch of speech-as-language is within the LgS.

But an utterance is not just a linguistic form, or an action of a certain type, whose meaning may depend on the activity pattern to which it belongs; its meaning is derived also from its thematic relations (including lexical cohesive relations) to parts of the same and to other discourses with which it shares a common (abstract) thematic system of specific meaning relations among the items in its thematic field. Utterances thus take meaning from and contribute to the establishment of a thematic context of situation in which, no less than in the interactional context of situation, the resources of LgS are deployed. In every community there is a semiotic of such abstract thematic systems (ThS) that enables language use to bridge across widely separated and structurally unrelated occasions of discourse and across social activities of widely varying (AcS) types. Also specified in the ThS are the thematic development strategies by which the thematic systems are constituted through discourse.

It is perhaps worth noting at this point, in anticipation of the next section, that ThS and AcS are rather different kinds of semiotic systems. Viewed paradigmatically, ThS specifies the meaning relations among all its items in a context-dependent way, representable as a set of nodes or hubs (the items) and connections labeled with their *specific* meaning relations (not the rather general taxonomic kinds of relations found in representations of lexical fields or semantic networks). Viewed syntagmatically, ThS establishes what one might generally call 'chains' or thematic strands across texts, which are not usually locally compact, i.e. chain members tend to be separated by shorter or longer stretches of intervening text, and many thematic lines may run in parallel simultaneously. There is no implied termination of a chain. AcS on the other hand, paradigmatically, is essentially a typology of activity-types and the act-type options available in each, while syntagmatically it establishes multi-level constituency structures that *are* locally compact, only occasionally simultaneous (where there are overlapping or ambiguous activity-types), and *do* have implied completions. These we will later describe as *multivariate* structures, distinguishing them from the *covariate* structuring by ThS. LgS for the most part is like AcS in these respects, except that some of the text-forming resources of language, its devices for linking compact (multivariate) syntagms to one another, are, as in the case of lexical cohesion, of the ThS type.

In this framework the status of the notion of register is that of an *intersemiotic,* constructed from the viewpoint of LgS to define how choices in AcS and ThS affect choices in LgS. The Register intersemiotic has inputs from the system of AcS and ThS and output to LgS; it enables one in effect to translate between meanings represented in terms of the relations among social actions and among socially shared thematic systems and meanings represented in language. The contribution of such a program, based in linguistic analysis, would be to tell us how AcS and ThS look from the viewpoint of language, to tell us what kinds of distinctions among social activities and thematic systems language is most sensitive to. But we need to recognize that projecting AcS and ThS out of analyses of the uses of LgS in a community will provide a specifically language-centered representation of AcS and ThS. If this can be done, it would represent an important contribution in itself. Certainly *any* model of the overall social semiotic system (LgS+AcS+ThS+ . . .) of a community will be built largely by analyzing language use, but it seems to me rather difficult to decide on the basis of LgS alone just how one should represent most usefully the AcS and ThS so as to make it relatively easy to see all the kinds of interrelations of the three in a community's conjoint use of them. So I would rather pose as the basic question *not* how AcS and ThS condition choices in LgS, but how choices in all three are patterned against one another *globally;* across different activity types, thematic systems, and occasions of language use.

Global Patterning

The notion of a *global patterning* in the deployment of these semiotic systems in relation to one another applies within the larger scale units of each semiotic as well as between them, as will all the notions introduced from here on. Consider first global patterns in the deployment of two systems in a text. These are essentially distributional patterns, in which we find that certain selections in one system are more likely to co-occur with some rather than other selections in the second system across the whole text. Halliday's analyses of transitivity system selections across the text of Golding's novel *The Inheritors* (Halliday 1971) and of selections in the systems of modality and tense in two long passages from Priestley's play *An Inspector Calls* (Halliday 1981) show global patternings in the deployment of these LgS resources against selections in the thematic systems invoked in these works (notions of causality in the world-descriptions of early humans in Golding, themes of social obligation and time-relations as human constructions in Priestley). Indeed Halliday's analysis, especially for modality in Priestley, also looks at the portrayal through modality shifts of a pattern of social interaction (Conflict and Confrontation, representable in AcS) that develops the social obligation themes, so that all three systems are seen as patterned against, or perhaps we should say *with,* one another. As Halliday emphasizes, the effect of the careful deployment of the systems in patterned relation to one another is to *foreground* themes which tie together the whole work (and in Priestley's case relate several of his works to one another). How *could* we select, from among all the possible thematic systems that are at least potentially relevant in complex texts like these, those which are more likely to ground a coherent reading of the whole, or of long parts of the text, *without* foregrounding devices? We know that mere number of repetitions of a word or a theme does not always give a criterion for identifying the central themes of a text, or even the significant connecting themes of different parts of a long, topically varied conversation. What does provide a foregrounding of themes is the global co-patterning principle that the same kinds of meaning relations be instanced through more than one semiotic system (or subsystem) and that these same foregrounding devices be employed across the text or set of texts.

We should be careful to note that the processes and devices of foregrounding are not necessarily consciously recognized by particpants other than the analyst; indeed they are usually quite invisible and 'automatic', tending to reproduce on every opportunity a particular mapping of kinds of doings, ways of saying, and things to be said onto one another in a fashion characteristic of a particular community.

In my own analyses of what people say and otherwise do in science classrooms (Lemke 1982), it is notable that the use of relational *vs.* material process clause-types closely follows shifts from the thematic systems of 'science topics' to those of 'classroom activities'. This is a global pattern, strengthening a separation or disjunction in the meaning system of classroom science between a 'world of Science' where things simply *are* as they are, and an ordinary, familiar world where people *do* things. The deployment of the transitivity system in the service of this disjunction is only one of many ways in which it is established and maintained in the discourse, and one that is quite unlikely to be recognized by the participants. Such a disjunction belongs, in these and many other texts in our community, to a global system of disjunctions that sustains an ideological mystification of science as describing the 'givenness' of the world, encouraging an acceptance of things as we are told they must necessarily be, and alienating most people from a world where, apparently unlike our normal world, our own human actions have no significant place.

These examples have mainly illustrated relations between LgS and ThS, but we could equally well demonstrate LgS/AcS relations by the ways in which deployment of modality in LgS is used to foreground and negotiate status relations between participants, or linguistic formulas for politeness used to accomplish mitigations of conflict, etc. In my work on classroom discourse there are very regular clause-level and discourse-level linguistic forms that mark out the actional structures of the special situation-type I have called Teacher-Student Debates (Lemke 1982: chapters 2 and 3). And it is also well known, and fairly well documented for the norms of a classroom science discourse (Lemke 1982: chapters 4 and 5) that in a given community not all thematic systems or even thematic development strategies may occur unremarkably in the course of enactment of a particular kind of social activity or when using a particular interactional strategy, illustrating the kinds of patterning of ThS against AcS in a community.

This framework for the analysis of intertextuality does not presume that texts dictate to us their relationship, or that there *are* existing relationships objectively there to be found out. Relations of meaning are *made* in human communities, and made differently in different communities. Of all the possible meaning relations within and between texts and social events only some are foregrounded by the particular meaning-making practices of a community. These become the basis for connections and disjunctions of texts and events, for specifying some kinds of relations in AcS and ThS and LgS and not others, for assembling a system of registers that places some texts together and separates others, thematic systems that relate some texts and not others, linguistic and actional and thematic structures that connect some utterances and other actions as parts of the same wholes, disconnected from others. To pursue this kind of analysis further, it is helpful to try to specify more carefully the two basic classes of relationships found in these semiotic systems on the basis of which connections within and between texts and events are made.

Covariate and Multivariate Structural Relations

Structural relations are relations on the syntagmatic axis. They are basically of two kinds. The first kind is quite familiar: a whole is defined by the relations among some finite set of functionally differentiated role-slots. For such wholes there are a finite set of roles and a finite set of relationships among them such that we can write a *structural formula,* say:

$$w = x + (y)^n + \ldots + z$$

including the possibility of recursion and that filling some roles may be optional (see Hasan 1979 for examples at the level of discourse structures). In a simple case, say $w = x + y$, two segments A and B (which may be syllables, words, stretches of text, acts, events, etc. and which are in part segmentable as such through the w-structure) may, if they meet the criteria to fill the x-role and the y-role respectively, be related as a whole of the w-type. Whatever we might say that A and B, taken in isolation, have in common, as parts of w they are filling functionally differentiated roles, and their relation is the relation of these roles, i.e. that of an x to a y. I borrow a term from Halliday and call such structures and the relations that constitute them *multivariate.* These structures tend to be *locally compact;* that is, it is noticeable if they are interrupted, and if they resume, the interruption is 'bracketed out' as not part of the structure and the interruption noted as unusual. Multivariate structures also imply a completion, once all their roles are filled; apart from recursions (and in ordered structures there is rarely—ever?—a recursive option in the last slot) the structure has been completed and anything following it must belong to another structure, though possibly of course another structure of the same type. Being completable in this sense, multivariate structures tend to come equipped with devices for internal expansion, postponing completion. *Recursive* options are one such device. (Recursive relations are called 'univariate' in Halliday's terminology; I take them to be a special case of multivariate relations.) Another device is *embedding,* in which, for example, a complete w-whole may be assigned the y-role in a superordinate w-whole.

Multivariate structures may be connected to one another by further multivariate relations, i.e. by occupying roles in higher order, larger scale multivariate structures, a familiar phenomenon in the constituency hierarchies of linguists and discourse analysts as well as in those of activity sequences. But this is not the only way in which multivariate structures may be tied to one another.

There is a second basic class of relations on the syntagmatic axis, with its associated type of structure. These *covariate* relations establish a connection between two or more segments of text or action on the basis that, in some wider context in part constituted *by* construing such a relationship between the segments (which are again partly segmented through their participation *in* the relationship), the segments belong to a system of meaning relations which specifies a particular relation between them. The simplest kind of system on the basis of which covariate structuring relations are construed is a typology, such that if A and B are, at some level of the typology, both members of the same class (i.e. share a type feature z) then there is a z-relation between A and B, and between them and any other member of the z-class. If A and B appear in a text, there will be at least a *weak* (i.e. a possible, not necesaarily foregrounded) covariate relation tying them to each other, and so tying together any larger multivariate structures in which they occur. If other members of the z-class appear in the text, there is a z-chain formed by their common ties to one another.

Notice how such a chain structure differs from a multivariate structure. A, B, C, etc. are not assigned to functionally *differentiated* roles, the relations are *homogeneous* in the z-system. They are not *orderable,* and there is no possible structural formula representation. Recursion is not a sensible notion for them since it does not define a special subclass of chains. Neither is embedding a distinctive feature. Chains are not normally locally compact; it is the rule, rather than the exception, for chain members to be distributed through a text rather than occur contiguously.

More complex covariate relations based in a typology are possible. A and B may not belong to the *same* class, but to contrasting classes at the same level of the typological hierarchy, or to different levels of the same hierarchy. Hasan's (1980) categories for lexical semantic ties (e.g. hyponymy, co-meronymy) illustrate these kinds of relations. But the kinds of relations in typologies tend to be as few as possible: typolgies and taxonomies are economical descriptions, creating the fewest possible classes at each level. More generally, A and B may have a covariate tie by virtue of belonging to a common thematic system. Thus 'book' and 'tome' or 'book' and 'magazine' or even 'book' and 'page' have covariate relations easily represented through a typological or taxonomic system, but 'book' and 'publisher' or 'book' and 'author' also have a covariate relation through the same thematic system, but their specific relations, not being of either a class-and-member or whole-and-part kind are not conveniently represented taxonomically. Halliday and Hasan have tried to use the notion of collocation, the frequency of co-occurrence *locally* in a set of texts, to justify non-taxonomic ties in the analysis of lexical cohesion (but later rejected by Hasan, 1981, for methodological reasons). This does not seem to me to be appropriate because: (1) collocation is not a *global* notion, it emphasizes that collocates occur *nearby* one another in texts, and (2) it is defined as a language system property, on the set of *all* texts, whereas clearly it is not just a property of A and B that they have a thematic tie; the tie they have depends on the context in which they occur and may in fact be specific to just one or a few texts. Collocation measures do often associate thematically tied items; this is expected for those thematic systems that are not highly specific to just some texts, and points to the fact that covariate relations often do occur locally in texts as well as globally. This is quite important as it bears on the relation between multivariate and covariate structuring in a text and we will return to it shortly.

Covariate structures can also be complex, though in a different way from the recursions and embeddings of multivariate structures. Chains can converge and diverge in the general sense that two tying criteria which have been making separate chains may, as the thematic context in the text shifts, come to be viewed as special cases of a unifying criterion; i.e. that foregrounded criterion may be membership in a class or system that is the union of the previously relevant ones. Or a single criterion and its chain may be contextually split into contrasting ones (even retroactively). The same set of segments may be covariately relatable in more than one system simultaneously, so sustaining two or more chains at once. And there may be 'pivoting' in which we can have a k-relation on A-B-C, and a j-relation on C-D-E if C belongs to both the k-system and the j-system.

   The pivoting kinds of chain relations make especially obvious the duality between text and system. Thematic systems are abstractions from texts; like all social meaning systems they must be created and maintained (and ultimately are changed) by the processes of social action. In this pivoting sequence A-B-C-D-E in a text, when A occurs all the systems to which it belongs are potentially relevant to its meanings. (Of course in practice even if it is the beginning of a text or action sequence, there will be plenty of other contexts narrowing the likelihood of relevance of those systems, but they too are part of its total social enactment.) When B follows A, especially if there is also a multivariate relation possible between them, so that A-B is taken as (the parts of) 'one event', there is a weak foregrounding of all the systems in which both A and B occur, and when C follows, the likelihood that the k-system is relevant becomes quite strong: the k-relation is foregrounded by its applicability to A-B, B-C, and A-C. Now D appears. It does not belong to the k-system, but C, perhaps with different meaning, and D do both belong to the j-system. When E comes along and strengthens the relevance of the j-system, both it and the k-system are foregrounded, and C becomes strongly polysemic or plurifunctional in this context. The multivariate relations among A-B-C-D-E will also play a role in the foregrounding, as in practice will the many possible system ties of the different elements. But where the effect is the strong foregrounding of the k-system and the j-system, this serves to strengthen and renew these systems. The foregrounding of pivoting of the k-j type globally in a text or set of texts may even serve to create, first in limited contexts and then perhaps more widely, a joint thematic system built from the union of these two. The strategies by which thematic systems are developed, invoked, renewed, and changed in texts, and the similar dynamic enactment processes and resources for all semiotic systems point to the great importance in any analysis of considering not just the 'synoptic' view (cf. Bourdieu 1977), which stands outside of time to describe the systems produced, but also the dynamic view which captures the dimensions of social meaning in *how* systems of relations are enacted. Only both views together can account for the dynamic metastability of social systems of action and meaning.

   The relations of covariate and multivariate structuring in a text are crucial to a unified inter/intratextual analysis. We noted before in discussing collocation that covariate ties do occur locally. They commonly occur *within* multivariate structures like the clause or clause complex. If there is a recursion in a multivariate structure, say $w = x + y_1 + y_2 + z$, there is no direct multivariate structural relation beyween y_1 and y_2, except that induced by their common relations to x and z (this is really a covariate tie through the y-class), but they may well have covariate relations. Halliday has pointed out (Halliday 1983) that there is no direct multivariate structural relationship between the constituents of embedded clauses and those of the clause in which they are embedded, but again we will often find covariate ties to increase the coherence across such multivariate boundaries (as in 'the man/who came *today*/will leave *tomorrow*'). But there is a more important reason why covariate ties occur within even simple clauses, akin to Hasan's principle of 'chain interaction'. How can thematic systems be formed and maintained, or changed? If you come to a text that relies on an unfamiliar thematic system, you can detect on the assumption that it is normally cohesive that there must be covariate relations presumed among many of its items, else it would not be normally cohesive without them. But how could you determine what they were? Mainly by looking at how through multivariate structures, which being few tend to be present (though not with the same distributions) in most texts, elements of known thematic systems with known relations were being multivariately related to items with unknown relations. If for example the known relations were used to construct chains, the multivariate relations of these chains that were foregrounded by occurring globally across the text (cf. Hasan's definition of chain interaction) would enable you to begin to construct a representation of the other, important abstract thematic systems of the text. Obviously this is easier to do with some texts than with others. It seems a reasonable hypothesis, generalizing from observations about text-specific thematic ties (cf. Hasan 1981 on 'instantial' lexical cohesion), that new thematic systems can only be built up (1) from prior ones, and (2) with the help of multivariate structures.

It is perhaps interesting to consider briefly at this point some of the traditional notions of how one text cites, refers to, or invokes another. Suppose I write (Hasan 1980) in my text. That action belongs to the activity-type of writing academic text, and it may function typologically in AcS as one or more of the acts: Acknowledgment-of-scientific-priority, Aknowledgment-of-debt-to-a-source-of-an-idea, Publicizing-a-colleague's-work, Claiming-authoritative-precedent-for-my-own-work, Identifying-the-source-of-a-quotation, Telling-the-reader-where-to-look-for-particular-information, etc. etc. These acts may be part of multivariate structures including those realized by global discourse patterns in the text which make us expect that there will be a list of References near the end of the text, tied to the segment in which (Hasan 1980) occurs by lexical repetition of "Hasan" and "1980" within the same structural subunit there. But what *is* the segment in which (Hasan 1980) appears? And *how* is it tied to a text described in the list of References? Some stretch of my text and some stretches in the cited text will presumably have covariate relations through a shared thematic system: the same key lexemes, or others synonymous with them in this thematic system, with the same or closely similar relations among them; or a set of relations and terms assimilable to the same abstract pattern. Of course other stretches in both texts will share thematic relations as well, but a particular passage or set of passages and a particular shared thematic system are foregrounded by the joint operation of the covariate and multivariate structures in each text (clauses, sentences, paragraphs, etc.) and between the texts (the joint multivariate structures of text organization in LgS—Academic Paper Format—and of an activity-type of scholarly practice—Tracing a Reference—in AcS that enable us to construe: Citing text-Reference text-Cited text). A good appreciation for how this works is obtained by considering how we decide that a citation is mistaken. Even if the multivariate indications take us to a particular page of the cited text, it is only through the further *thematic* relations of citing and cited text that a real intertextual meaning relation can be constructed.

Suppose a sentence appears in my text which is a *verbatim* replica of one in another text. In AcS its meaning depends on whether I use some multivariate device to signal that it is 'taken from' another text (*quotation* vs. plagiarism, or 'coincidence'), but in ThS its potential ties to other texts in which it occurs remain unaffected (*allusion*). An allusion to another text is not recoverable, i.e. the other text not specifiable, solely from the covariate relations, for all other texts which contain a replica, or a paraphrase, or a regularly transformed variant of the allusive text are equally candidates. Only by some additional multivariate means for identifying the canonical texts to which allusions are made is direct text-text connection possible. But very often it is not necessary that we be able to identify a specific text in relation to which this text is making part of its meanings: it may be enough that we read the text in relation to *some* of the other texts with which it shares a specific thematic system (some Halliday texts on register; some Hasan texts on lexical cohesion). We thus move from strongly foregrounded intertextuality in which both covariate and multivariate structural means are employed, to our normal and continuous operation of thematic systems which bridge between otherwise structurally unconnected texts.

IDEOLOGY AND INTERTEXTUALITY

If relations between stretches of text and social actions are not 'there' to be discovered already given, but are constructed by us with the available relations and structures of our semiotic systems, and if those semiotic systems are abstract representations of the kinds of relations and structures habitually made by us in our texts and actions, then the analysis of the meaning systems of a community, and how those systems are immanent in its social practices—including how the dual systems of meaning and action change or maintain themselves—is essentially the same as an analysis of the relations of systems and texts, an analysis which tries to show the global co-patterning of the system as we deploy them to make socially shared meanings.

The total meaning system of a community may be represented as a hierarchy of contextualization relations, each of which essentially tells *which* meaning relations among sets of entities obtain *when,* i.e. in what contexts (Lemke 1977, 1979). A segment of discourse has linguistic contextualizations, relating it to its co-text on the syntagmatic axis and to the system of linguistic forms paradigmatically; regarded as action, it has actional contextualizations relating it to the activities of which it may be regarded as a part and to the acts that in turn constitute it, as well as to the typology of possible actions; and it has as well thematic contextualizations relating it to other segments to which it can have thematic ties and to the thematic systems of ThS. These contextualization relations in a particular community are never independent of one another, but are globally co-patterned within the total social semiotic system of the community.

Suppose we have a set of episodes (texts, action sequences) and consider the wholes that could be made from them, either by simple concatenation, or by the addition of linking or framing episodes. We would have to take into account the textual, in the linguistic sense, coherence of the result, and what multivariate structures in AcS were available into whose functional roles the episodes might be placed. But the potential covariate ties of the episodes would not depend on whether there was a multivariate structure encompassing them or not, for they are freely intertextual as well as intratextual in their application. Some match, however, would have to be achieved between AcS multivariate structures and the fore-grounded thematic ties; some sequences of action 'make sense' thematically in a community and others do not. Given the activity type, there are constraints on thematic relations; given the thematic relations, constraints on the activity-types.

What enables us to link isolated segments is a meaning system that lets us see texts as *potentially* mutually contextualizing in *many* ways, but strengthen or weaken potential relational patterns through the global co-patterning of the ties in different semiotic systems. In doing this *consistently,* a community establishes that some texts and events have particular meaningful relations to one another (and hence *not* to still others), *and* that, more basically, there are some kinds of relationships that there can be between events, and texts, and not other kinds. The kinds of contextualization relations are limited, what is recognizable as an event or text, as some whole, as connected in any way, is limited, and the duality between kinds-of-relations and kinds-of-wholes is defined, limited, and specified in the same processes.

Every meaning system must make some selection from the set of all possible relationships. Meaningful relations can occur only insofar as not all possible patternings occur equally often. So it will always be the case that many connections will not be made, or not be made in particular contexts, in a given community. But some non-connections are disconnections, *disjunctions* that help to stabilize the systems of action and meaning in the community. These are relations which are not made, but which if they were made would tend to destabilize the overall system. They are contradictions in the system, inconsistencies, conflicts, that may appear to the analyst or outside observer, but not to most members of the community. These disjunctions cannot be isolated, but must form a global subsystem within the total system of meaning relations, each reinforcing the whole pattern of disjunctions, blocking one might say the alternate paths through the system that might lead to forbidden connections. A system of disjunctions is also a necessary feature of a social semiotic system; not only does it tend to stabilize the system, but it provides a reserve capacity for change, a potential adaptive flexibility in the system that tends to insure its continuity as a system even across significant changes. The system of disjunctions is not simply a negative system, a system of absences, for those absences must be rendered invisible. People will talk and act, but they must not do so, or not *meaningfully* do so socially, in ways that destabilize the system by exposing the disjunctions. So many of the connections that *are* made in the community, including its prohibitions, its notions of the necessary and the merely coincidental, serve to distract us from other not-made connections, providing alternative, displaced, or distorted ways of saying and doing things, ways of making meaningful relations that avoid making other connections. The notion that the belief systems of a community, and its social practices, are systematically distorted in the service of maintaining a social order is the basic assumption of the analysis of social ideology. Unfortunately, the notion of ideology is only framed in relation to macrosocial concepts of social organization and social stability, and does not provide a connection to micro-social analysis of actual human social practices, actions and texts, in a community. The notion of a system of disjunctions, which has only been sketched here (see Lemke 1982b), is framed in terms of a general model of the relations between texts and systems, or more generally between the dynamic processes of social practice and the systems of contextualization relations immanent in those processes, which makes it fruitful to try to analyze from intertextual relations the social ideologies at work in a community.

Why intertextuality? or more precisely, why focus on *global* rather than on local structures? With sentences we can make meanings we cannot make with words by themselves; nor do we stop with sentences, for we make meanings through the relations among sentences that we could not make with sentences. And we do not stop, as a community, with single texts; that is, we make meanings globally across texts that construct relationships with and out of the multivariate structural units we might call the locally compact 'parts' of a text, or texts or activities, or occasions of discourse. We make meanings through the relations, and the non-relations, of texts and actions that reach to the highest orders of contextualization, the 'deepest' patterns of our social system of action and meaning. If the disjunctions are to be analyzed, if the overall patterns of our social order are to be analyzed from actual social practices, we need a viewpoint that is not bound to 'a text', but can analyze relations that connect,and disconnect, across 'texts'.

The key to such a mode of analysis I think is an examination of how multivariate and covariate relations work together in structuring—which is to say creating, defining—the flow of socially meaningful action. In the terms with which we began, derived from the notions of register, it is the interplay across texts of the multivariate structuring relations of the semiotic of social action (AcS) and the covariate structuring relations of thematic systems (ThS), patterned against one another, and realized through the resources of the language system (LgS) that should be the focus of attention. Such a research programme carries forward to the intertextual level of analysis the core enterprise of functional linguistics: to describe the resources of language not in any imagined intrinsic, formal terms of its own, but in terms of what people do and can do with those resources. As we do more than we know we do, so we can do more than we now know how to do as a community. We, all of us, participate in remaking day to day the systems of action and meaning that limit us and sustain a social order that, because of those limitations, our community can see and respond to only in the system's own terms. The social practice of foregrounding those limitations through linguistic, actional, and thematic analysis can disrupt the most basic stability of our own social system, creating fundamentally new human possibilities.

REFERENCES

Bourdieu, P. (1977). *Outline of a Theory of Practice*. London and New York: Cambridge University Press.
Colby, B. N. (1973). A partial grammar of Eskimo folktales. *American Anthropologist* **75:** 645–662.
Gregory, M. (1967). Aspects of varieties differentiation. *JL* **3.**
Halliday, M. A. K. (1971). Linguistic function and literary style: an inquiry into the language of William Golding's *"The Inheritors"* In Chatman, Seymour (ed.), *Literary Style: a Symposium*. New York: Oxford University Press.
———— (1978). *Language as Social Semiotic*. London: Edward Arnold.
———— (1981). The de-automatization of grammar: from Priestley's *"An Inspector Calls"*. University of Sydney Department of Linguistics.
Halliday, M. A. K. (1983). *A short introduction to functional grammar*. University of Sydney Department of Linguistics.
Halliday, M. A. K. & Hasan, R. (1976). *Cohesion in English*. London: Longman.
Hasan, R. (1979). On the notion of text. In Petofi, J. S. (ed.), *Text vs. sentence*. Hamburg, Germany: Helmut Buske Verlag.
———— (1980). Text and context. *Sophia Linguistics* **6:** 44–59.
———— (1981). Coherence and cohesive harmony. Macquarie University, Department of Linguistics (North Ryde, Australia).
Hjelmslev, L. (1961). *Prolegomena to a Theory of Language*. Madison, WI: University of Wisconsin Press.
Lemke, J. L. (1977). The formal analysis of instruction. City University of New York, Brooklyn College School of Education.
———— (1979). Action, context, and meaning. Seminar paper, Department of Linguistics, University of Sydney.
———— (1982). *Classroom Communication of Science*. Final Report to the National Science Foundation (USA). Washington, DC: National Technical Information Service.
———— (1982b). Making Trouble. (Manuscript).
Martin, J. (1982). English text: system and structure (In preparation).
Propp, V. (1968). *Morphology of the Folktale*. Austin, TX: University of Texas Press.
Riffaterre, M. (1980). Syllepsis. *Critical Inquiry* **6:** 625–638.
Ure, J. N. (1971). Lexical density and register differentiation. In Perren, G. E. & Trim, J. L. M. (eds.), *Applications of linguistics*. Cambridge, England: Cambridge University Press.
Ure, J. N. & Ellis, J. (1974). Register in descriptive linguistics and linguistic sociology. In Uribe-Villegas, O. (ed.), *Issues in Socioloinguistics*. The Hague: Mouton.

How Does a Story Mean What it Does? A Partial Answer   **15**

Peter H. Fries
Central Michigan University

The basic question I ask about any text I analyze is virtually the one I asked in my title. 'How does this text mean what it does?' Part of the answer to that question involves the discovery of patterns in the language of the text which lead listeners or readers to interpret the text as they do. Of course, any text, once it has been created, contains an infinity of patterns. Since people cannot process and interpret an infinite number of patterns, the linguist cannot blindly search for pattern in the text, *any* pattern, and assume that *every* pattern so discovered will be significant and contribute to the interpretations given by readers or listeners. As a result, it would seem that the most efficient way to work would be to begin with a description of the interpretations of the text being analyzed, and then search for patterning in the language of the text which might be expected to account for those interpretations. This entails linking the choices of language made in the story to choices of language and meaning *available in the language system as a whole*. Underlying this approach is the assumption that choices of language form are significant only in so far as they lead to different meanings and interpretations.

The story I wish to analyze here, *Freddie Miller; Scientist,* is a story written for children in the fourth grade. The text is given in the appendix. It is the story of a young boy who is constantly in trouble with his family because he likes to tinker with things and usually ends up breaking them. First he tries to fix his sister's doll, but he turns it green in the process. Then he makes a wonderful mixture of chemicals and smells up the refrigerator with it. He then fixes his parents' alarm clock, and it goes off at three in the morning. Finally, his sister gets stuck in the closet and he redeems himself in everyone's eyes by fixing a light to calm her while she is stuck there. Clearly I did not choose this story for its literary merit. Rather it is a story which has been given to a large number of young children to read, and we have recordings of their oral readings and retellings which I wish ultimately to correlate with my analysis.

In this analysis, I wish to begin with a general notion of the overall structure of the story, and then to examine the details of the language used in the beginning of this story to show how certain structural elements are realized by certain semantic choices, and finally to show that the particular realization of an element in the beginning of the story (the problem) is followed up by repetitions of roughly the

[(<Placement>⃗) Initiating Event^] Sequent Event^⃗ Final Event [^(Finale) · (Moral)]

—Hasan unpublished

Figure 1. Structure potential of the nursery tale

same meanings in later portions of the story. In other words, I am taking a first step in what may eventually turn into a study of coocurrence restrictions between the realizations of elements within different parts of a story. Of course these goals require that the particular model of the overall structure of a text be one which has a more or less direct relation to meaning, and thus it should be easily interpretable in terms of meaning choices in the language.

Halliday, Hasan, Gregory and others have developed the notion of generic structure which seems to answer our need very well. It looks outside the text in such a way as to relate in a principled way features of the structures of the interactions between people to features of the meanings expressed at specific points within the texts which realize those interactions. In an interesting unpublished work, Hasan has tried to answer the question, 'What does one have to do to tell a nursery tale?' The basic outlines of her answer are given in Figures 1 and 2. Particularly important for my purpose here is the overtly semantic nature of the descriptions given in Figure 2.

Of course *Freddie Miller; Scientist* is not a nursery tale, and therefore it does not fit the structure Hasan describes exactly. For example, the semantic values she describes for placement do not describe the values found in *Freddie Miller; Scientist*. Indeed, given the way she describes placement, I doubt that *Freddie Miller; Scientist* has that function. However, even though *Freddie Miller; Scientist* is not a nursery tale, it seems to me that the story is similar enough to the structure which Hasan describes, that we can generalize and adapt her description so that it no longer describes just nursery tales, but provides a rough description of a much larger group of similar stories which includes *Freddie Miller; Scientist*. In particular, let me focus on the semantic tasks which are typically accomplished in the beginnings of stories. These are given in Figure 3. I have worded Figure 3 in terms of the tasks to be achieved rather than the particular values given in the achievement of any one task so that I do not limit my description to a particular genre such as the nursery tale. I have combined two of Hasan's elements (*Attribution* and *Habitude*) since

1. Character Particularization
2. Temporal (and Spatial) Distance
3. Impersonalization
4. Attribution
5. Habitude

—Hasan unpublished

Figure 2. Semantic properties relevant to the realization of placement

1. Character Introduction
2. Temporal and Spatial Placement
3. Choice of Personal Stance of Narrator
4. Characterization
   A. Attribution
   B. Habitude
5. Complicating Issue

Figure 3. Tasks typically accomplished in the beginning of stories

they seem to perform much the same function in a story, the description of norms of situation, of character, or of action to use as a basis for interpreting what happens later in the story. Finally I have added *Complicating Issue,* an item which I wish to discuss in this paper, and which I take to be implicit in Hasan's *Initiating Event.* In adding *Complicating Issue* to the list I do not wish to commit myself to saying that all stories must have such complicating issues, any more than Hasan would wish to say that all stories must have *Attribution* or *Habitude.* I wish merely to say that *Complicating Issue* does at least occur in some stories and that *Freddie Miller; Scientist* is one such story.

We now have a very rough sketch of the overall structure of a genre of stories which includes this story. Our next task is to examine how the author of *Freddie Miller; Scientist* achieved the tasks described in points 1)–5) of Figure 3.

1) CHARACTER INTRODUCTION

The first characters we see are *Poor Freddie* and *Elizabeth.* They are introduced with personal names, as if we already know them. (Personal names are much like pronouns in this sense.) All the other characters in the story are introduced by reference to Freddie.

his mother
your Uncle August
his Father

Even Elizabeth is immediately related to Freddie in the third sentence (*His little sister was heartbroken.*).

2) TEMPORAL AND SPATIAL PLACEMENT

This aspect of the story presents a problem for analysis. Readers I have consulted believe that the story is definitely placed near by—near both in space and in time. Yet few indicators (either spatial or temporal) exist in the language of the text which place it there. Certainly words such as *chemistry set, chemicals, refrigerator, alarm clock, bulb,* and *flashlight* help through our knowledge of the world, but in fact these items would do for any time since about 1920. Most readers I have talked to place the time setting much more recently than 1920. I have the feeling that the story took place in the very recent past (say the last five years or so) and this in spite of the presence of references to the transom, an object which I associate only with older buildings. Further, I obtain this sense of relatively immediate past well within the first 20 sentences, considerably before most of the vocabulary items mentioned above occur. This strong feeling of near spatial and temporal placement in the absence of clear and unambiguous signals in the text needs to be explained.

3) CHOICE OF PERSONAL STANCE OF THE NARRATOR

Freddie Miller; Scientist is narrated in the third person, thus there is an *I*, telling some *you*, the reader, about characters in the story. It is significant that the *I* never intrudes itself into the story to make obvious comments. There is no case where the narrator refers to himself. However, some narrator comments are present. We see in the first sentence that *Poor Freddie was in trouble again.* Certainly *poor* does not describe a characteristic of Freddie but rather is a description of the narrator's feelings about Freddie and the situation he is in. The narrator thus has a point of view and this point of view influences the telling. Clearly the central character is Freddie. All the other characters are related to him overtly. We get

> *his little sister*
> *Freddie's mother*
> *his Father*
> *your Uncle August*
> *his other uncles.*

Each of these phrases has two ways of taking Freddie as central, first the possessive, *his, Freddie's,* and *your* all refer to Freddie, and second, the relationships given take Freddie as central.

Further evidence for the narrator's point of view is the fact that the narrator often describes Freddie's thoughts and reactions directly, while the thoughts and reactions of the other characters are described only by the characters themselves. To put this in formal grammatical terms, Freddie may be the cognizant of mental processes both within quotations and within the narration. With five exceptions,[1] the other characters are cognizants of mental processes only within quotations.

---

[1] All of the exceptions to this last statement involve some sort of overt activity as well as a mental process, and therefore are not *simply* mental process verbs.

(48)   . . . when his parents *discovered* who had fixed the clock

(124)   Then *seeing* Freddie . . . "What are you doing in the kitchen with those things?" he *wanted* to *know.*

(127)   Mr. Miller *heard* the story three times—from Freddie, from Elizabeth, and from Mrs. Miller.

Finally we can see that the narrator takes Freddie's point of view in a number of descriptions. We have already seen this in the first sentence with *poor Freddie,* but it occurs elsewhere in the story as well. Sentences 14 and 15

(14)   She was always comparing Freddie with one of them [his uncles].

(15)   Good or bad, he was always like one of the uncles!

would seem to be a paraphrase of something Freddie might say, not his mother. Also note the narrator intrusion in the form of the exclamation mark. That should lead us to conclude that these sentences do *more* than report the facts. And indeed they can be seen to comment on them. The narrator disapproves.

4) CHARACTERIZATION

Chart 1 shows what the reader learns about each of the major characters of the story in the first 21 sentences. Chart 1, however, does not tell the whole truth. As I said earlier, sentences 14 and 15 (which occur under habitude for Mrs. Miller) do not merely report the facts, 'what always happens', they also comment negatively on these facts. This negative evaluation is achieved primarily by using the progressive form of the verb together with an adverb of extreme frequency.[2] Within the first 21 sentences of *Freddie Miller; Scientist* we find two clear instances of this usage (11 and 14). Two other sentences (15 and 12) convey the same effect, but use slightly different structures to do so.

(11)   —never letting well enough alone.

(14)   She was always comparing Freddie with one of them.

(15)   Good or bad, he was always like one of the uncles.

(12)   Freddie had heard a lot about Uncle August, and a lot about his other uncles too.

Sentence 11 shows that Mother doesn't like Freddie's actions. Sentences 12, 14 and 15 show that the narrator, taking Freddie's point of view, doesn't like what the mother typically does. Clearly evaluation, specifically *negative* evaluation, is important here. This notion is reinforced when we look at the other words and phrases characterizing the various participants in the story. Freddie is seen as poor and in trouble (now and frequently). He performs experiments which his mother thinks are queer (that is—strange, with the association of bad). Sentence (21)

---

[2] Quirk and Greenbaum (1973.41) describe this structure in the following words:

> The progressive (usually with an adverb of high frequency) can also be used of habitual action, conveying an emotional coloring such as irritation; e.g., He's always *writing* with a special pen—just because he likes to be different.

Chart 1. Characterization of the Four Major Characters of Freddie Miller; Scientist

A. *Freddie*

Attribution		Habitude	
(1)	Poor		
(1)	in trouble	(1)	again
		((6)	What queer experiment was it this time?)[3]
((11)	You are just like your Uncle August,)	((11)	—never letting well enough alone.)
		((12)	Freddie had heard a lot about Uncle August, and a lot about his other uncles, too.)
		((14)	She was always comparing Freddie with one of them.)
		((15)	Good or bad, he was always like one of the uncles!)
		(16)	. . . he loved to tinker with machines, tools, and chemicals.
		(21)	Sometimes he thought that a scientist's life was filled with disappointments.

B. *Mrs. Miller*

Attribution		Habitude	
(4)	Freddie's mother		
(4)	angry		
(5)	exclaimed		
((6)	"What queer experiment was it this time?")		
((11)	"You are just like your Uncle August,—never letting well enough alone!")		
		((12)	Freddie had heard a lot about Uncle August, and a lot about his other uncles too.)
(13)	had grown up [in Switzerland]		
		((14)	She was always comparing Freddie with one of them.)
		((15)	Good or bad he was always like one of the uncles!)
		(17)	What his mother called him depended on what he had done last!

---

[3] Parentheses indicate sentences which provide information about more than one character at the same time. Mrs. Miller's question 'what queer experiment was it this time?' not only shows her reaction to the situation and thus tells something about Freddie's situation, it also strongly implies that Freddie has been in this situation before.

Chart 1. *Continued*

C. *Mr. Miller*

Attribution	*Habitude*
(16) His father	(16) His father usually called him Tinker . . .

D. *Elizabeth*

Attribution	*Habitude*
(2) [had] doll	
(3) His little sister	
(3) heartbroken	

implies that Freddie is disappointed or unhappy. The people around him are unhappy with him. Mother is angry, Elizabeth is heartbroken. Of the 20 different items I have identified as describing the various characters, twelve either directly present a negative reaction (such as anger) or a negative evaluation, or imply such an evaluation. Clearly Freddie has a problem.

5) COMPLICATING ISSUE

This brings me to the last task authors typically accomplish in the beginnings of stories, the introduction of a Complicating Issue. Often such Complicating Issues are problems which must be solved, and the problem we have just identified for Freddie is perfectly adequate to motivate a story. Is there any evidence that this is indeed the problem which motivates this story? Notice our answer cannot be that this problem exists and therefore it is automatically the problem which motivates this story. We cannot assume that every problem which we the readers of a story are willing to regard as problems will be so important to the story that they will motivate the story. Rather, something within the language of the story must tell us the nature of the problem to be solved. Indeed, in the first section of *Freddie Miller; Scientist* it is easy to identify at least two very good problems, one of which is the negative evaluation of Freddie by his family, the other is the fact that Elizabeth's doll has turned green. This problem is also perfectly adequate to motivate the action of a story. It so happens that it does not motivate the action of this story and is dropped after sentence 21. This fact, coupled with what we have already seen would indicate that there are at least three ways that narrators tell their readers what are the problems which motivate their stories. First, within the beginning of the story, certain crucial meanings will be repeated which are connected or connectable with something that can be seen as a problem. Second, the words and phrases which convey these meanings will occupy positions of prominence, particularly in the beginning of the story. Finally, these meanings will be followed up throughout the remainder of the story. (That is, the reader must find out whether or not the problem has been solved.) In other words, a sort of cooccurrence restriction is set up between

Conjunctive Relations	Text

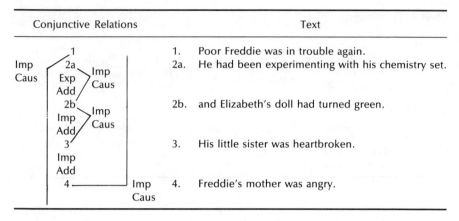

	1. Poor Freddie was in trouble again.
	2a. He had been experimenting with his chemistry set.
	2b. and Elizabeth's doll had turned green.
	3. His little sister was heartbroken.
	4. Freddie's mother was angry.

Figure 4. Conjunctive relations in the first four sentences of Freddie Miller; Scientist

the meanings which occur at the beginning of a story and those which occur at its end. Let us look at Freddie's problem in this light. First of all, what meanings related to a problem are repeated in the first 21 sentences of the story? Second, how are these meanings given prominence in these 21 sentences? Third, how are these meanings followed up in the remainder of the story?

We have already given a large portion of the answer to the first question. We have seen that terms involving negative evaluations of Freddie, of negative reactions to Freddie's actions, and of negative reactions by Freddie recur many times throughout this initial portion of the story. Every character mentioned in the beginning of the story (except Father) is unhappy, and Freddie is the cause. He deserves to be in trouble. This is captured in Figure 4, which describes the conjunctive relations within the first four sentences of the story. Here (2a) (an action of Freddie's) causes (2b) (a result of that action). (2b) in turn causes (3) (Elizabeth's reaction). Probably the whole of (2)–(3) causes (4) (Mrs. Miller's reaction). Finally, the whole of (2)–(4) appears to be the basis for saying (1).

Let me now move to the second question. How are these meanings given prominence in these 21 sentences? The first place to look is at the level of the information unit. The tonic syllable always falls within the constituent which is being treated as new. However, since I am dealing with a written story, and since I did not have time to record and transcribe a number of proficient readers to see where they placed their tonic syllables, I tried to get at the locus of new information indirectly. Halliday has said that there is a correlation between the clause and the information unit, such that one clause is usually said in one information unit. Further, the tonic accent, the signal of the locus of the new information in the information unit typically occurs on the last full constituent of the clause, provided that that constituent does not convey information which is recoverable from the context. I therefore pretended that the unmarked relation held for every clause in this section of the text and looked at what the result would be. Admittedly this is a very rough and ready approach, but the results are very interesting. Figure 5 provides the initial results.

1. Poor Freddie was *in trouble again.*
2. He had been experimenting *with his chemistry set,* and Elizabeth's doll had turned *green.*
3. His little sister was *heartbroken.*
4. Freddie's mother was *angry.*
5. "You've *wrecked that doll!*" she *exclaimed.*
6. "What queer experiment was it *this time?*"
7. "I was only washing the doll to make it look *like new,*" Freddie *explained.*
8. "I made *a special mixture.*"
9. But I guess I added *too many chemicals to the mixture.*"
10. "I guess you *did,*" Mrs. Miller *said.*
11. "You are *just like your Uncle August—never letting well enough alone.*"
12. Freddie had heard *a lot about Uncle August,* and *a lot about his other uncles* too.
13. All of them were living *in Switzerland,* where Mrs. Miller had *grown up.*
14. She was always comparing Freddie *with one of them.*
15. Good or bad, he was always *like one of the uncles!*
16. His father usually called him *Tinker* because he loved to tinker *with machines, tools, and chemicals.*
17. But what his mother called him depended on *what he had done last!*
18. "I think you should buy *another doll for Elizabeth,*" she was *saying now.*
19. "I want you to save half your allowance for it *each week.*"
20. Freddie nodded *sadly.*
21. Sometimes he thought that a scientist's life was filled *with disappointments.*

Figure 5. Unmarked foci of new information in the clauses of episode 1

First I mechanically underlined the last clause level constituent of each clause. I then looked at the underlined words in context to see whether they had either of two characteristics. First, did they belong to a small set of contrastive items (eg. *yesterday, today,* or *tomorrow.*)? *Again* (1) and *now* (18) each seemed to belong to such a group. Second, did the words convey information which was easily recoverable from context? *That doll* (5), *to the mixture* (9) and *for Elizabeth* (18) seemed to do so. In either of these situations I felt that the word was unlikely to contain the tonic syllable, and so I underlined the next preceding clause level constituent and drew an arrow pointing forward to indicate that the earlier constituent would be more likely to receive the tonic stress. The result of this procedure is that of the thirty clauses contained in the 21 sentences in this section of the story, 15 either end with evaluative terms, or have evaluative terms where the tonic would be likely to fall when adjustment for recoverable information is made. In other words, fully 50 percent of the clauses contain evaluative words where the unmarked focus of new information would fall, and hence, the evaluation would form part of the point made by those clauses. Negative evaluation is very definitely being emphasized in this section.

Negative evaluation is also being emphasized in another way in this section. Let us look now at the interpersonal interaction which takes place in the conversation given in this section. The text of the conversation is given in Text 1.

This conversation proceeds through five steps (described in Figure 6) corresponding roughly to the turns taken by the participants.

(M) 5. You've wrecked that doll!
(M) 6. What queer experiment was it this time?
(F) 7. I was only washing the doll to make it look like new,
(F) 8. I made a special mixture
(F) 9. But I guess I added too many chemicals to the mixture.
(M) 10. I guess you did
(M) 11. You are just like your Uncle August—never letting well enough alone.
(M) 18. I think you should buy another doll for Elizabeth.
(M) 19. I want you to save half your allowance for it each week.
(F) 20. Freddie nodded sadly.

Text 1. Dialog in the first twenty-one sentences

Before I begin the discussion of the dialog proper, let me first note that the dialog carriers *exclaimed* (after (5)) and *explained* (after (7)) support the analysis of the first two steps of the conversation into accusation followed by justification. These words *exclaimed* and *explained* were left out of Text 1 because they were not literally part of the dialog.

The whole point of the first portion of the conversation in Text 1 is the evaluation of Freddie's actions. The negative evaluations of sentences (5) and (6) with *wrecked* and *queer* are intensified by *this time*, with its implication that Freddie regularly performs "queer experiments". Freddie's justification uses *only*, a word which minimizes and limits the activity being described. He then introduces an admirable purpose and evaluates his mixture positively (*special*) and then introduces a bit of doubt through *I guess* as he presents his probable mistake. Note that he is unlikely to be really doubtful here, rather he uses *I guess* as a means of softening his responsibility. His wording is then echoed by his mother, in whose mouth *I guess* turns into great certainty. Indeed this certainty seems to extend throughout her part of the conversation. She does not use verbs of doubt or uncertainty. In her view Freddie is *just* like his uncle. He *never* lets well enough alone. Though she is willing to verbalize her demands in reasonably polite form with *I think you should* and *I want*, she is not uncertain as to what she wants. In the interchange in Text 1, Mother is constantly stating and asserting. Even in the question *What queer experiment was it this time?* she merely asks for the identification of an experiment which she has already characterized. Freddie, on the other hand, is responding. The difference between asserting and responding is likely to show up in the intonation patterns readers give this passage as well. Freddie's contributions are likely to be read with a

Step		Turn
1. Negative evaluation or accusation by Mother		Mother
2. Freddie's justification of his actions and admission of fault		Freddie
3. General evaluation by Mother	}	Mother
4. Proposal for restitution		
5. Agreement		Freddie

Figure 6. Interactive steps in the dialog in text 1

Situation
Problem
Solution
Evaluation
—Eugene Winter 1976

Figure 7. Fundamental information structure

falling-rising intonation (implying uncertainty) while Mother's lines are more likely to receive a simple falling intonation.

Finally it is quite clear in the first part of the dialog that Freddie is the one who is being evaluated. Of the first seven clauses in the dialog, the ones which focus on evaluation, Freddie is the explicit and overt theme in six, and is directly implied in the seventh, (sentence (6), in which what *queer experiment* refers to an experiment Freddie is known to have performed.) Only when we get to step 4, the proposal for restitution is the mother thematic. Thus Freddie is regularly the point of departure of the messages in the evaluation portion of the dialog. Thus the interaction in the dialog itself serves to make prominent Freddie's problem.

Now as I said earlier, we have to answer three questions when we identify how stories tell us what their problems are. I have already shown that meanings related to negative evaluation recur often in the beginning of this story. I have also just shown that these meanings are emphasized in this part of the story, first by their placement in the various clauses of the section, and second by being a major focus of the interaction between Freddie and his mother. The final task remaining is to show that this negative evaluation is followed up and emphasized in the remainder of the story.

First let me shift to a terminology for parts of the story which emphasizes the role of problems and evaluation (taken from Winter 1976). That is given in Figure 7. Not only does this terminology emphasize the problem-solution structures we have been talking about, it also provides a technique to distinguish episodes from sequences of events which do not constitute episodes. Episodes devote some space to evaluation, while mere sequences of events do not. Therefore, I took the presence of evaluation of some solution as defining an episode. I then made the chart of the overall structure of the story given in Chart 2.

As the chart shows, the story is divided into four episodes (1 through 4 in the first column). The next column shows the story level functions, while the third column gives the episode level functions. The last column shows which sentences were assigned to the various episode level functions.

Several points emerge from even a cursory examination of this chart. First, the cycling on the episode level is not complete, and the space devoted to those episode level functions that actually occur is not completely parallel. In episode 1 the situation and problem are not expressed overtly. Similarly the solution function in episode 2 is only implied. (Admittedly these functions are implied, and therefore recoverable to some extent. But that is a rather different matter from the overt expression of these functions.) Finally, the solution function of episode 4 is extremely long by com-

Chart 2. Overall Structure of "Freddie Miller, Scientist"

Episode No.	Story Level Structure	Episode Level Structure	Sentence No.
		Situation ⎫	implied (7)
		Problem ⎭	
1	Situation with Problem	⎧ Solution	2a, 7, 8
		⎩ Evaluation	1, 2b, 3, 4, 5, 6, 9, 10, 11, 18, 19, 20, 21. (12, 13, 14, 15, 16, 17, evaluate 11)
2	Solution 1	Situation	22, 23, 24, (+ evaluation of E#1)
		Problem	25
		Solution	implied (26)
		Evaluation	26, 27, 28 (F's), 29, 30, 31, 32, 33, 34, 35, 36 (M's), 37 (F's)
3	Solution 2	Situation	38, (+ evaluation of E#1&2)
		Problem	39, 40, 41
		Solution	49, 50, 51, 52
		Evaluation	42, 43, 44, 45, 46, 47, 48 (potential), 53, 54, 55, 56, 57, 58, 59, 60, 61, 62, 63, 64, 65, 66, 67 (actual)
4	Solution 3	Situation	68, 69, 70, 71, 72 (+ evaluation of E's 1–3)
		Problem	73, 74, 75, 76
		$Solution_1$	77a
		$Evaluation_1$	77b
		$Solution_2$	78, 79
		$Evaluation_2$ = Problem a	80, 81, 82
		Solution a	83–110
		Evaluation a	115, 116, 117, 118
		$Solution_2$ (reintroduce)	111, 112, 113, 114
	Evaluation	$Evaluation_2$	119–144

parison with the solution functions in the other episodes. In all of the episodes a great deal of space is devoted to the evaluation function. Charts 3 and 4 present a more graphic view of the relative amount of space devoted in each of the episodes of the story and in the story as a whole to each of these episode level functions. Chart 3 shows how many sentences are devoted to each episode level function, while Chart 4 shows how many processes are devoted to each episode level function.

How are these variations in the realization of the various episode level functions to be explained? The answers provided here can be no more than guesses, until they are checked against a large number of other stories. However, the stories I have

Chart 3. Sentences Devoted to the Various
Episode Level Functions

Episode	Situation	Problem	Solution	Evaluation	Total
1	—	—	2½	18½	21
2	3	1	—	12	16
3	1	3	4	22	30
4	5	4	34½	33½	77
Total	9	8	41	86	144

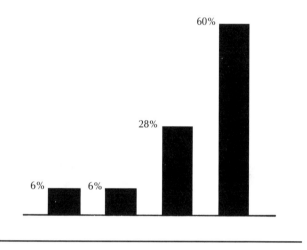

analyzed carefully do seem to fit the trends assumed in the explanations given here. It would seem that the initial situation and problem functions in episode 1 are not expressed overtly because they are not in focus. They are not in focus because, as can be seen in Chart 5, the story level function of episode 1 is to describe a story level situation which contains a story level problem. How or why the problem came about is really irrelevant, provided we at least see Freddie as the cause. Similarly, the solution in episode 2 is out of focus so long as we know that *Freddie* did some experiment, and that that experiment caused his mother's reactions.

One could probably make the same argument for the solution function in episode 4, except for one thing. Episode 4 is the location of the turning point of the story. This is where all those bad evaluations turn into good evaluations. Good narration technique should not merely tell us that Freddie deserves this good evaluation, it should also show us that he deserves it. Therefore, a great deal of space is devoted to narrating what Freddie did to help his sister.

I should say here that the segmentation of the story into episodes and into episode level functions is not a figment of my imagination, for it can be used to explain certain tendencies in the distribution of various linguistic phenomena. Chart 5

**Chart 4. Processes Devoted to the Various
Episode Level Functions**

Episode	Situation	Problem	Solution	Evaluation	Total
1	—	—	5	34	39
2	12	2	—	22	36
3	3	7	11	39	60
4	12	5	54	62	133
Total	27	14	70	157	268

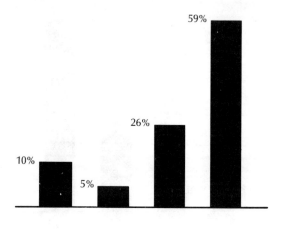

shows that the various process types do not occur uniformly throughout the story, but are strongly influenced by the type of episode level function in which they occur. For example, of the material processes which occur in this story, 50 (or 44%) occur in the evaluation functions of the various episodes while 44 (or 38%) occur in the solution functions of the various episodes. In evaluating these figures it should be remembered that 59% of the processes of the story are devoted to the evaluation function of the story while only 26% of the processes of the story are devoted to the solution functions on the episode level. Thus 44% should be compared with 59% and 38% with 26%. If we look at it the other way and ask about the types of processes which occur within the various functions, again we find significant skewing. Of the 70 processes which occur in the solution function of some episode, 44 (or 63%) are material processes and 13 (or 19%) are relational processes.

These two figures are to be compared with the total percent of material and relational processes in the whole story, which are 43% and 27% respectively.[4] (Incidentally, I suspect that the 19% figure for relational processes in the solution

---

[4] A x^2 analysis of the data presented in Chart 5 showed it was significant at the .0112 level.

Chart 5. Distribution of Process Types in Episode Level Functions

Episode Level Function	Process Types				Total
	Material	Relational	Mental	Verbal	
Situation	14	7	3	3	27
	52%	26%	11%	11%	100%
Problem	7	1	4	2	14
	50%	7%	29%	14%	100%
Solution	44	13	5	8	70
	63%	19%	7%	11%	100%
Evaluation	50	52	29	26	157
	32%	33%	18%	17%	100%
Total	115	73	41	39	268
	43%	27%	15%	15%	100%

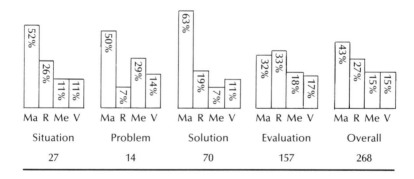

functions of the story is somewhat inflated, since most of the relational processes which I had difficulty classifying occurred here.)

A closer analysis of the distributions of specific sets of processes bears out the general analysis just presented. Figure 8 shows a preliminary analysis of the lexical sets encountered in the story. A lexical set is a group of words which are related via any of the traditional meaning relations (i.e., synonymy, antonymy, hyponymy, or meronymy. Occasionally I included strong collocational association as a relating tie.) Thus all the members of a lexical set are similar in meaning (see Figure 8).

If we look at the distribution of the processes from one set or from related sets we will see significant skewing from uniform distribution in the story. For example, the processes in sets 20) and 22) all deal with some variety of fixing, with 22) being a specific subtype of fixing. Chart 6 shows all instances of 20) which have an actor expressed overtly. The top 20 examples of the chart are all those in which Freddie is

Chart 6. Processes of Lexical Set 20 in Context

S	Episode Level / Function	Freddie	Others	Experiment	Fix	Chemistry	Mix	Machines, Tools, Etc.	Doll	Refrigerator	
2	Solution	he		experimenting		w his chem set					
5	Evaluation	you (=F)			wrecked				that doll		
7	Solution	I (=F)			washing				the doll		
8	Solution	I (=F)			made		spec.mix.				
11	Evaluation	[F]			letting w enough al.						
16	Evaluation	he (=F)			tinker	[w] chemicals		w machines, tools			the strange & the unknown
22	Situation	Freddie's		experim.s		chemistry	mixing				
23	Situation	[F]					mixture				
26	Evaluation	Freddie			made						
35	Evaluation	Freddie			cleaned out					the refrig.	
41	Problem	Freddie			fix			the clock			
43	Evaluation	I (=F)			fixed			it			
48	Evaluation	who			fixed			the alarm			
49	Solution	Freddie			worked			on it			
50	Solution	[F]			winding			it			
50	Solution	[F]			setting			it			
62	Evaluation	I (=F)			set			it			
64	Evaluation	he (=F)			fixed			the clock			
69	Situation	he (=F)			making			an elec. bell			
86	Solution	I (=F)			fix			a light			
29	Evaluation		Mrs. Miller		get . . . ready						supper
122	Evaluation		Mrs. Miller		getting . . . ready						supper
65	Evaluation		My bro Charles		tinkering			with clocks			

Chart 7. Processes of Lexical Set 22 in Context

| Episode Level | | | | | Location | |
S Function	Actor	Place	Parts	End	End	Path
9 Evaluation	I (=F)	added	too many chems.		to the mixture	
10 Evaluation	you (=F)	[added	too many chems.		to the mixture]	
70 Situation	he (=F)	got	the parts		in place	
96 Solution	he (=F)	taped	the batteries	end to end	on the ruler	
97 Solution	he (=F)	taped	the wire	tight	across the bott. of the end b.	up the sides of the two batt.
98 Solution	he (=F)	ran	the wire		to the bulb	
99 Solution	[F]	winding	it (= wire)		around the bott. of the bulb	
99 Solution	he (=F)	taped	the bulb		in place	
100 Solution	he (=F)	placed	the bulb		so that it touched . . . batt.	
102 Solution	he (=F)	taped	the bulb		in place on the ruler	
104 Solution	he (=F)	tied	a string		around the end of the ruler	

1. in trouble, fault, queer, well, good, bad, great, worst, wrong, wonderful, proud, worse, goody-goody
2. angry, heartbroken, disappointments, sadly, fun, happily, mind, enjoying, serious, angrily, seriously, tearful, cries, crying, afraid, scary, excitedly, excitement, frightened, laughing, smiled, fine, poor, sighed, exclaimed
3. queer, strange, unknown, discover, secret, surprise, experimenting, experiments, knew, forgot
4. dark, cloudy, strange, queer
5. harmful, wrecked, explode, safely, hurt, serious, worse
6. always, usually, sometimes, kept_____ing, again, was_____ing, once, each week, never, last, three times, this time, next, special
7. none, a lot, enough, many
8. day, night, week, morning, moment, minute, afternoon
9. breakfast, supper, eating, butter, refrigerator, kitchen
10. room, hall, cellar, closet, kitchen, stairs, door, transom, window
11. feel, heard, smell, smelling, seeing, hear
12. tell, told, called, calling, let_____know, exclaimed, explained, said, saying, thought, asked, sighed, shouted, reply, replied, answered, wanted to know, smiled, sighed
13. thought, knew, guess
14. corner, top, bottom, sides, end, front
15. mother, sister, father, parents, uncle, husband, brother
16. neighbor, teacher
17. home, school
18. school, teacher
19. scientist, experiment, experimenting, chemistry, chemicals, chemist, mixture, discover, field
20. tinker, fix, made, making, winding, worked, washing, cleaned out, wrecked, setting, experimenting, letting well enough alone, getting—ready, homemade, working, busy
21. works, give_____trouble
22. added, taped, ran, winding, placed, got
23. living, grown up, life, dead
24. machines, tools, clock, bell, alarm, siren, flashlight, light
25. wire, bulb, battery, tape, flashlight, parts, string, ruler
26. dark, night, light, glow
27. open, shut, opened
28. still, even, only
29. Switzerland, world
30. must, can't, likely to, would, might, surely, could
31. pretend, dream, dreamed, real
32. louder, faint
33. Freddie, Elizabeth, Mrs. Miller, Uncle August, Uncle Maximilian, Uncle Oscar, Uncle Charles
34. comparing, like, too, louder, so, enough, another, other, so . . . that
35. all, none, half
36. buy, save, allowance
37. library, book
38. cut, narrowed
39. went, gone, hurried, ran, came, go, be, get out, climbing

Figure 8. Lexical sets in Freddie Miller; Scientist

40. alarm, ring, bell, siren, went off
41. hope, wish, wanted, loved
42. sounded, look
43. alarm clock, wake
44. battery, electric, wire
45. couldn't, can't, can
46. turned, become
47. think, idea
48. found, had, catch, reach, keep, picked up, hold, pass
49. intended, decided
50. listen, heard, hear
51. stopped_____ing, kept_____ing, started, intended, began to
52. interesting, looked, listen, heard
53. taking, returned, pulling, pulled, get
general terms:
    thing, matter, happened, done

Figure 8. Lexical sets in Freddie Miller; Scientist (*cont'd*)

actor, the bottom three examples are those in which some character other than Freddie is an actor. Chart 7 shows all examples of 22). In this case Freddie is the only character who is the actor of this set of terms.

If we look at the distribution of these processes, several points become evident. First, all of those instances in which someone other than Freddie is actor of such a process occur in the evaluation function of some episode. Second, if we look at those processes of which Freddie is actor, we find that 15, or almost 50% occur within a solution function of some episode while only 11, or about 35% occur in some episode level evaluation function. However, not only is there a differential distribution of these processes in the various episode level functions, the roles these processes play in the clause level grammar seems to be quite different in the different sections. Since too few examples occur in the situation or problem functions to get a feeling for the different ranges, let me focus on the solution and evaluation functions. Of the fifteen processes which occur within the episode level solution functions, 12 occur in the direct narrative while 3 occur within some quotation by a character. By comparison, of the 11 examples which occur within episode level evaluation functions, only two occur in direct narration. Two others are found in the narrative but as complement of a mental process (e.g., *Freddie loved to tinker with machines, tools, and chemicals* (16)) and seven occur within quotations.

Similar non-random distributions can be demonstrated for other sets as well. Lexical sets 1) and 2) can be considered similar for the purposes of this story since 1) concerns evaluation good-bad while 2) concerns mental reaction. If we add to these two sets the various comparisons with the uncles, Chart 8 results. It will be seen that over 90% of the examples on this chart occur in some episode level evaluation function of the story.

Chart 9 summarizes the distributions of four different sets in the episode level functions of the story. Processes involving motion (lexical sets 39 and 53), the

Chart 8. Processes of Lexical Sets 1 and 2 and Comparisons in Context

	Emotion	Evalution	Comparisons	Episode Level Function
1 Freddie	poor			Evaluation
1 Freddie		in trouble		Evaluation
3 his little sister	heartbroken			Evaluation
4 F's mother	angry			Evaluation
5 she	exclaimed			Evaluation
11 you (=F)			just like your Uncle August	Evaluation
15 [he (=F)]		good or bad		Evaluation
20 Freddie	sadly			Evaluation
21 Scientist (=F)	disappointments			Evaluation
27 he (=F)	happily			Evaluation
34 Freddie's		fault		Evaluation
35 [Freddie]			just like your Uncle Maximillian	Evaluation
37 Freddie	mind			Evaluation
46 [Freddie]			just like Uncle Oscar	Evaluation
48 Freddie	enjoying			Evaluation
53 his teacher	angrily			Evaluation
60 Freddie	serious			Evaluation
63 Mr. Miller	angrily			Evaluation
64 you (=F)			just like Uncle Charles	Evaluation
66 Mr. Miller	sighed			Evaluation
67 [Mr. Miller]	seriously			Evaluation
73 Elizabeth's	tearful			Problem
80 His sister's	cries			Evaluation
89 Elizabeth	crying			Solution
114 [Elizabeth]	Don't be afraid			Solution
117 [Elizabeth]	scary			Evaluation
118 you (=F)		wonderful		Evaluation
120 she (=F)	excitedly			Evaluation
125 Elizabeth	excitement			Evaluation
128 I (=Mr. M)		proud of you		Evaluation
131 F's mother		proud		Evaluation
134 you (=F)			just like—	Evaluation
135			Uncle Maximillian	Evaluation
137			Uncle Oscar	Evaluation
139 She (=Mrs. M)	laughing			Evaluation
140			Uncle Charles	Evaluation
142			Uncle August	Evaluation
143 Mrs. Miller	smiled			Evaluation
143 Freddie	fine			Evaluation
144 he (=F)			just like you (=Father)	Evaluation

Chart 9. Distribution of Processes Belonging to Four Different Lexical Sets
in the Various Episode Level Functions

	Situation	Problem	Solution	Evaluation	
Verbs of Motion	3 17%	1 6%	10 56%	4 32%	18 100%
Fixing	4 10%	1 3%	15 52%	11 34%	31 100%
Emotion/Evaluation	—	1 3%	2 5%	37 93%	40 101%
Verbal Processes	3 8%	2 5%	2 5%	32 82%	39 100%
Sentences in Story	9 6%	8 6%	41 28%	86 60%	144 100%
Processes in Story	27 10%	14 5%	70 26%	157 59%	268 100%

process of fixing discussed earlier, processes involving evaluation or emotional reaction from Chart 8 and verbal processes (lexical set 12)).

Let me return to Chart 8 for one last point. Earlier we discussed the importance of negative evaluation and unfavorable reactions to the nature of this story. It follows, then, that any changes in such reactions should also be important for the story. And indeed, in Chart 8 we can see a definite change. Up to sentence 117, all the evaluations and reactions are negative. People are generally unhappy or angry. Freddie is in trouble. After sentence 118 all the reactions and evaluations are good. People are excited and laughing. Freddie is wonderful. Elizabeth's statement in sentence (116) that *"It's not so bad with the light"* says fairly directly that the presence of the light makes it (where *it* seems to be either the closet or the situation) not so bad. Of course the reader has just seen Freddie *think* of the light, *make* it, and *get* it to Elizabeth. Freddie, in solving Elizabeth's problem has solved his own as well.

We can now see that the problem which we identified as the problem which motivated the action of the story is indeed carried through the entire story and finally solved. In fact the meanings relevant to this problem are emphasized at the end of the story. Of the last 27 sentences of the story (sentences 118–144), 15 contain overt and direct evaluations of Freddie. If we add implicit and indirect evaluations of Freddie (for example, by filling in ellipses), this would add another 3 sentences which contain evaluations of Freddie. Thus, fully two-thirds of the last 27 sentences of the story contain at least one item which evalutes Freddie directly or indirectly. Again, as in the beginning of the story, many of the evaluative items in these sentences (19, to be exact) occur in the unmarked focus of new information in their respective clauses. The end of a story, like the end of a clause, is a place of prominence and again evaluations of Freddie are emphasized in this position.

Let me summarize what I have done. I have started with a rough approximation of the generic structure of this story. I have taken five major tasks which either are accomplished or tend to be accomplished at the beginnings of stories belonging to this genre, and have shown how these tasks have been accomplished in *Freddie Miller; Scientist*. In doing so, I have been forced to consider the contributions of the ideational, the interpersonal and the textual components of the language of this text. Indeed, one of the most satisfying aspects of the results obtained here is the integration of the results of the analysis of these radically different components of language. Not only is the transitivity system relevant to this analysis, but also mood, modality, adverbs of frequency, thematic structure, information focus, and so forth. Further these features are all seen to be relevant to the nature of the story *as a whole*. Looking at the story from the point of view of generic structure has made that possible.

In the analysis, I have made three simple working assumptions which ought to be verbalized so that they can be examined. First, I have assumed that important ideas tend to be repeated. I have therefore sought out and examined repetitions of meanings. (Of course repetitions of wordings is one way of signalling repetitions of meanings, but it is not the only way. Thus, though I am interested in repetitions of wording, I am also interested in various kinds of proximal repetition.)

My second assumption is that important ideas tend to be placed in positions of prominence. Prominence in the clause seems to be either thematic prominence (at the beginning) or informational prominence (at the end). The beginnings and the endings of stories also seem to be prominent for somewhat similar reasons.

Finally, I have assumed that meaning is conveyed only where there is choice. It should be obvious from the approach I have taken here that when I talk about choice I do not mean the random choice of an infinite sentence machine, but rather the choice of items within a context where certain goals are to be attained. The effect of this assumption is to say that to describe this story, or any story, we must link the choices made in telling this story to the choices that are available in the system of the language being used. We need for example to look at how this story relates to the potential of stories in this language. If we say that *Freddie Miller; Scientist* is oriented around a particular type of problem to be solved, how does this particular problem fit within the range of problems that are central to stories of this genre. Once we describe the range of such problems, we should be able to identify with greater accuracy the particular features of the wording of a text which indicate that a particular problem is central to that text. This is important, for its allows us to look at each text in two ways at the same time. On the one hand, we can look at it as an example of a type, which allows us to compare different texts. On the other hand this approach allows us at the very same time to pay attention to those features of the text which mark it as unique and distinguish it from all other texts.

Linking the choices made in telling one story to the choices available in the language system as a whole has another advantage as well, for by so doing, we can hope to move from the ex-post-facto analyses of texts which have already been produced and interpreted, to a predictive analysis of how to produce a text. We would like to say that if you are writing a story, and you wish it to be understood thus so, you should take such and such choices. Of course, given our present state of knowledge about language, texts and people, the dream of a predictive analysis seems unattainable and unrealistic. Perhaps even in the ideal world of complete knowledge of language, texts, and people such a goal will remain unrealistic. However, it is always fun to dream. If my analysis has been successful it has provided a tiny portion of the answer to the question in my title, and thus forms an even tinier portion of a step towards attaining that dream.

BIBLIOGRAPHY

Gregory, Michael & Carroll, Suzanne. (1978). *Language and Situation: Language Varieties and Their Social Contexts*. London: Routledge & Kegan Paul.

Halliday, M. A. K. (1978). *Language as Social Semiotic*. Baltimore: University Park Press.

Halliday, M. A. K. & Hasan, Ruqaiya. (1981). *Text and Context*. Tokyo: Sophia University.

Hasan, Ruqaiya. (1978). Text in the systemic functional model. In Dressler, Wolfgang (ed.), *Current Trends in Text Linguistics*. Berlin: Walter de Gruyter, pp. 228–246.

————.Unpublished. The structure of the nursery tale: An essay in text typology.

More, Lillian. (1963). Freddie Miller; scientist. In Betts, E. A. & Welch, Carolyn (eds.), *Adventures Here and There* (3rd edition), Betts Basic Readers, 61–68. American Book Company.

Quirk, Randolph & Greenbaum, Sidney W. (1973). *A Concise Grammar of Contemporary English*. New York: Harcourt Brace Jovanovich.

Winter, Eugene. (1976). *Fundamentals of Information Structure*. Hatfield, England: Hatfield Polytechnic, School of Humanities & Linguistics.

APPENDIX: FREDDIE MILLER, SCIENTIST

1. Poor Freddie was in trouble again.
2. He had been experimenting with his chemistry set, and Elizabeth's doll had turned green.
3. His little sister was heartbroken.
4. Freddie's mother was angry.
5. "You've wrecked that doll!" she exclaimed.
6. "What queer experiment was it this time?"
7. "I was only washing the doll to make it look like new," Freddie explained.
8. "I made a special mixture.
9. But I guess I added too many chemicals to the mixture."
10. "I guess you did," Mrs. Miller said.
11. "You are just like your Uncle August—never letting well enough alone."
12. Freddie had heard a lot about Uncle August, and a lot about his other uncles too.

13. All of them were living in Switzerland, where Mrs. Miller had grown up.

14. She was always comparing Freddie with one of them.

15. Good or bad, he was always like one of the uncles!

16. His father usually called him Tinker because he loved to tinker with machines, tools, and chemicals.

17. But what his mother called him depended on what he had done last!

18. "I think you should buy another doll for Elizabeth," she was saying now.

19. "I want you to save half your allowance for it each week."

20. Freddie nodded sadly.

21. Sometimes he thought that a scientist's life was filled with disappointments.

22. After the cut in his allowance, Freddie's chemistry experiments narrowed to those safely outlined in a library book.

23. But he still thought it more fun to pretend to be a great scientist, mixing the strange and the unknown.

24. None of the chemicals in his set was harmful or likely to explode.

25. Yet by accident he might discover a mixture that would change the world.

26. Then one day Freddie made an interesting mixture that was dark and cloudy, and had a queer smell.

27. "I'll keep this for a while." he thought happily.

28. "It's pretty good."

29. Later that day Mrs. Miller went to the kitchen to get supper ready.

30. When she opened the refrigerator door—well, this is what she told her husband:

31. "The worst smell!

32. I thought I would faint!

33. I thought the refrigerator would explode.

34. I knew it was Freddie's fault!"

35. While Freddie cleaned out the refrigerator, his mother kept saying, "Just like your Uncle Maximilian!

36. His clothes were always smelling of chemicals."

37. Freddie didn't mind being compared with his Uncle Maximilian, who was a real chemist with a company in Switzerland.

38. By accident Freddie's next experiment was in a field that had nothing to do with chemistry.

39. One day at breakfast his father said, "The alarm clock didn't ring this morning.

40. I hope it isn't going to give us trouble!"

41. As he was eating, Freddie decided to fix the clock.

42. Then the next morning, his father would say, "Why, the clock works after all!"

43. And Freddie would say, "I fixed it, Father.

44. It was easy."

45. There was only one thing wrong with this dream.

46. Freddie knew that his mother would say, "Just like Uncle Oscar—always so helpful."
47. As surely as he knew the alphabet, Freddie knew that Uncle Oscar must have been a terrible goody-goody.
48. Still, even Uncle Oscar couldn't keep Freddie from enjoying the moment when his parents discovered who had fixed the alarm.
49. Taking the clock to the cellar, Freddie worked hard on it.
50. Then, winding it and setting it carefully, he returned it to his parents' room.
51. At supper he was careful not to speak of the secret.
52. Once, however, he forgot himself; he looked at the butter and said, "Please pass the clock."
53. That night Freddie dreamed that his teacher was talking angrily to Father.
51. All the time the school bell was ringing, ringing.
55. The dream was so strange that Freddie told his parents about it at breakfast.
56. "That wasn't the school bell," said Mrs. Miller.
57. "The alarm went off at three o'clock in the morning!
58. It sounded like a fire siren.
59. It was enough to wake the dead."
60. "Three o'clock!" Freddie said in a serious voice.
61. "That can't be!
62. I set it for seven."
63. "You what?" Mr. Miller asked angrily.
64. When Freddie told how he had fixed the clock, Mrs. Miller said, "You're just like Uncle Charles.
65. My brother Charles was always tinkering with clocks in Switzerland.
66. Mr. Miller sighed.
67. "Seriously, Tinker, sometimes I wish you didn't want to be a scientist."
68. Then one afternoon, when Mrs. Miller had gone to visit a neighbor, Freddie hurried to his cellar worktable.
69. He was making an electric bell as a surprise for his mother.
70. Just as he got the parts in place, he heard a faint tapping and a voice calling, somewhere above.
71. When Freddie ran up from the cellar, he heard his sister's voice calling, "Freddie! Freddie!"
72. "Where are you?" he shouted.
73. "In the hall closet!" came Elizabeth's tearful reply.
74. "The door blew shut.
75. It's stuck!
76. I can't get out!"
77. Freddie tried, with all his strength, but he couldn't open the closet door, either.
78. "I'll get Mother," he called to Elizabeth.
79. He knew this could become a serious matter.

80. His sister's cries grew louder.
81. "Don't leave me alone.
82. "It's dark in here."
83. Freddie, trying to think looked up at the small window above the closet door.
84. He had an idea!
85. "Listen, Elizabeth," he called.
86. "I'll fix a light and drop it to you through the transom.
87. Then I'll get Mother.
88. All right?"
89. Elizabeth stopped crying.
90. "all right, Freddie.
91. But hurry.
92. It's very dark in here."
93. At once Freddie set to work seriously at something he had started for fun.
94. He ran to the cellar and picked up the small battery he had intended to use for his mother's bell.
95. In his tool box he found another battery, a ruler, a coil of copper wire, a small bulb, and tape.
96. Carefully he taped the batteries end to end on the ruler so that they touched.
97. he taped the wire tight across the bottom of the end battery.
98. Then he ran the wire up the sides of the two batteries to the bulb.
99. After winding the wire around the bottom of the bulb, he taped it in place.
100. Next he placed the bulb so that it touched the cap on the top battery.
101. The bulb began to glow!
102. Freddie taped the bulb in place on the ruler.
103. Now he had a homemade flashlight for Elizabeth.
104. He tied a string around the end of the ruler and hurried back upstairs.
105. Pulling the kitchen stepladder out into the hall and climbing up on it, he found the transom within easy reach.
106. "Elizabeth," he called.
107. "I'm going to drop this light down to you through the transom.
108. Catch it by the ruler and let me know when you can reach it."
109. The next minute Elizabeth cried, "I have it, Freddie."
110. "Hold it by the ruler," Freddie told her.
111. "Now I'll go get Mother.
112. Both of us together can open the door.
113. We'll be back soon.
114. Don't be afraid."
115. "All right," answered Elizabeth.
116. "It's not so bad with the light.
117. It's not so scary.
118. You're wonderful, Freddie."

119. That night, when Mr. Miller came home, Elizabeth was waiting for him at the front door.
120. "Father! We have something wonderful to tell you," she cried excitedly as she pulled him by the hand into the kitchen.
121. In one corner of the kitchen, Freddie was busy working on an experiment.
122. Mrs. Miller was getting supper ready.
123. "Now what's all this about, Elizabeth?" asked Father.
124. Then seeing Freddie . . . . "What are you doing in the kitchen with those things?" he wanted to know.
125. "But, Father," cried Elizabeth, dancing about with excitement.
126. "Wait until you hear what happened!"
127. Mr. Miller heard the story three times—from Freddie, from Elizabeth, and from Mrs. Miller!
128. "Tinker," he said, "I'm proud of you.
129. Elizabeth would have had a bad time without your help.
130. Sometimes it's worse to be badly frightened than it is to be hurt."
131. Freddie's mother looked proud, too.
132. "After this we must make some allowance for experiments that do not turn out so well.
133. Such quick thinking!
134. Freddie, you're just like . . . "
135. "Uncle Maximilian?" asked Freddie.
136. "No," his mother replied.
137. "Uncle Oscar?" Freddie made a face.
138. "No."
139. Now she was laughing, too.
140. "Uncle Charles? asked Mr. Miller.
141. "No."
142. "Then it must be Uncle August," said Elizabeth.
143. "No," Mrs. Miller smiled at them, and then she said something that made Freddie feel fine all over.
144. "Do you know, Father, he's just like you!"

Non-Thematic Re-Entry: An Introduction to and Extension of the System of Nominal Group Reference/Substitution in Everyday English Use

16

M. P. Jordan

Queen's University
Kingston, Canada

AIMS AND GENERAL BACKGROUND

The purpose of this paper is to place in a wider perspective established techniques of nominal reference in English texts, and to expand this sub-system of language by an introductory analysis of reasons for nominal substitution in non-thematic positions in the clause. This work accepts as a useful starting point the discussions in Halliday and Hasan (1976) dealing with nominal substitution techniques in English, but the complexity of the coherence sub-system demands that we delve more deeply into the techniques and patterns involved. Their analysis considers the overall structure of a text as determined by successive anaphoric references or "ties" in any position in the text; but it does not include discussion of "ties" within and between clauses or of the complex interaction of different participants or topics within the text. While they make a brave attempt to introduce systems of lexical cohesion, this broad area of coherence can now more usefully be separated and grouped within the overall sub-system by two separate branches of substitution-reference (associated and perspective). In addition the concept of collocation is seen to be an imprecise and occasionally misleading basis for the description of many instances of coherence within this sub-system. Thus this paper adds two distinct branches of coherence to the previously established framework, discusses the common inclusion of patterns of substitution and related techniques as themes of successive clauses, and introduces broad categories of reasons for non-thematic substitution.

The terms in the main title need some explanation. Although the usual meaning of theme is the initial part of a sentence, I am here more interested in the theme of a clause; and the presence or absence, for example, of an initial sentence adjunct will not materially affect the discussion. The main thrust of this paper is to explain how

322

nominal anaphora in clausal non-thematic positions occurs together with the more usual thematic connection.

The term "re-entry" needs more explanation. My concern here is not just with isolated single instances of nominal substitution within a text, but rather with textual patterns of such substitution. Any single substitution can be seen as an instance of anaphora during analyses of only two adjoining clauses, but the whole pattern of coherence of a larger text is better seen as a controlled mechanism by which the speaker/writer successively "re-enters" the topics or participants of this discourse into the text to provide more information about them. We will here be examining the ways by which educated users of English "talk about" the topic under discussion, and for this the speaker/writer has to continually "re-enter" that topic into the text so that we know what he is discussing at any point in the text. The term "re-entry" forces us to view this aspect of language as coherence in creative use rather than as a point-by-point analysis of each specific instance of coherence.

It should be clear that the term "substitution" is not broad enough for the means that writers re-enter a previously introduced topic. Although the terms "reference" and "antecedent" could be regarded in the broader sense of the topic being re-entered, the term "re-entry" seems more descriptive, stresses the creative development of text rather than analysis, and has not been used to mean different concepts as has "reference".

SPECIFIC BACKGROUND

In order to concentrate on some of the more complex issues involved with nominal cohesive systems in English, it is necessary to gloss over certain basic concepts with little further explanation. Some of these (substitution, repetition, synonymy, generic nouns, and superordinates) are discussed in Halliday and Hasan. To these I need to add re-entry by partial repetition, specifics, naming, acronyms, ellipsis and lists, and the entire system of basic nominal re-entry must also include grammatical techniques such as verbless and non-finite clauses, relative clauses, and apposition. What I call basic re-entry, then, is any technique which allows the writer/speaker to provide further information about a previously introduced topic without addition or alteration of the topic. Here is an example illustrating only basic re-entry.

(1)   Whilst making roller blinds, I had great difficulty in holding the tiny tacks that attach the blind to the roller. To hold *these tacks* in was virtually impossible until I had the idea of holding *them* in the teeth of a small hair comb. (*Practical Householder*, May 1980, p.14)

The topic of discussion for the final sentence is the nominal *the tiny tacks that attach the blind to the rollers*, and this is re-entered first as *these tacks* within the to-infinitive nominal as subject and then as *them* as object of *holding*. The substitutes are co-referential as the topic is not altered or added to in the substitution process. Note the coherence provided by repetition of *I* which overlies the meaning of the total text, and also the intra-sentential partial repetition of *the blind* and *the roller*.

Two other branches of coherence now need to be introduced: associated re-entry, and perspective re-entry. In associated re-entry something associated with the topic of discussion is re-entered into the text rather than the topic itself. For example, if the topic is a particular company, an associated re-entry could be *Its President*, where the topic (known as the "trigger") is in the possessive; or it could be *The half-yearly accounts* (untriggered) or *The Directors of the company* (triggered by prepositional post-modification). Triggering also occurs in appositives or as pre-modifiers. These and related concepts are based partly on work by Christophersen (1939) and Hawkins (1978), and are more fully discussed in Jordan (1981, 1982). Associated re-entry includes use of the partitives and is an extremely common and wide-ranging re-entry technique. Here is an example of associated re-entry:

(2)   A well-exposed blue spectrogram (dispersion 1.2×10^{-6}) of HR 8752 V509 Cas (IAUC 3382, 3390) was obtained on July 31 at the coudé focus of the Haute Provence 1.5-m reflector. No conspicuous emission is present, either at Hγ or at other wavelengths. No search was made for filling in of absorption lines in this spectral region, which is known to be very crowded. *A print and/or tracing of the plate* is available on request for detailed study of our material. (Central Bureau for Astronomical Telegrams, IAU, 3399, September 4, 1979)

The main topic of discussion is the spectrogram introduced as the subject of the first sentence. Of interest to us here is its re-entry as theme of the final sentence in the form of the associated nominal *A print and/or tracing of the plate,* which introduces something associated with the original topic and not just the topic itself. This is an instance of a "triggered" associated re-entry, as the synonym trigger (*the plate*) is overtly included in the new nominal; here a synonym is used, but any basic re-entry can be used as the trigger. Had the associated re-entry been simply *A print and/or tracing* with only implicit connection with the trigger, it would have been an untriggered associated nominal.

Perspective re-entry occurs when a clause or sentence rather than a nominal group is implicitly or overtly modified by a previously introduced nominal group. Out of its context, the second sentence in Example 2 would be meaningless, and it takes its perspective from the spectral region detailed in the previous sentence. The meaning *in this spectral region* is clearly an all-important factor in the meaning of the sentence even though no "tie" is overtly included; the same applies to untriggered associated re-entries, and both untriggered perspective re-entries and untriggered associated re-entries are linguistically recoverable as their triggered counterparts. In the third sentence of Example 2, the perspective re-entry is triggered by overt mention of *in this spectral region* to allow this to be re-entered into the relative clause. Perspective re-entries have several grammatical/semantic functions. In Example 2, it is constraining the meaning of the sentence to a previously introduced location as an adjunct, but in "We came to the mountain and climbed.", the second clause is given its location perspective as implicit object of the verb. Overt and implicit means and instrument perspectives are also common, and there are probably more uses of this branch of re-entry which remain to be identified.

Collocation does not provide a meaningful account of many instances of coherence as it would conflate associated, perspective and synonym re-entry and would also include antonyms, which are not re-entry devices; instead we need to use criteria of referentiality and the grammatical unit affected for definition of the types of coherence involved. The distinguishing criterion between associated and perspective re-entry is that the latter re-enters the topic as an overt or implicit adjunct or other grammatical unit within and modifying the clause or sentence; whereas with associated re-entry the topic is overtly or implicitly within and modifying a nominal group. Where the re-entry is untriggered it may not be easy to distinguish between the two types, as in the next example.

(3)   However, the recycled swarf does not have the same properties as the parent metal and could not supply the same market. To be economically feasible, new markets would have to be developed. (*GEOS*, Fall 1980, p.17)

However re-enters the previous paragraph and indicates the relation of "contrast" between the two paragraphs. The implicit re-entry *for the swarf* dominates the meaning of the second sentence, but is it untriggered associated re-entry (*new markets for the swarf*) or untriggered perspective re-entry (*to be developed for the swarf*)? Because of the lack of mobility of the possible sentence adjunct *for the swarf* to a position preceding the clause this is perhaps best seen as an untriggered associated re-entry.

BASIC DESCRIPTION AND EMPHASIS

The genre of "description" can be defined as discourse that relies entirely or almost entirely on various nominal re-entry techniques for its coherence. In its simplest form, description involves the successive re-entry of a single nominal group topic into each sentence and clause of the text. There are no clause or sentence re-entries (as with relations of logic, for example), no complications with two or more major participants or topics of description, no overlapping matrix clauses, and there is a single re-entry in each clause. In more usual form, description also includes "side patterns" of description (a sub-topic partially described before the main topic is again entered into the text for further description) and occasional occurrences of the complications just mentioned.

A further feature of basic description is that the re-entries are usually thematic, and this might indicate that thematic re-entry is the unmarked form. The occurrence of many well-formed texts that rely solely on thematic nominal re-entry and the simplicity of the coherence patterns involved both lend support to this conclusion, but there are very few instances in actual use in which the writer clearly has the choice of thematic and non-thematic use for the same meaning. It seems much safer to say that there is always some significant difference between thematic and non-thematic re-entry given the full context of the discourse and that this is not therefore primarily a matter of marking. Taken out of context, we can argue indefinitely about possible differences between, for example, an active non-thematic re-entry and a passive thematic re-entry; but within a context, these differences become more sharply definable. The following example illustrates this:

(4)   Suzi Gilstrap once thought she'd never move again, let alone rocket to TV fame.
        A freak accident four years ago left *Suzi*, 16, paralyzed from the waist down, but *she* is now one of Hollywood's most sought-after young actresses and *is* slated for a TV series of her own, much to her surprise and delight. (*New Woman*, June 1982, p.17)

In the first clause of the second sentence *Suzi* is re-entered as partial repetition in non-thematic position as object of *left*, and this breaks the chain of thematic re-entries by the substitute *she* and the ellipsis. Out of context, that clause could perhaps be seen as equivalent to "Suzi, 16, was left paralyzed from the waist down by a freak accident four years ago.", and it would be easy to see the non-thematic version as one of rhetoric choice, being equivalent in meaning to the original. But in context, we see that the rewritten version reduces the effect of the "surprise" between the first and second clause, which is signalled by *but* and reinforces the meaning of the first sentence. The reduction is caused by separation of paralysis from the second clause by the agent and the time adverbial.

Although it is possible in many descriptions to use thematic re-entry almost exclusively because of the simplicity of the coherence pattern of the information being communicated, in other genres non-thematic re-entry becomes an essential part of the writer/speaker's techniques if he is to convey all the meanings and subtleties that language is capable of.

Example 4 can loosely be regarded as illustrating how required emphasis is achieved by non-thematic re-entry. Two other forms of emphasis by non-thematic re-entry are shown in:

(5)   The only man-made structure you can see from the moon is the 1,500-mile Great Wall of China.
        But what you can't see from up there is *the damage that has been done to it*.
        People have chipped off *bits* for souvenirs and *stones* have been used for building (*Weekend*, April 2–8, 1980, p.28)

With the *But* mediating between what *you can see* and *what you can't see,* the pseudo-cleft provides clear emphasis for the contrast, and the re-entry occurs non-thematically in the triggered associate *the damage that has been done to it.* In the third sentence, re-entry first occurs non-thematically as the untriggered associated *bits* (of the wall) and then thematically as the untriggered associate *stones* (from the wall). Use of *People* as theme of the third sentence allows the tone of the article to be personal as opposed to the more formal ''Bits have been chipped off for souvenirs.'' with thematic associated re-entry.

Use of the personal pronouns *we, you* and *they* with non-thematic re-entry are other common means of creating an informal style and although there are thematic counterparts there are also definable differences in emphasis and tone in the text. Special emphasis is clearly achieved in the next example in which the re-entry is placed as agent in a passive structure to emphasize the theme:

(6)   The word *ulcer* usually brings to mind a harried, middle-aged executive, not a seven-year-old schoolchild. Yet even infants can be hit by *ulcers.* (*Woman's Day,* April 6, 1982, p.42)

The hypothetical *brings to mind* and the negation in the first sentence set up the true situation to come after the mediating *Yet.* The active counterpart ''Yet ulcers can even hit infants.'' does not have the same impact as the original with non-thematic re-entry, because the partial comparative affirmation (what is true of executives can also be true of infants) is less prominent.

SENTENCE COMPLEXITY AND GRAMMAR

Other reasons for non-thematic re-entry involve the length, complexity and grammar of the sentence including the re-entry, and these reasons are even more clearly not just a matter of rhetorical choice or marking. In fact many instances of non-thematic re-entry under this broad category do not have a thematic re-entry counterpart.

Obvious instances of sentence complexity with non-thematic re-entry are the use of matrix clauses, existential *there* and anticipatory *it,* and the grammars of the imperative and questions demand non-thematic re-entry for which there is no thematic counterpart in the context. Less obviously, non-thematic re-entry is used to avoid a long subject:

(7)   Concern over the lagging support of the general membership was the motivating force behind two papers tabled at the April meeting, both of which proposed remedial measures.
       Gordon Mackay presented a Notice of Motion wherein he proposed that to qualify for membership in the Chapter a point system be instituted based on

participation in Chapter and STC activities during the year. The notice is reproduced in this issue and will be debated and voted on at the first meeting of the next session. (*Stimulus,* April 1980, p.4)

The whole of the object of *presented* in the second sentence is a long associated nominal using a specific *Notice of Motion* to re-enter the more general *papers.* If the re-entry had been theme of the second sentence, it would have been "A Notice of Motion in which it is proposed that to qualify . . . year . . ." and this would normally be too long for an English subject; the non-thematic re-entry avoids this and also introduces the originator. The third sentence contains two basic thematic re-entries as the partial repetition *The notice* and then through ellipsis.

There are several other techniques for avoiding an overlong subject in English (e.g. existential *there,* anticipatory *it,* fronting and inversion) and this example of non-thematic re-entry fits that general pattern.

The occurrence of catenative verbs (Palmer 1974) also makes thematic re-entry difficult if not impossible because of the grammatical complexity needed to include many catenatives in the passive voice:

(8)   Streets in the 18th century were so smelly that people carried perforated silver boxes containing tiny sponges in vinegar, which they sniffed regularly.
The container was called a vinaigrette.
Sniffing the aromatic vinegar was also thought to ward off germs, and lectures on preventive medicine by Dr. William Henry helped boost *sales of vinaigrettes.* (*Weekend,* April 2–8, 1979, p.9)

The initial nominal of the final sentence incorporates a basic re-entry with added information (*aromatic*) to the previously introduced *vinegar* and is in thematic position, but the later associated re-entry *sales of vinaigrettes* is non-thematic, complementing the bare infinitive *boost.* Whereas "Sales of vinaigrettes were boosted by . . ." would be a reasonable alternative without the catenative *helped,* no alternative seems to present itself including *helped,* and the non-thematic re-entry must be accepted as the only possibility and therefore not marked.

Texts dominated by particle verbs or verbs that do not have a passive form also demand non-thematic re-entry:

(9)   The reason is probably as much to do with the insurance companies themselves as anything else. Collecting reliable statistics is a desperately slow business—and efficient underwriting depends on *it.* (*Professional Administrator,* February 1982, p.11)

This extract starts with the clause re-entry item *reason* as an untriggered associate of the preceding paragraph. The first part of the second sentence amplifies the reason and therefore comes under the semantic domain of *reason*, and the final clause explains the importance of collecting statistics. Of primary interest to us here is the non-thematic substitution *it*, for which there is no thematic counterpart because of the verb *depends on*.

Continuation of description of an associated topic is a further example of the need for non-thematic re-entry:

(10)   The 425 provides additional software options, including telecommunications and typesetting facilities. *Other options* include Supersoft, *which* increases the capacity of the machine to handle record processing and file management and AMtrain, *a* self-instructional training aid for operators. Of special interest to readers concerned with printing are *the AM Varityper CompSet and CompEdit connections which* allow output from the 425 to be used in standard phototypesetting applications. (*Professional Administration*, October 1981, p.10)

The thematic re-entry pattern (by the associate *Other options*, and *which* and the verbless clause for the side patterns) is broken by the non-thematic introduction of the co-ordinated associate *AM Varityper CompSet and CompEdit connections*. The clause containing this re-entry is inverted to allow the immediate continuation by re-entry of this associate into the relative clause, which contains another associate of the 425.

The clause *Other options include SuperSort . . . and AMtrain* introduces associations and communicates the association with the topic (*The 425*). I call these ''associating clauses'', and they can be seen as alternatives to triggered associations (in which the association is indicated in the nominal group) and untriggered associations (in which the association is deemed by the writer/speaker to be understood by his audience). To clarify this, for a trigger of the Imperial Chemical Industries Ltd., associated nominals could be triggered by *ICI's President, Frank Mills, Frank Mills, President of ICI*, etc. where the trigger is part of the nominal group or appositive. As an alternative the clause *The President of ICI is Frank Mills* is devoted solely to the introduction of the association and details of the type of association with the topic.

A final grammatical reason for non-thematic re-entry worth mentioning here is the inclusion of the re-entry within a clause of purpose or means:

(11)   The sex-mad male corpus of East Anglia are in for a shock. Scientists plan mass vasectomy operations in a bid to cut *the massive rodent populations!* (*Weekend* April 2–8, 1980, p.13)

The purpose clause cannot be adequately communicated with a thematic re-entry, making the non-thematic association obligatory. The trigger is in the form of the pre-modifying superordinate *rodent*.

COMPLEX RE-ENTRIES

This brief discussion would be incomplete without at least a mention of re-entries where the topic and re-entry are within the same clause, and where two or more participants or associations are involved in a single clause. Reflexive non-thematic re-entry within a clause is quite common:

(12   . . . there is no truth to the old wives' tale that *women with stretch marks* tear *their skin* during childbirth. (*Family Circle,* July 1980, p.25)

The nominal *women with stretch marks* is an associate of the topic *stretch marks,* and *their skin* is an associate of this sub-topic as a side pattern of detail. Reflexive associations also occur between clauses and can be thematic, but here we see the topic and non-thematic association bound as subject and object of a single clause.

Two or more participants can be involved in complex combinations of re-entries in a clause, and obviously only one can be theme, and the other(s) must be non-thematic. Alternatively the topics can be co-associates, associates of associates, etc. and familial terms *sibling, uncle,* etc. are appropriate means of describing the relationships between the various nominal groups, there often being several "generations" or levels of association. Some of the complexities are illustrated in Examples 1 and 8 and in the final sentence of Example 10. Further complications occur in the following example, which has specific models of word processing equipment as topic.

(13)   The operator performs all normal typing functions in the usual way. Typed text appears automatically on the display, which shows a one-third page segment of the page being processed. The operator is able to correct or revise displayed text, to produce it on the printer, and then record it on disk . . . (*Professional Administration,* October 1981, p.10)

The operator, which occurs twice as theme, is an untriggered associate of the topic. The untriggered perspective adjunct *on the machine* can be seen to apply to all the clauses, it being more specific as the triggered perspective *on the display* (of the machine) in the second sentence, and *on the printer* (of the machine) in the third sentence. In addition the sub-topic of "corrected text" is re-entered as object of the last two to-infinitive clauses in the third sentence.

To show some of the complexities of nominal re-entry techniques, see the nominal re-entries of Example 8 in Figure 1.

FINAL REMARKS

It should be apparent from even the introductory analysis offered here that nominal group re-entry occurs at all levels of language: within the nominal group itself, in

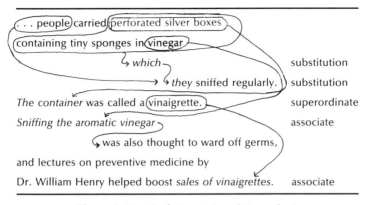

Figure 1. Nominal Re-entries of Example 8

the grammar of clause and sentence, in adjuncts, and between sentences, paragraphs and larger stretches of discourse. Re-entry within relative clauses, non-finite and verbless clauses, and appositives have their counterparts in independent clauses, sentences and paragraphs. The total system of nominal group re-entry can be seen as the thread of continuity in any text, as it is the means by which users of language tell their audience what they are "talking about" at any point in their communication. A deeper understanding of this topic would thus appear to warrant high priority in current linguistic research.

This paper and related earlier work has established, in skeleton form, the major techniques used in English to re-enter a nominal group into the text to permit further discussion of that topic. Minor gaps remain to be filled in and detailed examination of how each technique is used is also necessary, but the major related work now is the development of an understanding of how these techniques are used in combination in different genres. In particular, the ways writers enter new topics and participants and associate them with previously-entered topics or participants need detailed study in narratives, and the use of re-entry techniques and combinations in impromptu dialogue appears to be a fruitful area of development. Once we have a sound understanding of how the writer/speaker re-enters nominal topics into the text, it will be possible to integrate this knowledge with that of clause relations, in which clauses and sentences are re-entered into the text. In this work it should be clear that the indivisibility of grammatical study and the study of "text linguistics" has been taken for granted. Detailed matters of discourse cannot be separated from consideration of the grammar of the clause, as grammatical choices at any point in a text are contextually significant and often contextually constrained by the wider context and the communicative needs of the writer/speaker.

The notion of theme as starting point in a clause is a well-established and useful concept, but this analysis shows that it relates to more than just transitivity and voice. The choice of theme in a context can depend on the emphasis required; on the length, complexity and grammar of the clause; on interclause relations within a sentence, or on the need for two or more re-entries within a clause. It seems quite conceivable that major advances in our understanding of actual language use will require a theoretical approach which integrates our knowledge of nominal group, clause, and sentence grammars with the inseparable concepts of textual coherence. Winter's recent work (1982) is an important step in this direction.

REFERENCES

Christophersen, P. (1939). *The Articles: A Study of Their Theory and Use in English*. Copenhagen, Denmark: E. Munksgaard.

Halliday, M. A. K. & Hasan, R. (1976). *Cohesion in English*. London: Longman.

Hawkins, J. A. (1978). *Definiteness and Indefiniteness*. London: Croom-Helm.

Jordan, M. P. (1978). The Principal Semantics of the Nominals *This* and *That* in Contemporary English Use. Ph.D. Thesis (CNAA/Hatfield/Birmingham). U/microfilms 78-70,031.

————. (1981). Some associated nominals in technical writing. *Journal of Tech Writing & Communications*. **11/3.**

————. (1982). The thread of continuity in functional writing. *Journal of Business Communication* Fall.

Palmer, F. R. (1974). *The English Verb*. London: Longman.

Winter, E. O. (1982). *Towards a Contextual Grammar of English*. London: George Allen & Unwin.

RECENT RELATED WORK

Jordan, M. P. (1983). Complex lexical cohesion in the english clause and sentence. In *The Tenth LACUS Forum*. Columbia SC: Hornbeam Press.

Jordan, M. P. (1984). Structure, style and word choice in everyday English texts. *TESL Talk*, 15(1 and 2).

Jordan, M. P. (1984). *Fundamentals of technical description*. Malabar FLA: Krieger.

Jordan, M. P. (1984). *Rhetoric of Everyday English Texts*. London: George Allen and Unwin.

Jordan, M. P. (1984). *Fundamentals of Technical Prose*. Malabar FLA: Krieger.

'Rest' and 'Open Transition' in a   17
Systemic Phonology of English

J. C. Catford
University of Michigan

In accordance with a practice that is not uncommon among linguists, I might have entitled this paper ''Rest and Open Transition Revisited'', since much of what I have to say was originally worked out many years ago and presented in a talk at Edinburgh University in 1961. Its content, however, has been only partially published (principally in Catford 1965, 1966, 1977) and is not widely known. Moreover, I have, indeed, recently been 'revisiting' the topic and this is a further justification for putting it before you here.

The phonology of English can be described, as we know, in terms of a hierarchy of four units: *tone-group, foot, syllable* and *phoneme*. The first part of my paper deals with a phenomenon that occurs at the rank of the foot.

The elements of foot structure are commonly known as *salient* and non-salient, or *weak*. Salient is realized as a (strongly) stressed syllable in the first part of the foot, or (in a monosyllabic foot) occupying the whole foot. Weak is realized as one or more less strongly stressed syllable(s) occupying the remainder of the foot after the salient syllable. It is generally agreed that one must also posit what has been called 'silent stress' operating at the place of salient in some feet. As David Abercrombie has most cogently pointed out (Abercrombie 1965, 1971) a complete account of the rhythmic structure of English prose or verse is impossible without the recognition of 'silent beat' or 'silent stress'. Silent stress is a pause that does not interrupt the rhythm of an English utterance, and occupies the time-span of a stressed syllable, or of a whole foot, according to circumstances.

It is, for example, silent stress that takes up the time of an entire foot in the middle of the line:

To be or not to be . . . that is the question.

Since every normal foot begins with salient, realised as a stressed syllable, the convention has been adopted in systemic phonological transcriptions of English, of treating any initial unstressed syllables as being, in fact, the tail-end (the realisation of the element 'weak') of a foot with silent stress. Representing foot-boundaries by slant lines, and silent stress by a *caret* (ₐ), we can transcribe that line from Hamlet as:

/ ₐ To/be or/not to/be / ₐ /that is the/question/

The initial unstressed *to* is here represented as the final, weak, element of a foot whose salient is realized by silent stress. The same line may be rendered with three silent stresses as:

/$_\wedge$ To/be/$_\wedge$ or/not to be/$_\wedge$ /that is the/question/

and this is how the great 18th century actor David Garrick spoke the line, as we are told by Joshua Steele (1779).

I shall have something to say later about the procrusteanism inherent in the representation of *all* initial unstressed syllables (or 'pseudosyllables' as I shall call some of them) as if they had a silent stress before them. There is another kind of pausal, or pause-like phenomenon that can occur within the foot, but since this does not occur at salient (the locus of stressed syllables) it cannot be called 'silent stress'. I am referring to a brief pause, or, better, sustension (shown here by. . . .) that may serve to differentiate (b) from (a) in such pairs of sentences as the following:

1(a) /That was a/man-eating/fish/ (a barracuda perhaps?)
  (b) /That was a/man . . . eating/fish/ (A sea-food lover?)

2(a) /$_\wedge$I'll/be there from/tento/two/ (from 1:50)
  (b) /$_\wedge$I'll/be there from/ten . . . to/two/ (from 10:00 until 2:00)

The members of these sentence-pairs *could,* it is true, be distinguished from each other by silent stress, as in: 1(b) /That was a/man/$_\wedge$ eating/fish/.

The distinction I am referring to is *not* silent stress, however, since it does not occupy the place of salient, but is merely a momentary hesitation, or sustension, occurring in the middle of a foot.

This hesitation may be realized, though rarely, as an actual brief silence, produced as a rule by momentarily closing the glottis. More often, perhaps, there is no silent pause at all, the pausal effect being created by a prolongation of the preceding syllable. This prolongation may be effected by increasing the duration of the final consonant or of both the final consonant and the vowel.

Measurements were made of the durations of the vowels and consonants of the words *man* and *ten* in sentences 1(a,b) and 2(a,b) and of the words *cat* and *mantis* in the parallel sentences 3(a,b) and 4(a,b)

3(a) /That was a/cat-eating/fish/
  (b) /That was a/cat . . . eating/fish/

4(a) /That was a/mantis-eating/fish/
  (b) /That was a/mantis . . . eating/fish/

The data derived from these measurements are presented in detail in Table 1. The following, however, is a brief summary of the most important part of the data, indicating the *percentage increase* in the duration of the final consonant and of the immediately preceding vowel in the pre-pausal (b-sentence) realisations of *man, cat, ten,* and *mantis.*

	V	C
man	34%	50%
cat	38%	110%
ten	—	36%
(man)tis	11%	51%

These figures mean that the final /n/ of *man* in 'man . . . eating' is 50% longer than the final /n/ in 'man-eating': that the vowel of *man* in 'man . . . eating' is 34% longer than the vowel of *man* in 'man-eating', and so on.

It is interesting to observe that, though in every case the major increase is in the duration of the final consonant, the vowel /a/ of *man* and *cat* is also substantially lengthened (by more than 30%), while the /e/ of *ten* and the /i/ of *mantis* are either unchanged or only minimally lengthened. This no doubt reflects the well-known fact that the vowel /a/, alone among the English 'short' or 'checked' vowels, is noticeably susceptible to lengthening.

To come back from these merely statistical details, it is clear that we must recognize this particular kind of lengthening as a feature of English phonology. Since it may be realized either as an actual momentary cessation of sound, or, more

Table 1

		Foot	C	V	C	
man-eating:	duration	60.15	8.2	12.5	6.6	cs.
	% of foot	100	13.6	20.8	11.0	%
man∧eating:	duration	69.3	8.8	19.3	11.14	cs.
	% of foot	100	12.7	27.9	16.5	%
	% of increase	—	—	34	50	%
cat-eating:	duration	64.5	13.8	11.8	5.3	cs.
	% of foot	100	21.4	18.3	8.2	%
cat∧eating:	duration	75.5	13	19	13	cs.
	% of foot	100	17.2	25.2	17.2	%
	% of increase	—	—	38	110	%
(man)*tis*-eating:	duration	73.8	4.4	7.5	9.0	cs.
	% of foot	100	6.0	10.2	12.2	%
(man)*tis*∧eating:	duration	77.6	4.6	8.75	14.25	cs.
	% of foot	100	5.9	11.3	18.4	%
	% of increase	—	—	11	51	%
ten to:	duration	32.6	7.3	9.5	7.8	cs.
	% of foot	100	22.4	29.1	23.9	%
ten∧to:	duration	42.3	9.1	11.2	13.8	cs.
	% of foot	100	21.5	26.5	32.6	%
	% of increase	—	—	—	36.4	%

The effect of *rest* (∧) on preceding consonant and vowel: actual average durations in centiseconds, percentage of total foot-duration, and the percentage increase in these percentages in passing from utterance without rest, to utterance with rest.

commonly perhaps, as a sustension of the preceding consonant, which has the effect of a brief pause, it might as well be called by the musical term *rest*.

Moreover, being a pausal phenomenon in non-salient position, it is in complementary distribution with that other pausal phenomenon which occurs in salient position—silent stress. It seems reasonable, then, to regard both of these pausal phenomena as realizations of the same thing. We therefore want to call them by the same name: but since we obviously cannot label the unstressed, non-salient, hesitation 'silent stress' we are obliged to rename 'silent stress' *rest*. And this is what I have, in fact, long practiced. As Abercrombie has pointed out (1971 p. 154) 'rest' is but one of several names that have been given to the phenomenon of silent stress.

So we can now describe *rest* as a pausal phenomenon which can occur either at the element *weak* in a foot, or at the element *salient*. In this latter position it may also be called 'silent stress'.

I want to turn now to another English phonological feature, at a lower rank in the phonological hierarchy. It will be best to approach this new topic by way of some examples.

There are great numbers of minimal, or near-minimal, pairs of words or phrases in English that are differentiated as in the following examples, listed in two columns A and B

A	B
plight	polite
broke/Brock	baroque
train	terrain
claps	collapse
scum	succumb
sectors	seccateurs
Tiflis	syphilis
damsen	amazon
Skelton	skeleton
tusk	tussock
scalp	scallop
Sindh/sinned	synod
flatly	philately
cracks	Caracas
take part	take apart
some dresses	some addresses

The traditional way of describing the difference between the examples in the two columns is to say that in the items of list A we have either consonant clusters, or sequences of abutting consonants, whereas in the corresponding items of list B we have the same sequences of consonants separated by a short, unstressed, *schwa*-type vowel /ə/. There is, however, another way of describing this difference. The short schwa-like transition between consonants that we observe in the B-items may be regarded not as a vowel, but as nothing more than a particular way of making the transition between consonants—an 'open transition' in contrast to the 'close transition' between consonants exemplified in the items of the A list.

It is well known that one difference between English and French is that in what are universally accepted as sequences of consonants in English the second consonant follows extremely closely on the first one—the articulations of the two consonants may, indeed, overlap, so that there is no audible release of the first. In French, on the other hand, the first of two successive consonants is often quite clearly and audibly released. Thus in the English word *actor* the /k/ is not released until the articulation for the /t/ has been formed, and consequently the /k/ is virtually inaudible. In the corresponding French word, *acteur,* the /k/ is often audibly released before the /t/ is formed. We can describe this difference by saying that in French, the transition between the abutting consonants in *acteur* can be indifferently *close* or *open*, the latter probably being more usual. In English, on the other hand, the transition between the abutting consonants in *actor* is always *close*. This is necessarily the case, since in English, though not in French, the distinction between close and open transition is phonologically utilized—as in the examples listed above.

The precise nature of the difference between close and open transition between consonants depends upon their relative articulatory locations. It depends, that is, on whether the successive consonants are *homorganic* (articulated by the same part of the same organ, as in -pp- -ff- mb- etc.), *heterorganic* (articulated by completely different organs, as in -kp- -fs-, or by distinct and separately manoeuverable parts of the same organ, as in -kt-) or *contiguous* (articulated by adjoining parts of the same organ as in -tr- or -kj-).

The characteristics of close and open transition with respect to the three articulatory relations are as follows—the examples will be most convincing if the reader articulates each of them silently, several times, so that the proprioceptive sensations can be appreciated.

Homorganic

Close transition, as in *top part, tough fowl, nice seat*—articulatory continuity, that is, the articulators maintain their position unchanged throughout the two consonants.

Open transition, as in . . . *top apart,* so *tough a fowl, so nice a seat*—articulatory non-continuity, that is, the articulators are momentarily and minimally separated, or the articulatory channel is momentarily and minimally enlarged, and the original articulatory posture is immediately resumed.

Heterorganic

Close transition, as in *back part, tough kid,* or *plight*—articulatory overlap, that is, the stricture for the second consonant is formed before the stricture for the first is released. Measurements made by means of palate electrodes recording the making and breaking of tongue-palate contacts show that, in my pronunciation at least, the duration of the overlap averages approximately one third of the combined duration of the successive, overlapping, consonant articulations.

Open transition, as in *back apart,* so *tough a kid, polite*—no overlap, the stricture for the first consonant is released immediately before the stricture for the second consonant is formed, at the moment when the articulators are already moving towards the second stricture.

Contiguous

Close transition, as in *back yard* or *train*—articulatory accommodation, the articulation of the first consonant is accommodated to the articulation of the second one. In *back yard* the /k/ anticipates the palatal articulation of /j/ and its place of articulation is shifted forward (/k/ is palatalised). In *train* the apex of the tongue may anticipate the postalveolar location of /r/ and form the /t/-closure at that point. In my own pronunciation the tongue-tip goes first to the alveolar location but accommodates to the /r/ by immediately sliding backward to the apico-postalveolar /r/-location. This backward sliding motion is not only clearly kinaesthetically perceptible, but can be seen in real-time ultrasound tongue-scans.

Open transition as in *back a yard, terrain*—absence of accommodation. The /k/ in this case is velar and the forward tongue-shift to /j/ occurs immediately upon release of the /k/. In *terrain,* the shift of tongue-tip location from alveolar to postalveolar is performed by a minimal release, retraction and reapplication at the second position.

Open transition contrasts with vowel in such examples as these:

-CC-	-C · C-	-CVC-
(take the) cop part	. . . cop apart	copper part
		cop up, Art
a tough fowl	so tough a fowl	a tougher fowl
a brief lunch	a Brie for lunch	a briefer lunch
take part	take apart	take up art
make names	make an aim	make Ann aim

There are characteristic differences between open transitions and vowels with respect to duration, articulatory channel area, phonation and system, which can be summarized as follows:

Duration. In C·C, the duration of the open transition from C to C is extremely short. In CVC, the duration of the vowel is much longer. In a short study of 35 pairs, like *take apart* vs. *take up art* etc., the durations of the open transitions ranged from 1 to 6 cs., with a mean duration of 3 cs. The duration of vowels in the same environments ranged from 6 to 20cs. with a mean of 11 cs. Thus, on the average, vowels in −CVC− are nearly four times as long as open transitions.

Channel area. In C·C the articulatory stricture is minimally released: in CVC the articulatory channel is very much more widely opened than is necessary for the mere, minimal direct-path transition from C to C. As reported in Catford (1977 p. 221) a highspeed ciné recording of the lip movements in *cop apart* (C·C), *copper part* and *cop up, Art* (CVC) showed that while the labial orifice for the two vowel articulations reached maximum areas of 250 mm² and 220 mm² respectively, the maximum area of the articulatory channel for the open transition was only 20 mm². This is about the articulatory channel area of a wide-channel fricative or a narrow approximant. Experimenting with the silent articulation of such pairs as *cop apart* and *cop up Art* or *so tough a fowl* and *tougher fowl* one can easily feel the great difference between the minimal opening for open transition and the wider opening for the vowel.

Phonation. Open transitions may be fully voiced, partially voiced or totally voiceless. Thus the open transition between the first two consonants in such words as *potato, catharsis* can be voiceless. Again, in the sentence *He went to Trafalgar Square* the open transitions in *to* and *Traf* are normally completely voiceless. Vowels, on the other hand, are virtually always voiced: 'virtually' always, because there are occasions when English (RP) vowels are not voiced but whispered, or pronounced with creak, creaky voice or whispery voice. But they are never totally voiceless as open transitions can be.

System. In RP by far the commonest open transition has a neutral, schwa-like, quality. We may represent it as /ᵊ/. Many RP speakers also have open transitions with an ɩ-like and ʊ-like qualities, which we may represent as /ᶥ/ and /ᶷ/. It is difficult to find minimal triplets exemplifying all three, but they are represented in *a mission, emission,* and *omission* as in such sentences as:

1. We don't like a mission.
2. We don't like emissions.
3. We don't like omissions.

It is probable that some speakers of RP or near-RP do not possess the third transition, /ᶷ/. In any case, whether the system of open transitions consists of three terms, /ᶥ/ /ᵊ/ /ᶷ/, or only two, it is noticebly different from the system of vowels, consisting of six simple vowels /i, e, a, o, u, ə/ as in *pit, pet, pat, pot, put, putt* and 13 or so complex vocalic nuclei such as /iᵗ, aᵗ, iᵊ, eᵊ, əᵊ, əᵁ/ etc. as in *bead, bide, beard, Baird, bird, bode.*

Additional examples of open transitions contrasting with each other and with vowels are:

They lac*k q*uality	−CC−
They lac*k a q*uality	−C·C− /ᵊ/
They lac*k eq*uality	−C·C− /ᶥ/
A lac*quer q*uality	−CVC− /ə/
A lac*key q*uality	−CVC− /i/
Da*d m*ended it	−CC−
Da*d em*ended it	−C·C− /ᶥ/

Daddy mended it   −CVC− /i/
Dad amended it   −C·C− /ə/
Dadda mended it   −CVC− /ə/

Examples of contrast between /ᵁ/-transition and /u/ vowel are hard to come by, but the following are possible:

That's my bouquet.   / . . . bᵁkeᵗ/
That's my book A   / . . . bukeᵗ/

Is that Boleyn?   / . . . bᵁlin/
Is that bull in?   / . . . bulin/

The schwa-type transition /ə/ is by far the commonest: a rough check shows that in my own pronunciation the percentage occurrences of the three types are approximately /ə/ 90%, /ᵗ/ 9%, /ᵁ/ 1%.

So far, we have looked at open transitions only between consonants −C·C. But they also occur initially. That is to say, we can observe the difference between 'close' and 'open' in the transition between pre-speech zero (#) and an initial consonant, and we can contrast this with initial vowel. Some examples are:

#C-	# · C-	#VC-
pending	appending	upending
praised	appraised	upraised
Nemo	anaemic	un-emic
name	an aim	Ann aimed
state	estate	S. Tate
Brian	O'Brien	Oh Brian!

The difference between #C− and #·C is that in the close transition, the articulators are already fully in position for the articulatory stricture before the initiatory effort begins. In open transition, #·C, the pulmonic initiation begins at about the same moment as the articulatory organs begin to move together to form the articulatory stricture. In the third case, #VC−, the pulmonic initiation for the vowel starts long (ie. 10cs. or so) before the articulators begin to move into position for the C−.

If #C−, #·C− and #VC− all occur, it is reasonable to ask if an analogous set of three transitional possibilities exists for final consonants. In other words, do we have close transition −C#, open transition −C·#, and vowel transition −CV# between a final consonant and post-speech zero? The answer is no: at least not as three phonologically distinct possibilities.

It is true that something resembling the difference between close and open transition can be observed in unreleased versus released final consonants, especially stops. In the word stopᵀ, for example, with unreleased final [pᵀ] the initiatory activity ceases while the articulatory stricture is still in place, and this implies an abrupt, or close, transition from the consonant to zero, thus −C#. In stopʰ, on the other hand, with a final [pʰ], the articulatory stricture is released, allowing the energy in the pent-up initiatory air-stream to dissipate in a momentary aspiration. This relatively slow dissipation of the initiatory air mass constitutes a kind of gradual passage from −C to zero, somewhat analogous to the open transition from zero to C− in initial #·C. We might, then, say that with final consonants there is a possible difference between close transition (−C#) and open transition (−C·#) exemplified by the difference between final unreleased and released stops.

But in English this distinction is always optional, as a variable realization of final −C# in some varieties (some idiolects, accents and dialects). It is never linguistically, phonologically, pertinent, in the way it can be in languages that distinguish between unaspirated and aspirated voiceless stops.

In English, then, corresponding to the ternary opposition that occurs medially (−CC, −C·C, −CVC−) and initially (#C−, #·C−, #VC), in *final* position there is only a binary opposition, exemplified in such pairs as:

-C#	-CV#
cheat	cheetah
road	Rhoda
rose	Rosa
loaf	loafer
hip	hippy
boot	booty
cab	cabbie
race	racy

Now a legitimate question might be: "Why assign the analysis CV# rather than C·# to the items in the right-hand column? Since there is no phonological opposition between open transition and vowel in this position, could we not regard these as actually examples of −C·#, thus equating the final sound of *cheetah* with the open transition /ə/ in *cheat a man,* or the final sound of *hippy* with the open transition /ɪ/ in *epicure* etc.?"

The answer is that the *duration* of these finals associates them squarely with vowels, not open transitions. In 48 samples of words like *cheetah hippy* etc. the durations of the final vowel ranged from 13 to 28 cs., with a mean of 21 cs. This is almost twice the average duration of medial, interconsonantal, short vowels (−CVC−) and *seven times* the average duration of open transitions. Moreover, when some of the words with final −V listed here are placed in a non-final position they can *contrast* with obvious open transitions, in such pairs as:

They rowed *a*cross.   /ə/
Was Rhod*a* cross?   /ə/
Race *e*quality.   /ɪ/
A rac*y* quality.   /i/

Additional evidence for the non-occurrence of open transition in final position can be derived from the observation in Abercrombie's discussion of English disyllabic feet (1965:30,31) that the 'long-short' type of foot, exemplified by /Grey to/ in /ᴧ Take/ Grey to/ London/ or /tea for/ in /Tea for /two/ always implies a word-division between the two syllables. Occurrence of such feet, which typically contain an open transition, not a vowel, in their second 'syllable' only at word-division, of course implies their non-occurrence in absolute final position.

We have now looked at the occurrence of open transition between (−C·C−) and before (#·C−) consonants, and noted their non-occurrence after final consonants (*−C·#). We must now briefly consider their occurrence with vowels.

Consider such pairs of words as:

A	B
bid	beard
bed	Baird
good	gourd
tap	type
cup	cope

In the examples in Column A, the final consonant cuts off the vowel in full flight, as it were. That is to say, the tongue is still more or less in position for the vowel when the consonantal stricture is formed. This is particularly clear where the vowel-articulation and the consonant articulation are heterorganic, as in *tap* or *cup*, but it can also be observed in such words as *bid* and *good*. This kind of transition from vowel to consonant is clearly analogous to close transition between one consonant and another, and we can represent it as VC.

On the other hand, in the examples in Column B, the consonantal stricture is not formed until the tongue has already given up its articulatory posture for the vowel and has begun to make a /ə/-like, /ɩ/-like or /ʊ/-like transition to the consonant. This kind of transition is analogous to open transition between consonants, and we can represent it as V·C.

The vowels of at least one variety of RP thus fall into two major groups: simple vocalic nuclei V, and compound vocalic nuclei V·. At greater delicacy, the latter group falls into three sub-types, according as the transition is of /ə/-type, /ɩ/-type or /ʊ/-type. In the following lists of examples, compound vowels that are rare or occur only idiosyncratically, are enclosed in parentheses.

	V	V ·		
	V	**Və**	**Vɩ**	**Vʊ**
/i/	bid, hid	beard	bead	(*Theodore*)
/e/	bed	Baird	bayed	(*Beowulf*)
/a/	hat	heart	height	out
/o/	cot	court	coy	—
/u/	good	gourd	(ruin)	goo'd
/ə/	bud	bird	—	bode

There are also complex vowel nuclei, V··, such as /aᴵᵊ/ in *fire,* /aᵁᵊ/ in *tower* etc.

Pursuing the analogy with consonantal transitions we next consider the possibility of open transitions from consonant to vowel (−C·V−) from zero to vowel (#·V−) and from vowel to zero (−V·#). All of these may occur, but the first two types are very rare, and may be somewhat idiosyncratic in their occurrence. The following are examples arranged in contrasting lists.

CV	C · V	CCV
curse /kəᵊs/	coerce /kᵁəᵊs/	quern /kwəᵊn/
pourer /poᵊrə/	Peoria /pᴵoᵊrᴵə/	purer /pjoᵊrə/

#V-	# · V
ology /olᵊdʒi/	oology /ᵁolᵊdʒi/
oleo /əᵁlᴵəᵁ/	Aeolia /ᴵəᵁlᴵə/

-V#	-V · #
wheaty (-i)	wheatear (-iᵊ)
Nancy (-i)	Landseer (-iᵊ)
booty (-i)	bootee (-iᴵ)
khaki (-i)	car-key (-iᴵ)
chauffeur (-ə)	show-fur (-əᵊ)
cater (-ə)	Cato (-əᵁ)

It will be clear from the above that I am treating *open transition* as something *sui generis,* distinct not only from close transition, but also from *vowels.* In most descriptions of English, the open transitions /ᵊ/ /ᴵ/ /ᵁ/ are regarded not as forming a distinct system of units, but simply as instances of the regular vowels /ə/ /i/ /u/ under *reduced* or *minimal* stress. This means, of course, that they can be accounted for only in terms of a system of differential stresses.

One of the few scholars to recognize a special system of items corresponding in part to our open transitions is Bolinger (1981). But, as the title of his paper, *Two kinds of vowels, two kinds of rhythm,* shows, even he firmly associates his separate system of 'reduced vowels' with the vowels, rather than with open transition between consonants. Moreover, the examples of 'reduced vowels' that he adduces (specially on pp. 7–8) are quite heterogeneous. They include some that we would call open transitions, such as the ultra-short /ᵊ/ represented by *o* in *atom,* and the ultra-short /ᴵ/ represented by the *e* in *seduction.* But they also include some that are quite clearly *not* open transitions, such as the moderately long final vowels of *Minna, Minnie, Lhasa, Lassie,* and yet these, too, are classified as 'reduced vowels'. Bolinger gives examples, on p. 8, of contrasts between 'reduced' and 'full' vowels, and these include the pair *booty* (with final reduced vowel) and *bootee* (with final full vowel). Now this is one of the pairs we have listed above, as examples of contrast between final simple vowel $(-V\#)$ and final complex vowel $(-V\cdot\#)$. In a number of recordings of pairs of this type, we find that the mean duration of final $-V\#$ is 21 cs., and that of $-V\cdot\#$ is 25 cs. Both are obviously much too long to be counted as open transition. It is possible, in this and similar cases, that the surprising identification of final vowel with non-final transition is due to a difference of dialect or accent. But it seems more likely that it is due to the fact, mentioned above, that open transitions simply do not occur in final positions. Consequently, in the opposition *non-tense* vs. *tense* or *simple vowel* vs. *complex vowel* the simple vowel may be interpreted (or misinterpreted, as I would say) as an open transition, contrasting with a (full) vowel.

The establishment of open transitions as a category distinct from vowels leads to some curious consequences, relating to their syllabic status.

The normal carriers of syllabicity are vowels. The existence of syllabic /n/ in *eaten* etc. and syllabic /l/ in *bottle* etc. does not contradict this generalization, since these are widely conceded to be realizations of /ə/ + /n/ and /ə/ + /l/. Vowels, then, are the syllable-formers. Consequently if we deny the status of vowel to open transitions, we also deny them the status of syllable-formers. Thus the initial transition in *appending* and the interconsonantal transition in *catapult* or in *polite* are not the centers, or nuclei, of syllables, but merely of *pseudosyllables*. The word *catapult*, with the phonemic structure /CVC·CVCC/, thus consists of only two syllables. And the words *plight* and *polite* may both be regarded as monosyllables, each of them beginning with two consonants but differing in the way the transition between these consonants is made. The two words may be symbolized as *plight* /CCVC/ and *polite* /C·CVC/.

One consequence of recognizing the non-syllabic status of open transitions is that some cases of initial *rest*, or 'silent stress' become unnecessary.

Consider, for example, such sentences as:

1(a) Skewer that fish!
 (b) Secure that fish!

2(a) Praed Street's where we're going.
 (b) Parade Street's where we're going.

Since every foot begins with a stressed, salient, syllable the unstressed initial *Se-* and *Pa-* in the (b) sentences must be regarded as realizing the weak, final, part of a foot. Since nothing audible precedes that syllable, the assumption has to be made that this weak element is preceded by a silent salient or *silent stress* (a foot-initial rest) and the (b) sentences are conventionally transcribed:

1(b) /ʌ Se/cure that/fish

2(b) /ʌ Pa/rade Street's/where we're/going/

This procedure seems artificial and procrustean, but it can hardly be avoided so long as we regard *Se-* and *Pa-* as unstressed syllables, since such syllables cannot begin a foot. But the moment we recognize that they are merely pseudosyllables we remove the necessity for regarding them as realizing the weak element in an imaginary initial foot with 'silent stress' at salient! We can thus re-transcribe the sentences as:

1(a) /Skewer that/fish/
 (b) /S·cure that/fish/

2(a) /Praed Street's/where we're/going/
 (b) /P·rade Street's/where we're/going/

Clearly there are other cases where there is an initial unstressed chunk that *cannot* be regarded as a pseudosyllable, for example:

That man we met yesterday. . . .

which probably must be transcribed as:

/ₐ That/man we met/yesterday/. . . .

In such a case we must presumably continue to describe and transcribe in terms of an initial silent stress, or rest, and a question may well arise as to how many pseudosyllables can legitimately be tacked on to the beginning of an initial foot, but that is a problem I cannot pursue here.

I want to turn now to another, and more far-reaching, consequence of the recognition of the open transition and the pseudosyllable. In order to do this I must point out a difference between a systemic phonology of English and more 'traditional' approaches.

Most traditional phonologies proceed as if the phoneme were the basic or only fundamental unit. Every utterance is realized as a string of segmental phonemes, or, at most, a string of syllables. This string of segments or syllables is modulated by suprasegmental features superimposed upon it at various points.

On this view the *foot,* if recognized at all, would be regarded as a kind of derivative phenomenon—as a stress contour *resulting* from the varying degrees of stress carried by the successive syllables or phonemes in the string. In systemic phonology, however, we look at the foot from the opposite point of view. The foot is a stress-contour in its own right, and the causation operates in the opposite direction. It is the stress-contour of the foot that imposes different degrees of stress upon the successive syllables it dominates, according to their location within the foot.

One way of characterizing the difference would be to say that the traditional view represents a digital-to-analog conversion—you start with a digitized sequence of different stress-values from which you derive a continuous stress-curve. The systemic view is analog-to-digital—you start with a smooth stress-curve of a certain shape from which you derive a digitized sequence of different stress-values.

On the systemic view it would be misleading to say that there are as many feet in an utterance as there are stressed syllables: the correct version would be 'there are as many stressed syllables as there are feet'. For example, it is *not* the case that /*John was a*/*lighthouse*/*keeper*/ has three feet *because there are three stressed syllables, John light* and *keep*. On the contrary, there are three stressed syllables *because* there are three feet.

Feet are logically, and physiologically, prior to syllables or segments. The foot is a unitary quantum of 'vocal effort', that is, of *initiator power*. Initiator power is the force employed to initiate airflow in the vocal tract. It is the product of initiator velocity and the pressure-load imposed by the air driven forward by the initiator, or, more simply, for voiced sounds it is the volume-velocity of transglottal airflow times subglottal pressure. (See Catford 1977:80–84). The power-quanta, or stress-pulses, that constitute feet characteristically start with a rapid rise to a maximum followed by a slower decline, until the moment when the power build-up for the next foot begins.

We can picture the initiator-power curves of feet thus:

If a foot is realized by a single syllable, the power-curve is spread over the whole syllable. If there are several syllables in the foot, the first one, coinciding with the power peak, will be the strongest, or salient, syllable, subsequent ones being weaker.

This model of the initiator-power curve of the foot accounts for most of the observed stresses within a foot. But there is one rather common type of anomaly. This is where we have an apparently very weak syllable right in the middle of a foot, followed by a stronger syllable. An example might be /*Photŏgraphs*/*decŏrate*/ *archĭtects'* /*manŭscripts*/. In each of these feet, the middle syllable is extremely short and weak, and this seems to run counter to the view that the power-curve of the foot has an early peak and then steadily declines. The anomaly disappears, however, when we realize that the middle syllable in these feet is not, strictly, a syllable at all, but a pseudosyllable, containing an open transition.

In turns out, then, that we can account for four degrees of perceived stress in English without having any independent system of stresses at all. The strongest stress is the power-peak of a tonic foot, the next is the power-peak of a non-tonic foot, the third corresponds to the later, declining, part of the power-curve, and the fourth, and weakest stress, is that of the open-transition. Summarizing in a different way we can say:

1. Primary Stress = Salient in tonic foot.
2. Secondary Stress = Salient in non-tonic foot.
3. Tertiary Stress = Non-salient in any foot.
4. Weakest Stress = Open transition (pseudosyllable).

For example, we can display the stress-pattern of the sentence *John was a light-house keeper* as follows.

Power curve:

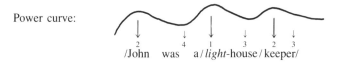

2   4   1   3   2   3

/John was a / *light*-house / keeper/

(The arrows imply that the initiator-power curve of the foot is imposing stresses upon the syllables, and not vice versa.)

And if we change the *footage* of the utterance the stresses of the individual syllables automatically rearrange themselves, as, for example, in:

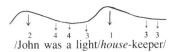

2   4 4   3   1   3 3

/John was a light/*house*-keeper/

In a similar way we can ring the changes on Chomsky and Halle's famous 'eraser' phrases:

2   1   3 4 2 3

/ /John's/*black*boarde/raser/ /

(. . . chalk remover for blackboard)

2   3   1 4 2 3

/ /John's black/*board*e/raser/ /

(. . . black eraser of boards)

2   2   1 4 2 3

/ /Johns/black/*board*e/raser/ /

(. . . eraser for black boards)

The necessary rearrangements of stresses automatically follow from (*1*) changes in tonicity, and (*2*) changes in footage (ie. in the locations of the divisions between feet). There is no need to invoke an independent system of stresses, or cyclical stress rules.

There are still some problems left relating to the theoretical status of open-transition within a systemic phonology, but enough has been said, I think, to show that the concept is a useful one in accounting for some aspects of English phonology. Moreover, I believe it closely reflects a certain kind of physiological reality—a point in its favour for those (like myself) who believe that this is what phonology is primarily concerned with.

Finally, there is something to be said for the recognition of open transition as a useful concept in the teaching of English pronunciation. A common error among foreign learners is to give too much 'value' to these extremely short and weak elements. Pointing out that these are not *vowels,* but merely ways of passing from one consonant to another, or from initial silence to a consonant etc. is very helpful in inducing a correct pronunciation of words like *t·morrow phot·graph ·dvantage* etc.

REFERENCES

Abercrombie, David. (1965). A phonetician's view of verse structure, and Syllable quantity and enclitic in English. Both in *Studies in Phonetics and Linguistics* London: Oxford University Press, pp. 16–25; 26–34 (respectively).

———. (1971). Some functions of silent stress. In Aitken, A. J. (Ed.) *Edinburgh Studies in English and Scots*. London: Longman, pp. 147–158.

Bolinger, Dwight. (1981). *Two Kinds of Vowels, Two Kinds of Rhythm*. Bloomington: Indiana University Club.

Catford, J. C. (1965). *A Linguistic Theory of Translation* London: Oxford University Press. (Chap. 1)

———. (1966). English phonology and the teaching of English. *College English* **May 1966.** 605–613.

———. (1977). *Fundamental Problems in Phonetics*. Edinburgh, Scotland: Edinburgh University Press.

Chomsky, Noam & Halle, Morris. (1968). *The Sound Pattern of English*. New York: Harper and Row.

A Systemic Phonology of Isthmus Zapotec Prosodies

18

Carol C. Mock

1.0. INTRODUCTION

Isthmus Zapotec, an Otomanguean language spoken by some 100,000 people in the Isthmus of Tehuantepec in southern Mexico, has several prosodic features in its phonology.[1] There is a durational type of stress accent (Pickett 1974; cf. Pickett 1951 for an alternative analysis), as well as two kinds of distinctive voice quality modification and four different pitch accents (Mock 1982). All these phenomena are intimately interrelated in Zapotec, and the present systemic analysis of them is relevant to the currently unresolved question of how tone is related to word-stress (Yip 1980) and to other phonetic properties like creaky voice and glottalization, features that often behave 'suprasegmentally' and have historical connections with tone (Anderson 1978).

It is the purpose of this paper to explore the interconnections among the prosodies of Isthmus Zapotec. The system networks developed here clarify the degree to which the prosodic oppositions of the language are restricted by phonetic correlations that are fairly common in other tone languages, such as the 'attraction' between glottalization and high tone, and an analogous affinity between laryngealization and low tone (cf. Hombert, Ohala & Ewan 1979).

In Isthmus Zapotec the domain of the prosodies is the morpheme and thus the network of systems generates the basic prosodic form of each morpheme. Surface-true phonetic patterns are developed from the underlying prosodic options via two sets of rules: association rules (a formal device borrowed from autosegmental phonology to simplify the description of prosodic structures), and realization rules. The association rules define how each prosody is tied to specific syllables within a morpheme, and the realization rules relate this underlying structure to the phonetic level, accounting for relatively simple conditioning factors such as the occurrence of a prosody in prepause position or in association with an accented syllable.

---

[1] I gratefully acknowledge the helpful comments made during my study of Zapotec prosodies by John Alsop, George N. Clements, John A. Goldsmith, D. Robert Ladd and Velma Pickett.

2.0. THE DURATION ACCENT

The duration accent of Isthmus Zapotec is an acoustic prominence characteristic of only one syllable in a word, a lengthening of the vocalic nucleus of the accented syllable to two moras (Pickett 1974), as shown in example (1).[2] When a post-accent syllable of the morpheme begins with a fortis consonant /p t k(c, qu) č(ch) s š(xh) m n:(nn) l: w(hu) y/, it is this consonant that is lengthened rather than the preceding vowel, as shown in (2); and when the vowel is glottalized, as in (3) and (4), the accent is heard only as heightened intensity and a raised register for the pitch carried by the syllable.

(1)   *rì*gà [rì:gà] 'husk'

(2)   *rà*tì [ràt:ì] 'dies'

(3)   *rà*'dè' [rà?dè?] 'receives a gift'

(4)   *rà*'tà' [rà?tà?] 'lies down'

The duration accent appears to be a redundant, configurative feature (Jakobson & Waugh 1979); it must be recognized, like syllables themselves, as an inevitable part of every major-class word (verb, noun and adverb), and its location in the word is only superficially contrastive, as in (5) and (6).

(5)   *rì*gà [rì:gà] 'husk'

(6)   rì*gà* [rìgà:] 'gets cut'

If we admit morpheme boundaries into the phonological description, it is possible to describe the accent as falling on the first syllable of every root morpheme.[3] In (6) rìGÀ 'gets cut' has an aspectual prefix rì- which is lacking in Rìgà 'husk'. Even without being ultimately distinctive, however, the duration accent is an important part of the phonological structure of words because it provides the focus for the pitch accents and laryngealization, and the limiting frame for glottalization. In addition, accented morphemes and unaccented ones (the enclitics, the proclitics and the affixes) have two slightly different prosodic system networks. In the space

---

[2] The standardized alphabet for Isthmus Zapotec is used throughout this paper, except that the tones have been added and stress is indicated by italicizing the accented syllable. In general the orthography uses the same phonemic symbols as Pickett 1960, but a few correspondences may need explanation: glottalized vowels are *a'*, *e'*, *i'*, *o'* and *u'*; laryngealized vowels are *aa, ee, ii, oo, uu; ch* /č/, *dx* /ǰ/, *xh* /š/, *x* /ž/, *nn* /n/ fortis, *l:* /l/ fortis. As in Spanish, *c* and *qu* are /k/, *g* and *gu* are /g/, and *hu* is /w/.

[3] In the clear cases, stem-initial accent always turns up, as for example in the verbs. But where no inflectional prefixes are present, it is harder to demonstrate where derivational prefixes end and stems begin; however, the number of words beginning with *b* and *g* is suspiciously high, and words with final accent tend to begin with these sounds. A very few words take the accent on the last syllable even though a synchronic analysis does not yield a prefix: chù*bi'* 'fig', gà*dxè* 'different', nàxì*ñá'* 'red'.

available we shall consider only the more interesting case: the prosodies of accented morphemes.

3.0. THE PROSODIES OF ACCENTED MORPHEMES

According to the traditional analysis, there are three phonemic tones in Isthmus Zapotec: high / ´ /, low / ` /, and low-rising / ˇ /. Two of them have striking sub-phonemic variants in accented syllables. Low-rising tone is a mid-rising glide there (7), and the phonemic high tone is a high-falling glide (8).[4]

(7) *ngǎ sǐ* [35.13] 'only that one'

(8) *guiúbà* [53.1] 'fast'

In the course of tonal analysis it has become evident that the high-falling glide should be seen as a complex phonemic tone / ˇ / which manifests an underlying sequence of the tones high (H) and low (L); thus (8) is revised to *guiûbà*. According to the present analysis phonemic high tone / ´ /, as opposed to the high-falling tone / ^ /, occurs in only three contexts: unaccented syllables as in (10), glottalized syllables as in (11), and in any high-pitched accented syllable that is both preceded and followed by a phonemic high tone as in (12).

(10) gù*lǔ*xú cá pè′   'precisely that catfish'

(11) *bé′*ñè′   'alligator'

(12) stà*l*:è b*íxí*dú′   'many kisses' (b*ìxì*dú′ 'kiss(es)')

3.1. Systemic Relations Among the Tones

Although these four phonemic tones represent accurately all the superficial contrasts of pitch, a more recent study by John Alsop has revealed severe tonotactic limitations. The main restrictions are as follows: there are only four common tone patterns in disyllabic morphemes that have a penultimate accent and plain vowels, as shown in (13).[5]

---

[4] The tones are identified phonetically according to the numerical system originally devised by Chao in 1920 to portray the tones of Chinese. In his representation, each numeral stands for a level tone, with 5 being the highest pitch and 1, the lowest. Gliding tones are indicated with two numerals, the first representing the beginning pitch of the glide, and the second its ending point; e.g. a mid-rising glide would be [35].

[5] Actually there is one other tone pattern that is quite frequent in disyllabic words: a rising tone on the first, tonic syllable, followed by a low tone on the last syllable. In many words of the autochthonous lexicon this melody obviously derives from the basic pattern *low + low-rising*, with the addition of a tonal morpheme; e.g. *xǔdxì* 'drunkard' derives from the adjectival *nà-xùdxǐ* 'drunk'. Many of the words that take this tone pattern are loanwords from Spanish; e.g. *mǎlè* 'comadre', *órà* 'when, hour' (Sp. *hora*).

(13) LOW-RISING + LOW-RISING   *mǐl:ǐ*   'mullet'
      HIGH-FALLING + LOW   *guiûbà*   'fast'
      LOW + LOW-RISING   *dùbǎ*   'maguey plant'
      LOW + LOW   *bìgù*   'tortoise'

If the tones were independently distinctive in each syllable of a word, we would expect to find many more different sequences of tones in disyllabic words of this sort.

In monosyllabic accented words, only three phonemic tones occur: high-falling, low, and low-rising, as shown in (14). But the monosyllables that have low-rising tone before a pause fall into two separate tonal classes when normal sentence-internal tone sandhi is taken into account, because some of

(14) HIGH-FALLING   *dxê*   'boy! (vocative)'
      LOW   *dè*   'ashes'
      LOW-RISING   *dǐ*   'curse'

these low-rising tones lose their rising glide to the following word, as in (15); and others do not, as in (16).

(15) *nguě*   'that one (distal)'
      nguè pé'   'precisely that one'

(16) *ngǎ*   'that one (proximal)'
      ngǎ pè'   'precisely that one'

These data and also the relations of regular tone sandhi among the tones, have led to a more abstract analysis of Zapotec tones (Mock 1982), in which there are only four tonal distinctions in accented morphemes, but each one is a double tone that extends across the whole morpheme: double high (HH), high-falling (HL), low-rising (LH) and double low (LL). Two tonal systems can specify all four double tones, as shown in (17).

(17)

$$
\text{accented morpheme} \begin{cases} \textit{Tone 1} \\ \rightarrow \begin{bmatrix} \text{High} \\ \text{Low} \end{bmatrix} \\ \textit{Tone 2} \\ \rightarrow \begin{bmatrix} \text{High} \\ \text{Low} \end{bmatrix} \end{cases}
$$

These double tones are not immediately interpretable in terms of phonemic tones or phonetic pitches, especially when voice quality modifications are also present.

Because their realizations sometimes depend on what is going on simultaneously in the voice quality systems, let us delay presenting the tonal realization rules until we have also considered glottalization and laryngealization.

3.2. Tonal Association Rules

The system network has morphemes as its domain, but the association rules and sometimes the realization rules as well refer to specific syllables within these morphemes; therefore some sort of syllable-recognition schema must be included in a complete phonology of the language, although such a schema is not presented here.

The double tones specified by the systems of (17) are borne by the duration-accented syllable of the morpheme, in the first instance. This relation can be stated formally as a tonal association rule, as shown in (18).

(18)   PRIMARY TONE ASSOCIATION

($\acute{\sigma}$ is an accented syllable, T_1 and T_2 are parts of a double tone, and the dotted line indicates the association.)

The examples of (19) illustrate this underlying association.

(19)   *mi* 1:i   *guiu* ba   *du* ba   *bi* gu
                  HH   HL   LH   LL

In that these double tones are associated with a single syllable of the morpheme, they are a type of pitch accent. What makes the Zapotec pitch accents more complex than those of other pitch accent languages like Tonga (Goldsmith 1981) or Japanese (Haraguchi 1977) is that *two* tones are tied to the accented syllable and thus four pitch patterns are possible rather than only two (accented *vs.* unaccented).

The underlying tone of any post-accent syllable of a morpheme is the result of automatic tonal spreading. The second part of each double tone is associated with both the accented syllable and any post-accent syllable the morpheme may have, according to rule (20), which is a limited version of Goldsmith's Well-Formedness Condition (Goldsmith 1976).

(20)   TONAL SPREADING

σ σ #
T_1 T_2

The application of this rule is illustrated in (21).

(21)   *mi* 1:i   *guiu* ba   *du* ba   *bi* gu
                  HH   HL   LH   LL

These two association rules identify each of the tones as a particular element in the tonal structure of the morpheme: T_1 always refers to the first tone of the accented syllable; T_2 is the second tone of that syllable and also the tone of any post-accent syllable which is part of the same morpheme. With the tonal associations in place, the realization rules can refer to the second tone of the pitch accent as such, whether it is manifested in the phonemic tone of just one syllable, or in the tones of two consecutive syllables.

3.3. Tone Sandhi

To explain the superficial tones of Zapotec utterances insightfully, it is necessary to understand three things: the underlying tones, tone sandhi, and various neutralizations accounted for in the realization rules. Tone sandhi is an automatic process in Isthmus Zapotec, by which any underlying LH pitch accent (or the LH tone of an unaccented morpheme, as well) 'spills over' into the following morpheme. If only the simplest data are considered, such as those in (22) and (23), it would seem as if the rise were merely delayed so as to add a high component to the following tone.

(22) *ndǎa* (LH), *làrì* (LL)   'piece, cloth'

(23) tì *ndàa lârì*   'a piece of cloth'

But when the full range of tonal data is taken into account, it becomes clear that the process is not a simple re-association; data such as those in (24) and (25) cannot be explained in that way.

(24) *guìdxǐ* (LH), *chùpǎ* (LH), ně (LH)   'sisal, two, and'

(25) tì *ndàa guǐdxǐ*   'a piece of sisal'
       chùpà ndǎa guǐdxǐ   'two pieces of sisal'
       nè *chǔpá ndǎa guǐdxǐ*   'and two pieces of sisal'

According to the most recent description (Mock 1982), tone sandhi only indirectly affects the superficial tone of the morpheme that follows an underlying LH, by contributing an underlying high tone (H or H_1) to it. The new tone replaces the original one, as stated in (26), and then the tonal realization rules operate upon the modified tone in a straightforward manner.

(26) L → H / LH ## _____

Thus in (25) the tone sandhi rule changes the underlying pitch accents of each morpheme that follows a LH tone, from LH to HH as shown in (27); and virtually every HH is subsequently lowered to phonemic low-rising tone by the realization rules.

(27)   chu̯pa ndaa gui̯dxi → chu̯pa ndaa gui̯dxi
            LH   LH   LH   LH   HH   HH

The tonal changes produced by tone sandhi are LL → HL and LH → HH in accented morphemes, and L → H in unaccented ones.

3.4. Systemic Relations Among Voice Qualities

The two voice quality modifications that affect Isthmus Zapotec vowels are prosodies just as certainly as the tones are. Glottalization has as its domain the entire morpheme, being manifested as a postvocalic glottal stop in each syllable. Compare (28) and (29) for nearly minimal contrasts between glottalized and plain vowels in disyllabic morphemes.

(28)   bé'ñè'   (HL)   'alligator'
        bèñè   (LL)   'mud'

(29)   rì-dù'bà'   (LL)   'gets carried'
        rì-dùbì   (LL)   'gets used up'

The other voice quality modification is laryngealization, or a 'broken' pronunciation of a vowel, as shown in the contrasting examples of (30–32). The phonetic effect is that of a single long vowel made creaky by a slight constriction in the larynx.[6]

(30)   dòo   (LL)   'rope'
        dù   (LL)   'maize tassel'

(31)   riàanǎ   (LH)   'stays'
        riànà   (LL)   'burns'

(32)   guǐidxǐ   (HH)   'tightly held'
        guìdxǐ   (LH)   'sisal'

Laryngealized vowels occur only in accented syllables; when the accent is lost (33) or it shifts (34), laryngealization disappears along with the duration accent.

(33) zèedá-zà → zèdá-zà   'walking along, comes walking'

(34) rèedà ně → rèdà-ně   'brings, comes with'

---

[6] Pickett (1951) transcribes them as VʔV sequences, but there is no clearly audible glottal stop separating the vocalic portions. Radin (1930) calls them rearticulated. Similar laryngealized voice quality occurs in a few other Mesoamerican languages as well; e.g. Yucatec Maya (Marshall Durbin, personal communication) and Chocho (Mock 1977).

Laryngealization is interpreted as a prosody rather than as a vocalic feature partly because of this intimate link with the duration accent, and partly because laryngealized morphemes that bear the LL pitch accent turn up with a predictable glottal stop on the post-accent syllable, as shown in (35). The absolute correlation between laryngealization and this glottal stop is taken as evidence that a single voice quality option is being realized, albeit differently, in both syllables of the morpheme.

(35) *riàa*nà' (LL)   'shaves oneself'
      *bèe*ndà' (LL)   'snake'
      *ziùu*là' (LL)   'long'

At first glance it would seem possible to set up a three-member voice quality system, as shown in (36).

(36) *Voice Quality*
      accented   ┌Plain
      morpheme →   ├Glottalized
                        └Laryngealized

But the distribution of the various pitch accents in morphemes with glottalized and laryngealized voice quality is oddly skewed. We have seen that morphemes that are neither glottalized nor laryngealized can bear all four pitch accents (cf. (13) and (19) above), but glottalized morphemes have only three pitch accents—HH, HL and LL,[7] as shown in (37); and laryngealized morphemes also bear only three of them—this time HH, LH and LL,[8] as shown in (38).

(37)   MONOSYLLABIC   DISYLLABIC
         rì-*ndǎ'*   (HH)   'gets bitter'   nà-*yàná'*   (HH)   'hot-tasting'
         rì-*ndá'*   (HL)   'gets hot'   nà-*yá'*nì'   (HL)   'clear'
         rì-*ndà'*   (LL)   'stinks'   nà-*yà'*quì'   (LL)   'burnt'

(38)   *nǔu*   (HH)   'there is'   nà-*dxǐíbǐ*   (HH)   'fearful'
         bǔu   (LH)   'charcoal'   nà-*chùu*chǐ   (LH)   'slippery'
         dòo   (LL)   'rope'   nà-*dxìíbì'*   (LL)   'smooth'

---

[7] Except if *gǎstí'* 'there is not' is considered a unitary glottalized morpheme in the LH class, rather than some sort of fused portmanteau.

[8] The one morpheme that might qualify as an exception is the question-introducer *ñêe*, whose HL tone may be induced by an intonational overlay. This is not the only case of intonational interference: at the other end of yes-no questions the interrogative final boundary marker *1ǎ* (H) has such an extraordinarily high rise that it has often been transcribed in the literature as bearing a phonemic high tone.

Thus there is some sort of constraint against the underlying LH pitch accent in glottalized morphemes,[9] and against the HL pitch accent in laryngealized morphemes. As a result of this lopsided distribution there are only two tonal contexts in which either glottalization or laryngealization can be chosen: HH and LL. The system network can capture this fact if we recognize two systems for voice quality, of which only the first is at the same degree of delicacy as the tone systems are:

(39)

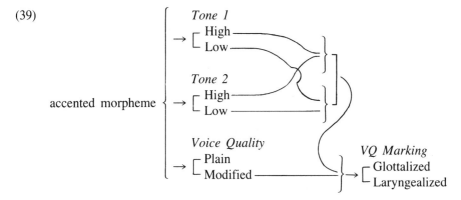

The first voice quality system here is very general. The option [modified] is realized as either one of the marked voice qualities: [modified] plus [HL] is glottalization, [modified] plus [LH] is laryngealization, and only in the tonal contexts [HH] and [LL] is there a straightforward *opposition* between glottalizing a morpheme and laryngealizing it, as shown in (40) and (41).

(40)   *nuǎ'*   (HH)   'laden down'   *nà-yǎná'*   (HH)   'hot-tasting'
       nǔu   (HH)   'there is'   *nà-yǎahuǐ*   (HH)   'funny'

(41)   rì-*dò'*   (LL)   'gets tame'   rì-*dù'ba'*   (LL)   'gets carried'
       rì-*dòo*   (LL)   'gets sold'   rì-*dùubà'*   (LL)   'approaches'

This lumping together of the two marked voice qualities, despite their opposition in certain contexts, is formally permissible in a systemic description because of its insistence on identifying the actual contexts in which putative phonological features are opposed. But in this instance the validity of the option [modified] is also supported by morphological alternations between laryngealized and glottalized vowels. There are two such cases, in which tonal morphemes which are superimposed on the verb create a HL pitch accent and simultaneously trigger a change from laryngealized to glottalized voice quality.

---

[9] Note that this is not a prohibition of *phonetic* rising tones followed by a glottal stop; the HH pitch accent is realized precisely as phonemic (and phonetic) low-rising tone in most contexts, as the realization rules below will show.

In the first case, inflection for first person plural forms entails adding not only one of the relevant dependent pronouns (*nŭ* (LH) 'we inclusive' or *dŭ* (LH) 'we exclusive'), but also raising the pitch accent of the verbal root. There are many laryngealized verbs whose base form has a LL pitch accent, but which bear a HL accent with the first person plural forms; with the change in tonal conditions their laryngealization is replaced by glottalization, as shown in (42) and (43).

(42) zú-*huàa* (LL)   'standing, stopped'
     pà má zú-*huá'* (HL) *dxìi*chì nù lǎ 'if we already are standing firm'

(43) guì-*dùuyà'* (LL)   'may see (potential aspect)'
     tí guì-*dú'*yà dǔ (HL)   'until we see'

Interpreting these data in terms of the system network, we can say that when the tonal context is changed by the addition of a tonal morpheme for first person plural, the entire second system of voice quality marking is knocked out of commission because its tonal entry conditions are no longer satisfied. The preceding system then becomes the terminal one, with its context-sensitive realization of the option [modified] as glottalization in the tonal context of HL.

As for the second case of alternation, the first component of a verb's pitch accent is changed to H in subordinate clauses, whenever the verb is inflected for either potential or completive aspect (John Alsop, personal communication). In these circumstances, even second and third person forms of the verb, which generally bear the basic pitch accent of the verb, end up bearing raised pitch accents, as shown in (44) and (45) below.

(44) *gù*ni (LL) bě   'he/she may do, may make'
     qué ràcà *là'*dxù nì *gû*nì bè nǐ   'you don't want him/her to do it'
                                                                    HL

(45) gù-*dxì*bà (LH) bě   'he/she may sew'
     qué ràcà *là'*dxù nì gù*dxì*bá bé nǐ   'you don't want him/her to sew it'
                                                                     HH

When laryngealized verbs with the LL pitch accent undergo this tonal change, many of them become glottalized, as shown in (46).

(46) *gùu*yà' (LL)   'may see'
     qué ràcà *là'*dxù nì *gú'*yà'   'you don't want (him/her) to see'
                                                       HL

Laryngealized verbs that have the LH pitch accent are not affected in this way, because HH is one of the tonal contexts that *does* permit laryngealization (47).

(47) *guià*anǎ (LH)   'may stay'
     qué ràcà *là'*dxù nì *guiǎ*anǎ   'you don't want (him/her) to stay'
                                                         HH

Similar relations seem to be common in other tone languages, although interlocking data on all the laryngeal phenomena have too seldom been presented together. Several languages of Mesoamerica exhibit similar traits: Yucatec Maya has contrastive tones on long plain vowels, but predictable tones on glottalized and laryngealized vowels (Marshall Durbin & Fernando Ojeda, personal communication; cf. Fisher 1976); in Chocho there is non-distinctive variation between a phonetic high-falling pitch and the combination of high pitch and a glottal stop (Mock, n.d.); tone and glottalization are also linked together in Otomi (Wallis 1968). Outside Mesoamerica, the same sorts of connections have been observed: both Acoma Keresan (Miller 1965) and Vietnamese (Han 1969) have laryngeal and glottal prosodies that apparently contrast directly with tones. Zahao, a Chin language of northwest Burma, has rising tones that can not occur in glottalized syllables, and similar phenomena are noted in Thai (Yip 1982).

There are many historical connections among such prosodic features as well. For example, the tonal accents of Swedish and Norwegian have the same origins as the glottal and laryngeal prosodies of Danish (Gårding 1973); and Hombert (1978) cites data from Vietnamese, Burmese, Lahu and Middle Chinese to the effect that when glottal stops disappear from a language, they often lead to either a rising or a high tone on the preceding vowel (cf. Matisoff 1970). A historical connection has also been established between low tone and laryngealization in Kiowa (Sivertsen 1956).

The asymmetrical distribution of tone with the two types of voice quality modification leads us to ask if there is any natural basis for the suppression of glottalization in the presence of a rising tone, and of laryngealization when a tone is falling steeply. As phonetic phenomena, both voice quality and tone are controlled at the larynx, making it reasonable to look for some sort of physiological interference. The phonetic research of Hombert and his associates suggests that the larynx moves *up* for both high pitch and glottalization, and *down* for both low pitch and vocalic breathiness (Hombert, Ohala & Ewan 1979). Hombert notes that apparently breathiness and laryngealization may be linked to low pitch in much the same way (Hombert 1978:96); and as a matter of fact, Zapotecan laryngealization is a reflex of Proto-Otomanguean *Vh* sequences (cf. the analysis of Rensch 1976).

The tonal constraints on how marked voice quality is manifested in Isthmus Zapotec harmonize with Hombart's data. The phonological opposition between laryngealized and glottalized voice quality is neutralized in the context of falling or rising pitch accents, and the form the neutralization takes in each case has its basis in the movements of the larynx, with glottalization following H_1 and laryngealization in the presence of L_1.

3.5. Voice Quality Association Rules

The next step, now that we have identified marked voice quality as being prosodic, is to indicate just how each option ties into the phonological structure of potential morphemes. The partial independence of voice quality from the pitch accents means that two separate tiers are needed, but because laryngealization and glottalization belong to the same series of prosodic systems, both of them can be represented on the same tier.[10]

Because association rules apply to the underlying forms of morphemes rather than to individual allomorphs, it is understood that they take effect before the realization rules do. The laryngeal rule, as shown in (48), simply associates the feature [laryngealized] with the accented syllable of the morpheme. The sort of prosodic structure it generates is illustrated in (49).

(48)   LARYNGEAL ASSOCIATION

                         ″
                         ¦   (″ is laryngealized voice quality)
                         ¦
                         σ́

(49)   ″
                  ¦
          na-*chu* chi   (↘ nàchùuchǐ) 'slippery'
            ¦   ⋀
            L   LH

There are two association rules for the [glottalized] option. The first one ties it to the last syllable of the morpheme, whether that syllable is accented or not:

(50)   GLOTTAL ASSOCIATION

                         ʔ
                         ¦
                         σ́ #

The second rule defines glottal spreading for disyllabic words:

(51)   GLOTTAL SPREADING

                        ʔ
                  ⸝----¦
          σ́ (#) σ́   (except if HH)

This rule states that glottalization spreads in an anticipatory way to a preceding accented syllable, except when the morpheme bears the HH pitch accent; the general case is illustrated in (52).

---

[10] There are no morphemes that are both laryngealized and glottalized distinctively at the same time. Laryngealized roots *do* take glottalized suffixes, however. In such cases, the glottalization is restricted to the suffix itself; e.g.

        ″   ʔ   ″   ʔ
        ¦   ¦   ¦   ¦
    ru- zaqui -a → ru- zaque ↘ rúzăaqué′
      ¦   ⋀   ¦   ⋀
      L   LL   HH   L (HH)

(52)   ʔ   ʔ
              | ⁄‾‾|
         bi cu   bi   cu
          ∧⁄   →   ∧⁄   (↘ bì'cù') 'dog'
         LL   LL

The accented syllable to which glottalization spreads must be in the same word, but need not belong to the same morpheme. For example, the glottalized contraction of the dependent pronoun *lù'* 'you, your' in (53) glottalizes the morpheme it is attached to:

(53)   ʔ   ʔ
                   | |
         li dxi -u→ *li* dx-u   (↘ *lì'dxù'*) 'your house'
          ∧⁄ | ∧ |
         LL   L LL   L

The first glottalization rule, (50) above, may need some special justification, because a phonetic glottal stop never appears at the end of a morpheme except in an accented syllable or before pause (see realization rule (71) below). Nevertheless, a morpheme-final association is supported both by comparative evidence and by the language-internal patterns we have seen. Data from other Zapotecan languages (e.g. the Villa Alta dialect of Sierra Zapotec) indicate that the original locus of the glottal stop must have been the morpheme-final position; and as we have seen, not all disyllabic glottalized morphemes in Isthmus Zapotec bear two glottal stops (cf. (40)), and nonglottalized stems can be glottalized with the addition of a glottalized suffix (53).

3.6. Realization Rules

Zapotec morphemes do not realize their full potential for glottalization, laryngealization and tonal contrast except as the nucleus of a phonological phrase (Pickett 1967); that is, in the presence of an unreduced duration accent and simultaneously before a pause. Thus an isolated or elicited word carries prosodic distinctions that are not apparent within longer phrases. Such fluctuation is not uncommon; Hyman (1977) notes that in many languages word-stress is often realized fully only in the tonic word of the intonational unit, and Waugh (1979) argues in favor of recognizing in-focus or strong positions within an utterance, in which the optimally distinctive variants are favored.

The realization rules below reflect this sort of variation; prepause position is often an important conditioning context, as is the location of the accented syllable.

The realization rules are much simpler if we set aside for separate description the phonological subclass of morphemes having all the characteristics portrayed in (54): glottalization, two syllables and a HH pitch accent.

(54) ?
         \
         σ́ σ́
         |
         HH

Whenever such morphemes need to be excluded from the general rules, this is indicated by the arbitrary symbol [-W].

We turn first to the tonal realization rules. The two pitch accents that begin with H tone have complementary realizations. In the HH pitch accent H_1 is realized as phonemic low tone, as stated in (55), regardless of whether the morpheme is also subject to marked voice quality.

(55) H_1 ↘ / ˋ / [3] | _____H_2
                                    [-W]

The examples in Section 1 of (56) (see Table 1) illustrate this realization; note that the disyllabic glottalized morphemes of Section 1c require a different rule.

The second rule for H_1 states that it is always realized as a phonemic high tone in the HL pitch accent:

(57) H_1 ↘ / ´ / [5] | _____L_2

Section 2 of the table shows this as the first part of a phonemic high-falling tone on plain vowels, and as phonemic high tone on glottalized vowels. (Recall that there are no laryngealized morphemes with the HL accent.)

There is only one realization for L_1, in all tonal contexts and with any of the three voice qualities:

(58) L_1 ↘ / ˋ / [3] | _____T_2

This phonemic low tone is present in the LH and the LL pitch accents, as shown in Sections 3 and 4 of the table.

The realization rules for the second tonal component of the pitch accent require narrower definition of particular contexts, with special attention to prepause position. We have seen that LH morphemes have alternate tone patterns before pause and in mid-utterance (see 3.3 above). This alternation is accounted for in the realization rules for H_2, the first of which is given in (59).

(59) H_2 ↘ / ˋ / [1] | L_1 _____ X (where X is not pause)

This rule states that the second tone of the LH pitch accent is always realized as (part of) phonemic low tone in mid-utterance. An alternative description of the context here would be to note that it always includes an underlying H, because tone

Table 1. (56) Paradigm of Accented Morphemes

			Realizations	
	Underlying Forms		Mid-utterance	Prepause
1. HH pitch accent				
a. Plain VQ	nga (∧ HH)	'that one'	ngǎ	ngǎ
	niru (∿ HH)	'in front'	nĭrú	nĭrŭ
b. Laryngealized	nu (″ ∧ HH)	'there is'	nŭu	nŭu
	stipi (″ ∿ HH)	'whistle'	stĭipí	stĭipĭ
c. Glottalized	ma (ʔ ∧ HH)	'already'	mǎ' Z	mǎ'
	dama (ʔ ∧| HH H)	'owl'	dàmá / dámá	dàmá' / dámá'
2. HL pitch accent				
a. Plain VQ	dxe (∧ HL)	'boy!'	dxê	dxê
	guiuba (∿ HL)	'fast'	guiûbà	guiûbà
b. Glottalized	da (ʔ ∧ HL)	'rotten'	dá' Z	dá'
	beñe (ʔ ∕| ∿ HL)	'alligator'	bé'ñè	bé'ñè'

(continued)

Table 1. *Continued*

	Underlying Forms		Realizations	
			Mid-utterance	Prepause
3.	**LH pitch accent**			
a. Plain VQ	*di* ∧ LH	'curse'	*dì* . ˙.	*dǐ*
	benda ∿ LH	'sister'	*bèndà* . ˙.	*bèndǎ*
b. Laryngealized	″ ∣ *nda* ∧ LH	'piece'	*ndàa* . ˙.	*ndǎa*
	″ ∣ *bitu* ∿ LH	'bud'	*bìitù* . ˙.	*bìitǔ*
4.	**LL pitch accent**			
a. Plain VQ	*ru* ∧ LL	'cough'	*rù*	*rù*
	benda ∿ LL	'fish'	*bèndà*	*bèndà*
b. Laryngealized	″ ∣ *sa* ∧ LL	'music'	*sàa*	*sàa*
	″ ∣ *benda* ∧ LL	'snake'	*bèendà*	*bèendá'*
c. Glottalized	ʔ ∣ *le* ∧ LL	'fence'	*lè'* Z	*lè'*
	ʔ ∧ *tixhi* ∿ LL	'trunk'	*tì'xhì*	*tì'xhì'*

sandhi invariably changes any underlying L to H immediately after LH (see (26) above). In any event, the rule applies to both plain and laryngealized vowels, as shown in Section 3 of the table. Recall that H_2 is associated with both syllables of disyllabic morphemes and thus the realization rule above will provide a phonemic low tone in each syllable of the morpheme.

H_2 is realized as a phonemic high tone in a diverse set of contexts:

(60) $H_2 \searrow$ $/\,'/[5]$ | a) $H_1 \underline{\quad}$ X   (where X is not pause)
                                  [-W]

            b) $\acute{S}$ $/\,/$
                  $\wedge$
                  $L_1\underline{\quad}$

Rule (60) states that in mid-utterance the HH pitch accent ends in a high tone (except for the disyllabic glottalized subclass)—as shown in Section 1 of the table; and that monosyllabic LH morphemes bear a phonemic low-rising tone in utterance-final position, as shown in Section 3 of the table. This one rule accounts for most of the superficial low-rising tones of Isthmus Zapotec; note that except before pause, it is the HH pitch accent that gives rise to most of them, rather than the LH accent.

Both the LH and the HH pitch accents have special prepause realizations which are expressed in rule (61).

(61) $H_{(2)} \searrow$ $/\check{}/$ [13] | $H_2 . \underline{\quad}$ $/\,/$ (where . is a syllable boundary and
                                         [Y]   Y is not [glottalized])

This rule states that any nonglottalized post-accent syllable bearing an underlying H acquires a low-rising glide in utterance-final position. Thus disyllabic HH morphemes have a second rising tone before pause, unless they are also glottalized, as is evident from Sections 1a and 1b of the table.[11] Similarly all the disyllabic LH morphemes end in a rising tone, as shown in Section 3 of the table. Rule (61) is written so as to exclude not only the glottalized morphemes of Section 1c, but also glottalized enclitics which have been perturbed to H by a preceding LH morpheme, such as pè' and lù' in (62), and basically high-toned enclitics like rí' in (63).

(62)   ʔ   ʔ
                  | |
            ŋue pè   →   ŋue pè   ($\searrow$ ŋuè pé')   'precisely that one'
            $\wedge$ | (tone $\wedge$ |
            LH L   LH H
                 sandhi)

[11] The influence of glottal stops on the manifestations of tone in Zapotec might almost be taken as evidence for an asymmetry seen as axiomatic among tonal scholars: 'It is virtually always segments which influence tone; tone rarely, if ever, influences segments' (Schuh 1978:224). The difficulty with this is the assumption that glottal stops always behave as segments rather than as prosodies. The relations between glottal stops and tones in Isthmus Zapotec are interprosodic; and only if glottalization is interpreted as a prosody does Leben's Convention (10) hold true for the language—that tonal processes are indifferent to segmental factors (Leben 1978:183).

$$\begin{array}{ccc} \text{ʔ} & & \text{ʔ} \\ | & & | \\ ria\ \text{lu} & \to & ria\ \text{lu} \\ \wedge\ \ | & & \wedge\ \ | \\ \text{LH L} & & \text{LH H} \end{array} \quad (\searrow ri\grave{a}\ l\acute{u}') \quad \text{'you get clean'}$$

(63)   *bèndà rí'*   'this fish' (*bè*ndà LL)

Glottalization is pertinent to the realization of L_2 as well, but in rather a different way. Rule (64) specifies that L_2 is realized as phonemic low tone(s) in either plain or laryngealized morphemes:

(64) $L_2 \searrow / \ ^\vee / \ [1] \ | \ T_1 \underline{\quad}$ (where Y is not [glottalized])

                                    [Y]

The application of this rule is illustrated in Sections 4a and 4b for the LL pitch accent; the examples in Section 2a have both falling and low tones as a result of this rule. But in the accented syllable of glottalized morphemes (Sections 2b and 4c), another rule for L_2 cuts off any tonal realization at all:

(65) $L_2 \searrow \varnothing \ | \ T_1 \underline{\quad\quad\quad}$
             [glottalized]

This 'nonrealization' rule is made necessary by the way glottalization intersects with the duration accent. A glottalized syllable never has a long vowel unless it bears a phonemic rising tone (an underlying HH). The phonetic pitch of the accented syllables of *bé'ñè'* and *dá'* in Section 2b is a short, nongliding high, and the accented syllables of *ti'xhì'* and *lè'* in Section 4c have short low tones. It is as if the glottal stop consumes the second mora of the accented syllable, and also the tone that is associated with it.

The realization rules for voice quality are less complex than the tonal rules we have just considered. The rules attached to the option [modified] are not strictly speaking realization rules, but function instead much as the tone sandhi rule does, to reassign phonological features to a morpheme at a single level of abstraction:

(66) modified $\to$ glottalized $| \ H_1 L_2$

(67) modified $\to$ laryngealized $| \ L_1 H_2$

(68) modified $\searrow \varnothing \ | \ \alpha T_1 \ \alpha T_2$

Rules (66) and (67) simply state that the option is to be rewritten as [glottalized] in HL morphemes and as [laryngealized] in morphemes that bear the LH pitch accent. The third rule here says that in the other two tonal contexts—HH and LL—the option is merely an entry condition to the second voice quality system.

The main rule for the [laryngealized] prosody (69) does not specify any syllabic or tonal context, because the laryngeal association rule above automatically links laryngealization to accented syllables.

(69) laryngealized ↘ /VV/ [vocalic creakiness]

Examples of laryngealization in combination with various pitch accents are to be found in Sections 1b, 3b and 4b of the table. In morphemes that bear the LL pitch accent, laryngealization co-occurs with a predictable glottal stop, as stated in rule (70); see the examples in (35) above, as well as the one in Section 4b of the table.

(70)   laryngealized ↘ (/VV/ and) /ˈ/ [ʔ] | CV.CV___ / /

As mentioned earlier, glottalization is associated with both the accented syllable of a morpheme and with any post-accent syllable (except for the disyllabic glottalized HH subclass, in which glottalization is restricted to the post-accent syllable). Given these associations, the realization rules merely insert glottal stops into the segmental structure of a morpheme at the previously specified locations, according to particular external circumstances. As stated formally in the first part of rule (71), the glottalization associated with any accented syllable is realized as a post-vocalic stop unless the following sound is a sonorant consonant /n m l r/. At the same time it is also realized as another post-vocalic stop in prepause position in any post-accent syllable, as shown in the second part of the rule. The examples in Sections 1c, 2b and 4c of the table are pertinent here.

(71)   glottalized ↘ /ˈ/ [ʔ] | a)   ś   Z   (where Z is not a sonorant
                                              CV___   consonant)

                                       b)   ś   ś   / /
                                                          CV___

In all contexts except those relevant in rule (71), the glottalized feature is not realized at all:

(72)   glottalized ↘ Ø | a) ś -Z   (sonorant consonant)

                                 b) ś X   (where X is not pause)

This 'nonrealization' rule accounts for the absence of word-final glottal stops in disyllabic morphemes (and in unaccented ones) in mid-utterence position, as shown in Sections 1c, 2b and 4c of the table, as well as the 'disappearance' of the word-final glottal stop in several examples cited earlier—the second part of (43), and the word là'dxù in examples (44–47).

To summarize the patterns which we have examined so far, the tones of the pitch accents interact with voice quality in accented morphemes in such a way that the opposition between laryngealized and glottalized voice quality is neutralized in half of the tonal contexts; and the underlying pitch accents are themselves neutralized in various positions: LH and LL 'merge' in mid-utterance, if we discount the tone sandhi effects of LH; while HH and LH 'merge' in monosyllabic morphemes before pause. The effect of all these interrelated neutralizations is to reduce the superficial prosodic complexity. The actual stream of speech contains far fewer glottal stops, laryngealized vowels and tonal contrasts than are present in the basic forms of the morphemes.

3.7. Disyllabic Glottalized HH Morphemes

The realization rules just presented adequately describe the tones and voice quality modifications of most accented morphemes, but there are a few morphemes whose prosodies do not behave this way, most of which belong to the special subclass of disyllabic glottalized morphemes bearing the HH pitch accent. The elicitation forms of such morphemes are quite different from those of other HH morphemes; their superficial tones following any syllable with a superficial high tone, however, suggest an underlying HH, and there is a gap in the paradigm of glottalized morphemes which they fill very nicely, assuming that they do bear a HH pitch accent.

These morphemes are phonologically peculiar in several ways. Their glottalization is limited to the *post*-accent syllable, for one thing.[12] This peculiarity can be captured via a special glottal association rule:

(73) LIMITED GLOTTAL ASSOCIATION

$$\begin{array}{c} ? \\ | \\ \acute{\delta}\ \acute{\delta}\ \# \\ HH \end{array}$$

This subclass also has an unusual set of tonal patterns. To begin with, they are the only morphemes that have a phonemic high tone on the post-accent syllable without also having a high or rising tone on the accented syllable; cf. the examples of (74).

(74) *dàmá'*   'owl'
      bì-*cùtí'*   'worm'
      rì-*gàbá'*   'gets counted'

Another peculiarity is that the accented syllable does not perturb following a LH morpheme, as shown in (75); cf. the normal tone sandhi of (76).

---

[12] The same tonal pattern is repeated in words that take the glottalized suffix for first person singular, which changes the pitch accent of the preceding stem to HH; e.g. *lìdxì*(LL) plus (HH)-*a'* → *lìdxé'*. Note that in this case the tones of laryngealized stems behave in a more transparent way; e.g. *xìñì'* (LL) plus (HH)-*a'* → *xíñé'*.

(75) *chùpà dàmá'*   'two owls' (*chùpǎ* LH)
     nè *dàmá rí'*   'and this owl / these owls' (ně LH)

(76) *chùpà bí'cù'*   'two dogs' (*bí'cù'* LL)
     nè *bî' cù rí'*   'and this dog / these dogs'

Finally, it is the only class of morphemes whose low tone changes to high after any morpheme-final superficial high tone, whether the preceding morpheme would normally cause tone sandhi, as in (77), or not, as in (78).

(77) *huàgà* què né *dámá rí'*   'that rat and this owl'   (què LH)
     nè *chǔpá dámá* què   'and those two owls'

(78) nà*quìchí dámá rí'*   'this owl is white' (nà-*quìchí'* HH)
     nè bí-*cútí rí'*   'and this worm' (bì- L)

The tonal change itself is unusual for Isthmus Zapotec, because an accented low tone normally perturbs to a high-falling tone, whereas in these words there is only a barely perceptible glide [54]. All these facts require a separate set of rules. It seems best to start with a special tone association rule such that H_2 is tied only to the post-accent syllable:

(79) SPECIAL TONE ASSOCIATION RULE

$$\begin{array}{cc} & ? \\ & | \\ σ' & σ' \# \\ | & | \\ H_1 & H_2 \end{array}$$

This leaves H_1 unassociated, with only the accented syllable available for it. The nature of the duration accent makes it necessary that there should be a tone associated with each mora of the accented syllable. In this case, it means that H_1 will have to be doubled:

(80) H_1 DOUBLING

$$\begin{array}{ccc} & ? & \\ & | & \\ σ' & & σ' \# \\ \wedge & & | \\ H_1 & H_1 & H_2 \end{array}$$

With this set of underlying associations, the realization rules for this class of morphemes can be written quite simply, as follows:

(81) $H_2 \searrow$ /ˈ/ [5] | ?
                     | |
                     | /ˈ/___σ' #
                     | |
                     | H_2

(82) $H_1 \searrow \ /\ [3]$ | ?

           $Y\_\_\_\ \acute{S}\ \#$ (where Y is not $/\ /$)

           H_2

The special condition Y specifies the preceding context as 'not $/\ /$'; that is, as being either phonemic low tone or utterance-initial position.

A stable high tone manifests H_2 in these morphemes:

(83) $H_2 \searrow /\ \prime /\ [5]$ | _____
                                           | [glottalized]

The unusual element in the realization rules for H_1 here is the intrusion of a superficial tone as a relevant prosodic context. This peculiarity indicates that the realization of the $H_1 H_1$ is delayed, or ordered after all the other realization rules have applied. It is one of the few cases in which specific rule ordering is necessary in a systemic phonology of Isthmus Zapotec prosodies.[13]

4.0. CONCLUSIONS

In this account we have seen how a systemic phonology sorts out the paradigmatic contexts in which each opposition is functional. Specifically, for accented morphemes there is an intricate interdependence between the pitch accent options and modified voice quality such that glottalization and laryngealization are functionally opposed only in the tonal contexts HH and LL. Once the prosodic features have been selected via the system network, association rules link them to specific segments, and realization rules detail how each feature is manifested. The use of association rules is a formal innovation, but the concept of independent prosodies, and its corollary, the need to state explicitly how they tie into the segmental structure of a language, have always been important in systemic phonology.

This account has illustrated the necessity of recognizing more than one prosodic (or 'autosegmental') tier for some languages. It has also marshalled evidence pertinent to the quest for the phonological universals of laryngeal phenomena, particularly by highlighting the ways in which tone and voice quality modification interact.

REFERENCES

Alsop, John. (n.d.). Isthmus Zapotec tone patterns: system of tone perturbation. Unpublished manuscript.

---

[13] The tone sandhi rule is ordered first in any event. In a purely autosegmental treatment of these data (Mock 1982), more rule ordering is used.

Anderson, Stephen R. (1978). Tone features. In Fromkin, Victoria A. (ed.), *Tone: A Linguistic Survey*. New York: Academic Press, 133–175.

Fisher, William M. (1976). On tonal features in Yucatecan dialects. *Mayan Linguistics* **1**.29–43.

Fromkin, Victoria A. (ed.) (1978). *Tone: A Linguistic Survey*. New York: Academic Press.

Gandour, Jackson T. (1978). The perception of tone. In Fromkin, Victoria A. (ed.), *Tone: A Linguistic Survey*. New York: Academic Press, 41–76.

Gårding, E. (1973). *The Scandinavian word accents*. (Lund University Working Papers). Lund, Sweden: Lund University Press.

Goldsmith, John A. (1976). An overview of autosegmental phonology. *Linguistic Analysis* **2**.1.23–68.

———. (1981). Accent in Tonga: an autosegmental account. In Clements, George N. (ed.), *Harvard Studies in Phonology* **vol. II**. Cambridge, MA: Linguistics Department, Harvard University, pp. 178–187.

Han, M. S. (1969). *Vietnamese Tones*. Los Angeles, CA: Acoustic Phonetics Laboratory, University of Southern California.

Haraguchi, Shosuke. (i977). *The Tone Pattern of Japanese: An Autosegmental Theory of Phonology*. Tokyo: Kaitakusha.

Hombert, Jean-Marie. (1978). Consonantal types, vowel quality and tone. In Fromkin, Victoria A. (ed.), *Tone: A Linguistic Survey*. New York: Academic Press, 77–111.

Hombert, Jean-Marie, Ohala, J. J. & Ewan, W. G. (1979). Phonetic explanations for the development of tones. *Languages* **55**.37–58.

Hyman, Larry M. (1977). On the nature of linguistic stress. In Hyman, Larry M. (ed.), *Studies in Stress and Accent* (SCOPIL 4). Los Angeles, CA: Department of Linguistics, University of Southern California, pp. 37–82.

Jakobson, Roman & Waugh, Linda R. (1979). *The Sound Shape of Language*. Bloomington, IN: Indiana University Press.

Leben, William R. (1978). The representation of tone. In Fromkin, Victoria A. (ed.), *Tone: A Linguistic Survey*. New York: Academic Press, 177–219.

Matisoff, James A. (1970). Glottal dissimilation and the Lahu high-rising tone: a tonogenetic case-study. *Journal of the American Oriental Society* **9**.1.13–44.

Miller, W. (1965). *Acoma Grammar and Texts*. Berkeley, CA: University of California Press.

Mock, Carol C. (1977). *Chocho de Santa Catarina Ocotlán*. Archivo de Lenguas Indígenas de México, **vol. 4**. México, D.F.: Centro de Investigación para la Integración Social.

———. (no date). Chocho field notes. Unpublished papers.

———. (1984). Las alternancias tonales en el zapoteco del Istmo. In Solá, Donald F., Suñer, Margarita & Rodrigues, Aryon (eds.), *Proceedings of the tenth PILEI Symposium*. Ithaca, NY: Latin American Studies Program, Cornell University, pp. 268–311.

Pickett, Velma B. (1951). Nonphonemic stress: a problem in stress-placement. *Word* **7**.60–65.

———. (1960). The grammatical hierarchy of Isthmus Zapotec. *Language* **36**.1, Part 2.

———. (1967). Isthmus Zapotec. In Wauchope, Robert and McQuown, Norman (eds.), *Handbook of Middle American Indians* **vol. 5**. Austin, TX: University of Texas Press, pp. 291–310.

———. (1974). *Zapoteco del Istmo*. Archivo de Lenguas Indígenas del Estado de Oaxaca, **vol. 1**. México, D.F.: Instituto de Investigación e Integración Social del Estado de Oaxaca.

Radin, Paul. (1930). A preliminary sketch of the Zapotec language. *Language* **6**.64–85.

Rensch, Calvin R. (1976). *Comparative Otomanguean Phonology*. Indiana University Publications, Language Science Monograph no. **14**. Bloomington, IN: Indiana University Press.

Schuh, Russell G. (1978). Tone rules. In Fromkin, Victoria A. (ed.), *Tone: A Linguistic Survey*. New York: Academic Press, 221–256.

Sivertsen, E. (1956). Pitch problems in Kiowa. *International Journal of American Linguistics* **22**.117–130.

Wallis, Ethel. (1968). The word and the phonological hierarchy of Mezquital Otomi. *Language* **44**.76–90.

Waugh, Linda R. (1979). Remarks on markedness. In Dinnsen, Daniel A. (ed.), *Current approaches to phonological theory*. Bloomington, IN: Indiana University Press, pp. 310–315.

Yip, Moira J. W. (1980). The tonal phonology of Chinese. Ph.D. dissertation, Massachusetts Institute of
    Technology. Reproduced by the Indiana University Linguistics Club, Bloomington, Indiana.
————. (1982). Against a segmental analysis of Zahao and Thai: a laryngeal tier proposal. *Linguistic
    Analysis* **9**.79–94.

On the Signalling of Complete Thoughts

19

James Monaghan
The Hatfield Polytechnic
England

In Monaghan (1982) I discussed some of the ways of intonationally signalling text structures and remarked on the at times complex relationships between the phonological and the lexicogrammatical signalling of meaning in speech situations. The basis of my approach was the familiar Neo-Firthian dispersal of the total meaning of the text in its context into the various modes of meaning signalled by the various relevant aspects of the speaker's behaviour. I noted that these strands of meaning were not mutually predicted in an absolute sense, but are rather made more or less probable by their common role in simultaneously signalling the resultant meaning of the whole speech event. In the present paper I propose to examine some of the ways of expressing the notion of completeness in text structure. My aim will be to work towards a reexamination of the utility of the concept of the sentence, but first I propose to look at other ways of expressing completeness in texts.

The speech event as a whole may be compared to a structure under tension, such as a spider's web or a mobile, where the constituent parts, as well as playing their roles in the total functioning of the whole structure, also partake in an equilibrium with other constituents. The pull of each part is reinforced or neutralised by the pulls of other parts so that the final result is that the structure achieves a stable shape consonant with its function, e.g. catching flies or looking nice. In the same way, the different aspects of the text language are part of the unified semiogenic event of communicating in a social situation. Each linguistic choice both contributes to the total meaning by what it expresses, and by how this expression relates to other expressions in its context. The complexity inherent in such an intricately balanced web of relationships, especially in dialogue, is one of the main sources of the richness of potential meanings available to speakers.

Grammar, phonology and lexicology all contribute to the explication of the various strands of linguistic meaning and, although each mode of expression operates within its own constraints and possibilities, they are all locked together by the requirement that the totality of signals must make sense in its context. In other words, each phonological pattern, each grammatical structure, each member of a lexical collocation at a particular place in an utterance embodies constraints from what has gone before at its own level but also from the expectations being set up by what is simultaneously occurring at the others. All participants in the speech event have a knowledge of what the ongoing language is predicting as well as what it is contributing itself. The hearer is able to range ahead of the speaker in terms of the likely developments both in content and expression. He may even use this ability to drop out of close monitoring of what is being said for varying periods, and this can lead to occasional problems as in the case of the 'Yes dear' jokes of the cartoons. It also partially explains why we fail to observe the 'errors' in spontaneous speech until we come to transcribe recordings. A speech error, properly so called, is something that causes a breakdown of communication.

This might seem obvious but recent linguistic writings have displayed a surprising tendency to lump together positive restructurings with slips of the tongue, lapses of concentration and other events prejudicial to getting the message across. In speech it is a sign of competence as a communicator when a speaker notices that the audience is not following and rephrases in order to improve matters. Even scholars deservedly famous for their work with real speech sometimes suffer lapses, as when Crystal (1976:24) finds it necessary to excuse the fact that it is possible in speech "to start a new sentence before the old one is finished, to break the syntax by introducing a clarification, to be vague and imprecise" on the grounds that "people need to relax". Not only are such features characteristic of speech situations where the speakers are anything but relaxed, such as when politicians are being grilled by a hostile interviewer, they can also be utilised in subtle ways. The anacolouthon *I was hoping that you—would you tell him the news for me?*, made up by Huddleston (1976:2) to illustrate ill-formedness, can be used to make a request combining the polite circumlocution *I was hoping that you might tell him the news for me* and the more direct *Would you tell him the news for me?*. It is simply nonsense to say that the combination of the two sentences must be seen as evidence that "a person's use of his language may not reflect his knowledge of it". The core of a speaker's knowledge of his language *is* how to use it and any grammatical theory that fails to take this into account is correspondingly weakened, even as an abstract theory. When it comes to explaining how speakers use language to live, it is useless.

As well as continuously monitoring the reactions of his audience, the hearer is also under the influence of the familiar patterns, both sequential and simultaneous, that are predicted by each part of the utterance. We are all aware of the 'automatic pilot' which tends to put the utterance onto the tramlines of highly predictable sequences as soon as certain patterns are initiated. In contexts where the phatic element is important, the appropriate fluency will be purchased by keeping to the well-worn tracks. Where it is important to be precise, original or creative, the speaker will often reject the first structure that comes to mind and hesitation will result. Hesitation signals are important signs that the speaker, although he is not at that precise moment proceeding with his contribution to the text, does not see his turn as complete and proposes to continue it in due course.

This is only one aspect of the pervasive textual meaning of completeness, which derives from the understanding between participants in the speech event that the speaker will stop at some point, and that in the course of his turn he will indicate in various ways that his message is to be taken as subdivided into sections. The signals of final completeness and internal sectioning are to be seen at all levels of language and gesture. They subdivide what we have to say into packages or quanta of information, such that each package is more intimately structured internally than externally, i.e., although each quantum or package of the meaning has its own degree of absolute completeness, it is more semantically independent of its context than its constituents are of each other, and this semantic independence is echoed in the expression. Each package is represented as a step in the progress of the utterance towards its goal, the point. When we ask someone to get to the point we are appealing to this tacit assumption that there ought to be some kind of unity in what a speaker says and that when this has been achieved he will stop. Each internal marker of finiteness indicates that the package just completed is to be understood as a whole in relation to the other wholes bounded by the same signals.

Various textual units are important in signalling completeness. At the level of graphic layout there is the paragraph. In textual phonology, a unit with similar functions to the paragraph has been termed *pitch sequence* (Brazil, Coulthard & Johns 1980:61ff), *paratone* (Brown 1977:86) and *tone-unit sequence* (Crystal 1969:240ff). This unit is seen as being made up of units characterised by pitch movements like Halliday's *tone groups* (Halliday 1967), although Brown, Currie and Kenworthy (1980:29) prefer the term *pause-defined unit*. Both the paratone and its constituent units are crucially defined by differences in voice pitch, and function to indicate information packaging. We will look at this in more detail below. In the lexicogrammar, the lexical set and the collocation play an important but neglected role in the chunking of information, but preeminent in any discussion of completeness is the sentence.

I propose to review some important ways that intonation indicates completeness and incompleteness in dialogue, before reviewing some problems that speech analysis presents to the concept of the sentence. In this latter discussion I will show that phonological and lexical information have to be taken into account in our discussion of the sentence because this helps us to avoid some of the problems that traditional approaches to the sentence have entailed.

As part of the large number of intonational systems to which speakers react in dialogue, Brown, Currie and Kenworthy 1980:33ff) describe five. These are ''(i) affective meaning (ii) interactional structure (iii) topic structure (iv) information structure and (v) speech function''. The information and topic structure systems are, from the point of view of the signalling of completeness, terminal systems. The information structure is concerned with labelling items in the text as new or contrastive, while the topic structure system signals whether the passage relates to an already established topic or not. New lexical items as well as a new topic are signalled by a rise in pitch, which thus demarcates the item as different from what has gone before. Interactional structure is about the signalling of whether the speaker wishes to conclude his turn, when he may select a low terminal to indicate finality. By speech function is meant the signalling of ''who it is that is accepted by the participants as the repository of the relevant knowledge'' (Brown, Currie and

Kenworthy 1980:181). A terminal rise to high pitch in this system signals that the speaker is not sure of the truth of what he is saying and is inviting confirmation, whereas a low terminal presupposes that the speaker and the hearer are in agreement. Finally, the affective system signals empathy by shifts up in pitch. Its importance from the point of view of the completeness systems is in the supportive use of tone carriers like *mhmh,* whose role is to provide voiced sounds without any other content that would interfere with the pitch-signalled meanings. These are used by listeners to indicate that they are listening and wish the speaker to continue, or, if the end of a package has been signalled, that they are in agreement with what has been said and need no further clarification on that point.

These empathy signals contrast with interruptions, which occupy the other end of the same cline. As part of ongoing research French and Local (1982) have described quite delicate distinctions in the language of incomers and turn-occupants. A turn-competitive incoming is spoken both higher in pitch and louder than the incomer's norm for openings and louder than the ongoing speech. Even if the turn-occupant has no lexicogrammatical signals to go on, he will either acquiesce in the bid to take over the floor by tailing off in loudness until he is inaudible, or he will resist the incoming by speaking slower and louder. On the other hand, remarks from listeners which are not intended as a bid to complete the turn and initiate a new one are spoken more quietly and less loudly than the norm. These asides or interjections are reacted to almost immediately by the turn-occupant stopping and allowing the aside to be finished before he continues his turn.

These are only some of the ways the packaging of information is signalled phonologically, and the phonological mode is only one level of textual meaning. Each individual proposition expressed has to be fitted into a particular niche in the larger propositional structure that is the text. This packaging of meaning is every bit as 'semantic' as the expression of the propositions themselves. In fact the choice of whether to express a given meaning as word, group, clause or sentence and the parallel decisions on the phonological level are merely steps on the way to greater delicacy of expression.

Dialogue exhibits many examples of how meanings at one level will sometimes work harmonically and sometimes contrapuntally with meanings at another. The speaker must continually signal completeness of various types within his own turn and also inform his audience when he has finished, and if he wants them to take over the topic. Changeover sequences are full of signals which the current linguistic handbooks do not handle adequately. While it is easy to isolate the point where a speaker stops, or is stopped, and another takes over it is often difficult to relate this in a principled way to traditional categories, such as *question* and *interrogative.* Even with perfectly acceptable sequences, the kind that you only notice as special when trying to describe them, you often find that people respond with *yes* or *no* to structures with none of the classic signals of questions, and do not answer those that do. This has been noted by Bald (1980) on the basis of an analysis of 309 examples of *yes* and 63 examples of *no* in the Survey of English Usage, but problems arise with non-polar answers too. A case in point is to be found in extract I.

Extract I

Lynn	Can you not tell Sylvia about the time when the safe came down the stairs?
Neill	I wonder if Sylvia wants a cup of tea.
Sylvia	[laughs]
Neill	Sylvia, do you want a cup of tea?
Lynn	Shouldn't he? Shouldn't he tell you about the time when the safe came down the stairs?
Sylvia	Mhmh.
Neill	Fine. Sylvia will have a cup of tea.
Lynn	Oh of course. By all means . . .

Sylvia is the only one who knows she is being recorded and so she is saying as little as possible. Lynn and Neill only allow each other to complete their turns in one out of the three changeovers they share, although it is hardly an interruption in either of the other two cases. Lynn and Neill's last two utterances are particularly interesting. Neill's *Fine* etc. can be seen as appropriating Sylvia's preceding response although it would be equally good as an answer to Lynn's previous question. Lynn's final remark associates her with Neill's previous statement in a way not unlike an answer to a request for permission. Winter (1982:19) characterises a question as not a sentence, but a demand for a sentence. Certainly the crucial feature of any structure that we would want to count as a question is that it should signal interactional incompleteness. Extract I shows speakers creatively attributing different kinds of status to parts of the text which are not obviously what they are being treated as. This will be a complicating factor in any analysis.

The major problem for the definition of sentence, the classic completeness signal in traditional grammar and rhetoric, is applicability. The definition in the OED written by Henry Bradley seventy years ago is as good as most more recent ones. He defines the sentence as "a series of words in connected speech or writing, forming the grammatically complete expression of a single thought". More recent definitions have usually dispensed with the insistence on the connected speech or writing but more crucially they have emphasised the grammatical completeness to the detriment of the semantic unity on the grounds that form provides a better tool to recognise a sentence than meaning. One can certainly sympathise with this point of view. However, in text analysis, it is more important to be able to divide the text into its inherent informational constituents than that all these constituents should be unambiguously labelled as sentences or non-sentences. The text and its internal information packaging is a semantic matter relevant to how speakers use language to mean, but the sentence or any similar metalinguistic concept is only a tool to help us explicate the text.

Nevertheless, the concept sentence is often of use in isolating important aspects of the structuring of text information, although in speech it frequently requires phonological signalling of a kind which has been too often neglected. If we take the notion of a complete thought as referring to a package of textual meaning which the speaker has chosen to present as (relatively) independent of its context, we can say that the sentence is crucial among the various ways of signalling such a package.

The emphasis on the packages being *presented* as complete portions of text information allows us to avoid irrelevant philosophizing about the completeness of thoughts and the formulation 'relatively' allows us to distinguish between degrees of completeness.

This is because hardly any sentences used in communication are designed to stand wholly alone. Each is inextricably bound up with what goes before and what comes after and the fictitious sentences of the grammarians derive their unnaturalness from this fact. Nevertheless, the semantic relations in texts across sentence boundaries are, by the nature of the sentence, presented as being different from those within a single sentence structure. This is one of the most important uses of the Neo-Firthian distinction between sentence and clause. The clause is the highest purely grammatical unit and as such it has a fairly abstract status. It only achieves its connection with reality and the here-and-now in living texts by its realization in sentence structure.

The sentence is pivotal between grammatical and textual structure. Winter (1982:178) describes it as "the executive function of clause". This I understand as meaning the clause in action. A simple sentence or uncoordinated main clause is to be interpreted directly in the thematic structure of the unfolding text. Subordinate clauses, on the other hand, have their propositions mediated by their superordinate clause. In other words, the sententiality of a clause is one kind of statement about the degree of independence the message expressed has in relation to the surrounding clauses. Although at one level, the level of clause relations (Winter 1979), each clause is to be interpreted in the context of the preceding and succeeding clauses, the point at which the sentence boundary occurs is another choice point with its own meaning. In the case of coordination the matter is particularly complex. A coordinated clause, although not signalled as interpretable through a superordinate, can be taken out of the main thematic sequence and phonological cues play an important part in this as we will see below.

The phenomenon of completeness within an incomplete sequence of clauses can be signalled in various ways. We are all familiar with grammatical incompleteness in sequence sentences in texts but not enough has been made of the fact that incompleteness is unmarked in answers. The response *Teach* is much more likely to the question *What are you going to do when you leave university?* than any longer sequence. The effect of the incomplete clause structure is to signal that the hearer must interpet the utterance as being in particularly close semantic relationship with the preceding statement, in this case the relationship of answer to a question. The same reason explains the naturalness of the truncated sequences *Fine* and *Of course. By all means* in extract I. *Fine* repeats by evaluating Sylvia's presumed agreement to have tea, while Lynn's two Adjuncts can only be interpreted along with Neill's preceding sentence. This shows that the participants are cooperating in the creation of this text and are not, at this point, at cross purpose.

A similar signalling of incompleteness is to be found in the use of lexis, and it is connected with the concept of lexical fulfilment. It is a commonplace that grammatical, or empty, words and lexical items are two ends of a single cline. The examples which are usually adduced to illustrate this point are usually grammatical items with lexical aspects such as complex prepositions. More important are the items which Winter (1977:13) calls "Vocabulary 3 Word" and I call *lexical connectors*. They are items like *reason, problem* etc., in sentences like *I know of only one good reason* or *This is the central problem*. Although all the places in the grammatical structure of these sentences are occupied and the sentences are therefore grammatically complete, the items *reason* and *problem* are unfulfilled in the sense that they can only be understood in relation to the context. Their whole function is to characterise some part of the message as being a reason for something and a problem. At the same time they set up a relation in their texts with other parts which are characterised as results and solutions respectively.

Lexical fulfilment, like grammatical completeness, is an important boundary signal within a text, and its opposite forces hearers to interpret across clause and sentence boundaries. Thus a tension is set up between the notion of sentence as a complete semantic package and these ways of linking across the boundary. Just as a grammatical ellipsis links the structure where it appears with the structure where the 'missing' element is to be found, so a lexically unfulfilled item draws its clause together with the parts of the text where it is fulfilled. In fact, the kinds of complete and isolable sentence most grammars discuss are few and far between in texts. They are by their semantic disconnectedness important boundary signals in the sentence/clause-relation overlay that characterizes most texts.

In fact, the supersentential linkage in real texts has been one of the main grounds for doubting the validity of the concept for the analysis of discourse. This has been particularly true of speech although similar observations have been made about written texts (Monaghan 1979). Most speech is characterized by parataxis or, as it is often called, 'loose' coordination as against hypotaxis. Most authors write as if the facts of speech were in some way inferior to the features of elegant reflective prose. Bernstein's middle class groups use a high proportion of subordination as against the working class sample (Bernstein 1962). If these figures are accurate it would seem to indicate that the middle class groups spoke more like a book than the working class groups. It is interesting to note also that frequent use of coordination and simple sentences is one of the aspects that schools try to discourage in the written English of their students. The watchword is often 'repetitive', and "variety and the ability to construct complex sentences" (Withington 1982:16) is a goal of much teaching of composition. A related problem is the teaching of punctuation, because many students cannot readily grasp the at times rather rarefied rules of the English sentence punctuation. This derives from what Crystal and Davy (1969:46) describe as a linguistic problem for analysis of informal conversation.

> Informal conversation is characterised by a large number of loosely coordinated clauses, the coordination being structurally ambiguous: it is an open question whether one takes them as sequences of sentences or as single compound sentences.

The problem of the teacher, and of the linguists who try to approach the problem of the structure of spoken English in terms of the categories of written language, is the same. We even get systems of intonation based on readings of prose passages, or even of isolated sentences. As Brown, Currie and Kenworthy (1980:17) point out, 'post-syntactic' intonation "does not arise from the sorts of constraints which apply when speech is produced spontaneously." Among these constraints is the fact that while in writing we are confined to lexicogrammatical signals with a few punctuation marks, in speech we have at our disposal a range of devices that have not yet been adequately described. As Crystal himself notes, (1976:22),

> the point is that in speech, intonation and pause (and related features) provide us with continua along which we can range—as if we were able to vary the degrees of size or blackness of our punctuation marks

Some of the realizations of the different types of punctuation mark have been discussed in a recent study of unscripted oral narrative (Withington 1982). She found that, although by far the most common way of linking sentences was by *and,* in speech there are so many realizations of what in writing we are forced to write as 'big *And*' or *and,* that there is no feeling of repetition. Variation can be seen in both the prosodic and the segmental aspects of the realization of *and* (and *mutatis mutandis* for other connectors). There are differences of preceding and following pauses, pitch, syllable length, stress and phonetic realization. Examples of pause length variation can be seen in the following extract (where pause length is roughly indicated by the number of hyphens. . . . //-and then four of US //--ə:—put our rifle SLINGS //--under this chappie's SHOULDERS //—and--heaved UP // and tried to pu-and we couldn't pull him OUT // . . . (H. .86–90). Examples of the variation in phonetic realization are the familiar 'weak forms' of the introductory phonetics books, [n], [n̩], [ən], [æn], and [ænd]. These are not mere reflexes of stress choice elsewhere but are themselves important expressions of the different status that can be given in speech to the connector we hypostatize in writing as *and.* A good example of the kinds of difference that is possible is the following extract: . . . //—-[ənd ə:] she says don't take on ABOUT it // she says it's not done you any HARM // she says [n̩] I was in a HOLE // . . . (D.3.82–84).

All of this, and much more in transcriptions of spontaneous speech, serves to remind us of the primacy of speech and the artificiality of the picture of basically writing-oriented rules that underlies so much of contemporary linguistics. It is emphatically not the case that speech forces us to ignore rules that we 'know' in our heart of hearts are true. Rather the rules of all the grammars we can write are pale reflections of the ability of speakers to create not trivially novel grammatical structures, but new meanings in situations. The very prescriptive nature of so much grammar and lexicology is an attempt to make up for the loss of the ability of the speaker to make creative variations on familiar material in concrete situations. The relative poverty of the written mode has forced more and more of the signalling into grammar and lexis. Although all but the most arcane, and therefore usually foreign e.g. Latinate, constructions and vocabulary are equally to be found in speech as in written prose, the writer is forced to give much more attention to the lexicogrammar to compensate for the lack of a way to communicate his living voice.

In this context the concept of the sentence as the expression of a complete thought takes on a new function. Of course we cannot count thoughts. Of course we cannot say where one thought ends and the other begins. In living speech, however, we are continually offering parts of the language as the expression of wholes which are to be interpreted both in themselves as well as in relation to each other. The grammatical pattern which makes up the canonical sentence is one of these boundary markers, and the speaker can choose to take advantage of it. Simultaneously, he can modulate the absolute nature of this boundary by various means, lexical, phonological and paralinguistic. Any description of real speech must try to keep all these factors in mind.

ACKNOWLEDGMENTS

I wish to thank Peter Fries, Michael Halliday and Kenneth Pike for commenting on the lecture on which this paper was based and thus improving it. I am also indebted to Winifred Crombie, Alex de Joia, Geoffrey Turner and Eugene Winter, who suffered the first draft. I take responsibility for not making even more use of all this wisdom.

REFERENCES

Bald, Wolf Dietrich. (1980). Some functions of *yes* and *no* in conversation. In Sidney Greenbaum, Geoffrey Leech and Jan Svartvik. (eds.), *Studies in English Linguistics for Randolph Quirk,* London: Longman, pp. 178–191.

Bernstein, Basil. (1962). Social class, linguistic codes, and grammatical elements. *Language and Speech.* **5.**221–40.

Brazil, David, Coulthard, R. M. & Johns, C. M. (1980). *Discourse Intonation and Language Teaching.* London: Longman.

Brown, Gillian. (1977). *Listening to Spoken English.* London: Longman.

Brown, Gillian, Currie, Karen & Kenworthy, Joanne. (1980). *Questions of Intonation.* London: Croom Helm.

Crystal, David. (1969). *Prosodic Systems and Intonation in English.* Cambridge, England: Cambridge University Press.

Crystal, David. (1976). *Child Language, Learning and Linguistics.* London: Edward Arnold.

Crystal, David & Davy, Derek. (1969). *Investigating English Style.* London: Longman.

French, Peter & Local, John. (1982). Turn-competitive incomings, *Journal of Pragmatics* **6.**

Halliday, M. A. K. (1967). *Intonation and Grammar in British English.* The Hague: Mouton.

Huddleston, Rodney. (1976). *An Introduction to English Transformational Syntax.* London: Longman.

Monaghan, James. (1979). Some proposals for a cotextual approach to coherence in English texts. In Vandeweghe, Willy & van de Velde, Marc. (eds.), *Akten des 13. linguistischen Kolloquiums.* Gent. 1978, **vol. 2.** Tübingen, Germany: Niemeyer. 371–380.

Monaghan, James. (1982). On the phonological signalling of text structure. *The Eighth LACUS Forum, 1981.* In Gutwinski, W. & Jolly, G. (eds.). Columbia, SC: The Hornbeam Press.

Winter, E. O. (1977). A clause-relational approach to English texts. *Instructional Science* **6.** Special issue.

Winter, E. O. (1979). Replacement as a fundamental function of the sentence in context. *Forum Linguisticum*. **4**.95–113.

Winter, E. O. (1982). *Towards a Contextual Grammar of English*. London: George Allen & Unwin.

Withington, Jean M. (1982). *Inter-Clause Connections in Spoken Narrative*. Unpublished M.A. thesis, Hatfield, The Polytechnic.

Author Index

Subject Index